APPRECIATION OF EDWIN ARLINGTON ROBINSON

APPRECIATION OF
EDWIN ARLINGTON ROBINSON

---

28 Interpretive Essays

Edited by
RICHARD CARY

WATERVILLE, MAINE
COLBY COLLEGE PRESS

LIBRARY
AUG 1 9 1970
UNIVERSITY OF THE PACIFIC

FOR THE 100TH ANNIVERSARY OF MAINE'S MOST ILLUSTRIOUS POET

BORN DECEMBER 22, 1869

Shall there not one arise
To wrench one banner from the western skies,
And mark it with his name forevermore?

FOREWORD

PUBLIC acclaim of Edwin Arlington Robinson was long in coming. His first, self-published, self-distributed booklet of forty-six poems—*The Torrent and the Night Before* in 1896—was greeted pleasurably by Edward Eggleston, Harry Thurston Peck, and Nathan Haskell Dole; it received approximately a score of notices in the columns of the Boston *Evening Transcript, Bookman, Dial, Independent, Christian Register, Harvard Monthly, Outlook, Sewanee Review, Poet-Lore, Literary World,* and others; it cropped up as far afield as the Denver *Times,* Chicago *Record,* and New Orleans *Daily Picayune.* Yet it created no visible stir.

The Children of the Night in the following year fared no better although printed and issued through regular commercial channels. The same soft disregard attended his third volume, *Captain Craig* (1902), despite reviews in the larger metropolitan dailies of New York, Boston, and Chicago, and favorable nods from Clinton Scollard, Frank Dempster Sherman, Bliss Carman, and Thomas Wentworth Higginson, all moguls of literary taste in this time. What opened the gate, at least ajar, was the intervention of Theodore Roosevelt, then president of the United States. His belated appraisal of *The Children of the Night* in the *Outlook* of August 12, 1905, inspired widespread ironies on his qualifications as a critic of literature. Nonetheless, it aired Robinson's name for the first time in such important quarters as the New York *Post* and the *Saturday Review of Books* of the *Times.* Beyond this, the irrepressible Teddy persuaded the firm of Scribner's to bring out a new edition of *The Children* and to admit Robinson's poems to the magazine.

It sparked no instantaneous reversal: Robinson did not wake up to find himself famous among editors. From 1906 through 1910, twelve of his fifteen published poems appeared in *Scribner's.* After three years of almost total drought, in 1914-1915 Robinson gained entree to the *Atlantic Monthly, Poetry,* and *Harper's Weekly.* His major breakthrough, however, came in February 1916 with publication of *The Man Against the Sky.* The New York *Times* book section was pointedly generous with space after repeated neglect. Amy Lowell joined William

Stanley Braithwaite, Harriet Monroe, Padraic Colum, and Louis Untermeyer in an harmonious cantata of praise. The effect was to elevate a new star to the galaxy.

Each of Robinson's volumes thereafter engaged the attention of prestigious critics—Odell Shepard, Stark Young, Carl Van Doren, William Rose Benet, Conrad Aiken—and the poet himself assured a broad following with his Round Table romances, *Merlin* (1917) and *Lancelot* (1920). In 1927 he achieved unprecedented acceptance with *Tristram*, last segment of his Arthurian trilogy. It was chosen a book-of-the-month by the Literary Guild of America, and it attracted the third of his Pulitzer Prizes. Up to this point examination of Robinson's esthetic had been largely confined to reviews in newspapers and periodicals, with an occasional interview (notably Joyce Kilmer's in the New York *Times*), and a slim list of cogitative essays, the best of which—by John Drinkwater, J. C. Squire, and Charles Cestre—were later incorporated in their books.

The great generality of these early critiques was either too restricted in range or too brief to cover the subject. Three years after *Tristram* Robinson became fair ground for the academic journals, skittish though they were then about discussing living authors. From that date, longer, deeper, and—yes—more somber studies of Robinson's art became customary. In the three and a half decades since his death a substantial body of instructive commentary has come into being. The editor's intent relative to this material has been twofold: to mark the centennial of Robinson's birth with an appropriate salute to his genius, and to convene within a single, accessible volume the most acute and useful of these far-flung assessments.

Excepting the lyrical tribute by Archibald MacLeish which inaugurates this volume, all essays were selected on the basis of sufficient length to do justice to the topic. Each is complete and independent in itself; there are no extracts or chapters from books. Indeed, no essay already collected in a book by its author is here repeated. For maximum value to students of Robinson's work a diversity of critical methods and ideological approaches is offered: probings into his philosophy, religion, psychology, and sociology; close readings of individual poems; contrasts of his romantic and realistic manifestations; his aptitudes in specialized verse forms; cluster views of his short poems, long poems, later poems, poems of the known and the imagined; his characters, male and female; his poetic principles and strategies of practice; his urge toward the novel and the drama; his position in literary history; and the man himself. *"The feast of reason and the flow of soul."*

RICHARD CARY

Colby College
Waterville, Maine

CONTENTS

ON REREADING ROBINSON

ARCHIBALD MACLEISH

REREADING Robinson it occurs to you that something came into American poetry—American literature—with E.A.R.: something not easy to define. It wasn't his characteristic form, the dialogue or monologue or dramatic scene, the narrative condensed to its essential crystal. Browning had already polished that device and Browning had been read in the United States. Neither was it Robinson's peculiar attitude toward style, his mastery of syntax—the taut, deliberate purposefulness of the sense of the words riding the sound of them like a skillful surfer on his changing wave. Others had practised the syntactical arts also: that long, intricate sentence at the start of *Avon's Harvest* tastes, if you break the meter, like Henry James.

What is it then that strikes you as new, as first seen, in Robinson's work—new, I mean, as of the time when it was written? Not a new world, certainly: Robinson was no explorer of the undiscovered, though he had a curiosity about the dark. Not a new music: Robinson's tunes are simple and familiar—often too familiar. Not a new way of seeing. There are fewer visible images in Robinson than in most: Dante's eternal squinting tailors never got to Tilbury Town. No, what strikes you as you read Robinson now—what catches your ear first and then your half attention and after that your speculating mind is not so much the shape or sound or even substance of what is being said as the manner of the saying.

What is new is the speaker. And I mean the *speaker*, not what is meant or implied by such terms of the contemporary critical vocabulary as "Mask" or "Persona." Robinson's mask was his face, his own for all purposes—business-like glasses, trim moustache—but his way of speaking in his poems was his way of speaking in his poems, for otherwise he rarely spoke. He had—he developed in his work—a Voice in the sense in which Villon had a Voice which gave humanness a different

Reprinted by permission, *Colby Library Quarterly*, VIII (March 1969), 217-219.

timbre, and Sappho had a Voice which sharpened the taste of life, and Li Po had a Voice which made a place for laughter—a place which all the sententious solemnity of Chairman Mao and all the ranting of his mechanized adolescents have not been able quite to drown.

I am not comparing E.A.R. with Villon and Sappho and Li Po: I respect his integrity too much. I am saying only that he made for himself a Voice in the same sense they did. His poems were new poems under the sun not because form or theme or style was new but because the speaker was: new as a man and new too as a man of his time and country. We say, when we do not think what we are saying, that Whitman's was the American voice, but clearly it wasn't. Whitman celebrated America—what it was and what it might have been—but the voice in which his America was celebrated was no more American than the rhythms. Delete the place names and the geographical evocations and you are out at large on the timeless, placeless tone of the lyric self. Or we say, more carefully, that Thoreau's voice was American, as indeed in many ways it was, but not in the essential way. Thoreau's was the voice of the American idea, alive and talking back to the universe, but it did not *sound* in the native tone: it sounded of Thoreau.

With Robinson it was the other way around by both measures. He did not speak for the American idea. When he mentioned America there was a glint in his voice like the glint of his glasses.

> You laugh and answer, 'We are young;
> O leave us now and let us grow'—
> Not asking how much more of this
> Will Time endure or Fate bestow.

And certainly he never celebrated the blond young continent and its innocent dream. But when it comes to the Voice itself, to the speaker spoken in the Voice, Robinson was more American than either and therefore—the world having moved in the direction it has—more modern, for if Crèvecoeur were to ask his famous question now he would have to reply that his American is well on his way to becoming modern man. (Perhaps he would add, Hélas!)

Fifty years ago readers took the tone of Robinson's for "downeast" and thought of Head Tide and Gardiner when they heard his voice. Fifty years ago Richard Cory who "was always human when he talked" and persuaded us that he "was everything / To make us wish that we were in his place" but who, one summer night, "Went home and put a bullet through his head" was an introverted Yankee. But those fifty years have passed and few would make the provincial application now. The irony is applicable on too broad a stage.

And of course it is the irony that makes Robinson so particularly our own. He speaks for us in our inexplicably aborted time as no one else, even among the very great, quite does. His tone knows truths about us we don't know ourselves—but recognize. We don't despair—not quite—and neither does Robinson. But we don't hope either as we used to and Robinson, with no bitterness, has put hope by as well. His is the after voice, the evening voice, and we neither accept it nor reject it but we know the thing it means.

It is all in that extraordinary poem he put into the mouth of Ben Jonson entertaining a Stratford Alderman and explaining Shakespeare's "old age"—his forties.

> The coming on of his old monster Time
> Has made him a still man; and he has dreams
> Were fair to think on once and all found hollow.
> He knows how much of what men paint themselves
> Would blister in the light of what they are;
> He sees how much of what was great now shares
> An eminence transformed and ordinary;
> He knows too much of what the world has hushed
> In others, to be loud now for himself. . . .
> But what not even such as he may know
> Bedevils him the worst: his lark may sing
> At heaven's gate how he will, and for as long
> As joy may listen but *he* sees no gate
> Save one whereat the spent clay waits a little
> Before the churchyard has it and the worm.

THE ARTHUR OF EDWIN ARLINGTON ROBINSON

E. Edith Pipkin

Despite twentieth-century critics who have not hesitated to include the *Idylls* in their revolt against Victorianism, the Arthurian conception of the average reader is still largely Tennysonian. Such a reader, as a rule, gives little thought to the long history of the story of Arthur and its multiplicity of elements. Says Caxton: "Herein may be seen noble chivalry, courtesy, humanity, friendliness, hardiness, love, hate, virtue and sin." Usually, however, Malory is known only in bits or at second hand. In one respect certainly our high schools have done their work well. The timeless figures of Arthur, Guinevere, Lancelot, and Merlin are seen through Tennysonian glasses.

Accordingly, when Mr. Edwin Arlington Robinson decided to re-handle the Arthurian legend, he found his reading public emotionally conditioned by Tennyson. Many seemed to wonder at his choice, seeming to feel that Tennyson had left very little for another poet. When *Merlin* was published in 1917, Mr. Robinson was quite frequently judged in terms of Tennyson: he was either like or unlike Tennyson, not so good as Tennyson or better. Eventually, however, it was recognized not only that Mr. Robinson is very unlike Tennyson, but that he has given a highly individual view of the situation at Camelot. So significant a thing has he done that no less critic than M. Charles Cestre has declared that what the Greek dramatists did for Greek myth, Mr. Robinson has done for Celtic myth.

His Arthurian poems, *Merlin, Lancelot,* and *Tristram* are marked by a strong dramatic handling. Mr. Robinson has, indeed, a real genius for recognizing the essential scene, presenting it with the necessary fullness of detail, holding an emotional tone and moving from crisis to crisis. In fact, Amy Lowell once said of him that in spite of his austerity

Reprinted by permission, *English Journal,* XIX (March 1930), 183-195.

and restraint, he had a real liking for the melodramatic. In his Arthurian trilogy, by an exclusion of irrelevant material, a reduction of the dramatis personae, and a limiting of the time of the action, he has gained freedom for a dramatic, humanly significant presentation of the old theme.

Not only are the poems dramatic, however; they are tragic. In *Merlin* and *Lancelot* the element of tragedy, depending as it does on some fatal weakness of the characters themselves, takes on a certain stark austerity. *Tristram* alone, presenting the eternal theme of two "star-crossed lovers," shows in some degree a lightening of the tragic effect. *Merlin*, perhaps more a tragedy of the spirit than *Lancelot*, has a quieter, more reflective quality, but it is nevertheless very real, this soul tragedy of a highly integrated personality, doomed to spiritual failure. For a full realization of the overwhelming ruin that overtakes Camelot, we must consider both these poems together.

In this cumulative tragic effect Mr. Robinson's Arthurian poems stand in sharp contrast to the more recently published *Midsummer Night and Other Tales in Verse*, a group of Arthurian poems by John Masefield. Robinson's poems are in their very essence drama. The dramatic effect is carefully prepared for and sustained. Mr. Masefield's poems are, as their title declares, tales and deal with individual episodes, their action being completed in a much narrower compass. Mr. Robinson, as a poet, is distinguished by precision rather than melody. Masefield's poems, marked by metrical experimentation and the use of archaic expressions, are interspersed with hauntingly beautiful passages. Much closer in spirit to medievalism than are *Merlin, Lancelot,* and *Tristram,* the *Tales* of Mr. Masefield give us once again magic, love, fighting, and vengeance. Robinson, however, omitting the trappings of medievalism, foregoing all pictures of the court when chivalry was at its height, stresses the human element and gives us real persons acting each on each, developing, growing and disintegrating under the pressure of emotional strain.

One of Mr. Robinson's most distinctive traits is his psychological understanding. Searching the souls of men, he sees their weaknesses, even their contemptible littlenesses, but he also sees their aspiration, their gallantry in the face of insuperable odds, and their puzzled bewilderment at some of the insoluble mysteries of life. His Arthurian figures are no mere puppets in medieval dress; they are men and women, highly individualized and yet universal.

Usually Arthurian stories depict Arthur in his role of king. The early chronicles devoted themselves to his personal exploits, but the emphasis soon shifted, and the romances presented Arthur "the monarch in position," Arthur the head of the chivalric society at Camelot.

Malory's Arthur, indeed, starts his career as an individual, but soon withdraws into regal seclusion. Engrossed in cares of state, he is blind to the human crisis that is threatening his own household. When Guinevere is brought to trial after her disastrous dinner, Arthur innocently chides, "What ails you that you cannot keep Lancelot at your side?" After the crash comes, he acknowledges, "I am sorrier for my good knights' loss than for the loss of my fair queen, for queens I might have enow, but such fellowship of good knights shall never be together in no company." In his Arthur, Tennyson gives us an idealized conception of kingliness working high purposes in a world of sin. He omits altogether, as not fitting the character of his stainless king, the story of Arthur's incest and the birth of Modred. For his attempt to burn the Queen, Tennyson substitutes, "Let no man think but that I love thee still."

In striking contrast, Robinson subordinates the king to the man. His Arthur is introspective, highly wrought, emotionally disturbed; his nerves are worn raw by vague fears and suspicions. Instead of being primarily the ruler, he is even neglecting his public obligations as more than one character attests. Instead of showing the traditional blindness to the Lancelot-Guinevere situation, he is acutely aware of it. In the long hours of his sleepless vigil after Merlin's visit, he visualizes the "cold eyes of Guinevere"; he mutters to himself, repeating Merlin's words, " 'The love that never was!' Fool, fool, fool, fool!"

Moreover, love has always played a disproportionate part in Arthur's life. Merlin says of him:

> The king, who made of love
> More than he made of life and death together,
> Forgot the world and his example in it.

Accordingly, Arthur is represented, as in Malory, as being the father of Modred, a fact which is generally known at court. Lamorak bluntly phrases it:

> Arthur, he being Arthur and a king,
> Has made a more pernicious mess than one
> We're told, for being so great and amorous.
> . . . .
> And there again did Merlin warn the king.
> The story goes abroad, and I believe it.

In *Lancelot* we have the fruition of the doubts and fears with which Arthur has lived for two years. He comes in on the morning that Guinevere is to be burned:

> Like a sick landlord shuffling to the light
> For one last lookout on his mortgaged hills.

He is torn between the wish that he were dreaming, vain regrets for the false hunting that precipitated the crisis, and a desperate effort to convince himself that he is acting justly. This ends, however, with the piteous cry,

> What have I sent those boys to see?
> I'll put clouts on my eyes, and I'll not see it!
> Her face and hands and her little small white feet,
> And all her shining hair and her warm body—
> No—for the love of God, no—it's alive!
> She's all alive, and they are burning her.
> . . . . Her eyes
> Are what I see—and her white body is burning!
> She never did enough to make me see her
> Like that—to make her look at me like that.
> There's not room enough in the world for so much evil
> As I see clamoring in her poor white face
> For pity. Pity her, God! God! Lancelot!

This is Arthur at his most tragic moment. Since his love had come to mean more to him than his kingdom, its tragic culmination meant more to him than the loss of his kingdom. With the conclusion of this scene the story of Arthur as a person ends. After this he becomes a shadowy automaton, played upon by the hate of Gawaine. At the end there is no marvelous story of Arthur's passing. We are told,

> Arthur was dead,
> And Modred with him, each by the other slain,
> And there was no light left of all who fought
> On Salisbury field, save one, Sir Bedivere,
> Of whom the tale was told that he had gone
> Darkly away to some far hermitage
> To think and die. There were tales told of a ship.

Innumerable tales of magic have gathered around the figure of Merlin. We can imagine what he might become in the hands of a poet like Coleridge or Walter de la Mare. Robinson makes scant use of the supernatural as such, yet a brief consideration of the older versions enables us to see more clearly the changes he has made in the spirit of the story. Malory does scant justice to Merlin, presenting with provoking terseness the end of his career. Merlin, he tells us, "fell into a dotage" and was "assotted on one of the damsels of the lake that hight Nimue." For a real understanding of Merlin we must go beyond Malory. Robinson's *Merlin,* at least in its treatment of Vivian, is perhaps a little more akin to the ordinary or Vulgate *Merlin* than to the *Suite de Merlin.*

Merlin's father was a devil, straight from hell. Merlin was to have been the means of circumventing Arthur and the chivalric ideal, but through his mother's prayers he was turned from evil designs. Although Merlin frequently resorted to deeds of pure Celtic magic, he was regarded more seriously as prophet, his dire predictions frequently striking terror to the hearts of his listeners. The Nimue of this story is an innocent, childlike girl, who acts, not from malice, but from the desire to have Merlin to herself. Merlin, fully aware of what he is doing, yields to her entreaties to tell her the charm. For the most part she stays by him. "For in you," says she, "I have set all my hope, and I abide no other joy but of you, and ye be my thought and desire."

In his *Merlin* Robinson has almost done away with the supernatural. Vivian's charms are the magic which hold Merlin in Broceliande, not any mysterious spell of waving arms and mysterious passes.

> She sings
> To Merlin, till he trembles in her arms
> And there forgets that any town alive
> Had ever such a name as Camelot.
> So Vivian holds him with her love, they say.

Lacking supernatural powers, Merlin has simply a greater insight, a greater power to see into the heart of things than other men. He is a man who has lived out of time or in the world of abstract thought. He says,

> I saw
> Too much and that was never good for man.
> The man who goes too far alone goes mad—
> In one way or another.

Like the Merlin of the Vulgate version he is entirely aware of what he is doing when he turns his back on the life of thought, on Camelot and Arthur. Arthur expresses it,

> You, yourself,—God save us!—
> Have gone down smiling to the smaller life
> That you and your incongruous laughter called
> Your living grave. God save us all, Merlin,
> When you the seer, the founder, and the prophet,
> May throw the gold of your immortal treasure
> Back to the God who gave it, and then laugh
> Because a woman has you in her arms.

For a time Merlin luxuriates in the flattery of Vivian's attentions, the sense appeal of her beauty, and the creature comforts of the life at Broceliande. This life, however, disintegrates his moral and spiritual fiber. When he returns to Camelot, beardless, arrayed in purple silk, Arthur at first feels that the old Merlin has gone. But he soon acknowledges,

> But you are Merlin still or part of him.

In this speech Arthur gives the reason why Merlin cannot be entirely happy in the life of dalliance and sort of Lotos-eaters' oblivion of the outside world. He is Merlin still. His "avenging, injured intellect" will let him have no peace. Change is coming in Camelot, and

> A mightier will than his
> Or Vivian's had ordained that he be there.

Merlin delays, however, dreading the final step, knowing that he personally will never come to the Light. At last he sets out, "old and gaunt and garrulous." Dagonet sees,

> An old face
> Made older with an inch of silver beard,
> And faded eyes more eloquent of pain
> And ruin than all the faded eyes of age
> Till now had ever been, although in them
> There was a mystic and intrinsic peace
> Of one who sees where men of nearer sight
> See nothing.

This is Merlin, the seer who tried to reach a personal happiness by disavowing his qualities of insight and wisdom. Such happiness as he attained was transitory. At the end he may have reached a certain personal tranquillity because he has returned to his own native element, the life of thought, but he is powerless either to aid Arthur or to save Camelot.

Not quite the innocent Nimue of the Vulgate Merlin and certainly not the malicious creature of the later versions, Vivian shows conflicting impulses. She has both a capacity for scheming and a willingness to sacrifice for love. Robinson has spent a good deal of care in delineating Vivian. We can visualize her dark beauty in a "fragile sheath of crimson" or dressed in green "like a slim cedar." She is sophisticated, is given to little poses, and has a habit of making demands to test her power. In her the possessive instinct is highly developed. She can brook no rival, whether it be a king and kingdom or simply a detached mood of her lover's. Yet after Vivian has proved to herself that she is first with Merlin, she does not like the Merlin whom she has changed.

> Pitying herself,
> She pitied the fond Merlin she had changed,
> And saw the Merlin who had changed the world.

She seems to have no love for this groping, hesitating Merlin and veers between a perverse desire to hurt and a pitying gentleness. Merlin, however, pronounces her

> Warm and kind and overwise
> For woman in a world where men see not
> Beyond themselves.

In spite of everything, he seems sure of his power over her, declaring

> No other love than mine
> Shall be an index of her memories.

Even before Guinevere's name was linked with that of Lancelot, she was frequently portrayed as untrue to Arthur. Her name at times became a synonym for unfaithfulness. Originating in the fashion of courtly love, the story of her love affair with Lancelot for a long time bore the stamp of its artificial origin, but finally the somewhat wooden figures of Guinevere and Lancelot came to life, becoming two of the best-known lovers of all times. The traditional Guinevere, although always beautiful and queenly, frequently exhibited a spiteful jealousy. Malory, not overfond of Guinevere, the disrupter of the knightly order, followed this general conception, portraying her, however, as being faithful to her love to the end. On the other hand, Tennyson debases his Guinevere. She may finally recognize the highest when she sees it, but she loses in her own self; she is no longer one of the fated lovers of history.

In Robinson's Guinevere we have a new perspective, for we see the situation through her eyes. Having lived through her jealousy, she can now refer to it casually.

> And for a time
> Before you went—albeit for no long time—
> I may have made for your too loyal patience
> A jealous exhibition of my folly—
> All for those two Elaines; and one of them
> Is dead, poor child, for you. How do you feel,
> You men, when women die for you? They do,
> Sometimes you know. Not often, but sometimes.

She is now facing an entirely different problem. Lancelot is torn between his love for her and his new-found desire to follow the Light. Recognizing the difference, she calls into play all her resources. Guinevere's love for Lancelot is her dominating passion. For her there is only Lancelot, and he is aware of this.

More single in her purpose than Lancelot, Guinevere experiences no division in her loyalties. Less spiritually complex, she has greater intensity and strength. She sees things objectively in the clear, cold light of reality. She does not gloss over; there are no halfway measures in her judgments. Unmindful of Arthur's love for her, she sees the inescapable fact of the faggots. She bursts out in protest over going back to Camelot,

> To be his wife?
> To live in his arms always and so hate him
> That I could heap around him the same faggots
> That you put out with blood?

At the end, too, Guinevere is still stronger than Lancelot. Having once renounced her love—and in so doing Guinevere does not follow after any mystical Light but firmly allies herself with the existing religious order—Guinevere stands firm in her determination. The long nights in the Tower have taught her a new sense of values. She says to Lancelot,

> Forgive me.
> I could not let you go. God pity men
> When women love too much—and women more.

Now she has forgiven the faggots. Once she pleaded with Lancelot for France; now she waves aside his suggestion, deciding for them both.

In contrast to Guinevere's singleness of purpose, Lancelot is a person of divided loyalties. He is allured by the Light; he is held by the white and gold of Guinevere. Yet his love for her has not the glowing ardor of tragic young love such as we see in *Tristram*. Habit has incorporated this love into his scheme of life, but it has been rudely touched by disillusionment. The old fire has been replaced by a brooding tenderness for Guinevere. Impelled by all his better impulses to follow the Light, yet Lancelot cannot conceive existence without Guinevere. He is

> A moth between a window and a star,
> Not wholly lured by the one or led by the other.

A man of delicacy of perception and keenness of insight, he sees the situation in Camelot in all its ugliness. He condemns himself as one who has served his king "with a cankered honor." During the battle before Joyous Gard Lancelot, still hesitant, cannot throw himself wholeheartedly into the contest. He is still troubled by his betrayal of Arthur. Tormented by the death of Gareth and Gaheris, he visualizes with all its hideous details the scene of their killing.

In his decision to return Guinevere to King Arthur's court, Lancelot is trying to prevent another and more dreadful war, to bring some slight measure of healing to the war-torn realm of Camelot. Having allowed himself to slip into a habit of indecision, he now finds it necessary to fight desperately for the right as he sees it. He realizes that where Guinevere is concerned, he is not entirely master of himself. Small wonder is it that he, in his desperation, seems to strike out blindly, inflicting needless wounds.

Lancelot says of himself,

> When the great gods are playing,
> Great men are not so great as great gods
> Had led them once to dream.

In these lines he has given us a clue to the evaluation of his own character. He had aspirations toward greatness, but the tangled web of circumstances and his own innate qualities prevented the realization of these ideals.

Just as Mr. Robinson has given us a modern, psychologically complex group of Arthurian characters, so he has breathed a new spirit into the legends themselves. He is dealing with modern standards and modern complexities of thought. In such a world the ethics of tournaments, battle fields, and courtly love have little place. Instead of Malory's frank delight in a good fight, of Tennyson's sublimation of the idea of war, he introduces a new element into Arthurian story: utter war weariness. The poems are filled with such references as,

> How many of these tomorrows
> Are coming to ask unanswered why this war
> Was fought and fought for the vain sake of slaughter?

In the same way he gives hints of the future place of woman in society. Merlin persists in the idea that the torch of woman, together with the light that Galahad found, will work out in the final salvation of the world. Furthermore, Mr. Robinson has discarded the miracle-working, mystic elements in the story of the Grail. It has become merely a symbol of a light that leads men on, luring them to ideals as yet ill-defined, but clear enough to make them dissatisfied with the existing social order.

One of the most commonly repeated criticisms of Mr. Robinson is that he is a pessimist. His works are certainly marked by a pervading sense of the tragedy of life, a recognition that certain fundamental problems are in themselves puzzling and bewildering. Yet he himself disclaims the label of pessimist, saying, "In point of fact, I recommend a reading of my work to anyone who wishes to become an incurable optimist." Mr. Robinson, being a thoughtful, reflective man, is used to meeting the skepticism of his day; clear-eyed, he sees the case for it. He, however, is not stampeded by it. Again and again in his work, although the references are sometimes so vague as to be tantalizing, we see an insistence on spiritual values.

> There was a light wherein men saw themselves
> In one another as they might become,
> Or so they dreamed. . . . .
> . . . . They all saw something.
> God knows the meaning or the end of it,
> But they saw something.

With Santayana, he seems to think that life is animal in origin, spiritual in its possible fruits. Accordingly, he puts emphasis on the value of man's aspirations. In the Arthurian poems, in spite of failure, utter and desolating, the two outstanding figures, Merlin and Lancelot, are both still striving. Their individual lives have met defeat; they themselves have been instruments in bringing about the tragic fate of their society. But in neither is there a surrender of the spirit. In the face of such a will to hold on, we see with Merlin,

In each bewildered man who dots the earth
A moment with his days a groping thought
Of an eternal will.

Tristram, the poem of the Arthurian trilogy to receive the greatest popular acclaim, offers both in the method of treatment and in spirit a striking contrast to *Merlin* and *Lancelot.* Its story is the great love story of medievalism, the roots of which strike deep into our racial heritage. The last of the great legends to be annexed by the Arthurian cycle, it remained loosely connected. Like the original story, Mr. Robinson's *Tristram* stands just on the edge of the Arthurian legend. Its events do not take place at Camelot; with the exception of Gawaine, the characters of King Arthur's court receive merely casual references.

Tristram, on the whole, is less dramatic than the other two poems. There are sharply etched scenes that live in our memories, but there are also occasions when the action seems to lag. To compensate for this, there is a lyrical, ecstatic quality in the love of Tristram and Isolt, a quality which doubtless goes far toward explaining the popularity of this poem. *Tristram* is tragic, but the tragic element lacks the grim austerity of *Merlin* and *Lancelot.* The tragic end of the lovers depends not so much on their own weaknesses as on outer circumstances. Their worst offense has been that they have failed to speak. At Joyous Gard, however, they experience a happiness so perfect that any other emotional experience would be in the nature of an anticlimax. One feels that the end is as it must be. The very name of Tristram signifies one born for sorrow. These lovers

Are not for the fireside, or for old age
In any retreat of ancient stateliness.

At the end we feel that Mark was right in his conclusion:

"There was no more for them," he said again
To himself or the ship, "and this is peace.
I should have neither praise nor thanks of them
If power were mine and I should wake them."

In his characterization of Tristram and Isolt, Mr. Robinson has not departed so widely from the traditional conception of their characters as he did in the cases of Merlin, Arthur, and Guinevere. They are still the eternal lovers. Their speech has a modern ring. Their passion is depicted with a realistic definiteness of detail that individualizes it for modern readers, but it is essentially the same story, the oldest love story of such length of which we have knowledge, the theme which has attracted story-tellers from Beroul and Gottfried to Swinburne, Arnold and Wagner. With Tristram we feel "the shuddering, unreal miracle of Isolt"; we see her

> Isolt of the dark eyes—Isolt
> Of the patrician, passionate helplessness,
> Isolt of the soft waving blue-black hair.

Tristram is still

> Tristram, the loud-accredited strong warrior,
> Tristram, the loved of women, the harp-player,
> Tristram, the learned Nimrod among hunters.

On the other hand, there is a new note struck in the handling of some of the minor characters. Good and evil mingle in Mark. He is neither the noble king of the older versions nor the contemptible creature whom Malory depicts. Unattractive physically, "ordained to wait on lust and wine and riot," he still has his generous impulses. The death of the lovers comes, not through him, but through Andred, and Mark, too, seems a victim of circumstances. Isolt of the white hands is drawn with a new tenderness. She is a pathetic figure, living with her dreams, searching the horizon for a ship which does not come, sadly acknowledging at the end,

> I would have been the world
> And heaven to Tristram, and was nothing to him.

Again unlike *Merlin* and *Lancelot, Tristram* is not weighted with overtones and undertones of meaning and of musing on the fate of man and society. There may be a casual reference, as when Tristram decries a loveless marriage, speaking of Isolt as

> The bartered prey
> Of an unholy sacrifice, by rites
> Of Rome made holy.

The main theme of the poem, however, is love between man and woman, and such abstract ideas as we find deal with love, its place in the human scheme of things, and the relationship of man and woman. The poem is a glorification of love, and Isolt gives expression to its dominant idea when she says,

> My life to me is not a little thing.
> It is a fearful and a lovely thing.
> Only my love is more.

TILBURY TOWN AND CAMELOT

EDNA DAVIS ROMIG

FOR ONE who has three times received the Pulitzer prize and has been given honorary degrees by our greatest colleges, who has an output of poems equalling in volume that of the poets in the great tradition, who has established a sure reputation in his own span of years, further acclaim would appear over-measure. Yet I feel that there are a few things to say of Edwin Arlington Robinson that have not yet been said.

The things that have been said have been well said. From several small volumes we learn that Mr. Robinson is now a man of sixty-two years, living in New York City during the winter, at the MacDowell Colony, Peterborough, New Hampshire, in the summer—presiding, it is said, with gracious hospitality at the large table where American artists forgather for retreat and creative work. We learn that Edwin Arlington Robinson was born at Head Tide, Maine, reared in the small town of Gardiner, where very early the little boy made poetry for his mother; that in due time he went down to Harvard for two years, but did not stay to take a degree; that for several years afterward he lived in poverty in New York City; that in 1896 he brought out at his own expense *The Torrent and the Night Before,* a slender book of thirty-nine pages, dedicated "To any man, woman, or critic who will cut the edges of it. I have done the top." We learn also that in 1897 he had Richard Badger and Company bring out *The Children of the Night,* with the text running from pages 11-121; that neither of these books brought any real recognition; that not until after Houghton, Mifflin, and Company had brought out *Captain Craig,* in 1902, and Scribner's had brought out an edition of *The Children of the Night,* in 1905, a volume of which fell into the hands of Theodore Roosevelt, who reviewed it for *The Outlook,* did the trend of things begin to change. President Roosevelt saw to it that Mr. Robinson had more chance to develop what his

Reprinted by permission, *University of Colorado Studies*, XIX (June 1932), 303-326.

review called "an undoubted touch of genius, a curious simplicity and good faith." A consularship in Mexico was offered Mr. Robinson, which he refused; then a place in the New York Custom House was opened, but this position of security he gave up in 1909, because he wished to devote his whole energy to writing. In 1910 Scribner's published *The Town Down the River.* The next year Mr. Robinson became a guest at the MacDowell Colony. His life from then until the present has been one of steady work and of steadfast devotion to the art in which he has shown a singular integrity.

And how do we rank Edwin Arlington Robinson? To speak in absolutes of the present is often embarrassing; to forecast a future position is futile: the years have a way of settling things in a fashion that often makes contemporary criticism ridiculous. History has impressive illustrations of contemporary heroes passing into quick obscurity, of obscure artists in time looming large. The critics of Mr. Robinson have almost unanimously pronounced him the greatest poet America has had, excepting only Walt Whitman. But American criticism is not always judicial; it is accused of the same mutual service that is attributed to American politics. There are little trinkling rivulets of gossip slipping out here, darting out there, from the fountainhead of culture on Manhattan. In the last decade there has been rumor of guilds and embargoes, even of bosses and gangs. One hears much of the fine art of *jacketeering.* And so each critic must largely handle his own case before a somewhat skeptical jury. The position that I shall take here is more extreme than that I have found anywhere in my reading.

It is my opinion that Mr. Robinson is not only one of the greatest poets of America—if not the greatest—but one of the greatest in the literature of the Occident, ranking with the greatest names of European, British, and American *makers.* The only thing we have to guide us in making our approximations of the present are those judgments that time has made of art in the past. Why do we rank as great Homer, Aeschylus, Dante, Cervantes, Shakespeare, Goethe? Why is Chaucer greater than Cowper, Whitman greater than Whittier, Shelley greater than Southey? The answer usually is that the great ones are those who excel both in conception and technique, both in vision and art. There must be vigor, intensity, power, beauty; there must be dramatic validity or essential truth. Does the poetry of Edwin Arlington Robinson have these elements? If so in what degree?

Mr. Robinson is, as anyone realizes who reads his poems extensively, a master of technique. He has superbly used every verse form—couplet, quatrain, sonnet, triolet, villanelle, ode, ballad and ballade, free verse, blank verse—and he has made all these traditional forms take on new life and new power. His vocabulary is probably the largest of all vocabularies, excepting neither that of Shakespeare nor that of Milton. He has utilized every poetic device: vivid diction, swift figure of speech, suspense, climax, initial parallelism, balance, antithesis, repetition, echo, interlacing, refrain, alliteration, assonance, lilting cadences, discordance, long rhythms, free rhythms. It is interesting to note that Mr. Robinson early wrote speech rhythms or "talking verse," that Mr. Frost was later to make peculiarly his own, and that he was also the earlier to use understatement and the diminished ending.

Indeed Mr. Robinson is more the innovator and creator than many of us realize. As one critic has said, "Tilbury Town was founded eighteen years before ground was broken along Spoon River."[1] And his portraits of Tilbury folk are on a much larger canvas than is generally known. Some are drawn on a vast scale with an amazing fidelity to detail. Some are as swiftly moving and as vivid, I risk saying, as those in Chaucer's Prologue; in fact, I think of the Tabard Inn as I think of the Chrysalis inn and Tilbury streets. There is not quite the naive realism or the quaint savor, but there are variety and objectivity close to life. And the characters of Camelot are as significant. The breath of life has been blown into these legends; and the men and women who people them are vitalized by the mind and spirit of today. If one should want proof of the creative capacity of Mr. Robinson, let him study *Tristram,* study it as to structure, as to characterization, as to style. Let him lay it beside all the other Tristan or Tristram versions: beside those of medieval Britain, of the French poets, of Gottfried von Strassburg, of Malory, of the nineteenth century poets—Tennyson, Swinburne, Matthew Arnold—of Thomas Hardy, of a score of our minor contemporaries in the frail poetry journals. Not until then will he realize how perennial is this interest in tragic human love, how moving and how passionate the story is today when motivated by the complex psychology that we may be beginning to understand. One is rather shaken by the beauty and the power with which Mr. Robinson has given life to the age-old legend.

The faults most commonly attributed to Mr. Robinson's poetry are obscurity and pessimism. Many lose patience with those "twists of language that are admittedly Robinsonian." His mannerisms of repetition and circumlocution displease, for instance like this from *Roman Bartholow.*

> There was a man once who believed himself
> Nearer to God, and by the way of reason—
> Where few may see, or seeing may dare to go—
> Than all the martyrs by the way of faith.
> Now I am not so sure that he was there—
> Though I believe it; and if I believe it,
> For all my needs I know it. Yes, he was there;

And where he was, he is,—a little scarred
Tonight, but nowhere else than where he was.[2]

Yet parallels are not wanting in some of the greatest books we have. And often this very trait gives a verbal magic, a subtle implication and power. Take this from *Cavender's House*—

If he was to learn
Too late for nature, it was not too late
To learn; although it was too late for envy
Of others who had married safer faces.[3]

Merlin has this, an echo that runs through many poems, the tragedy of man seeing too much:

I saw too much when I saw Camelot;
And I saw farther backward into time,
And forward, than a man may see and live,
When I made Arthur king. I saw too far,
But not so far as this.[4]

Some readers find the meaning of his poems obscure. They do not know whether his characters are real characters or ghosts of characters, whether the dramatis personae are persons or thoughts going on in the mind of the protagonist—fears, hallucinations, memories, regrets, aspirations. At least we find Mr. Robinson not alone before the bar on such a charge. There have been readers and critics, producers and scholars who have debated the question of Hamlet's madness and Banquo's ghost. Mr. Robinson is sometimes difficult, but so is Milton. He is often profound, with a predilection for something near the boundary line of the real and the unreal; but *Faust* indicates that Goethe was similarly interested. Any artist will not prove quite transparent who deals with the symbolism of human destiny.

The pessimism of Edwin Arlington Robinson is often a tangible thing. Detached passages, quoted lines, that are pessimistic could be piled up in quantity equal to the whole output of some of our contemporary minor poets. For example there is in "Captain Craig" a passage more realistic and even more wretched than Shakespeare's Seven Ages:

Yes, I have cursed
The sunlight and the breezes and the leaves
To think of men on stretchers or on beds,
Or on foul floors, things without shapes or names,
Made human with paralysis and rags;
Or some poor devil on a battlefield,
Left undiscovered and without the strength
To drag a maggot from his clotted mouth;
Or women working where a man would fall—
Flat-breasted miracles of cheerfulness
Made neuter by the work that no man counts
Until it waits undone; children thrown out
To feed their veins and souls on offal....[5]

But can we judge a poet by excerpts—at least a poet like Mr. Robinson, in whom there is so much of the organic whole? Would one seeing a writhing figure in a Sistine fresco say that Michelangelo was a pessimist? Seeing the Laocoon say that those Rhodian sculptors were pessimists? Reading the soliloquy of Hamlet or the curses of Lear say that Shakespeare was a pessimist?

There is too much of the dramatic in this poetry for it to be called pessimistic. Robinson is essentially a dramatist. He sees life much as Euripides saw life. And his tragedy is often tragedy in the purely Aristotelian sense. While only *Merlin, Lancelot* and *Tristram* show a great movement greatly moving toward catastrophe, he is constantly catching characters in conflict, he is constantly concerned with cause and effect. Mr. Robinson believes that tragedy grows out of character, character snarled by heredity or environment; that tragedy is tragedy wherever there is misunderstanding, frustration, failure. His tragic character may be a great man caught between conflicting loyalties, a great man tragic because he comes unknowingly into some predestined fate. Destiny—"there may be chance in this, there may be law,"—looms large and man, in his greatness or littleness, his dreams or his disillusionment, climbing to shining triumph or stumbling into chaos, man is tragic in his very humanity. He may be a perfect column flawed or he may be "one more foiled obscurity." He may be Richard Cory, Miniver Cheevy, Malory, Nightingale, Cavender, Roman Bartholow, Matthias, Timberlake, Lancelot, Merlin, Guinevere, Tristram, Isolt of the White Hands or Isolt of Ireland. Tilbury Town or Camelot—human tragedy is much the same. Fernando Nash, *The Man Who Died Twice,* is one of Mr. Robinson's significant tragic heroes. Fernando Nash, the giant that had been reduced, the "massive aggregate of the whole man disintegrated," the man who threw his scepter away and went wallowing, is the one who reproaches himself,

> All you had not then was only waiting
> To make of that which once was you a torch
> Of sound and fire that was to flood the world
> With wonder, and overwhelm those drums of death
> To a last silence.[6]

And Fernando Nash, who had in him the early ambition to be a singing fire and who had lost his aspiration in the drums of death, is still a tragic character; in the Aristotelian sense he is a victim of clashing destinies, in the modern sense he is a character falling into decay through some tragic fault. There is catharsis in his struggle, and there is at least the tragic illumination when out of his waste and ruin he comes to the realization that

God was good
To give my soul to me before I died
Entirely, and He was more than just
In taking all the rest away from me.
I had it, and I knew it; and I failed Him.[7]

Mr. Robinson's definition of the tragic hero would unquestionably be kin to the description he gives Fernando Nash:

There was in the man
With all his frailties and extravagances,
The caste of an inviolable distinction . . . .

There was the nameless and authentic seal
Of power . . . .

Crippled or cursed or crucified, the giant
Was always there.[8]

Lacking in Mr. Robinson is that dramatic range of personalities that we find, say, in Shakespeare; Mr. Robinson's characters, however, are blood and bone characters, and they speak in modulations of their own. For example, Laramie does not speak as Natalie speaks, and neither as Genevieve and Alexandra speak. Vivian is strikingly modern in her manner and as real as life. One wonders where Mr. Robinson goes for copy. Queen Morgan has tones and words, gestures and emotions that differ strikingly from those of Isolt of the White Hands and Isolt of Ireland, who in their turn, are different women by more than the color of their eyes and hair. Lancelot and Tristram have individual traits and accents; Lazarus, Rembrandt, Hamilton and Burr, John Brown, Merlin, Gawaine, Dagonet, Sir Lamarek—each becomes a character, convincing and valid. Whether in persons dramatically presented or in the shorter sketches, there is very real vitality. Mr. Flood, Uncle Ananias, Old King Cole, Isaac and Archibald—these are supremely human characters, humorously presented, but in the humor there is a profound understanding of the more somber shades in human experience. The sketch of Shakespeare in "Ben Jonson Entertains a Man from Stratford" is at once the most original and the most understanding in literature. The mother who sees in her commonplace son something shining in transcendent glory,

As upward through her dreams he fares,
Half-clouded with a crimson fall
Of roses thrown on marble stairs,[9]

reveals both pathos and absurdity, a combination surprisingly close to life. The tenderness of Charles Lamb pervades each line of "The Poor Relation":

They go and leave her there alone
To count her chimneys and her spires

. . . .

Her memories go foraging
For bits of childhood song they treasure.[10]

And so, while we may miss the staccato notes and the great sweeping spaces where strong winds blow, in the accents and the habitat of these characters; while we may regret that there is not the dramatic energy that moves through all human experience, we do realize that Mr. Robinson has both depth and breadth surpassing most poets. Too often those who make comment, have not read or else forget the virility of *Lancelot,* where the drama often moves with Elizabethan vigor:

They went unwillingly,
For they are new to law and young to justice;
But what they are to see will harden them
With wholesome admiration of a realm
Where treason's end is ashes. Ashes. Ashes!
Now this is better. I am King again.
Forget, I pray, my drowsy temporizing,
For I was not then properly awake . . . .
What? Hark! Whose crass insanity is that!
If I be King, go find the fellow and hang him
Who beats into the morning on that bell
Before there is a morning! This is dawn!
What! Bedivere? Gawaine? You shake your heads?
I tell you this is dawn! . . . . What have I done?
What have I said so lately that I flinch
To think on! What have I sent those boys to see?
I'll put clouts on my eyes, and I'll not see it!
Her face, and hands, and little small white feet,
And all her shining hair and her warm body—
No—for the love of God, no! it's alive!
She's all alive, and they are burning her—
The Queen—the love—the love that never was!
Gawaine, Bedivere, Gawaine! —Where is Gawaine!
Is he there in the shadow? Is he dead?
Are we all dead? . . . .
I cannot see her now in the smoke. Her eyes
Are what I see—and her white body burning!
She never did enough to make me see her
Like that! to make her look at me like that![11]

So speaks the broken Arthur, in anguish and repentance. But he is direct and simple when he later speaks to Sir Lucan, who relates bombastically, with not a little of Polonius in his polysyllabic indirections, what he has come to tell:

The penal flame had hardly bit the faggot,
When, like an onslaught out of Erebus,
There came a crash of horses, and a flash
Of axes, and a hewing down of heroes,
Not like to any in its harsh, profound,
Unholy, and uneven execution.
I felt the breath of one horse on my neck,

And of a sword that all but left a chasm
Where still, praise be to God, I have intact
A face, if not a fair one. I achieved
My flight, I trust, with honorable zeal . . . .
I found a refuge; and there saw the Queen
All white, and in a swound of woe uplifted
By Lionel, while a dozen fought about him,
And Lancelot, who seized her while he struck,
And with his insane army galloped away,
Before the living, whom he left amazed,
Were sure they were alive among the dead.[12]

There is that passage of poignant simplicity where the Fool speaks in *Merlin:*

Dagonet's quick eye
Caught sorrow in the King's; and he knew more
Of what was hovering over Camelot.
"O King," he said, "I cannot sing tonight.
If you command me I shall try to sing,
But I shall fail; for there are no songs now
In my old throat, or even in these poor strings
That I can hardly follow with my fingers.
Forgive me—kill me—but I cannot sing."[13]

A single reading of all that Mr. Robinson has written will leave the student in possession of a remarkably rich store of human types, of human experience, of the ideas that must always occupy the thinking man.

"I like Edwin Arlington Robinson because he is intellectually bracing," writes one of my friends. As I type this paper, I am listening between sections to the broadcast talks from Geneva; those speakers at the Disarmament Conference would find more passionate expression of the ideas they so sincerely set forth, and much of the same deep insight, in page after page of Mr. Robinson's poetry. Not only Captain Craig speaks in fierce denunciation of war; characters, one after another, cry out bitterly, sardonically, pityingly. Gawaine is as powerful as any when he says in *Lancelot,*

If war be war—and I make only blood
Of your red writing—why dishonor Time
For torture longer drawn in your slow game
Of empty slaughter? Tomorrow it will be
The King's move, I suppose, and we shall have
One more magnificent waste of nameless pawns,
And a few more knights. God, how you love
This game!—to make so loud a shambles of it,
When you have only twice to lift your finger
To signal peace, and give to this poor drenched
And clotted earth a time to heal itself.[14]

It may be Mr. Robinson speaking—for at times he does intrude, as Shakespeare did before him, putting his own words upon the lips of a character in some high moment—but Sir Lucan says,

Not even in the legendary mist

Of wars that none today may verify,
Did ever men annihilate their kind
With a more vicious inhumanity,
Or a more skilful frenzy.[15]

In a colloquy between Lionel and Lancelot, where the speeches have the swiftness and the verve of intelligent communication and the courtly brilliance that Mr. Robinson so often secures, Lancelot is explaining to Lionel the arrival through the rain of messengers not from Arthur,

For these who come,
If I be not immoderately deceived,
Are bearing with them the white flower of peace—
Which I could hope might never parch or wither,
Were I a stranger to this ravening world
Where we have mostly a few rags and tags
Between our skins and those that wrap the flesh
Of less familiar brutes we feed upon
That we may feed the more on one another.[16]

For Mr. Robinson poetry is a vehicle for thought, a medium for the communication of principles, beliefs, reflective analysis. He discloses the fallacies of what some label Democracy, discloses the complacence, the "tireless legislation," the determination of Demos—

I'll have it all alike and of a piece—
Punctual, accurate, tamed, and uniform,
And equal. Then romance and love and art
And ecstasy will be remembrances.[17]

He makes his characters denounce

the world's easy measurement of ruin
And its inch-ruling of the infinite.[18]

He sees in us all the same ignorance and the shame that moved man when he crucified Christ—and continues to crucify Him.

Mr. Robinson's attitude, says Lloyd Morris, is the "realist's recognition of the ironic discord between material experience and spiritual ideals." Any detailed study of his poetry will reveal how much Mr. Robinson is heir to his time and place. He is a reasoning man. He cannot take traditional beliefs and traditional attitudes simply for the sake of tradition. He sees clearly the danger if not the doom of an over-mechanized civilization. He scorns standardized mediocrity. He hates complacence. He denounces—by implication—prevailing judgments of success and failure. He faces courageously new approximations of truth. His spiritual struggle is something that of Tennyson's but it has gone further. The most poignant expression of his scientific doubt is that tremendous one in *Lancelot:*

God, what a rain of ashes falls on him
Who sees the new and cannot leave the old![19]

But there is still the tinge of New England in Mr. Robinson—the hue of the Puritan, the shade of Thoreau and of Emerson. The transcendentalist comes out again and again:

> There is a fenceless garden overgrown
> With buds and blossoms and all sorts of leaves;
> And once among the roses and the sheaves,
> The Gardener and I were there alone.
> He led me to the plot where I had thrown
> The fennel of my days on wasted ground,
> And in the riot of sad weeds I found
> The fruitage of a life that was my own.
>
> My life! Ah yes, there was my life indeed!
> And there were all the lives of humankind;
> And they were like a book that I could read,
> Whose every leaf, miraculously signed,
> Outrolled itself from Thought's eternal seed,
> Love-rooted in God's garden of the mind.[20]

The same note re-echoes through many poems. The seed, any growing thing, music, the gleam—the figure varies; but the idea is pervasive, from the first poems to the last that have so far appeared: in, through, beyond, above human life, shattered or ludicrous, tragic or comic, there is something of perfection, some kinship with a something that we cannot understand—

> the rhythm of God
> That beats unheard through songs of shattered men
> Who dream but cannot sound it.[21]

The vision, the light, the Gleam, the Holy Grail—this figure is used to symbolize human understanding, sympathy, the love of man for woman, the love of a mother, conceptions of a new social order, religious faith, the mystic seal:

> Alone, remote, nor witting where I went,
> I found an altar builded in a dream—
> A fiery place, whereof there was a gleam
> So swift, so searching, and so eloquent
> . . . . I awoke . . . and was the same
> Bewildered insect plunging for the flame
> That burns, and must burn somehow for the best.[22]

Arthur, lonely and seeing at least the pathos of his lost cause, says in his grief to Merlin,

> "Yet I'll not ask for more. I have enough—
> Until my new knight comes to prove and find
> The promise and the glory of the Grail,
> Though I shall see no Grail. For I have built
> On sand and mud, and I shall see no Grail."—
> "Nor I," said Merlin. "Once I dreamed of it,
> But I was buried. I shall see no Grail."[23]

Guinevere, seeing Lancelot troubled and repentant, partly in sorrow and partly in the wisdom and insight with which Mr. Robinson endows his women, says:

> "Lancelot,
> I say the dark is not what you fear most.
> There is a Light that you fear more today
> Than all the darkness that has ever been."[24]

That which forsakes the light, that forgets the glory, constitutes the tragic element of man.

> There were somewhere
> Disfigured outlines of a glory spoiled
> That hovered unrevealed and unremembered,[25]

he writes in *The Man Who Died Twice.* And it is only to the five or six of all the men in Tilbury Town, only the few "who had found somehow the spark in him" that Captain Craig reveals his tremendous humanity. This Light may be a fearful thing; it may mar comfortable ease, self-satisfaction, complacence. Many characters know the truth of this. Sir Bors felt something of it when he says to Lancelot:

> "And I saw once with you, in a far land,
> The glimmering of a light,"

Angrily he goes on,

> "The Light you saw
> Was not for this poor crumbling realm of Arthur,
> Nor more for Rome; but for another state
> That shall be neither Rome nor Camelot."[26]

But Lancelot knows the secret of his failure,

> "The Vision shattered, a man's love of living
> Becomes at last a trap and a sad habit."[27]

And at last, after his farewell to the nun who had been Guinevere,

> Over the land
> Around him in the twilight there was rest.
> There was rest everywhere; and there was none
> That found his heart. "Why should I look for peace
> When I have made the world a ruin of war?"
> He muttered; and a Voice within him said:
> "Where the Light falls, death falls . . . .
> And in the darkness comes the Light."[28]

In different temper, and yet with the same symbolism are those strong lines in "Captain Craig":

> Forget you not that he who in his work
> Would mount from these low roads of measured shame
> To tread the leagueless highway must fling first

And fling forever more beyond his reach
The shackles of a slave who doubts the sun.
There is no servitude so fraudulent
As of a sun-shut mind; for 'tis the mind
That makes you craven or invincible.[29]

And so we find the poetry of Edwin Arlington Robinson the poetry neither of pessimism nor the glorification of failure. For instance these eight lines have been quoted to show the morose poet:

Tumultuously void of a clean scheme
Whereon to build, whereof to formulate,
The legion life that riots in mankind
Goes ever plunging upward, up and down,
Most like some crazy regiment at arms,
Undisciplined of aught but Ignorance
And ever led resourcelessly along
To brainless carnage by drunk trumpeters.[30]

But taken in its context, this second "Octave" has no morbidity; it is a clarion call from that spendid poetry of the "Octaves." "Octave I" has as its key the fact that

We shrink too sadly from the larger self.[31]

"Octave IV,"

While we are drilled in error, we are lost
Alike to truth and usefulness

. . . .

We are too proud of death and too ashamed
Of God, to know enough to be alive.[32]

"Octave V,"

Our days are whirled and blurred
By sorrow, and the ministering wheels
Of anguish take us eastward, where the clouds
Of human gloom are lost against the gleam
That shines on Thought's impenetrable mail.[33]

"Octave VI" could have been written by Emerson, though it still has the full identity of Mr. Robinson:

When we shall hear no more the cradle-songs
Of ages—when the timeless hymns of Love
Defeat them and outsound them—we shall know
The rapture of that large release which all
Right science comprehends; and we shall read,
With unoppressed and unoffended eyes,
The record of All-Soul whereon God writes
In everlasting runes the truth of Him.[34]

The same recurrent thought, voiced by Mr. Robinson or by some character in Tilbury Town or Camelot, takes on a lofty dignity in "Octave XIV":

> Though the sick beast infect us, we are fraught
> Forever with indissoluble Truth,
> Wherein redress reveals itself divine,
> Transitional, transcendent. Grief and loss,
> Disease and desolation, are the dreams
> Of wasted excellence.[35]

and vivid imagery in "Octave VIII":

> There is no loneliness:—no matter where
> We go, nor whence we come, nor what good friends
> Forsake us in the seeming, we are all
> At one with a complete companionship;
> And though forlornly joyless be the ways
> We travel, the compensate spirit-gleams
> Of Wisdom shaft the darkness here and there,
> Like scattered lamps in unfrequented streets.[36]

When a review in *The Bookman* of *The Torrent and the Night Before,* pointed out that to Mr. Robinson the world was not beautiful but a prison-house, Mr. Robinson replied in a letter which was later quoted in the editorial section (March, 1897): "I am sorry that I have painted myself in such lugubrious colors. The world is not a 'prison-house' but a kind of spiritual kindergarten, where millions of bewildered infants are trying to spell God with the wrong blocks." There is much in Mr. Robinson's poetry to indicate a desire for education out of this kindergarten. Doubtless the best short poem to give expression to this desire is the sonnet "Credo."

Dramatically, the idealism is expressed by Captain Craig, who confesses himself to be

> Cliff-rubbed wreckage on the shoals
> Of Circumstance

but who can still say,

> It is the flesh
> That ails us, for the spirit knows no qualms,
> No failure, no down-falling: so climb high,
> And having set your steps regard not much
> The downward laughter clinging to your feet
> Nor overmuch the warning; only know
> As well as you know dawn from lantern-light
> That far above you, for you, and within you,
> There burns and shines, and lives unwavering
> And always yours, the truth. Take on yourself
> But your sincerity, and you take on
> Good promise for all climbing: fly for truth,
> And hell shall have no storm to crush your flight,
> No laughter to vex down your loyalty.[37]

This poet cries out against

> the cursed waste
> Of life in the beneficence divine

Of starlight and of sunlight and soul-shine
That we have squandered in sin's frail distress.[38]

This mortal surge
That beats against us now is nothing else
Than plangent ignorance.

The challenge is that we rise above this ignorance, that we face life undaunted, that we hear the music, follow the vision. There is a robust poetry in Mr. Robinson. Here is a full, strong expression of idealism in "L'Envoi":

Now in a thought, now in a shadowed word,
Now in a voice that thrills eternity,
Ever there comes an onward phrase to me
Of some transcendent music I have heard;
No piteous thing by soft hands dulcimered,
No trumpet crash of blood-sick victory,
But a glad strain of some vast harmony
That no brief mortal touch has ever stirred.
There is no music in the world like this,
No character wherewith to set it down,
No kind of instrument to make it sing.
No kind of instrument? Ah, yes, there is;
And after time and place are overthrown,
God's touch will keep its one chord quivering.[39]

Finer than this, and more significant poetry, is the long poem, "The Man Against the Sky." To break this spendid composition up into quotable fragments is to do it grievous wrong; it is a unit of singular integrity, and it is Edwin Arlington Robinson at his truest. Somewhere he says,

I have not drugged a clamoring vanity
With lies that for a little while may seem
To sweeten truth.[40]

In this poem Mr. Robinson makes no attempt to sweeten truth; he catches the age-old echo of elemental doubt and the wistful human wish that destiny is something high and good, or why are we here—we struggling, striving, yearning humankind? The same note is in Hebrew poetry, in Anglo-Saxon and Germanic poetry; and here it is again in "The Man Against the Sky."

Shall we, because Eternity records
Too vast an answer for the time-worn words
We spell, whereof so many are dead that once
In our capricious lexicons
Were so alive and final, hear no more
The Word itself . . . . ?

What have we seen beyond our sunset fires
That lights again the way by which we came?
Why pay we such a price, and one we give

So clamoringly, for each racked empty day
That leads one more last human hope away . . . .
If after all that we have lived and thought
All comes to Nought,—
If there be Nothing after Now,
And we be nothing anyhow,
And we know that,—why live?
'Twere sure but weaklings' vain distress
To suffer dungeons where so many doors
Will open on the cold eternal shores
That look sheer down
To the dark tideless floods of Nothingness
Where all who know may drown.[41]

This poem, Mr. Robinson writes me,* is the one that he thinks best represents his poetic vision.

And this poem with its vivid, its radiant, opening shows the sheer beauty which is again one of the qualities that make Mr. Robinson a major poet:

Between me and the sunset, like a dome
Against the glory of a world on fire,
Now burned a sudden hill,
Bleak, round, and high, by flame-lit heights made higher,
With nothing on it for the flame to kill
Save one who moved and was alone up there
To loom before the chaos and the glare
As if he were the last god going home
Unto his last desire.[42]

Miltonic elevation marks the next lines:

Dark, marvelous, and inscrutable he moved on
Till down the fiery distance he was gone,
Like one of those eternal, remote things
That range across a man's imaginings
When a sure music fills him and he knows
What he may say thereafter to few men,—
The touch of ages having wrought
An echo and a glimpse of what he thought
A phantom or a legend until then . . . .
Who moved along the molten west,
And over the round hill's crest
That seemed half ready with him to go down
Flame-bitten and flame-cleft.[42]

Though the beauty is usually more intellectual than sensuous, there is nevertheless in many poems a tonal magic and a richness of imagery:

When Avon, like a faery floor,
Lay freighted, for the eyes of One,
With galleons laden long before
By moonlit wharves in Avalon.[43]

Innumerable pictures colored like some old master's canvas:

The lady Vivian in a fragile sheath
Of crimson, dimmed and veiled ineffably
By the flame-shaken gloom wherein she sat . . .[44]

With a long-kindling gaze that caught from hers
A laughing flame, and with a hand that shook
Like Arthur's kingdom, Merlin slowly raised
A golden cup that for a golden moment
Was twinned in air with hers; and Vivian
Who smiled at him across their gleaming rims
From eyes that made a fuel of the night
Surrounding her, shot glory over gold
At Merlin, while their cups touched and his trembled.[45]

There is Isolt of Ireland, with her "violet eyes and Irish pride and blue-black Irish hair," whose

low voice tells how bells of singing gold
Would sound through twilight over silent water.[46]

And there is Tristram, who has been in the forest and is to return in happiness to Isolt:

Leaves and flowers,
Wild roses for Isolt encumbered him,
But were no bulk or burden as on he rode,
Singing, and seeing always in the firelight
He would find shining at his journey's end—
Isolt, always Isolt. She was not there,
He fancied smiling; she had never been there,
Save in a dream of his; the towers and walls
Of Joyous Gard were only a dream of his;
But heaven had let him dream for a whole summer,
And he was dreaming still as he rode through
The silent gate, where there were silent men.

. . . .

He passed them on his way to the still door
Where joy so often entered and came out.
A wonted sense of welcome failing him,
He summoned it from the twilight on the stair
And half began to sing with a dry throat
That held no song. He entered the same room
Where first Isolt had found him waiting for her,
And where, since then, he had so often found
Isolt, waiting for him. She was not there.[47]

And Tristram goes from place to place, comforting himself that she was away by chance; but the only sound in the whole house is that of his own pounding heart, and at last he stands alone,

More like a man of bronze than a man breathing.

He stumbles to a couch and sits staring until Gawaine enters.

Tristram arose,
Propping himself with pride and courtesy,

And stood there waiting for Gawaine to tell him
As much as he might tell.

When he hears that Isolt has been taken back to Cornwall,

Tristram, the doom of his prophetic mother,
Dropped like a log; and silent on the floor,
With wild flowers lying around him on the floor—
Wild roses for Isolt—lay like a log.[48]

Tristram is full of vivid beauty; often a poignant loveliness gives overtones to passages such as this:

Incredulous after Lancelot's departure
From Joyous Gard, Tristram alone there now
. . . . saw the ocean
Before him from the window where he stood,
And seeing it heard the sound of Cornish foam
So far away that he must hear it always
On the world's end that was for him in Cornwall.
A forest-hidden sunset filled long clouds
Eastward over the sea with a last fire,
Dim fire far off, wherein Tristram beheld
Tintagel slowly smouldering in the west
To a last darkness, while on Cornish rocks
The moan of Cornish waters foamed and ceased
And foamed again. Pale in a fiery light,
With her dark hair and her dark frightened eyes,
And their last look at him, Isolt of Ireland
Above him on the stairs, with only a wall
Waist-high between her and her last escape,
Stood watching there for him. . . . [49]

The poem closes with these lines that run like a fugue through the whole
whole composition:

And white birds everywhere, flying, and flying;
Alone with her white face and her grey eyes,
She watched them there till even her thoughts were white,
And there was nothing alive but the white birds flying,
Flying, and always flying, and still flying,
And the white sunlight flashing out to sea.[50]

An exquisite delicacy lifts lines and whole poems into grace and music. There are "women who are like slim cedars," and "Sappho, and the white leaves of her song." There is love which "like a wild wine" goes singing through one of those in Camelot; and in Tilbury Town one who sits

with aching arms and hardly catch
A few spilled echoes of the song of songs.[51]

Again and again we hear "the broken flutes of Arcady"—

A lonely surge of ancient spray

Told of an unforgetful sea,
But iron blows had hushed for aye
The broken flutes of Arcady.[52]

There is lyric tenderness in unforgettable passages, perhaps none more lovely than Guinevere's words to Lancelot when he is seeking to find a way out of his confusion and despair:

Were you to give a lonely child who loved you
One living thing to keep—a bird, maybe—
Before you went away from her forever,
Would you, for surety not to be forgotten,
Maim it and leave it bleeding on her fingers?
And would you leave the child alone with it—
Alone, and too bewildered even to cry,
Till you were out of sight?

But Mr. Robinson never holds any lyric note long enough to thin out his music, never intensifies a delicate emotion until it hints of the mawkish. These lines gain in intensity by the fact that almost at once Guinevere rises to a whipping reproach in words not far below Elizabethan scorn:

The queen in me would hardly go
So far off as to vanish. If I were patched
And scrapped in what the sorriest fisher-wife
In Orkney might give mumbling to a beggar,
I doubt if oafs and yokels would annoy me . . . .[53]

And then with a wistful wisdom, with just an edge of the sardonic, she confesses to Lancelot that she cannot see why their love need hurt his Vision—

She looked away: "If I were God," she said,
"I should say, 'Let them be as they have been.
A few more years will heap no vast account
Against Eternity, and all their love
Was what I gave them . . . .'
If I were God, I should say that to you."[54]

There is haunting sadness in the farewell at the convent in Almesbury, where Lancelot leaves forever and the golden queen Guinevere, seeing, as he rides away, her dim hands and still face. . . . . "Only as a bar of lost imperial music," is one of the phrases of the "Credo," and as such we hear this elusive lyricism—tender, understanding, wise, and proud, and occasionally serene.

Again, there is in Mr. Robinson's poetry a superb suggestiveness. To isolate lines from their context is not difficult, even though the passages have a singular integrity in the architecture of the poems; to quote those best illustrating this excellence is most difficult. There are those dynamic sketches of Shakespeare in "Ben Jonson Entertains a Man from Stratford," there are unforgettable landscapes and portraits of groups and dramatic situations, there are symbols that flash forth the significance of some magnificent idea. For swift description, for packed phrasing, for sheer craftsmanship these lines from *Merlin:*

> Away into the sunset where he saw
> Once more, as through a cracked and cloudy glass,
> A crumbling sky that held a crimson cloud
> Wherein there was a town of many towers
> All swayed and shaken, in a woman's hand
> This time, till out of it there spilled and flashed
> And tumbled, like loose jewels, town, towers, and walls,
> And there was nothing but a crumbling sky
> That made anon of black and red a ruin
> A wild and final rain on Camelot.[55]

In *The Man Who Died Twice* there is this picture of folly, the wastrels

> hating the magnificence they cursed,
> Seeing not the beauty or the use of it,
> They soiled with earthy feet the shining floor,
> Flinging the dregs of their debaucheries
> From crystal cups against the gleaming walls
> Of Life's immortal house.[56]

And there is the last, the twenty-third, of the "Octaves":

> Here by the windy docks I stand alone,
> But yet companioned. There the vessel goes,
> And there my friend goes with it; but the wake
> That melts and ebbs between that friend and me
> Love's earnest is of Life's all-purposeful
> And all triumphant sailing, when the ships
> Of Wisdom loose their fretful chains and swing
> Forever from the crumbled wharves of Time.[57]

Than this, I know no finer poetry of Immortality, of that soaring mystic imagination that reaches out to Infinity.

Beauty, then,—beauty of chaste simplicity, of movement, of color, of rich imagery, of poignant loveliness, of exquisite delicacy, of lyric tenderness, of superb suggestiveness—is an element strangely overlooked by those critics and readers who find only a tone too drab, an attitude too pessimistic; who remember only the cutting satire of some of the social figures, and a method obscure and eccentric. Indeed, the more we move among them, the more we come to realize that as varied as life itself are the moods and thoughts, the scenes and situations, the men and women of Tilbury Town and Camelot. This is an inspiriting thing: A man among us speaks in our own time, in our own tongue, with all the accents of contemporary speech, with all the facets of contemporary psychology, with all the gradations of contemporary condition in our social life—those of the home, the school, the church, the market, the laboratory, the streets, the inns—and we have Tilbury Town; he speaks in our own time, in our own tongue, and we have Camelot and

Joyous Gard. There are illusions and delusions, hopes and fears, visions, wrongs, aspirations, misunderstandings, frustrations, ecstasy, renunciations, joy, tragedies; young boys and old men, girls and aged mothers, the wealthy, the impoverished; kings and clowns undergoing what Bacon called *the wrong of time*—all seeking happiness, success, triumph, pleasure, "the lost imperial music," the Holy Grail. Here indeed is the Golden Thread, twining through human experience from the misty morning of King Arthur's court down to the age of the automobile and the aeroplane, from legendary Britain to the after-war America.

It is on evidence such as this that I build my case for the greatness of Edwin Arlington Robinson. There is vigor, there is intensity, there is power, there is beauty, there is dramatic sweep of real characters in real action, there is profound feeling for the grief and tragedy of man, there is essential art. I believe that his poetry is infinitely greater than the poetry of Walt Whitman, though Whitman as an Original will remain always significant in the history of American poetry. I believe that he surpasses much and equals most of Tennyson and Browning. If he has not the voluptuous beauty of Keats, the flaming lyricism of Shelley, he has more depth and far more range. He is transcendently above Victor Hugo, Musset, Lamartine, Verlaine, Gautier. I believe that he falls not far below Goethe in his intellectual conception of poetry, and that while he has nothing to equal the structure of *Faust,* he seizes upon more actual human experience. He has as great an ethical center as has Wordsworth, and is a surer artist. The great epics are greater than anything Mr. Robinson has done because of their high purpose and their sustained unity—their energy and elevation are supreme.

What Mr. Robinson may write yet, we do not know. But knowing his attitude toward art and life, we may be assured that he will not slip in the secure position he has so long and so honestly built up. He may not be our best-beloved poet, as our best-beloved music is rarely that of the greatest symphonies. But to one whose ear is attuned to Beethoven and Bach only the finest music can make appeal. In poetry there cannot be a great popular response to the "time-sifted few." Time may do strange things by the way of evaluation; but in the old and high tradition, this man is heir to the best. Edwin Arlington Robinson belongs, I think, among the Great Men. Somehow I find singularly fitting to foretell his own future position among the great poets of the Western world his closing lines, written in 1906 to Broadway:

> Here, where the white lights have begun
> To seethe a way for something fair,
> No prophet knew, from what was done,
> That there was triumph in the air.[58]

**Editor's note:* Facing page 318 of this article is a facsimile of the letter Robinson wrote Mrs. Romig from New York, dated January 7, 1932:

"It is difficult to answer your letter for lack of anything very specific to say, but taking your questions in order I might say something like this:

1. My interest in poetry goes back almost as far as I can remember.
2. There were not only days, but several years, when patience (with and without work) and faith were my main supports.
3. Perhaps 'The Man Against the Sky' comes as near as anything to representing my poetic vision— as you are good enough to call it.
4. I cannot attempt to say what will happen to poetry in America during the next two or three decades. A new light is likely to shine at any time.

I fear this will not be of much use to you in your talk on my work, and can only hope, with many thanks, that my work will serve you better."

---

1 Ben Ray Redman, *Edwin Arlington Robinson* (New York, 1926), 14.
2 *Roman Bartholow*, 816-817. All quotations from Robinson's works are by permission from the Macmillan Company; page references are to the 1930 edition of his *Collected Poems*.
3 *Cavender's House*, 966.
4 *Merlin*, 297.
5 "Captain Craig," 126-127.
6 *The Man Who Died Twice*, 930.
7 *Ibid.*, 955.
8 *Ibid.*, 956, 957.
9 "The Gift of God," 8.
10 "The Poor Relation," 46.
11 *Lancelot*, 392.
12 *Ibid.*, 395.
13 *Merlin*, 256.
14 *Lancelot*, 405.
15 *Ibid.*, 395.
16 *Ibid.*, 409.
17 *Cavender's House*, 975.
18 "Demos and Dionysus," 917.
19 *Lancelot*, 385.
20 "The Garden," 86.
21 "Captain Craig," 143.
22 "The Altar," 92.
23 *Merlin*, 253, 254.
24 *Lancelot*, 379.
25 *The Man Who Died Twice*, 953.
26 *Lancelot*, 403.
27 *Ibid.*, 417.
28 *Ibid.*, 448, 449.
29 "Captain Craig," 166.
30 "Octaves," 101.
31-36 *Ibid.*, 100-107.
37 "Captain Craig," 151.
38 "Two Sonnets," 89.
39 "L'Envoi," 108-109.
40 *The Man Who Died Twice*, 954.
41 "The Man Against the Sky," 68-69.
42 *Ibid.*, 60.
43 "The White Lights," 340.
44 *Merlin*, 269.
45 *Ibid.*, 276.
46 *Tristram*, 657.
47 *Ibid.*, 698-699.
48 *Ibid.*, 702.
49 *Ibid.*, 673.
50 *Ibid.*, 729.
51 "Captain Craig," 158.
52 "Ballade of the Broken Flutes," 78.
53 *Lancelot*, 418.
54 *Ibid.*, 419-420.
55 *Merlin*, 308.
56 *The Man Who Died Twice*, 951.
57 "Octaves," 107.
58 "The White Lights," 340.

ROBINSON AS MAN AND POET

HARRIET MONROE

THE DEATH of Edwin Arlington Robinson in early April was a sorrow to his friends, and a shock to his admirers who, after gathering too slowly, had become a large and loyal audience. But, as one surveys his symmetrically rounded life in its completeness, it becomes impossible to grieve for him — the elegy should be a song of triumph. In youth he had outlined an austere and difficult pattern to live by, and with rare precision he had devoted his later years to filling in the design with strong lines and ardent delicate colors. His work was done. Bad health had begun to undermine his strength and threaten his creative power. I am told he felt that it was time for his story to end.

My mind goes back to our first meeting. It was in 1906, when numerous devotees of the arts were summering in beautiful Cornish, and Robinson had come to New Hampshire to spend a few days with his friend and mine, William Vaughn Moody, the poet and playwright. "A mighty good poet — very simple bare style," Moody had said of this author of three neglected books of verse. And when I read the long narrative, *Captain Craig*, the latest of them, I realized that this poet of the lean phrase and the nutty flavor was no Victorian, though I could not foresee that in his ascetic style and realistic approach to subject a "new movement" was beginning which was destined to lead poetic art away from Victorian tradition and practice.

I found him shy, quiet, reticent, holding off from easy intimacies. I doubt if anyone in Cornish, after his brief visit knew any better than before what was going on in his mind. His instinct for isolation, for self-dependence, was strengthened during these difficult years by the public endorsement of it; for apparently only a few friends cared what he was thinking or writing, and even the outspoken admiration of President Theodore Roosevelt did not avail to sell his books. It brought him, however, a clerkship in the New York Custom House, which for

Reprinted by permission, *Poetry,* XLVI (June 1935), 150-157.

a few years eased the strain of poverty. When even that strain seemed more endurable than the dull routine of such an office, he resigned, encouraged by a few slight evidences of increasing interest in his work.

The habit of isolation grew upon him, however, though it never tempted him toward egoism. A certain humility and self-distrust tempered the fine steel of his character, and made him proof against adulation — when at last it came, emphasized by three Pulitzer prizes — and against the reverent affection felt for his leadership by the writers and other artists who spent many summers with him at the MacDowell Colony in Peterboro. Here he seemed to unbend more than in New York and Boston, where most of his later life was passed. When I stopped for three days in 1926 to see the Colony, I felt better acquainted with him than ever before; especially over the billiard-table, for he was the local champion and I from childhood had always been tempted by a cue. In this congenial atmosphere, encouraged by Mrs. MacDowell's warm friendship and wise sympathy, he not only wrote most of his later books, but became more companionable, and perhaps happier, than he had ever been before.

When Mrs. MacDowell, showing me the cottages, interrupted him one morning, he had just finished *Tristram* — "a poem Miss Monroe will *loathe!*" he exclaimed with a smile and a guttural emphasis on the verb. The verb was too strong, but I never followed with sympathy the excursions to Camelot of this far-traveler who had scarcely stepped west of New York, and only once crossed the sea to England. What I thought of *Tristram,* after the Literary Guild's powerful boost had started it toward its record sale, may be found by the curious in *Volume XXXI* of *Poetry;* and what I thought, and still think, of Robinson's work in general was first printed as an editorial in January, 1925, and now opens my book of essays, *Poets and Their Art,* and is partly repeated in the biographical section of *The New Poetry.* Indeed, there is no modern poet whom I have written about more explicitly in terms that I would ratify today; so that anything I might add in the way of tribute or criticism would be mainly repetition.

It might be interesting, however, to study the psychology of the man — the effect of his rather solitary habits on his work, the action and reaction between the life of his mind and spirit and that of his senses and perceptions. His perceptions were acute, and his keen imagination was always at work on them, enlarging and intensifying the record of experience. At first, during and soon after his youth in "Tilbury Town" — otherwise Gardiner, Maine, it was close and personal experience which he recorded and intensified in such poems as "Richard Cory," "Dear Friends," "Amaryllis," "Lorraine," "Aunt Imogen," and "Captain Craig," the earliest and one of the most humane of his long narratives. He had known such individuals personally, and they were usually a sorry lot. In his Maine village, as in so many small New England towns, the people were mostly the unadventurous, the frustrated, the failures; for braver souls had sought braver fortunes in the growing cities and spacious plains out westward. Thus it was the pathetic or comic or tragic residue of ineffectual citizenship that Robinson came in contact with during his mind's formative period, and it would seem that his studious and loyal sympathy with such twisted characters gave a sombre coloring to his imaginative studies of humanity through the rest of his life.

For again and again he repeats the theme of human failure, giving it dignity, and once or twice almost tragic splendor, in making it deal with the frustration of genius. "Captain Craig" aspires to this theme, for the garrulous old codger, its hero, was "one of Apollo's pensioners" —

> Sage-errant, favored of the Mysteries,
> And self-reputed humorist at large —

a man primed full-up with iconoclastic Socratic wisdom which the poet, in Plato's fashion, proceeds to set down and amplify. We find the theme repeated with variations, or at least hinted at, in certain lyrics and sonnets, in his latest long narrative, *Amaranth,* and especially in the best one of all, *The Man Who Died Twice,* published over a decade ago. A variant of this motive may be found in the triangle tales — *Roman Bartholow, Cavender's House, Glory of the Nightingales, Matthias at the Door, Talifer* and the rather futile Camelot series, in which the frustrated talent (it has rarely the flash and color of genius) is a talent rather for life than for art, and the frustration comes through ill-assorted marriage and consequent love-entanglement.

These are all tales of spiritual failure; and if, during the past ten years, they have become more and more theoretic and remote — abstractions mind-conjured rather than living figures — that may be the penalty the poet paid for his life-long reserve, for his retreat from close contacts, from intimate experience. Into his adult province no child ever entered. He observed keenly the world's blasting of its most precious souls, and the psychological discords which ruined them, but he observed these from his study, from the sacred enclosure where his mind worked them over into the richly orchestrated harmonies of his blank verse.

The Man Who Died Twice, published ten years ago, was more strictly a soul-biography than any of the later poems; and more loftily the record of a soul equipped for high achievement, born to be a great artist in music but self-ruined and self-betrayed. Fernando Nash is a grand figure in his fall, and the element of the grotesque, a note of tragic irony which is pitiful rather than bitter, emphasizes the riddle of the man's destiny when he is found beating Salvation Army drums in a village street. The poet's blank verse plays orchestral measures in honor of the agony of genius; the solemn fall of the lines strikes on the heart like the slow march of a regiment passing with dirges to a hero's burial. More than twenty years of practice and discipline had gone by since the stark rhythms of "Captain Craig" sounded their new tune, and gradually the poet had achieved wonderful power over his instrument until, in the climax of this symphonic poem, it rolls out magnificent harmonies.

The climax of this poem was perhaps also the climax of the poet's career. Certainly he never surpassed it in any of the later narratives. Some of these seem repetitions, reminding us of that fateful line,

> The way of custom being the way of death.

They show an increasingly theoretic contact with life, achieved by thinking rather than by imaginative brooding over the hints supplied by direct experience. The three Camelot poems especially record a retreat from life; the famous old tales were a refuge, to retell them in modern terms a tempting mental exercise.

But Robinson was not always concerned with failures; a number of his poems celebrate successes. Not only a few beautiful brevities like "Cliff Klingenhagen," "Flammonde," "Eros Turannos," "Uncle Ananias," and the adorable "Mr. Flood's Party," in all of which a spiritual triumph is wrung out of meagre and reluctant destinies, but also in the longer monologues uttered by or about the Apostle Paul, our own apostolic John Brown, Theodore Roosevelt "the revealer," and Shakespeare and Lincoln. These monologues do not always quite achieve their aim. Paul talks too long and too placidly; Roosevelt's lively and engaging personality is not generously revealed, and Lindsay and Sandburg have done vastly better with the half-mythical John Brown, to whom Robinson accords only one great line, the last of the hero's monologue:

> I shall have more to say when I am dead.

But Shakespeare's clash of magnificent powers with

> The mystery that's his — a mischievous
> Half-mad serenity that laughs at fame
> For being won so easy —

this is presented, in "Ben Jonson Entertains a Man from Stratford," with a complete mastery which ought to silence forever the Baconians and other theorists who try to strip the man Shakespeare of his glory. And "The Master" is a great Lincoln poem, second only to Whitman's magnificent elegy among the many tributes which have been written in verse and prose.

Robinson's life-work is itself a great success-story. He would deny this if he were alive to sum it up with a final estimate; he would say it was all fragmentary and ineffectual, a faint projection from the knowledge in his mind, the sympathy in his heart. Measuring the distance between aspiration and achievement, he would feel, like his own Shakespeare, that his struggle

> Against the fiery art that has no mercy

had ended in defeat, or at least in a drawn battle that brought no feeling of victory.

But for us the story is heroic, the achievement is a triumph. Against all odds this poet kept the faith. Through lean years of obscurity he wrote memorable poems, inheritors of what we mortals call immortality. His fame is now ours to cherish, his life ours to admire. To his fellow-countrymen especially they become a proud heritage of beauty.

E. A. ROBINSON'S LATER POEMS

DAVID BROWN

THE PUBLIC response to the narrative poems of Robinson which appeared after *Tristram* was chilly. The poems were praised, but usually with a hovering air of disappointment or uneasiness. The enormous popular success of *Tristram,* largely the result of the friendly advertising efforts of Robinson's literary admirers, has blinded critics, if not to the true value of the later poems, at least to their significance in Robinson's career. It is still too early to predict the measure of permanence which these poems will enjoy in relation to the earlier ones. Robinson himself rarely felt disposed to justify a particular work, or even to judge it, in terms of such finality.

> One accent of the Holy Ghost
> The heedless world has never lost,

Emerson had said, and Robinson shared this optimistic fatalism concerning his own works. For him each poem presented a problem which he sought to solve with that concentrated and devoted art which many fellow-craftsmen have admired. Although it is too early to judge the relative permanence of these later volumes, it is possible to accord them a closer critical attention than they have received.

They achieve in varying degree the final aim of Robinson's maturest purposes in art and thought. They succeed in approximating the total artistic intention of Robinson's personality from his own point of view, whether or not they succeed, or ever will succeed, in satisfying the needs of readers. If we approach them in this light, we can see in them elements that will teach us not only an increased regard for this group of poems, but perhaps also a new appreciation and understanding of the meaning of the earlier and much more popular volumes.

This meaning may be sought in two ways: in a description of the art-form toward which Robinson had been striving, and in a formula-

Reprinted by permission, *New England Quarterly,* X (September 1937), 487-502.

tion of the underlying convictions of which his art is the concretion. An understanding of both these matters leads one to the inevitable opinion, I believe, that *Cavender's House* is immeasurably greater in its artistic achievement than *Tristram* — not that this necessarily means that it is a greater poem. The mere fact that it is not generally felt to be a special kind of triumph in relation to Robinson's earlier works justifies an attempt to set a value on its significance — and with it, in some measure, the significance of the later narratives — *The Glory of the Nightingales, Matthias at the Door, Talifer, Amaranth,* and *King Jasper.*

If we glance back at the earlier forms in which Robinson was interested, and in which many of his most popular poems were written, we shall see that from the beginning of his career, he had been concerned with contemporary characters and character-types. It is no accident that the most frequently quoted of Robinson's poems should be "Richard Cory," in which the tragic story of a life is told in sixteen verses. There are many such studies in the early volumes — "Reuben Bright," "Cliff Klingenhagen," "Aaron Stark," etc. As he grew in maturity Robinson developed this character study in two ways: first, by means of a more elaborate poetic form in which to treat character, as in the blank-verse narrative, "Isaac and Archibald"; second, by an increased abstraction of the character-type itself within narrow limits. One has but to compare "Richard Cory" (1897) with "Job the Rejected" (1921) to satisfy oneself as to the increased complexity of the character who serves as theme and the increased abstraction of the point in character which interests Robinson. Interest in contemporary character was fundamental with Robinson, however, and this background should always be kept in mind in a consideration of the later long narratives. These are in origin character-studies of more extended scope.

Abstraction may occur in terms of an increased inclusiveness of the moral type depicted, or in terms of symbols. Robinson used this second method, also. From his earliest volume we may gather evidence that the symbol appealed to him as a device for suggesting a more inclusive world of experience than the particular contains. "Luke Havergal" is such a poem from *The Children of the Night.* The title suggests a character-portrait, but the mode of art is quite unlike that of "Richard Cory," being more lyrical and connotative.

> Go to the western gate, Luke Havergal,
> There where the vines cling crimson on the wall,
> And in the twilight wait for what will come.
> The leaves will whisper there of her, and some,
> Like flying words, will strike you as they fall;
> But go, and if you listen she will call.
> Go to the western gate, Luke Havergal —
> Luke Havergal.

This same early volume gave evidence of further interests. It contained a great many more philosophical or reflective poems than have since appeared in the *Collected Poems.* The interest that Robinson had in character was always a double one — he was attracted to what might be called a special case of significant character as in "Richard Cory," but frequently he was more attracted to the significance in more general terms. Characters often were but illustrations of a truth, and Robinson thought much in moral abstractions about the truth. Thus, we find didactic poetry, in which Robinson attempts to versify some of his convictions. The title-poem of *The Children of the Night,* "Credo," "The master and the slave go hand in hand," and the "Octaves" exhibit Robinson's concern with a poetry whose appeal should lie in deftly formulated thought on a multitude of life's meanings. This neo-classical element in his work has often been noted.

In the form these poems take, as with the studies of character, we may notice the existence of the lyrical method as well as of that of intellectual abstraction. In his philosophical poems one discovers a larger kind of symbolism and its effect of emotional abstraction. In the first volume it finds its best expression in "The Wilderness."

> The songs that call for us to-night, they have called for men before us,
> And the winds that blow the message, they have blown ten thousand years;
> But this will end our wander-time, for we know the joy that waits us
> In the strangeness of home-coming, and a woman's waiting eyes.

Such poems are "The Klondike" in *Captain Craig,* the title-poem of *The Town Down the River,* and "The Man Against the Sky."

These types can not be kept wholly separate, and indeed the last-mentioned poem is essentially a union of the two methods of philosophical poetry. It will be sufficient if one notices that there are two distinguishable interests of Robinson's mind: a desire to depict character, and a desire to convey abstract truth; and that each of these interests finds two predominating modes of expression: intellectual abstraction, and the emotional abstraction of symbolism.

Robinson continued to write short poems of these different kinds throughout most of his career. But he very early began the search for something more inclusive of all these interests. In the much-neglected "Captain Craig" one finds most of them at work, not wholly in harmony. The poem concerns an extraordinary character, originally suggested by an actual acquaintance, whose nature presents the paradox of success and failure in life, a theme to which Robinson was often to return. The flow of the captain's talk, earnest, whimsical, trifling, profound, touches this question constantly. Captain Craig, however, is not simply a character whose nature is interesting in itself; he is an opportunity for the setting-forth of the practices in contemporary American life by contrast with its professed ideals. "If I was interpreting anything in Captain Craig," Robinson wrote to Charles Eliot Norton, "it was America, I should say, rather than life. I do not mean to leave a final impression of anything more than hope, more or less obfuscated, may be, but still good-natured and real." Running through the poem is the picture of a professed Christian charity that finds itself uncertain and timid, not to say cruel, in face of the disreputable. The "hope" of which Robinson speaks concerns rather more than hope for America, however, for Robinson uses the captain as the mouth-piece of a faith in man which serves as the answer to the pessimism which prevailed at the end of the nineteenth century.

"Captain Craig" is not wholly a successful poem. The reason for its partial failure lies in the inadequacy of its artistic technique. The setting and narrative are far too thin to sustain the theme for nearly two thousand lines of blank verse; they do not disguise the extent to which the poem is a didactic soliloquy by Robinson himself. He had too many things to say, and no adequate concrete material in which to embody them.

Robinson, of course, was not speaking merely for himself, and he was no tramp. In so far as "Captain Craig" is not soliloquy, it is a kind of "dramatic monologue." This device of art was another of Robinson's interests. Every reader knows the highly successful dramatic monologue on Shakespeare, "Ben Jonson Entertains a Man from Stratford," and it is commonly assumed that Robinson achieved more success in this form than he actually did. It is further assumed that he used it often — as he did not. His most conspicuous failures in verse are attempts at the dramatic monologue as Browning perfected it. Two early poems in this form were not included from his first volumes in his *Collected Poems* — "For Calderon" and "The Night Before." "An Island" — Napoleon speaking about the time of his death — has rarely seemed a success to his readers. "Rembrandt to Rembrandt" seems less powerful now than it appeared to the first reviewers in 1921. The form of dramatic monologue did not suit Robinson's temper, for he could not rest content with a character's state of mind at an exciting moment in its history. He had to see it all around and to present what it meant.

The few notable successes in this form, it may be noted in passing, invert Browning's technique. Browning made obscure people who had failed express a faith which was their spiritual success in advance of the great who achieved recognition. Robinson was interested directly in the characters of the great, and approached them — St. Paul, Lazarus, Shakespeare — through the meditative soliloquies of contemporaries. His successful dramatic monologues, thus, are less dramatic than meditative.

Something similar to direct narrative was necessary for Robinson's art, and his experiments and achievements in this form are notable. His human interests were too complex for the way of simple story, as Tennyson had used the form. He had small concern about the picturesque, which has often served to disguise poverty of thought and emptiness of feeling. Even the larger world of beauty was not primarily a concern of his temperament. Thus, in his narratives, his purposes demand the suppression of picturesque action so that people may be set talking, for he was interested in the analysis and judgment of character. Many readers thus come to feel that they have been unreasonably cheated of the facts in such poems as "Captain Craig," "Tasker Norcross," and "Avon's Harvest." He had difficulty, indeed, with the manipulation of the details of plot and was not, perhaps, very inventive in this respect.

It is likely that one important reason for Robinson's use of the Arthurian material was the release it afforded him from the supplying of those external facts which were outside his interest. The plots were ready-made, and the reader could supply whatever he did not care to give. Hence, *Merlin, Lancelot,* and *Tristram* each presented him with a setting and plot for that triangular character relationship of husband-wife-and-friend which he was often to use in contemporary settings. Thus the Arthurian poems are to be regarded as transitional in the development of Robinson's art, though we need not stress the point too much. *Merlin* and *Lancelot* could have taught him all he needed to know; the *Tristram* probably contained its own inherent and compelling appeal to the author of the other two.

Robinson was striving to gain mastery of a form for the presentation of contemporary life in which he could achieve at once the immediacy which is necessary in the presentation of vital action and the detachment which is necessary for conveying his sense of its meaning. He needed for the expression of his total talent an opportunity for detached analysis of soul which the lyric or dramatic monologue resists. At the same time he needed a form in which he could express the sense of immediate contact with a soul which is more the function of drama and dramatic monologue than of poetic narrative. Drama set him too much within the requirements of actual description of psychological states and forbade him the exercise of judgment and reflection which were his supreme gifts; mere narrative required too much decoration and too much attention to externals.

In *The Man Who Died Twice* he approached his form in those sections which recorded a dream. There, with a character selected from the modern world, he could draw on a wealth of tradition and knowledge and poetic symbol in the record of a dream world. The character was an artist, however, and literature is more intelligible to the mass of men when it is not written about artists. *Roman Bartholow* took the way of symbols in part: a redeemer who betrayed the redeemed, a lover who emerged from delusion, a dead soul who sought real death. These things were of more value than many Tristrams or Merlins or Lancelots in the development of Robinson's search for a modern art. But there was still something perhaps a trifle thorny and obscure about Robinson's themes, and unquestionably much that failed in general interest about the characters. There is also — wherever Robinson is unsure of himself — a kind of irrelevant and capricious whimsicality of detail, which may be a mask to cover a half-consciously perceived difficulty. A restraint in enthusiasm for these two works is always understandable.

It is with *Cavender's House* that Robinson's goal is achieved, for here the diverse intentions of his art are fused into a lucid unity. The story is clear and powerful: Cavender, who had twelve years before murdered his wife, Laramie, in a sudden fury of jealousy, has returned to his house and the scene of the crime. In the moonlight he converses with the apparition of his dead wife, and the result of their conversation is his conversion to a new mode of action. The poem ends with the suggestion that he will give himself up to justice. This is the "plot." But the details of the poem are symbolical rather than real, and one learns from the opening lines

> Into that house where no man went, he went
> Alone . . .

that the immediate action is a mental or spiritual one of which the details are symbols. The "house" is Cavender's spiritual world, the shade of Laramie is not an apparition but a concretion of all Cavender knows, loves, suspects, and repents concerning his dead wife. These symbols carry one, thus, into a more inclusive world than the world which they factually present. Furthermore, though in the form of a narrative which records the conversation of two beings, there is really but one speaker at a decisive moment in his life. In this derived sense, the poem is a dramatic monologue. And finally, the poem, though depicting much of the "psychology" of crime and punishment, is directed in its total effect to the exposition of a larger moral perception than is derivable from the mere description of psychological states. It is the presentation of a "conversion" which is the result of Cavender's learning to shift the grounds of his suffering and questioning to a higher plane of truth. For twelve years he has been asking himself the wrong question, namely, whether or not he had been right in his suspicion of Laramie's infidelity. Since Laramie in the poem is no more than what he knows of her, she can not answer. But she can talk with the voice of Cavender's conscience once it has learned to acknowledge the truth.

> How do you know the stone you cast that night
> Was not your fear, hammered to look like love
> By passion and sick pride? Love would have been
> The death of you far likelier than of her,
> If there was to be death. Love, would you call it?

From then on, Cavender's suffering finds the door open toward self-knowledge and peace. The poem, thus, is at once a narrative poem, superficially in its technique; a dramatic monologue, in its essential situation; and a symbol of the nature of a moral issue in its total meaning.

Perhaps the scope and significance of the art of this poem have not been fully realized by critics. In its inclusiveness there is argument for regarding it as one of the richest of modern poems — if not in achievement, then at least in intention. We have seen much experimentation in poetic art since the turn of the century in America; there has been much restlessness among poets concerning the form which would hold the diverse experiences of modern minds. The varied experimental forms have exhibited too plainly their own necessary limitations, and hence even among much that is of high excellence there often remains for the readers a dissatisfaction and sense of incompleteness which the limits of the form create. In a fully rounded work of imagination symbols alone will not do. They rarely carry one far into an objective world, as Eliot's *Waste Land* proves. But, on the other hand, a mere narrative, whatever the subject, can not be found to include the diverse experiences of modern liberal minds, as Benet's *John Brown's Body* shows. Tennyson's heroic effort to make the Arthurian material national failed with astute English readers, and no one has succeeded since. Furthermore, abstract studies of a moral universe, in which Robinson had great interest, and which he managed to objectify in "The Man Against the Sky," do not of themselves allow of extension into a long poem. Finally, Browning had done all there was to do with the dramatic exposition of a significant psychological state. Robinson, having himself experimented, as we have seen, and achieved in art-forms illustrative of all these purposes, sought to fuse them in one. In *Cavender's House* the fusion is accomplished.

It is significant that after this poem Robinson did not return to the court of King Arthur. His nearest approach was to a monarch of modern industry, called King Jasper. The long narratives which follow, though none until *King Jasper* is so perfect as *Cavender's House*, are tragedies or tragi-comedies — *Talifer* is a comedy throughout — of modern life, in which a moral problem of modern life is viewed reflectively through the words of a small group of characters when (or shortly after) the moral struggle has been brought to an issue. All of them are more than they say as narrative, for all are symbolical and psychological in method and moral in intention. Robinson had developed the management of narrative which he needed for these in the Arthurian stories. *Cavender's House* taught him how to apply the technique with assurance to modern life. *Matthias at the Door*, *The Glory of the Nightingales*, *Talifer*, *Amaranth*, and *King Jasper*, though certainly works of varied merit and interest, are all assured in their technique and deft in construction.

Along with the development of skill in the manipulation of his form, Robinson shows a growing development in clarifying his underlying convictions about human nature and in revealing them through his characters. Poets, to be sure, resent strict formulation of their ideas, since the formulation is often to them a pale substitute for their poems. Critics of Robinson have yielded to this poetic prejudice in order to escape the necessary labor of exposition. Yet this is just the critic's function: the translation of poetic into intellectual experience. Had it been tried more often on Robinson, we should have had greater respect for his later poems.

In "The Children of the Night" he had spoken of the duty of reverence for "the Self which is the Universe" as an antidote to the breakdown of faith in a cosmic protector of the soul and of the impossible theology which served for current explanation of him. One might say that the whole body of Robinson's imaginative concretion of experience in poetry embodies some aspect of his faith in "the Self which is the Universe." Among many mechanisms in the modern world for the dispersion of the self — in the cosmic urge, in the subliminal unconscious, in the structure of the braincells, in the hormones or the genes, in a kind of accidental atomic consciousness — he clung tenaciously to the conviction that every self has its own sense of identity. He *believed* in separate selves, and, from all any one has ever written about him personally, he was exceedingly charitable toward their validity as such in real life. The early studies of the people of Tilbury Town are evidence of an interest which continued, grew, and expanded in the range of its moral inclusiveness throughout Robinson's life.

Yet he recognized in each self a power of illusion with respect to its own nature, and he shows that out of the illusions of selves grew suffering, defeat, distortion, and misdirection of effort. The early poems rarely reveal the nature of the illusion, resting content to set forth the evidence of a struggle that implies a battle of soul which has gone on in a realm deeper and more serious than the conventional. Richard Cory shoots himself for an unexplained reason that reminds us merely that separate selves have dissatisfactions more subtle than want of wealth and social approval and comfort. But the later poems reveal more clearly the nature of human dissatisfactions which are thrown up into self-consciousness by some shock that breaks the glass of illusion. In the alien face and hostility of Young Hebron, King Jasper learns to look on an action of his past which he had never faced — and, it may be added, he learns to triumph over himself while he goes down to defeat superficially.

For Robinson, the Self, with its perpetual power of absorption of the exterior world and with its sudden mysterious needs that arise to shatter its own previous self-knowledge, was the mystery, fascination, tragedy, and comedy of human nature. Perhaps as a young man at Harvard he had heard William James say that "the self is separated from the not-self by an ever-shifting line of demarcation"; or that "each of us dichotomizes the Cosmos in a different place." With or without this influence on his thinking, Robinson sought to build his moral judgments on the fundamental truth of the two propositions, with the infinite variety in human values that they imply.

He constantly sets the problem of an individual self against one of the many theories which men use to explain or justify or excuse an action. It is important to understand the exact *locus* of his interest. He is so frequently described as subtle, brooding, obscure, uncertain, dubious, that one may be certain that the essence of his faith and conviction has been misunderstood. Many readers apprehend easily enough his actual doubt of the familiar modern and ancient theories of human nature but do not perceive in him the existence of a centre of faith. He say, for instance, of Cavender

> He had come because
> The world he wandered was a world too small
> Where there was not that house. Some chemistry
> Of fate, forestalling him, had long ago
> Combined his coming with necessity,
> Perhaps, if that would help. It would not help.

Properly read, this passage says that for Cavender, whatever the truth of the theory may be, the issue is not one of natural determinism, and that the theory has no bearing or relevance to his problem. But there are moments when such a law has great relevance, as when Mallory, intent on murder, finds Nightingale stricken with arthritis and ataxia. Cavender's problem is to free his mind of a false and illusory question, which, however it may have come into being, is his question and concerns his soul.

Each of the long narratives deals with a single character faced with the problem of determining its destiny after an event which shatters its illusions. Captain Craig, the tramp and failure, can speak triumphantly from his death-bed of his joy in values superior to success. Roman Bartholow, having emerged from despair through the help of Penn-Raven, is suddenly brought to face the illusion inherent in his love for Gabrielle and his gratitude to Penn-Raven through the shock of his discovery of their treacherous love. The very title of *The Man Who Died Twice* is symbolic of the relation of self-knowledge and illusion in terms of life and death. Matthias is brought to a true conception of his own nature after the deaths of Garth, Natalie, and Timberlake — which are the means for bringing his consciousness to the recognition of his selfishness in competition with men, in love, and in friendship. Matthias may live in hope, and may not go the way of the rest to death, for his spirit has been made alive by his casting out of self-deception. Talifer manages to free himself from an absurd aberration in love to return to Althea. *Amaranth,* though it is the poorest of the later narratives, makes Robinson's point most clear of all by putting the problem of self-knowledge in the simplest of terms. Here all the characters live in a nightmare-land of the unreal because they have known themselves so little as to have found the wrong occupations in life. The search of each character is for the discovery of the inevitable in his own soul, which is the true principle of life, which is Amaranth, "the flower that never fades." The moral sanity of men rests, as Robinson presents them, on the psychological veracity of their own self-awareness.

Once one has understood the symbols of these later poems and has isolated the central issue, a good deal of their alleged obscurity disappears. They never become easy, of course, but they become clearer if one avoids the error which unconsciously obscures much criticism of Robinson. In *Matthias at the Door,* for instance, readers are likely to be especially affected by the melancholy deaths of Garth, Natalie, and Timberlake, whom they understand more readily than Matthias, and to suppose the poem singularly morbid and sad. Sad it is, of course, where so much unnecessary misery is to be found. But readers should not forget Matthias, concerning whom the poem is written, and who ends — not, to be sure, a happy man — but a free soul. Robinson is sad in mood perhaps only in the extent to which he is constantly willing to put life at its worst in order to reveal most forcefully the point in which it is the ultimate value. The great tragedy for Robinson is suicide.

> My penance [Laramie says] is that I may say no more
> Of life than that you are to learn of it
> A best way to endure it to the end.

This is the negative and the stoic aspect of Robinson's point of view. But it should not be forgotten that he strives constantly to isolate the point of human freedom, and to reveal its direction. Throughout his poems there is always a symbol of life itself, freed from the chains of self-deception — the Light, God's music, "the flower that never fades," Zoë.

The fact that Robinson builds his morality on the principle of self-knowledge identifies him with the prevailing outlook of the modern world in its liberal aspects, and distinguishes him from the Victorians, whose late representatives were his early teachers. Browning inveighed against "the unlit lamp and the ungirt loin," setting thereby his concept of morality in action rather than in awareness. Browning was willing to abandon criticism of the end of an action, and is transitional between the more characteristic Victorian outlook of Tennyson, who could satisfy his moral sense in the idea that the ruin of the Round Table was a proper consequence of Guinevere's adultery. Virtue for Tennyson lay in the discipline of good actions, for Browning in the enthusiastic and honest pursuit of one's own activity, and for Robinson in honesty of soul itself. He returns to the Socratic maxim that "knowledge is virtue," meaning self-knowledge. This simplification of his conviction explains the reason for his suppression of action in his narratives.

But Robinson's conception of the *locus* of the moral problems of men is not a complete break with the past. In an important sense he continues herein a lost aspect of his inherited Calvinism, though he alters its sanctions from the theological to the psychological. Critics have talked of his Puritanism, observing how frequently conscience gnaws the souls of Robinson's characters. But the thing goes deeper into the more profound Calvinistic belief that men are strong or weak by nature, which, put in its simplest terms, means that men have separate natures. Robinson, emancipated from the uncharitable Calvinistic judgment of the weak, has pity for them. And furthermore, he has freed himself from that identification of the good with the conventional which is characteristic of a corrupt Puritanism. Strength or weakness, being spiritual to Robinson, are constantly depicted in ironical relationship to conventional judgments and habits. Most of his characters discover that what they had thought strength is predatory and, hence, mere weakness. It is not an accident that the first strong soul depicted by Robinson should have been the philosophical tramp, Captain Craig, and that his last weak one should have been the industrial monarch, King Jasper. Men like Cavender, Matthias, Nightingale, and Talifer have a deluded assurance which some event humbles and drives back on their inherent sources of strength. A fate dwells in them which is themselves. The process of its discovery is often painful, disillusioning, and humiliating. These men find themselves in learning the limits of their bondage to necessity.

With these as his convictions, it is natural that Robinson should present souls as in triumph or defeat over illusion. Self-knowledge is triumph for those characters with native strength of soul. The weak, gazing into the eyes of Amaranth, commit suicide or vanish. In the light of this opinion of Robinson's beliefs, the common accusation that he is pessimistic seems naive. Optimists and pessimists are perhaps both necessarily naive. But triumph rings so frequently in the conclusion of Robinson's poems that it seems strange there has been little notice taken of it. Surely *Cavender's House* can be called pessimistic only by one who believes it a sign of pessimism simply to write poetry about murderers, or *Matthias at the Door* pessimistic only by those who think it a sign of pessimism to deal in death. Yet to save their souls from death and frustration as Matthias and Cavender do is plainly a kind of conversion. Robinson is not an optimist only because he often accepts a second-best as valid. He is a pessimist only in the measure that he detects an element of illusion and fatality in all lives.

These last poems of Robinson, thus, are very essential to an exact estimate of his work. Read as they deserve to be, they take on a significance which none of Robinson's critics has sought to emphasize. Each of them, with varying power, embodies in concrete form Robinson's most mature convictions about life. As a group, each separate poem having its peculiar vitality, they convey to us the joy and grief of being ourselves among much the modern world has discovered that is not ourselves. To have held fast to a faith in the value of self-knowledge between the years 1869-1935, when so many superficial mechanisms have been born, grown up, and been exploited by art, yet to have kept due reverence for the dignity and solemnity of the element of chance or uncertainty or the illusory which surrounds the conditions of human life, is to have triumphed at once over pessimism and optimism, despair and hope.

THE OPTIMISM BEHIND ROBINSON'S TRAGEDIES

FLOYD STOVALL

I

THE CRITICAL world has been slow to make up its mind about Robinson's poetry. Definitely skeptical at first, it has only gradually learned to understand him, and even now approves him with more respect than admiration. Until recently it has been the fashion to call him a pessimist. In a review of his first volume, *The Torrent and the Night Before,* he was charged with representing the world as a prison-house.[1] His reply, now famous, was "The world is not a 'prison-house,' but a kind of spiritual kindergarten, where millions of bewildered infants are trying to spell God with the wrong blocks."[2] Undoubtedly Robinson meant to deny that man is doomed to be forever bewildered. Although now an infant, he will certainly grow up; eventually he may be able to "spell" God.[3] The statement, however, has been persistently misinterpreted. Robinson himself may later have wondered whether the sentence was not ambiguous, for when questioned about it in an interview a few years ago he said, as if half disapproving of it, "I was young then and it was a smart thing to say."[4]

Among those who continued to cling to the "prison-house" idea, Amy Lowell was the first to make anything like a comprehensive study of Robinson's work. She calls him a "disinherited Puritan,"[5] in whom the qualities that were a tonic to his New England ancestors have become a poison.[6] She sees his life as a "continuous fight between himself and himself, between the old Puritan atavism and the new, free spirit" that is abroad in modern America, and she believes every poem that he wrote reflects this inner struggle and frustration, is "his dual self personified."[7] "His preoccupation," she decides, "is with the unanswered question: 'Is the Light real or imagined, is man dupe or prophet, is faith unbolstered by logic an act of cowardice or an expres-

Reprinted by permission, *American Literature,* X (March 1938), 1-23.

sion of unconscious, pondering intellectuality?' "[8] But she discovers no answer to these questions. Even more pessimistic is the view of Clement Wood, to whom the whole "message" of Robinson's poetry is that mankind has failed[9] and that the poet himself is sunk in a dungeon of black despair.[10] T. K. Whipple is hardly more encouraging. He agrees that Robinson's theme is "always defeat—always failure";[11] and that, although he is aware of a glimmering transcendental "light," it is only "a surmise and a hope, rather than a faith—no more than enough to make us go on living."[12] He finds in the poems no other remedy for inevitable failure than "the negation of life," the "repudiation of the world."[13]

The poet has had defenders, however, who deny that he is a pessimist. Lloyd Morris, one of the first of these, thinks Robinson an idealist, possibly under the influence of Josiah Royce,[14] to whom "the intuition of truth is the 'light' which somehow reveals itself to us in a world in which the spirit is burdened by thwarted hopes and humiliated ideals."[15] To make Morris's position clear I quote at length:

> His counsel is one of positive acceptance; follow the light no matter where it may lead you; follow it in spite of the fact that the wisdom of material experience may believe you a fool, in so doing lies the way of wisdom and the way of virtue; develop your own potentialities to the fullest, no matter what they may be, for in so doing you are fulfilling your destiny. This is hardly a philosophy of quietism or of pessimism, and critics who have read such philosophies into Mr. Robinson's poetry seem simply to have misinterpreted a devotion to ideals so profoundly exclusive that it results in a supreme indifference to their material consequences. This attitude of mind is likewise the explanation, it seems to me, of what some of his critics have felt to be a doctrine of "success through failure." The failure which they see is, for Mr. Robinson at least, not failure; it is merely the realist's recognition of the ironic discord between material experience and spiritual ideals.[16]

In this interpretation Morris comes close to a right understanding of Robinson, but I believe he is mistaken in thinking the poet's devotion to ideals was so exclusive that it resulted "in a supreme indifference to their material consequences." That would mean that Robinson saw for himself and for all men no alternative but to accept defeat in the world of experience or retreat altogether into the world of spiritual ideals. Morris's view, therefore, is very much like Whipple's: that for Robinson, to follow the light is to repudiate the world.

Similarly Ben Ray Redman, another enthusiastic supporter of Robinson, reads in his poems nothing more cheering than the history of a futile struggle between the forces of light and darkness, "the old unending conflict of Ahura Mazda and Agri Minos."[17] Mark Van Doren, in an excellent essay on the poet, has this to say in the same strain:

> Ideally the world for him is filled with pure white light; he speaks of "the gleam" as often as he speaks of "the Word," and they are the same. . . . Yet Mr.

> Robinson is acutely aware that the world we move in is for the most part dark—perhaps completely so—to our eyes. We are "bewildered infants," and the fact that we are trying to spell God rather than some other word does not mean for Mr. Robinson that we should or do succeed. The desire is important. The achievement is undeniably feeble. Mr. Robinson emphasizes this aspect of our twofold life so powerfully and so consistently that we are tempted to behold him as a man without hope.[18]

Yet Van Doren quotes Robinson, in a passage immediately preceding the above, as saying that none but "superficial critics" could call him a pessimist. "In point of fact," he is reported to have said, "I recommend a careful reading of my books to anyone who wishes to become an incurable optimist."[19] In a recent article one who knew Robinson well says: "E. A. used to refer to himself as an 'insane optimist,' because he saw the possibilities of good in thwarted lives that seemed wholly evil."[20]

The fullest critical study that has been made of Robinson's work is that of Professor Charles Cestre, of the University of Paris, who says: "Robinson's poetry, at its highest, overleaps the barriers of realism and expands in the sphere of liberated thought, where reason and faith, transcending the accidents of mortal life, descry the beauty and hopefulness of ultimate values."[21] Professor Cestre seems here to agree with Lloyd Morris that there is an "ironic discord" between the real and the ideal, and that man must transcend the world of actualities in order to discover any ultimate values. This judgment is stated more specifically by the French critic in the following sentence: "Robinson's teaching may be summed up in Emerson's words: 'Man is a golden impossibility.' "[22] If this means that man can never hope to attain what at a given moment he conceives as an ideal, it is not true of either Emerson or Robinson. The quotation is, in fact, inaccurate. What Emerson really said was, "A man is a golden impossibility."[23] What he meant is made clear by this sentence in his next paragraph: "Every man is an impossibility until he is born; every thing impossible until we see a success."[24] That is to say, the impossible or ideal is forever becoming the possible or real. There is no impassable barrier between them. Emerson's idealism, therefore, is not an escape from reality with all its imperfections, but a foreseeing of the ideal, the impossible, that is some day to be made possible and the real. Behind the perpetual decay and death of the living world lies the promise of rebirth and perpetual growth.

Robinson's idealism is of the same type. Yet Robinson is something of a realist, and is determined, like Crabbe and Zola, not to let his hopes for the future blind him to the frequent ugliness of actuality.[25] Emerson affirms what, intuitively, he knows of general truth. Standing remote from the stream of life, he sees far enough through time backward and forward to chart the direction of its movement, but he loses the individual object in the flux. Robinson describes what he sees of particular fact. His is the dramatic method, and he deals of necessity with particular individuals and situations. He brings the living organism into the laboratory, where we observe it pass quickly from birth through growth and decay to death. Robinson sees life in its immediacy, therefore, as a tragedy of change.

He does not reiterate in his tragedies the familiar lament for the loss of a cherished possession. His is an impersonal and cosmic emotion: the protest of a stable creation against inevitable dissolution, the outcry of elemental matter at the ravages of time. He contemplates with the same melancholy wonder the phantom-haunted regions where Greek civilization rose and fell,[26] the desolate village left stranded by the shifting currents of modern business,[27] and the lonely house abandoned to ruin and decay.[28] He beholds with a more poignant sadness the incessant change of the physical body. The whole pathos of human mortality is limned in the picture of Amaryllis grown ald, and now dead within sound of the pulsing life of a great city;[29] and in three short stanzas of "For a Dead Lady" he sums the incredible sorrow of poets in all ages before the sight of beauty

> shattered by the laws
> That have creation in their keeping.

Robinson's dominant theme is not physical decay, however, but the growth of the human mind in its pursuit of truth through time and change. He frequently represents truth by the symbol of light. Written with a capital it is the ineffable Word, the transcendental reality that endures within and behind this phenomenal world.[30] Without the capital it is knowledge, or truth in its pragmatic sense.[31] In this dual use of an identical symbol Robinson suggests that in the mind's pursuit of ideal truth it must follow the ways of worldly knowledge. Man should therefore study the laws of his own self-development as well as the laws that govern his relations with others and with society as a whole. If he lacks knowledge, or if knowledge comes too soon or too late, he will fail in one way or another, and his failure will almost certainly have tragic consequences for himself or for those with whom he is associated. With adequate knowledge man makes painful progress, individually and socially, towards his ideal of the perfect life. This is the extent of Robinson's optimism.

For convenience in analysis I have divided the poems into three classes: studies of separate lives, studies of small group relationships, and studies of the evolution of civilizations.

II

An examination of Robinson's poems devoted to the study of separate lives fully substantiates the statement, cited earlier in this essay, that he saw possibilities of good in every person.[32] But these possibilities cannot be fully realized unless the person in whom they inhere is able to focus his energies upon an object consistent with the conditions, whether of heredity or environment, under which he works. Thus Miniver Cheevy fails because his sentimental attachment to an imaginary past and his preference for illusion above reality leave him spiritually dead. Not unlike him are Lingard, the moon-calf, and Clavering, who sees

> Too far for guidance of to-day,
> Too near for the eternities.

Leffingwell, it seems, has followed a light that "lured him with high promises" and then went down, driving him to secret despair and sycophancy.[33]

In three of Robinson's best-known poems may be observed the different effects of economic change on the lives of three typical men. Old Eben Flood, with money and friends gone, finds comfort in solitude and the friendly jug, but maintains the appearance of self-sufficiency. Bewick Finzer, on the contrary, loses his self-respect with his fortune, and continues a humiliating existence through the largess of former friends. The third man, an anonymous miller, goes quietly down to his idle mill and hangs himself.[34] With fuller knowledge of their spiritual resources these men might have survived their material losses.

Others there are who fail in the very lap of material prosperity. Their tragedy is, ironically, in knowing too well their own spiritual poverty. Of these the one most often mentioned is the imperially rich, graceful, and gracious gentleman, Richard Cory, who shot himself for no reason that his envious neighbors could see.[35] Presumably he had come to know an ideal of life that made the life he lived unendurable. Like Richard Cory and equally rich, Briony also "knew too much for the life he led," and it is hinted that he became insane.[36] The tragedy of Tasker Norcross is somewhat more complicated. Though he came of an old and distinguished family, he had no spiritual wealth in himself and discovered none in the world without, where

> his tethered range
> Was only a small desert.[37]

He knew too much for illusion, but not enough for vision; and his life clearly shows that though

> the worst of all
> Our tragedies begin with what we know,[38]

they feed upon our ignorance, and they consume us unless we can know always more and more.

Robinson knew that a great many are happier with their illusions. In *Amaranth,* one of his last long poems, he is concerned particularly with the problem of self-knowledge. Amaranth, who is for every man a mirror of truth, is made to say:

> Dreams have a kindly way,
> Sometimes, if they are not explored or shaken,
> Of lasting glamorously. Many have lasted
> All a man's life, sparing him, to the grave,
> His value and his magnitude.[39]

Others are troubled by doubt and cannot rest until they have learned the truth. Sometimes the truth kills, as it did in the case of Pink the poet and Atlas the painter, who have not the strength of character to accept it and live by it. Miss Watchman, the novelist, lived for a long time deliberately in the world of illusion because she liked writing more than she liked truth or life.[40] But Fargo, the chief character of the poem, who was a capable maker of pumps but who had wished to be an artist, heard Amaranth's warning voice in time and had the courage to flee from the world of delusion into the world of reality and truth, where he lived usefully as a pump-maker. There he came to "know the best there is for man to know," which is "the peace of reason."[41]

Another aspect of the same problem is revealed in the conversation between Nicodemus, who has talked with Jesus and believes in him, and the high priest Caiaphas, who thinks Jesus either a madman or a charlatan.[42] Caiaphas says, "The laws that were our fathers' laws are right," but Nicodemus knows that there is no life in them; "they are the laws of death." He understands that Christ is the true life, but he will not act upon his knowledge. Tasker Norcross saw his own darkness but not the Light, and so he could not change; Nicodemus saw the Light, but he was afraid to face change alone. Hence both remained spiritually dead; for, as Nicodemus tells Caiaphas, "they are the dead who are afraid of dying."[43]

In contrast with these who saw their darkness yet could not escape from it, others, like Fargo, passed through the darkness to the light, though not unscathed. Flammonde, for example, with most of the virtues of a cultivated and benevolent gentleman, had a moral weakness that permitted him to live upon the generosity of his neighbors. There was some "satanic sort of kink" in his brain that limited and distorted his powers.[44] There was no such "kink" in the brain of Aunt Imogen, who acknowledged at last that her hunger for motherhood would have to be satisfied in the love of her sister's children. She saw the truth and was able to adjust herself to it.

> There were no dreams,
> No phantoms in her future any more,[45]

and so she won a sure though modified happiness. More tragic is the story of Fernando Nash, who might have become a great composer, but who found knowledge too late to save for himself and for the world the creative genius with which he was endowed, having first destroyed himself with dissipation while struggling with the shadows of defeat.[46] Captain Craig had also passed through the darkness which is death, but he had saved more of his original power because he was a philosopher. He knew that failure is of the flesh, not of the spirit,[47] and that through ruin and failure beats unheard the rhythm of God, which is fulfilment unexpressed.[48] It is revealed to him that in the slow search for the truth that is within us and above us,[49] "what men lose man gains."[50]

> Look east and west
> And we may read the story: where the light
> Shone first the shade now darkens; where the shade
> Clung first, the light fights westward—though the shade
> Still feeds, and there is yet the Orient.[51]

Captain Craig bequeathed to his young friends the wisdom he had purchased with a lifetime of defeat, hoping that the light he found too late might yet be effectual through them.

The characters so far considered have been imaginary, or at least unknown to the public. I have now to examine some of the historical characters about whom Robinson wrote poems. Each of these was successful in the sense that each achieved a degree of fame, yet they all failed to reach the high goal they set for themselves and so failed to that extent. In most cases their sense of failure was due to the fact that they measured success in terms of immediate rather than ultimate results.

Napoleon conquered half the world and then lost it, to die on a rat-infested island because he could not be content with less than all.[52] Shakespeare, though

> lord of more than England and of more
> Than all the seas of England in all time
> Shall ever wash,

could not be happy because he was not lord of the manor in Stratford.[53] Soaring above the sphere of ordinary minds, he looked with impatience upon the world in its slow advance, yet could not separate himself wholly from it. Rembrandt, however, because his "demon willed it," followed his vision so far that he was lost to his short-sighted contemporaries, who left him to starve.[54] The aims of John Brown and Toussaint L'Ouverture were more definite and altruistic than any of these, and they pursued them with more confidence though with less immediate success. John Brown was glad he had not foreseen the human suffering his course was to involve, for then he might have wavered and failed. His last words were, "I shall have more to say when I am dead."[55] Toussaint also died, betrayed and in a dungeon, before his work was complete, yet from the beginning he knew what the outcome would be, impossible though that outcome seemed. He

saw long ago
More than a man could do, till it was done,

and now it was done, and more and better, he believed, was yet to be done.[56] These heroic lives illustrate the temper of Robinson's individualism. He believed, as he makes Paul say, that

the few at first
Are fighting for the multitude at last,[57]

and that too often they are neglected or persecuted by the very people they would lead out of the darkness up to the light.

III

In the poems thus far examined Robinson deals primarily with that aspect of tragedy in which it is seen to affect separate lives. I proceed now to the consideration of those poems, including many of the long narratives, in which he delineates the passions out of which tragic situations arise and traces their interrelated effects on the lives of two or three persons in a social group. The two passions that work most havoc are love and hate, and they are sometimes so inextricably woven together in the minds of perplexed mortals as to be almost indistinguishable.

Avon's Harvest, the one poem of this group in which love is no part of the motivating force, is a psychological study of the devastating effects of hate and its two shadows, remorse and fear. By some inexplicable chance the elemental antagonisms that give life to nature had so arranged themselves in Avon and his schoolfellow that they must hate each other. Avon was aware that the antidote for hate is love, but he had "no kindlier commodity than hate,"[58] and he knew no alchemy by which hate may be transmuted into love.

That such an alchemy exists, however, is revealed in another drama of hate, *The Glory of the Nightingales.* Malory, a physician, and Nightingale, a capitalist, are in love with the same woman. Nightingale loses, but gets revenge in causing his rival's financial ruin, as an indirect result of which the woman dies. Malory then, after some years have elapsed, goes to Nightingale's house intending to kill him and then commit suicide; instead Nightingale, who has long been in poor health, kills himself after transferring all of his wealth in trust to Malory to build and operate a great hospital and biological laboratory. After Nightingale's death Malory says of him:

> I cannot know,
> For certain, that your way, dark as it was,
> Was not the necessary way of life.
> There was in yours at least a buried light
> For time and man; and science, living in time,
> May find at last a gleam nearer than yours,
> For those who are not born to follow it
> Before it has been found.[59]

The necessary way of life leads through suffering and evil and death, but it is not an evil way, nor is death the end. Hate is a darkness in which sometimes there is a buried light of knowledge that may, in time, lead to love.

A score or more of Robinson's shorter love poems are simplified versions of the familiar triangle plot. With few exceptions they tell of lost love ending in the death of one or more of the principals, in permanent separation, or in hate and distrust concealed under a mask of happiness.[60] Sometimes the interference of a circumstance ever so slight and apparently innocent will destroy the delicate balance of conjugal happiness. It may be no more than silence when a word of truth would forestall the gossip and suspicion that undermine faith;[61] it may be the bare suggestion of hypocrisy in a minister's unwonted religious zeal that arouses his wife's contempt and distrust;[62] it may be a chance encounter that revives and old romance at a moment when the nerves of both husband and wife are on edge;[63] or it may be a woman's idealization of another man, now dead, whose wraith separates her from her lover more completely than a living man ever could.[64]

In each of these domestic tragedies love is lost because it is either an illusion that is shattered by the impact of truth, or else an unguarded truth that is undermined by doubt. Disillusion and doubt, however, are not the inevitable conclusion of married love.[65] In the story of Annandale and Damaris we see that love may be true and lasting, not because it is an overwhelming passion, but rather because it is passion tempered with human understanding. Annandale says that Damaris knows the way God made his fur to lie:

> So all goes well; and with our wits
> Awake, should go indefinitely—
> Sufficient without subterfuge,
> Harmonious without history.[66]

This, which is love as the world permits it, is far from that ideal of which the fond lover dreams. Yet thus it has been ever since man found the Tree of Knowledge and was driven out of Eden, and thus perhaps it will continue to be until he finds his way back past the flaming sword to the Tree of Life. Knowledge lives and moves with time, but love without knowledge, which is passion, lifts against time a citadel whose walls begin to crumble before they are finished. The passionate lover builds on earth his paradise of love, and then comes the inexorable angel with the flaming sword. And so Merlin, who saw farther backward and forward into time than any other man, lived in harmony with time and kept his youth until he abandoned knowledge and the world to follow passion to Vivian's gardens at Broceliande. Then time had its revenge upon him;[67] for, although knowledge returned to him when passion was spent, old age came with it and weariness both of love and of the world. Ironically, yet not inaptly, after the illusion is gone, Vivian refers to their retreat as Eden, for says she,

> We have had
> A man and woman in it for some time,
> And now, it seems, we have a Tree of Knowledge.[68]

Merlin's passion could not endure because it was but a temporary reversion from the intellectual to the sensual plane of activity brought about by the mind's unwillingness to face defeat. As for Vivian, she was moved more by vanity than by love in her desire to win and hold the king-maker and prophet, for whose greatness of mind she had no genuine sympathy. Thus the reasons for the failure of their love were in themselves. Tristram and Isolt of Ireland, on the contrary, found in love the fullest expression of their nature, and there was neither degradation nor design in their abandonment to passion. This was true especially of Isolt, who by temperament as well as by circumstance was more completely shut away from worldly interests than most women of her time and station. Yet she knows intuitively that such love cannot long endure in an imperfect world, and so she tells Tristram while they are still safe at Joyous Gard:

> We are not for the fireside, or for old age
> In any retreat of ancient stateliness.
> If that were so, then this would not be so.[69]

Their failure, if indeed they failed, was due to causes that lay outside themselves and beyond their control.

The serpent had waited in Vivian's garden from the beginning but there was no serpent at Joyous Gard, where Tristram and Isolt found their paradise islanded in time. Yet it lasted for only one brief summer, and then time rolled over it, leaving no more than enough to make a deathless story.

Of the Arthurian poems only *Tristram* is concerned exclusively with love. *Lancelot,* like *Merlin,* subordinates the tragedy of lost love to the greater tragedy of a dying world.[70] Yet Guinevere's loss is greater and more pathetic than Vivian's, perhaps because it is more human. Again time, with its gift of knowledge, plays havoc with the house of love.

But it is another knowledge than Merlin's that comes between Lancelot and Guinevere; and its mystic symbol, the Grail, is a beacon that leads through darkness towards another and a brighter world than Arthur's. Lancelot, having seen the light, must follow it wherever it leads; but Guinevere, who has seen no light and who foresees no new world, clings desperately to Arthur's crumbling world until it lies in ruins all about her. Their love was molded to the pattern of chivalry, and when the law of change discarded chivalry for a new pattern the old love would not fit. The creative will, which is the pulse of life and yet sometimes as cruel as death, cast Guinevere aside in order that Lancelot might go forward.

Knowledge is the fertile soil from which all new life springs, and just as surely today as when Adam first wandered in the garden of the world, the price of knowledge is death. This is the theme of three long poems of Robinson's: *Cavender's House, Roman Bartholow,* and *Matthias at the Door.* Knowledge came to Cavender through dark ways that involved the murder of his wife, long years of consequent remorse and self-examination, and final submission to the law. It is not easy to see what good can come of these melancholy events. Yet Cavender sees something, for while communing with himself on the spot where his crime was committed, he is on the point of taking his own life when he hears the phantom voice of his dead wife, which is the voice of his wiser self, saying:

> Eternity may have time and room to show us
> How so transformed a fabric may be woven
> Of crimes, corruptions, and futilities,
> That we shall be confounded with a wonder
> At our not seeing it here. Yes, there is hope;
> And there is hope deferred by too much haste—
> Or so there might be. It's all rather dark.[71]

If Cavender speaks for the author, as I believe he does, this is an affirmation of his belief that in some way which we cannot now understand, but which we or our successors on earth may eventually come to know, what we call evil may prove in its effects to be good.

The good that is to come of Cavender's evil may not appear in this life. Roman Bartholow, however, is more fortunate, since he can look forward, after he has been spiritually reborn, to a long lifetime of usefulness. The whole story is too complicated to be told here. It must suffice to say that he married and took his young wife, Gabrielle, away from the society she loved to a lonely country house. There he gave himself up to abstruse studies and soon was lost in a dark despondency which was a kind of death-in-life. Then came his strange friend, Penn-Raven, whose magnetic personality and persuasive reasonings won him back to life and hope. In the meantime, however, Gabrielle's love for Bartholow had been irrecoverably lost, and Penn-Raven, against his will, had fallen desperately in love with her. At the last Penn-Raven departs after being denounced as a blackguard by Bartholow, Gabrielle drowns herself in the river, and Bartholow emerges free and strong and buoyant with hope and energy. The knowledge which Penn-Raven possessed but could not put to use, when transferred to Bartholow became active for his own and for the world's betterment. Gabrielle was sacrificed because she chanced to stand in the way of this transfer. It was not a matter of rewards and punishments, but the functioning of a will beyond human control. Bartholow, for reasons which neither he nor Penn-Raven understood, was an instrument of this will. As Penn-Raven tells him:

> Your doom is to be free. The seed of truth
> Is rooted in you, and the fruit is yours
> For you to eat alone. You cannot share it,
> Though you may give it, and a few thereby
> May taste of it, and so not wholly starve.[72]

For Gabrielle the poet felt a deep pity, yet he could not alter her destiny, which was to die in order that Bartholow might live more effectively. She was

> a woman doomed never to live—
> That he who had adored her and outgrown her
> Might yet achieve.[73]

But it is in *Matthias at the Door* that the optimism behind Robinson's tragedies is most clearly seen and stated. The poem is the record of a succession of catastrophes by means of which Matthias, complacent over his material success, is made to know himself and through self-knowledge to be reborn. His instruction began when his friend Garth, who had grown desperate through failure, one day crawled into a dark cave in the rocks to die by his own hand. Matthias's friend Timberlake, whose life he had saved when they were young by pulling him out of a burning building, had deliberately thrown himself and his talents away in order that Natalie, whom they both loved, might marry Matthias. This she did and was unhappy for twenty years, when, after Garth's death, the secret was revealed. A few months later she committed suicide in Garth's cave, leaving Matthias dejected and bitterly scornful of this "accident of nameless energies" which we call life.[74] Gradually, however, with the assistance of Timberlake, who was slowly dying, his better self was born out of the ruins, and he turned his face to the future with renewed hope. To show how this happened it will be necessary to introduce several quotations, in which may be found the essence of Robinson's wisdom.

Before his death, Timberlake, who does for Matthias, in part, what Penn-Raven does for Bartholow, talks at length to his friend, and from this talk I excerpt the following lines:

> If you had eyes inside you, and you may,
> To read a little further into your book—
> Well, you would be surprised at what is there
> For you to find. If it had not been there,
> I might have hated you for saving me,
> When we were young, out of that burning house.
> There was a price for that, which I have paid
> As well as I was able. Natalie paid,
> And you are paying still. We are like stairs
> For one another's climbing, and are never
> Quite told which way it is that we are going
> While we are climbing higher, or think we are.
> I have not always thought so; but you have,
> Matthias, and I have watched you going up
> While you were going down. You are down now
> As far as you will go—if you remember
> That you are like a book with pages in it
> You have not read, and cannot read in the dark.[75]

Finally Matthias, contemplating suicide also, goes down into the cave for a soul-searching colloquy with himself. He hears what seems to be Garth's voice saying to him:

> Nothing is wasted, though there is much misused—
> Like you and me, Matthias, who failed together,
> Each in a personal way. You, having more
> To fail with, failed more thoroughly and abjectly,
> But that was not the end. I shall go on,
> Where you'll not follow me. You will go back,
> Where I'll not follow you. And in that fashion
> We shall go on unconsciously together,
> And consciously apart, to the same end.
> It's all a matter of our not going too fast.[76]

Later in the same colloquy he recognizes in Garth's voice much of Timberlake and something of himself:

> We are prisoners now and pupils in a school
> Where often our best rewards appear to us
> To be our punishments. There's no escape.
> To sleep with earth between you and the sun
> Is not to escape from earth, or from the sun.
> It seems a mystery that so many should live
> Who are not born, but that's the infinite way,
> And one that is not altered or improved
> By protest or denial, or by rebellion.[77]

And when Matthias questions what is to be the end of all man's striving, the voice replies:

> You will be happier to forget the end,
> Or more than revelation or conviction

Tell you to see, and to make what you may
Of your apportioned means. The end will wait
For all your most magnificent and protracted
Progressions and expansions, and be still
Sufficiently far away.[78]

And so, when the voice is silent, Matthias is ready to go back and begin life over again:

He must go back again; he must be born,
And then must live; and he who had been always
So promptly served, and was to be a servant,
Must now be of some use in a new world
That Timberlake and Garth and Natalie
Had strangely lived and died to find for him.[79]

The reassuring fact in this tragic story is that Garth and Timberlake and Natalie have not died in vain, though the justice of their sacrifice is something not to be found in the book of human wisdom. Phoenix-like, Matthias is reborn from the ashes of his dead self; and thus the modern seer reaffirms an ancient truth.[80]

IV

Most of Robinson's poems, as I have shown, are studies of the spiritual development of an individual either in his separate life or in his relations with other members of a small group. Several poems written in his later years, however, have as their theme the development of society as a whole, and describe the life and death of civilizations as stages in the advancement of the human race. The first of these were the Arthurian poems *Merlin* and *Lancelot.* After them came a group of contemporary studies in the volume *Dionysus in Doubt,* and finally the allegorical poem *King Jasper.*

In the decay of Arthur's kingdom and the appearance of the Grail, suggesting the advent of a new ideal to supplant the medieval ideal of chivalry, Robinson saw a notable illustration of the universal law of change by which, under the impulse of the creative will in nature, the human world slowly evolves. Merlin, who is the primary instrument of this impersonal will, made Arthur king because he perceived in him a mirror in which every man of that age recognized himself as he would like to be.[81] Arthur believed Merlin was Fate, yet Merlin could do no more than show the king what in his heart he already knew,[82] and what every man knew when he knew himself in his ideal self, which was the king. All went well so long as Arthur remained men's highest conception of themselves. But then,

There was a Light wherein men saw themselves
In one another as they might become—
Or so they dreamed,[83]

and afterwards there was no more peace in Camelot. Whatever cannot change must die, and Arthur, who believes "that what has been, and is, will be for ever," cannot change.[84] Lancelot, who has seen the Grail, knows that "a played-out world . . . had best be dead" in order that a new world may be born.[85] Although he himself does not die physically, he must go through an agonizing spiritual death and rebirth, and many people must suffer and die in order that he may go so far even as the threshold of the new world. As he rides away into the darkness towards the light after his last sad parting from Guinevere, the will that is not his and yet works through him speaks to him from within:

> Where the Light falls, death falls; a world has died
> For you, that a world may live. There is no peace.[86]

Merlin sees and speaks the truth thus:

> When I began with Arthur I could see
> In each bewildered man who dots the earth
> A moment with his days a groping thought
> Of an eternal will, strangely endowed
> With merciful illusions whereby self
> Becomes the will itself and each man swells
> In fond accordance with his agency.
> Now Arthur, Modred, Lancelot, and Gawaine
> Are swollen thoughts of this eternal will
> Which have no other way to find the way
> That leads them on to their inheritance
> Than by the time-infuriating flame
> Of a wrecked empire, lighted by the torch
> Of woman, who, together with the light
> That Galahad found, is yet to light the world.[87]

Arthur's world had to go because the time had come when the eternal will could no longer find adequate expression through the will of one man imposed upon an entire nation. Henceforth authority was to be less concentrated. Moreover, love, which had been apart from the affairs of life, was to be introduced more and more into them to leaven the sternness of the older law. There was to be a long period in which the power and freedom of the individual steadily increased. Eventually, with the development of an equalitarian philosophy, the freedom of the individual, which before had been suppressed by the authority of an arbitrary king, was threatened by the authority of the misguided multitude. And so in his later poems Robinson foresees the dissolution of the individualistic civilization of the modern world by the combined forces of mechanism, utilitarianism, and equalitarianism.

He first approached the problem as early as 1920 in the short poem "Demos," in which he says that democracy is foiled by a false equality which obscures the truth that

> the few shall save
> The many, or the many are to fall.[88]

Five years later he returned to it in two long poems in the volume *Dionysus in Doubt.* In the first, which is the title poem, he seems to have been provoked to expression by the national prohibition amendment, but it is the subjection of the individual will to the will of the majority that he objects to most strenuously. Dionysus is made to say to the poet and to all Americans:

> An ultimate uniformity enthroned
> May trim your vision very well;
> And the poor cringing self, disowned,
> May call it freedom and efficiency.
> Others would somewhat rather call it hell,
> And rather not be quite so free
> To blend themselves with mediocrity.[89]

In the second poem, "Demos and Dionysus," Demos is the god of the multitude and the advocate of a mechanized and what he calls a "rational" society in which love and art will be scorned and all people will be alike. Dionysus is the god of wine and of life, of love and art, and of all that enriches and differentiates the individual as a separate being moved by feeling and imagination and true reason. Demos says:

> We have had too much
> Of the insurgent individual
> With his free fancy and free this and that,
> And his ingenuous right to be himself.
> What right has anyone now to be himself,
> Since I am here to fix him in his place
> And hold him there? And as for your fit world,
> I'll have it all alike and of a piece—
> Punctual, accurate, tamed and uniform,
> And equal. Then romance and love and art
> And ecstasy will be remembrances
> Of man's young weakness on his way to reason.[90]

Dionysus, who undoubtedly speaks Robinson's opinion, prophesies to Demos that such a

> delirious clumsy leap
> From reason to the folly you call reason
> Will only make of you and of your dupes
> A dislocated and unlovely mess
> For undertakers, who are not yet born
> To view the coming ruin that is to be
> Their occupation and emolument—
> If your delusion for a time prevail,
> As like enough it will.[91]

Though Demos may for a time prevail, Robinson is certain that Dionysus will eventually rule; that love and art and freedom will return. Dionysus says,

> I may go somewhere, for a while,
> But I am one of those who have perforce
> To live and to return.[92]

In Robinson's last poem, *King Jasper,* he describes the revolution which in "Demos and Dionysus" he foresees, with its annihilation of capital wealth and the civilization that rests upon it. The characters are individuals, yet they are also symbols. As young men Jasper and Hebron were friends and partners. Jasper loves power and is not over-scrupulous in his methods of acquiring it; he is the business manager of the firm. Hebron is a scientist, an inventor, a lover of truth for its own sake; he cares little for power, and is content to work behind the scenes. Jasper sees how he can grow rich through Hebron's ideas, but he does not tell Hebron, whose health begins to fail through overwork and undernourishment. After Hebron dies, Jasper, grown rich and powerful, becomes King Jasper. He marries Honoria, who stands for custom and convention, and all the codes and fixed laws by which society resists change. Young Jasper, their son, represents the liberal-minded younger generation. He is eager for change and is rather scornful of his old-fashioned parents; yet he is bound to them by ties of nature which he cannot escape, and when their world falls he falls with it. Young Hebron has something of his father's inventive genius, but not the scientist's love of truth. He represents the doctrinaire and fanatical revolutionary, the human counterpart of the god Demos. The young woman Zoë is, as her name reveals, a symbol of life—life which is beauty and truth eternal, yet forever unseizable and forever escaping from outworn forms and passing into new forms. She has many of the characteristics of the god Dionysus. She is the woman of Merlin's vision who is to save the world, for she combines the beauty of the chivalric ideal with the truth which the Grail revealed. Although she loves young Jasper, it is the law of her nature that she must remain free; hence she will not bind herself by ties of marriage. And in the end, when young Jasper dies in the general catastrophe, Zoë escapes to wait for wiser men who in some future age shall build a better and a more stable society.

This poem leaves no doubt of Robinson's faith in the intrinsic worth of humankind. Some time, we are assured, man will know enough to know his own worth and use it. As Zoë says,

> All a man sees is less than what he is
> Without it, if he knew.[93]

But it all takes time, and when knowledge comes too soon or too late it brings inevitable death. Zoë cannot be domesticated in Jasper's world because the time for that has not arrived; there, she tells him sadly,

> I'm like a child trying to be at home
> In the wrong house. The wise one said to me
> That I must always go my way alone.[94]

Nor can young Jasper follow her into the new world to come, because he is bound within the life-pattern that produced him, and that is King Jasper's capitalistic world. It will be remembered that the Grail brought a light in which men saw themselves in one another as they might have become. Zoë knew that some day all men would live by that light, but she did not know when that day would come. To King Jasper, who thinks many must toil and suffer that a few may be kings, she says:

> We should all be kings,
> Or queens, if we could see ourselves in others.
> But that's a long, long way from where we are;
> And a few suffocatings and blood-drenchings
> Of helpless heroes who will not know why,
> Or what it means, will show the devil's ahead,
> With banners and with music of all nations.
> The devil is an impartial patriot,
> Unprejudiced as he is promiscuous.
> Today the devil is more than God. Tomorrow
> He will be more, and more. Out of it all
> He'll come with crutches, and not the devil he was.
> Father, don't ask me when, for I don't know.[95]

Thus Robinson looks beyond the tragedies of persons and societies and beholds life as an eternal and creative will evolving through a succession of changing patterns towards an ideal of perfection. Since this creative will rises to actuality only in the forms which it creates and inhabits for a time, the law of change requires that old forms shall decay and die in order that new and higher forms may come into being. In man, the highest of these forms, the will begins to know itself and the law of its evolution. Through knowledge, therefore, man may hope to hasten and direct the process of evolution. This, surely, is not a philosophy of escape or of pessimistic acceptance, but a dynamic belief in the power of the human mind to overcome, in time, most of the difficulties that beset mankind, and to make of this unsettled world, in the words of Dionysus,

> a world
> Fit for a self-defending human race
> To recognize, and finally to live in.[96]

---

1 *Bookman*, IV (February 1897), 509-510.
2 *Ibid.*, V (March 1897), 7.
3 In Robinson's play *The Porcupine* (New York, 1915), one of the characters says to another (p. 137): "Yes, Rachel, —that's just about what we are—children. The best and the worst, the wisest and the silliest of us—children. Tumbling, blundering, groping children,—getting our heads bumped and our fingers burned, and making ourselves generally uncomfortable. But all this needn't keep us from growing, or from looking now and then as if we had not committed the unpardonable sin in being born."
4 Nancy Evans, "Edwin Arlington Robinson," *Bookman*, LXXV (November 1932), 680.
5 *Tendencies in Modern American Poetry* (New York, 1917), 24.
6 *Ibid.*, 28.

7 "A Bird's Eye View of E. A. Robinson," *Dial*, LXXII (February 1922), 134.
8 *Ibid.*, 28.
9 *The Poets of America* (New York, 1925), 119.
10 *Ibid.*, 141.
11 *Spokesmen* (New York, 1928), 46.
12 *Ibid.*, 50.
13 *Ibid.*, 57. For other views somewhat similar, see Bruce Weirick, *From Whitman to Sandburg in American Poetry* (New York, 1924), 184-192; Harriet Monroe, "Edwin Arlington Robinson," *Poetry: A Magazine of Verse*, XXV (January 1925), 205-217; and Alfred Kreymborg, *Our Singing Strength* (New York, 1929), 297-315.
14 *The Poetry of Edwin Arlington Robinson* (New York, 1923), 66. Nancy Evans (*op. cit.*, 680) quotes Robinson as saying, "I'm afraid Mr. Morris was on the wrong track. But if you want to find out about my 'Transcendentalism,' read *The Man Against the Sky* and *Matthias at the Door*—it's in those poems.
15 *Ibid.*, 68.
16 *Ibid.*, 69.
17 *Edwin Arlington Robinson* (New York, 1926), 64.
18 *Edwin Arlington Robinson* (New York, 1927), 30-32.
19 *Ibid.*, 30.
20 Louis V. Ledoux, "Psychologist of New England," *Saturday Review of Literature*, XII (October 19, 1935), 4.
21 *An Introduction to Edwin Arlington Robinson* (New York, 1930), 22-23.
22 *Ibid.*, 24.
23 From the essay "Experience," *Complete Writings*, III, 66.
24 *Ibid.*, III, 69.
25 See the poems "Zola" and "George Crabbe" in *Collected Poems of Edwin Arlington Robinson* (New York, 1937), 85, 94. (All references to the poems are made to this edition unless otherwise stated.) Concerning "Zola" Robinson later wrote to a friend: "When I wrote that rather pinfeatherish Zola sonnet, I had read only *l'Assommoir*, and I have read only one of his books since then" (Laura E. Richards, *E. A. F.*, Cambridge, Mass., 1936, 14).
26 "Villanelle of Change," 80-81.
27 "The Dead Village," 88.
28 "The House on the Hill," 81-82.
29 "Amaryllis," 84-85.
30 Cf. "Credo," p. 94; "The Book of Annandale," 206; and "The Man Against the Sky," 66, 68.
31 Cf. "Octave XII," "Captain Craig," *passim*, and "Sainte-Nitouche," 214.
32 The only exception I can think of is Aaron Stark (p. 86), the morose, snarling miser who was glad to be hated and who laughed at the alien pity of kinder folk. One is inclined to believe that even he would prove to be less contemptible if the secret of his private life were known. Sometimes a man's best side is not remembered until after he is dead (as in "An Old Story" and in "Charles Carville's Eyes"), or an entire life may be redeemed by a noble death (as in "The Rat").
33 See the short poems, "Miniver Cheevy," "Calverly's," "Clavering," and Leffingwell."
34 The poems are "Mr. Flood's Party," "Bewick Finzer," and "The Mill."
35 See the poem "Richard Cory."
36 "Fragment," 49.
37 "Tasker Norcross," 507.
38 *Ibid.*, 505.
39 *Amaranth*, 1324.
40 *Ibid.*, 1378.
41 *Ibid.*, 1392.
42 "Nicodemus," 1162-1164.
43 *Ibid.*, 1164.
44 "Flammonde," 5.
45 "Aunt Imogen," 188. A recent biographer (Richards, *op. cit.*, 59) says of Robinson: "He told his sister-in-law that in 'Aunt Imogen' it was himself that he was revealing—or concealing, as you will."
46 *The Man Who Died Twice*, 921-957.
47 *Captain Craig*, 151.
48 *Ibid.*, 143.
49 *Ibid.*, 151.
50 *Ibid.*, 150.
51 *Ibid.*, 153.
52 "An Island," 323-330.
53 "Ben Jonson Entertains a Man from Stratford," 23.
54 "Rembrandt to Rembrandt," 589.
55 "John Brown," 490.
56 "Toussaint L'Ouverture," 1186.
57 "The Three Taverns," 469.
58 *Avon's Harvest*, 554.
59 *The Glory of the Nightingales*, 1072.
60 Cf. "Another Dark Lady," 41-42; "The Story of the Ashes and the Flame," 84; "The Clinging Vine," 8-11; "Eros Turannos," 32-33; "Genevieve and Alexandra," 49-50; and others.
61 "Lizette and Eileen," 49-50.
62 "An Evangelist's Wife," 528.
63 "London Bridge," 493-499.
64 "Late Summer," 525-528.
65 As shown, for example, in "Firelight," 510-511; in "Vain Gratuities," 576-577; and in "Rahel to Varnhagen," 513-520.
66 "Annandale Again," 1205. See alsc "The Book of Annandale," 195-211.
67 *Merlin*, 287.
68 *Ibid.*, 294.
69 *Tristram*, 695.
70 This theme will be more fully treated later in the essay.
71 *Cavender's House*, 994.
72 *Roman Bartholow*, 825.
73 *Ibid.*, 855.
74 *Matthias at the Door*, 1126-1127.
75 *Ibid.*, 1137.
76 *Ibid.*, 1148.
77 *Ibid.*, 1150.
78 *Ibid.*, 1150.
79 *Ibid.*, 1154.
80 To prove that he could be amusing and that he could make a poem with a happy ending, Robinson wrote *Talifer*, a novel in verse, which, in plot, is very similar to *Roman Bartholow* and *Matthias*. But tragedy is averted in *Talifer* because one of the group of characters is benevolent and wise enough in the ways of human nature to cause mis-

takes to be corrected before they lead to tragic consequences.

81 *Merlin*, 293.
82 *Ibid.*, 282.
83 *Ibid.*, 306.
84 *Lancelot*, 383.
85 *Ibid.*, 436-437.
86 *Ibid.*, 448.
87 *Merlin*, 307.
88 "Demos," 472.
89 *Dionysus in Doubt*, 867.
90 "Demos and Dionysus, 917.
91 *Ibid.*, 916.
92 *Ibid.*, 917.
93 *King Jasper*, 1455.
94 *Ibid.*, 1469.
95 *Ibid.*, 1471-1472.
96 "Demos and Dionysus," 916.

TRISTRAM THE TRANSCENDENT

FREDERIC IVES CARPENTER

I

THE *Tristram* of Edwin Arlington Robinson is more than a fine narrative poem. Published in 1927, it looms already as a landmark in modern American literature, and also as a challenge to criticism. Perhaps the publication of Robinson's letters will illuminate the problem which it raises, but there is little likelihood that they will answer it. For the problem is not so much individual as national. Briefly, it is this: How could a poet morally and intellectually disciplined and even inhibited as Robinson was, suddenly write a poem describing vividly and celebrating wholeheartedly one of the most passionate love stories in all literature? Not only that—how could be achieve with it his greatest triumph? Did he all at once deny the heritage of his New England past? Or was there some unsuspected spark hidden in the old puritanism, which finally flamed in him?

Whatever the cause of *Tristram*, the effect was immediate and unquestionable. The poem at once achieved a success almost unparalleled in its combination of quantity with quality; the reading public and the professional critics united to praise it. What is even more unusual, the author himself felt it to be his masterpiece. Subsequent writers have largely confirmed the verdict. But since the different critics have interpreted it differently, even while agreeing on its greatness, the history of the poem is worth reviewing.

Before its publication, the Literary Guild chose *Tristram* for its book of the month—an unheard-of honor for a long narrative poem. Soon after publication, the book appeared on the best-seller lists, rivaling even novels in the number of its sales. Financially, it marked the author's first success; when *Tristram* was out, Robinson admitted, "I had a little money to invest."[1] And for the third time, it won him the Pulitzer Prize.

Reprinted by permission, *New England Quarterly*, XI (September 1938), 501-523.

The professional critics, of course, were partly responsible for this. The unanimity of their enthusiasm was remarkable. Mark Van Doren and Lucius Beebe wrote full-length articles in its praise.[2] Ben Ray Redman called it "the greatest poem that has yet been written in America."[3] Percy Hutchinson's comment in the New York *Times,* May 8, 1927, was headlined "American Poetry at its Best." Lloyd Morris described it as "not only the finest of Mr. Robinson's narrative poems, but among the very few fine narrative poems in English."[4] The *Bookman* declared, editorially, in June: "Here is a book that your great-grandchildren will know, even if you neglect it;" and Herbert Gorman, in the July number, added: "One may be quite dogmatic in asserting that this is the finest long poem that has ever been produced in this country."[5] Nor was the enthusiasm limited to America. In France, Professor Cestre wrote in glowing terms of this "*chef d'oeuvre,*" this "*couronnement d'un effort créateur.*"[6] And the conservative *London Times Literary Supplement* called it a masterpiece by "one of the most magnificent of modern American poets."[7] In fact, the only major exception to the enthusiasm was that of Conrad Aiken, who considered it "a comparative failure."[8]

But book reviewers have often been mistaken. Perhaps a better index to the significance of *Tristram* is suggested by the change of attitude of representative critics toward Robinson following the publication of the poem. Thus, in 1923, Louis Untermeyer had written: "His language is indirect, but it is not that which brings his poetry to a halt at the very peak of greatness. It is not that he is devious in the way he gives himself, but that, in the sense of complete abandon to an emotion, he never gives himself at all."[9] But later, in praising *Tristram,* Untermeyer wrote: "Robinson, as though reacting against the charge of Puritanism, abandoned himself to a drama passionate and headlong."[10] Likewise T. K. Whipple modified his criticism of Robinson's "constitutional reserve" and "emotional chariness" with the highest praise of *Tristram.*[11]

Finally, Robinson himself felt that the poem contained his best work: "He supposed that he was up about as well in *Tristram* as anywhere."[12] And to an interviewer he expressed the belief that his best poetry was "somewhere" in the Arthurian poems, because "the romantic framework enabled me to use my idiom more freely."[13] Similarly, Robinson spoke of *Tristram* as extraordinary for him, because of the precipitancy with which it was written: ". . . my largest output was 110 lines, one day when I was going strong in the latter part of *Tristram.*"[14]

This coincidence of enthusiasm on the part of the reading public, the critics, and the author also, is rare enough. In one way or another, the flame had been lit. But more remarkable than this general acceptance, perhaps, is the effect which the writing of the poem produced on the author. His letters have not yet been made public, but his literary executor has summarized their import (not, be it noted, in any specific discussion of *Tristram*). The rereading of these letters, he said, gave "a strong impression that E. A. had put so much vital force into the writing of *Tristram,* had worked on it and lived in it with such utter concentration, that his health never again was what it had been."[15] The flame was a real fire, that had burned. It was not the reflected light of a long-ago, literary love, but a variety of authentic emotional experience.

But why had the spark flamed so suddenly? To many there seemed no connection between the Robinson of the early poems and the Robinson of *Tristram.* All at once he seemed to have abandoned the intellect for the emotions, to have abandoned morality for the precipitancy of passion, to have lowered (or raised) himself suddenly from the plane of metaphysical abstraction to the plane of flesh-and-blood reality. The majority of critics and readers alike gave themselves up to the enjoyment of the new love poem with a sigh of relief, accepting it as a gift of God, not inquiring too meticulously whence the strange gift had come. "Here," they thought, "is an end to all troublesome, outworn transcendentalism."

But was *Tristram* really so simple and unmoral a poem as these critics thought? "There are no abstract themes in it," Mark Van Doren wrote. "The elements which compose it have nothing of metaphysics in them; there is no Light. . . . We have simply two people in love."[16] Would it not be more accurate, and more revealing of the development of modern thought, to say rather that *Tristram* implied, and as it were incarnated, the intellectual ideas which Robinson had formerly described explicitly? Moreover, the poem did give certain explicit formulation and development to the most fundamental of these ideas.

Second, did *Tristram* actually abandon the tiresome morality which had troubled the course of the earlier narratives? "The poem is singularly free of ethical implications,"[17] wrote Lloyd Morris. And Herbert Gorman declared: "In *Lancelot,* love was for the sake of the Light; in *Tristram* love is for itself and builds a world out of itself."[18] But did not *Tristram* rather suggest how "love" and "the Light"— which in *Lancelot* had been divided — might achieve a certain tragic harmony? And are the "ethical implications" absent, or merely latent?

Certainly, the subject matter and mood of *Tristram* are different from those of Robinson's other poems. These differences are obvious. But do they justify us in separating *Tristram* from the rest of the poems, or in saying that it lacks intellectual significance?[19] Does not *Tristram* rather illustrate the natural development of Robinson's literary thought, and therefore achieve "the completest and most characteristic expression of his genius"?[20] This interpretation is not entirely orthodox and has never been fully developed. But if true, it is highly significant. And it is important, not only for the understanding of Robinson's poetry but for the interpretation of American literary thought as a whole.

First, this essay will suggest the continuity of *Tristram* with the rest of Robinson's poetry, particularly with his other two Arthurian poems, *Merlin* and *Lancelot.* Second, it will describe the significant differences between his *Tristram* and other versions of the history, both medieval and modern. Third, the ideas implicit and explicit in the poem will be developed in relation to the transcendentalism of Emerson, whom Robinson greatly admired, both as poet and as thinker.[21] Finally, perhaps, *Tristram* may emerge, not as the denial and refutation of the transcendental tradition in American literature, but rather as the most recent and one of the most fully realized and satisfying embodiments of it.

II

Merlin was published in 1917, *Lancelot* in 1920, and *Tristram,* after a longer interval, in 1927. These three narrative poems group themselves naturally together, not merely because they deal with Arthurian material but because they deal primarily with the problems of romantic love. And these three poems describe progressively three distinct but related types of that love. In the language of Emerson, these are: "Initial, Daemonic and Celestial Love."

Merlin deals with the "initial" type of love—that of the senses. In it there is no admixture of the spiritual. The descriptions of Merlin and Vivian at Broceliande contain much beauty—so much that one wonders at Robinson's capacity for imagining pure pleasure—but the beauty is cloying. Merlin has renounced wisdom and power for mere sensuous enjoyment. In him men see

> A pathos of a lost authority.[22]

He has shaved off his beard, to regain youth, but has "gone down smiling to the smaller life." In other words, his love for Vivian, being sensuous only, has led to nothing but dissatisfaction and defeat. The lovers tire of each other and eventually part. It all comes to nothing.

Lancelot deals with a different type of love—partly sensual, partly spiritual. In it there is more than caprice—compulsion enters also. Fate drives the lovers on, but against their wills. Unlike the simple Vivian and the deluded Merlin, Lancelot and Guinevere do what they know to be wrong. In the introductory lines Lancelot is described as seeking to escape from his infatuation—"the Light" commands him away. But the insane vengeance of Arthur and his own inner conflict force him to carry off Guinevere to his retreat at Joyous Gard, and there to defend her. But he knows himself foredefeated: "The Light came and I did not follow it."[23] When, at the end, he and Guinevere discuss a second attempt at escape, they recognize the justice of their lot. What raises *Lancelot* above *Merlin,* then, is the purposefulness of the inner conflict—Lancelot's love was not a mere sensuous escape but a true struggle of loyalties. An inner daemon drove him on against his conscious sense of duty. The result was war, psychological and actual:

> And ever the Daemonic Love
> Is the ancestor of wars
> And the parent of remorse.[24]

Tristram, on the contrary, describes a love which is neither a sensuous escape from thought, like Merlin's, nor a conscious conflict of loyalties, like Lancelot's. Compare the descriptions of Broceliande and those of Joyous Gard, and the difference becomes obvious. Instead of *Merlin's*

> "fruits and wines and many foods
> Of many savors, and sweet ortolans,"[25]

there is, in *Tristram,*

> knowledge born of all endurance . . .
> Passion and comprehension beyond being[26]

Where Merlin's sensuous love denied "knowledge" and "comprehension," Tristram's created them. And in contrast to Lancelot, Tristram's love, being all-inclusive, suffered no division:

> Stronger than God,
> When all was done the god of love was fate,
> Where all was love.[27]

For Tristram, all was love. He had merely followed the transcendental counsel: "Give all to Love." And significantly, it had been Guinevere who had brought Isolt to Joyous Gard, and Lancelot who had given to Tristram his island for their love.[28] The unhappy and divided lovers symbolically offered their unattained happiness to those who could consummate it.

The events, internal and external, which motivate and make possible this consummation may be suggested later—the question here is of continuity. Whatever the causes, the three loves of Merlin, Lancelot, and Tristram came to three different but obviously related ends. Merlin's ended in spiritual defeat; Lancelot's ended in suffering, which, however, promised the hope of salvation; Tristram's ended in spiritual victory.

The final lines of the three poems make clear this continuity. They describe progressive developments of the same theme. Thus *Merlin* concludes:

> Colder blew the wind
> Across the world, and on it heavier lay
> The shadow and the burden of the night;
> And there was darkness over Camelot.

But in *Lancelot,* the darkness lightens, and there is hope of dawn:

> He rode on into the dark, under the stars,
> And there were no more faces. There was nothing.
> But always in the darkness he rode on,
> Alone; and in the darkness came the Light.

But with *Tristram,* the dawn has come. King Howel says:

> "When the dawn comes, my child,
> You will forget."

But Isolt of the white hands replies:

> "The dawn has come . . .
> And wisdom will come with it. If it sinks
> Away from me, and into the night again—
> Then I shall be alone, and I shall die,
> But I shall never be all alone—not now."[29]

Not alone at the end, like Lancelot, nor shrouded in night, Isolt watches the sunlight:

> She watched them there till even her thoughts were white,
> And there was nothing alive but white birds flying,
> Flying, and always flying, and still flying,
> And the white sunlight flashing on the sea.

Clearly, Robinson intended this white sunlight to be symbolic, and to contrast with the earlier darknesses.

More subtly, but no less clearly, the three poems are contrasted with regard to the theme of "peace." The three loves produce three different states of mind, not only in the lovers but in the onlookers; for love is not only individual but social in its implications. Thus Merlin, it was falsely reported,

> "wears the valiance of an ageless youth
> Crowned with a glory of eternal peace."

But no, his peace is not real:

> Dagonet, smiling strangely, shook his head:
> "I grant your valiance of a kind of youth
> To Merlin, but your crown of peace I question;
> . . . I look not to Merlin
> For peace, when out of his peculiar tomb
> He comes again to Camelot.[30]

This false peace, which Merlin foolishly sought, Lancelot at last finds is not for him. Rather, it is for him to suffer, in order that others may find:

> "Where the Light falls, death falls; a world has died
> For you, that a world may live. There is no peace.
> Be glad no man or woman bears for ever
> The burden of first days. There is no peace."[31]

Merlin found false peace; Lancelot found hope in change. But those who have lived life to the full may find peace at the end. Such—as King Mark mused—were Tristram and Isolt:

> "There was no more for them—and this *is* peace."[32]

And he repeats the theme in the lines immediately following.

Similarly, Robinson contrasts the three loves in their relations to "time." Merlin, seeking to find youth in light love, fell afoul of time:

> "I see the light,
> But I shall fall before I come to it
> For I am old. I was young yesterday.
> Time's hand that I have held away so long
> Grips hard now on my shoulder. Time has won."[33]

But in contrast, the central theme of *Tristram* is the triumph of true love over time:

> "Why should he wish to live a thousand years?
> Whether your stars are made of love or fire,
> There is a love that will outshine the stars,
> There will be love when there are no more stars."[34]

And constantly the theme is repeated:

> "It was not time
> For you or me, when we were there together.
> It was too much like always to be time."

Unlike Merlin and Lancelot, for whom love alone was not enough but seemed merely a means of escape from time, Tristram's love, by filling life to the full, triumphed over time. The theme has philosophic implications—of which, more later. But whatever the exact meaning of the idea, it runs like a thread of unity through the Arthurian poems.

III

Robinson's *Tristram,* then, is not only an unusual poem by an individualistic poet—it also forms one of a series of three Arthurian narratives which describe progressive aspects of the idea of romantic love. But the outlines of the legend of Tristram were traditionally fixed. Therefore it was inevitable that Robinson should change the old plot and mold the old characters to his purpose. In general, the changes which he introduced into the plot are comparatively few, although significant; but the characters have become wholly the instruments of his poetic imagination.

Robinson's plot differs in three important aspects from the conventional legend. In the first place, Tristram's passion for Isolt of Ireland is described as gradual, and as it were, cumulative, rather than merely love at first sight. Ordinarily the lovers consummate their passion on the ship—they are both impetuous and disloyal. Robinson, by postponing the consummation of their love, gives to it the dignity not only of maturity but also of honesty. Following as it does after Tristram's quarrel with Mark and his exile, it ceases to be disloyal, either to liege-lord or to friend. In both these aspects Tristram's love is distinguished from Lancelot's whose love for Guinevere was impetuous:

> "I saw your face, and there were no more kings,"[35]

and whose love was also disloyal, because Arthur was Lancelot's king and his avowed friend.

In the second place, Robinson described the meeting of Tristram and Isolt at Joyous Gard, not as a stolen tryst but as an unexpected encounter, managed by others. Tristram himself does not steal Isolt, nor does he even arrange the meeting. On his way from King Arthur's court, he is left by Lancelot at Joyous Gard, as Isolt is also left by Guinevere. Instruments of fate, the two guilty lovers make possible the happiness of the two innocent lovers, whom only an arbitrary authority has separated. If this device seems somewhat indirect, the mechanism is not over-emphasized, and the psychological result remains satisfying.

Finally, Robinson ends the story not with the incident of the white sail, the treacherous words of Isolt of Brittany, and the rather melodramatic death of the lovers, but with the sunlight musings of Isolt. From a tale of lawless passion, treachery, and revenge, the story has become one of a passion purified by suffering, of joy beyond sorrow, and of the slow growth of wisdom.

But these changes of plot have been motivated by more subtle and significant changes in the characters of the four chief protagonists. Tristram himself has changed in subtle ways. And, strikingly, Robinson has described this change as occurring gradually, in the very process of the tale as he tells it. At the beginning, just as in the old legend, Tristram is described as impetuous and warlike, having slain Isolt's kinsman, Morhaus, in battle. But to his mind, this killing marks the beginning of evil:

> "When a man sues
> The fairest of all women for her love
> He does not cleave the skull first of her kinsman."[36]

This killing also marks the beginning of wisdom for him. But wisdom is slow: when he discovers Andred spying upon him and Isolt, he beats the man violently, thus earning his undying hatred and sealing his own death warrant. When Mark appears and he is again tempted to warlike resistance, he pulls his sword from the scabbard, but puts it back again, choosing exile rather than resistance. Later he neither seeks to win Isolt by violence, nor, once he has found her, to keep her at Joyous Gard by force of arms. He has now become not the valiant warrior of the old tales, but "the child of thought." In contrast again with Lancelot, who snatched away Guinevere by violence[37] and whose stay at Joyous Gard was troubled by civil war, the mature Tristram refuses to resort to violence, and enjoys his love freed of the fear of defeat and death. This non-resistant wisdom might even have won him final physical victory, but for Andred. From the valiant, violent knight of the conventional legend, the Tristram of Robinson has developed into the wise man who will no longer resist evil with evil.

A similar development occurs in the character of King Mark. Other modern dramatists, beginning with Richard Wagner, had attempted to describe Mark sympathetically.[38] But none had seen in him the potentialities for good suggested by Robinson. Appearing at first as the more or less conventional villain of the old legend, Mark, like Tristram, develops, because he possesses a nature "not so base as it was common." Indeed Mark may represent the reincarnation of the god Demos, whose dialogue with Dionysus immediately preceded the writing of *Tristram*. For Mark, like the proverbial common man, possessed the elements of goodness and wisdom which, if realized sooner, might have averted the tragedy. Near the end of the tale he is given one of the most profoundly moving soliloquies in it.[39]

In keeping with the changed characters of Tristram and Mark, Isolt of Brittany also has changed—perhaps more profoundly than they. Since she both introduces and concludes the poem, and since it is suggested that she alone is to know the sunlight wisdom of the new day, her significance is obvious. Robinson has lavished upon her his greatest gift of psychological analysis. She seems most nearly like the heroines of his other narratives, and therefore, perhaps, least like the traditional Isolts of Brittany. Her love is not selfish, but pure. And like all of Robinson's best characters, she gains our admiration by remaining true to her inmost nature, not seeking to win Tristram by feminine wiles or to deceive him by treachery. But when all is said, she still seems somewhat unsubstantial, living in a dream world mostly:

> "yet I must have
> My dreams if I must live, for they are mine."[40]

She becomes most real when contrasted most sharply with the other Isolt.

Superficially like the traditional heroines of the old legend, it is Isolt of Ireland, nevertheless, who makes the poem unique. Never elsewhere did Robinson so completely realize a character so passionate and direct. She seems foreign to the puritan tradition in her headlong abandon. Yet this very passionate Isolt of Robinson's has gone far beyond the original of the Celtic legend, and even the later European tradition. For she is no longer pagan, nor is her love merely the sensual love of earth:

> "It was not earth in him that burned
> Itself to death; and she that died for him
> Must have been more than earth."[41]

Compare Robinson's heroine with Swinburne's, and the radical difference becomes clear. Swinburne's, like most of the Isolts of the past, is only the passionate lover, self-abandoned to emotion. But Robinson's Isolt is the passionate lover, who also is capable of spiritual growth and wisdom:

> Till tears of vision and of understanding
> Were like a mist of wisdom in their eyes.[42]

The character of this dark Isolt suggests the reconciliation of passionate, physical experience with the old ideal of wisdom.

The Merlin of Robinson's early poem had once prophesied concerning the means of realizing this ideal:

> "the torch
> Of woman . . . together with the light
> That Galahad found, is yet to light the world."

And Dagonet had repeated after him:

> "The torch of woman
> . . . and the light that Galahad found
> Will some day save us all."[43]

Now this cryptic and seemingly un-puritan prophecy finds realization in *Tristram,* where the dark Isolt points to salvation through passionate love (the torch of woman), while Isolt of the white hands realizes the ideal of purity, which Galahad found.

IV

The contrast between Robinson's *Tristram* and other versions of the legend suggests that his poem possesses definite ideal implications. These, moreover, are related to a philosophy of life, which may be described as transcendentalism. Certain passages in the poem explicitly suggest this philosophy, without ever defining it. What is the meaning of it all?

In *Tristram,* the key word is clearly "time." Indeed, the constant repetition of this word would become monotonous, were it not for the wide variety with which it is used. "Time," almost like a concrete character, takes shape and grows as the poem progresses, until, in the final love scenes, it emerges as a consciously intended and consciously expressed idea. Its poetic virtue, of course, lies partly in its evocative vagueness; but we may define it prosaically as "the routine experience of daily life." The theme of the poem is the transcending of "time," or the world of routine experience, by the ecstatic intensity of the mystical or passionate experience.

Throughout the poem, whenever Tristram and Isolt of Ireland appear together, the theme of "time" introduces them. Thus the third canto begins:

Lost in a gulf of time where time was lost,

and continues:

Time was aware of them,
And would beat soon upon his empty bell
Release from such a fettered ecstasy
As fate would not endure.

The seventh canto again begins with

Isolt alone with time, Isolt of Ireland,

and later apostrophizes the lovers:

But let these two that were not shadows
Be as they were, and live—by time no more
Divided until time for them should cease.
They were not made for time as others were,
And time therefore would not be long for them. . . .[44]

Always Robinson describes the experience of the two lovers in terms of time, suggestively. But as the love scene at Joyous Gard develops, Tristram himself formulates the idea more explicitly:

"Time is not life. For many, and many more,
Living is mostly for a time not dying—
But not for me. For me a few more years
Of shows and slaughters, or the tinsel seat
Of a small throne, would not be life. Whatever
It is that fills life high and full, till fate
Itself may do no more, it is not time.
Years are not life."[45]

Later he repeats the theme to himself.[46] And finally Isolt echoes it to affirm the final, spiritual victory of the two lovers, in the face of death:

"How shall we measure and weigh these lives of ours?
You said once that whatever it is that fills
Life up, and fills it full, it is not time.
You told my story when you said that to me,
But what of yours? Was it enough, Tristram?

> Was it enough to fly so far away
> From time that for a season time forgot us?
> You said so once. Was it too much to say?"
> ". . . It was enough,"
> He said.[47]

Repeatedly, and with progressive self-consciousness and clarity, the idea of "time" recurs. By filling their lives with something other than time, the lovers have escaped from time. They have "islanded their love" for a season in Joyous Gard. They have achieved spiritual victory by transcending time. But as the idea develops, one becomes conscious of a certain ambiguity in it. On the one hand the words "escape," "isolation," and "flight from time" suggest the other-worldly idealistic tradition, the ivory tower of romanticism, and the defeatist philosophy of much post-war literature. On the other hand, the phrases "fill life full" and "defeating time," and also the whole-souled happiness of the lovers' life at Joyous Gard, suggest an opposite philosophy of realization in this world, of immediate experience and of spiritual victory. How, then, did Tristram "transcend" time? Did he conquer time or escape from it?

The answer to the question depends partly upon the point of view. If one takes the position of Mark the materialist, agnosticism and pessimism follow:

> "I do not know
> Whether these two that have torn life from time
> Have failed or won . . .
> Now it is done, it may be well for them,
> And well for me when I have followed them.
> I do not know."[48]

Robinson himself occasionally seems to take the pessimistic view: death is best; the only peace is that which follows death. And many critics have developed this interpretation. T. K. Whipple calls the escape from time ". . . an escape, that is, from this world, from this life."[49] And Mark Van Doren, in praising Mark's soliloquy, has made it the key to Robinson's philosophy. Is transcendentalism, then, a philosophy of escape from this world, and of defeat?

The analysis of *Tristram* presented earlier in this essay suggests the opposite conclusion. If Tristram's "escape from time" had been truly "an escape from this world, from this life," it would have ended in spiritual defeat, as Merlin's attempted escape ended. Time cannot be conquered by cowards—only those who have passed beyond the fear of death can conquer it. If Tristram had fled to Joyous Gard to escape the vengeance of his king, as Lancelot did, and had taken recourse to arms, he would have failed, whether or not his arms had won. Nor was there anything of the Hamlet in this modern Tristram, "child of thought." For in him knowledge did not inhibit action and the consummation of love. On the other hand, wisdom developed through experience, and as the crown of experience. And this wisdom was not other-worldly, or negative.

"Time," it has been said, is the key word. If Tristram had sought truly to escape from time, he would always have been at enmity with it. But this he never was. Rather, he and Isolt have used "time" itself in order to conquer "time." From the beginning, time has been "on our side,"[50] because the two lovers did not seek stolen love, nor did they offer armed resistance: "Praise God for time," Tristram exclaimed:

> "Praise God for time,
> And for such hope of what may come of it
> As time like this may grant. I could be strong,
> But to be over-strong now at this hour
> Would only be destruction. The King's ways
> Are not those of one man against another,
> And you must live, and I must live—for you."[51]

These are not the words of one who seeks an escape from life in this world. They are rather the words of one who knows that there is a time for all things, and that the renunciation of love and of action at one time may lead to the consummation of love and to the fullness of life at another. *Tristram* describes the achievement of the fullness of life, in this world, in the due course of time.

V

In American literature and thought, two philosophies of life have always struggled for supremacy. The more common of these, popularly identified as "pragmatism," has preached that "time is money," that waste of time is waste of value, and that daily, routine application to work offers the way both to worldly and spiritual success. Economically, this is based on "the labor theory of value," and derives from the mechanistic assumption that one moment is as good as another. Not only is the amount of work which a man can accomplish measurable absolutely in terms of "man-hours," but as a corollary, the amount of experience which a man can realize per hour is likewise limited, and measurable quantitatively. Work neglected is money lost; action neglected is experience lost. "Let us then be up and doing!"

But this mechanical, "pragmatic" philosophy has never gone unchallenged. Even in America, and in the eighteenth century, the evangelists attacked it—men could achieve salvation (*i.e.*, success) not by works, but only by grace. Opposed to Franklin, Jonathan Edwards sought to convert men's souls, not gradually, but suddenly. In the nineteenth century, transcendentalism continued this opposition: Time is not value, because routine repetitive action is unimportant in comparison with new intuitions, new inventions. Nature is saltatory and impulsive.[52] Moreover, daily routine is insignificant in comparison with the ecstatic moment: "We must be very suspicious of the deceptions of the element of time," wrote Emerson. "It takes a great deal of time to eat and sleep, or to earn a hundred dollars, and a very little time to entertain a hope or an insight which becomes the light of our life."[53]

But this "transcendentalism" which denies the supreme value of "time," has always been accused of other-worldliness—of seeking merely to escape from "time." This accusation has seemed credible, partly because of the evangelical and puritan origins of transcendentalism, partly because of certain ambiguities in the philosophy itself. Emerson sometimes spoke as though a man's salvation were purely a personal affair of "self"-reliance, which could have no practical effect on the world, and also as though it belonged to a purely intellectual realm beyond worldly experience. Robinson, primarily interested in psychological and intellectual analysis, sometimes followed him. But Robinson's poetry did develop and clarify two "transcendental" ideas which had often been misunderstood. First, it proclaimed repeatedly that individuals who suffer defeat and death "in time," while gaining "spiritual" salvation, actually do influence the world about them so powerfully that their individual deaths seem unimportant. Second, Robinson's *Tristram* emphasized that those ecstatic moments which transcend "time" by their intensity and power are not merely intellectual insights but deeply felt moments of living experience.

Robinson, like Emerson and Thoreau before him, took John Brown as a historic example of transcendentalism. The individual who dies for a principle does not fail, even in a temporal sense: "I shall have more to say when I am dead."[54] His individual death teaches men wisdom, even though too late to "save" his own body. Thus Mark laments that understanding came to him too late to save Tristram and Isolt, who had almost won victory by not resisting:

> "And what might once have been if I had known
> Before—I do not know."[55]

But Mark, though capable of understanding, was not capable of true wisdom:

> "there are darknesses
> That I am never to know . . ."

This wisdom remained for Isolt of Brittany, who, in her own way, shared the suffering and the wisdom of the other two. Like Zoë in Robinson's allegorical poem *King Jasper*, Isolt of Brittany becomes almost the embodiment of that principle of life which progressively learns wisdom through experience. Toward the end, Zoë exclaimed:

> "Leave me, and let your poor, sick, stricken soul
> Suffer until it feels; and let it feel

> Until it sees. You will have died meanwhile,
> But who knows death?"[56]

So Merlin, Lancelot, and Tristram progressively had suffered, felt, and seen; they had died meanwhile, but others lived who had learned wisdom from them, and on whom the sunlight shone.

But what of the individuals who had died? What was their compensation for self-sacrifice? Was it merely that they had followed "the moral law?" Was it merely that they had enjoyed the satisfaction of an ecstatic moment of insight? Was it merely that, not resisting, they had "given all to love"? The Emersonian language had been mostly negative. Most of Robinson's other poems had even described wisdom as divorced from positive realization in this life. But *Tristram* for the first time described the ecstatic moment as a period of such intense experience that its quality was worth more than the quantity of a lifetime of daily experiences:

> "Now listen, while I say this:
> My life to me is not a little thing;
> It is a fearful and a lovely thing;
> Only my love is more."[57]

The question in *Tristram* is not one of self-sacrifice or the denial of life in this world for "salvation" in the next, but rather of realization of values in this world. Tristram "transcends" the old mechanical philosophy that one moment of experience is worth as much as another, but *Tristram* does not deny the philosophy of experience. In this one poem, Robinson realized, for the first and perhaps the only time, the positive implications which had lain implicit in the transcendental philosophy from the beginning. Transcending "time," Tristram gained wisdom without sacrificing the fullness of life in this world.

---

1 Rollo W. Brown, *Next Door to a Poet* (New York, 1937), 49.
2 Mark Van Doren, *Edwin Arlington Robinson* (New York, 1927), 77-90; and Lucius Beebe, *Edwin Arlington Robinson and the Arthurian Legend* (Cambridge, 1927).
3 New York *Herald Tribune*, Books, (May 8, 1927), 3.
4 *Nation*, CXXIV (May 25, 1927), 586.
5 *Bookman*, LXV (June 1927), 466; *ibid.* (July 1927), 555.
6 C. Cestre, *Revue Anglo-Américaine*, V (December 1927), 97.
7 Reviewed September 22, 1927, 640.
8 *New Republic*, LI (May 25, 1927), 22.
9 *American Poetry Since 1900* (New York, 1923), 66.
10 *Modern American Poetry* (New York, 1936), 141.
11 *Spokesmen* (New York, 1928), 61-63.
12 Brown, *Next Door to a Poet*, 81.
13 *Bookman* (November 1932), 676. Interview reported by Nancy Evans.
14 Brown, *Next Door to a Poet*, 74.
15 Louis V. Ledoux, "Psychologist of New England," *Saturday Review of Literature*, XII (October 19, 1935), 16.
16 Mark Van Doren, *Edwin Arlington Robinson* (New York, 1927), 77.
17 *Nation*, CXXIV (May 25, 1927), 586.
18 New York *Evening Post*, "The Literary Review," (May 7, 1927), 3.
19 The two most recent, and most excellent, studies of Robinson's philosophy have largely neglected *Tristram*. See Floyd Stovall, *American Literature*, X (March 1938), 1-23; and David Brown, *New England Quarterly*, X (September 1937), 487-502.
20 Lloyd Morris, *Nation*, CXXIV (May 25, 1927), 586.
21 See, for example, Robinson's letter to D. G. Mason in the *Yale Review*

(June 1936), 861. "He [Emerson] really gets after me."
22 *Collected Poems* (New York, 1929), 249. Permission to quote from this volume has been granted by the publishers, Messrs. Macmillan and Company.
23 *Collected Poems*, 439.
24 Emerson's *Poems*, Centenary Edition (Boston, 1903), 113.
25 *Collected Poems*, 239.
26 *Ibid.*, 675.
27 *Ibid.*, 676.
28 *Ibid.*, 676.
29 *Ibid.*, 727.
30 *Ibid.*, 238.
31 *Ibid.*, 448.
32 *Ibid.*, 721.
33 *Ibid.*, 295.
34 *Ibid.*, 690.
35 *Ibid.*, 376.
36 *Ibid.*, 614.
37 When he wrote *Lancelot*, Robinson apparently had not yet planned his contrasting version of *Tristram*, but referred contemptuously to "the stolen love" of Tristram and Isolt (page 400) and later to Isolt as a dark temptress (page 416) as in the old versions of the tale.
38 See Maurice Halperin, *Le Roman de Tristan et Iseut dans la Littérature Anglo-Américaine au XIXe et au XXe Siècles* (Paris, 1931).
39 *Collected Poems*, 720-722.
40 *Ibid.*, 726.
41 *Ibid.*, 727.
42 *Ibid.*, 675.
43 *Ibid.*, 307, 309.
44 *Ibid.*, 675.
45 *Ibid.*, 682.
46 *Ibid.*, 693.
47 *Ibid.*, 713.
48 *Ibid.*, 722.
49 *Spokesmen*, 54.
50 *Collected Poems*, 618.
51 *Ibid.*, 618.
52 Compare Emerson's essays "Experience" and "The Method of Nature."
53 From the essay "Experience," *Works*, III, 85.
54 *Collected Poems*, 490. The last line of "John Brown."
55 *Ibid.*, 721.
56 *Ibid.*, 1482.
57 *Ibid.*, 685.

E. A. ROBINSON AND THE COSMIC CHILL

Hyatt Howe Waggoner

THE MOST persistent theme in the poetry of Edwin Arlington Robinson is the problem of man's place in the universe—one which he shared with other thoughtful minds in his generation. John Burroughs, in the mid-nineties, wrote:

> Feeling, emotion, falls helpless before the revelations of science. . . . The universe is going its own way with no thought of us. . . . This discovery sends the cosmic chill, with which so many of us are familiar in these days.[1]

For this cosmic chill Robinson, in the first poem in his first regularly published volume, *The Children of the Night,* and again in the last poem he published before his death, attempted to set forth a remedy. Moreover, poem after poem between gave evidence of his preoccupation with the "revelations of science." After the appearance of *Captain Craig* in 1902, both his consideration of the problem and his final solution of it are conditioned by the same conception of the universe so eloquently set forth by Bertrand Russell in "A Free Man's Worship," in 1903. From this time on, Robinson was painfully aware of the significant question that sprang inevitably from the interpretation of natural science which to Russell seemed the only honest one:

> That man is the product of causes that had no prevision of the end they were achieving; that his origin, his growth, his hopes and fears, his loves and beliefs are but the outcome of accidental collocations of atoms; that no fire, no heroism, no intensity of thought and feeling, can preserve an individual life beyond the grave; that all the labours of the ages, all the devotion, all the inspiration, all the noonday brightness of human genius, are destined to extinction in the vast death of the solar system, and that the whole temple of man's achievement must inevitably be buried beneath the debris of a universe in ruins—all these things, if not quite beyond dispute, are yet so nearly certain, that no philosophy which rejects them can hope to stand. Only within the scaffolding of these truths, only on the

Reprinted by permission, *New England Quarterly,* XIII (March 1940), 65-84.

firm foundation of unyielding despair, can the soul's habitation henceforth be safely built.

How, in such an alien and inhuman world, can so powerless a creature as Man preserve his aspirations untarnished?[2]

Robinson's lifelong attempt to build the habitation of his soul on some foundation other than the "unyielding despair" recommended by Russell forms an episode in the larger story of the impact of science on thinking men of the last century and of our own, a story with which, in a general way, we are all familiar. But Robinson's reaction has a peculiar interest for us, an interest beyond that which inheres in it as merely a bit of concrete evidence for a generalized concept about cultural history. For his poetry has perhaps been as often misinterpreted, as grossly misunderstood, as that of any other American poet. For a generation it was usual for critics either to deplore Robinson's "pessimism" or to applaud it as intellectual honesty, and largely because of it, to welcome him to that group of writers who, in the second and third decades of this century, prided themselves on having put away false hopes and having faced the unpleasant facts. More recently, Professor David Brown[3] and Professor Floyd Stovall[4] have showed us the strand of "optimism" in the tragedies; and Frederic I. Carpenter has pointed out the transcendental elements in "Tristram."[5] Altogether, he has been interpreted as a fatalist, a pessimist, an intellectual brother of Dreiser, a Victorian, an optimist. A brief survey of some of the aspects of Robinson's reaction to science may throw a little light on this critical confusion, at the same time that it supplies a bit more evidence for the historian of general movements in literature.

I

Enough is now known of Robinson's childhood and youth to justify at least a conjecture as to when and how he became aware of the main current of contemporary thought and its significance for the problem of man's place in the universe. Hagedorn tells us that the boy early showed a tendency toward brooding melancholy, and that he "looked at life across the emblems of death, trying to find out what it meant from the foreshortened perspective of the graveyard."[6] Added to this melancholy were shyness and an increasing sense of inferiority. Robinson himself has said of these years that he would sit in a rocking-chair for hours "and wonder . . . why the deuce I should ever have been born."[7] There were periods of great loneliness, made more terrible by his sensitivity to the pain he saw all around him, in his family and in Gardiner. Nor was he free from physical suffering himself; a blow on the ear suffered in school in childhood gave him pain and, worse, caused him great anxiety, for the doctors warned that the deafness in one ear which resulted might be only the first step in a progression that could end in death or insanity. Oppressed, then, by periods of severe pain, filled with premonitions of early death or insanity, lonely, and fearfully aware of all the suffering of those dearest to him (his brother Dean was a tragic failure; his father was ending a sturdy life with a lingering death; his mother was unhappy, frustrated by the suffering of her son and husband), Robinson, at the age of twenty, was not one to remain complacently immune to the pessimism in the air.

Even before going to college he had ample opportunity through his reading, to become acquainted with the new temper of thought. Hagedorn, in his chapter on the years from 1889 to 1891, tells that among the writers whom Robinson most enjoyed in his voluminous reading were Swinburne, Matthew Arnold, Hardy and Housman. And once he had started his two-year Harvard career, his opportunities to feel the spirit that was soon to produce Haeckel's *Riddle of the Universe* and Russell's "A Free Man's Worship" were doubled, for now reading was supplemented by personal contacts. He probably got less of this insidious new spirit from his classes than from his friends, but he got something from both. In high school he had taken the scientific course to avoid Greek, and though he had no real interest in science, had found that chemistry amused him and that the course was easy and fairly pleasant; at Harvard, however, the going was harder. His courses were mostly in the field of English, but from a sense of duty he included also logic, psychology, and the history of philosophy. Though he "hated" logic "worse than hell itself" and disliked the other two, he could hardly have studied philosophy and psychology without becoming more fully aware of the philosophic import of science.[8]

Robinson's distaste for abstract, systematic thought made him somewhat resistant to the influence of his courses, but this is not true of the influence of his friends. With them he met frequently—the group called itself the "Corncob Club"— to "debate the dicta of Gates or Wendell or Royce or the fruits of their own reading."[9] Philosophy was an ever-recurrent topic for heated discussion by the group, and such discussions gave Robinson more than a taste of agnosticism and materialism, for Mowry Saben, who "dominated the discussions," had absorbed the new radicalism thoroughly.

> Robinson, silent, repressed, felt a new sense of life stirring in him at the luxuriant outpouring of Saben's pagan gospel.
>
> He was lonely, and hungry for friendship, and let the dynamic hedonist know that he wanted him to be his friend. . . . He was in Saben's room almost daily. Saben's heterodoxies and his morals made him uneasy; and logic, he felt, could go too far. "Your philosophy would clip an angel's wings." But he admired Saben's intellectual endowment, most brilliant in the fields in which Robinson

himself was lacking; and he liked the robustious iconoclast for the warmth which underlay his rhetoric.[10]

The more Saben argued, the firmer became Robinson's conviction that materialism was not the answer:

He had no systematic philosophy and no exalted opinion of the sages who had conceived the systems; but he admitted a mystic element in his thinking, though he would not defend, or even formulate it. "I can't argue," he would say, but Saben was conscious of an underlying conviction as firm as Plymouth Rock.[11]

Saben never was able to convince Robinson of the soundness of his position. Several years later the poet wrote to Arthur Gledhill: "The universe is a great thing, and the power of evil never put it together. Of that I am certain and I am just as certain that this life is but a little scene in the big show."[12] Yet Saben's importance in Robinson's intellectual development cannot be doubted. When, a few years later, in 1902, they met again, Robinson found his old friend "as amusing and disturbing as ever."[13] The "disturbing" quality of Saben's views probably did more than Robinson's reading in his courses at Harvard to bring the sad conclusions of science intimately before the thoughtful and melancholy poet.

From the time of his withdrawal from Harvard in 1893, after his father's death, to that of the publication of *The Torrent and the Night Before* in 1896, he was searching consciously for a philosophy of life.[14] In Gardiner again, he shared his philosophical interests and nourished his desire for companionship with three friends, who together hired a room over a dry-goods store for meeting and talking. One of the "Quadruped," Linville Robbins, called by the rest "The Scientist," did the most to fill Saben's place, for he was "fresh from courses in geology and excited by his first contact with the theory of evolution."[15] They met almost every night, and usually the talk ran to philosophy:

They were all eager and intelligent readers and the talk ran over books and ideas, though Blair might reach for his fiddle when Robinson and Robbins, who were given to speculation, turned to the *whence* and *why* of things. Robinson was aware that the younger man had been caught in the gears of the mechanistic system on the rebound from a theology his intelligence would not let him accept; and, with an inherited passion for untangling twisted skeins, determined to set him straight. Plagued by the pain in his ear, desperately needing a refuge, he himself was reaching up from a conception which he called "materialism" to a rarer climate which he called "idealism." "Idealize yourself!" he would exclaim. "Take your mind off the material and focus it on the real existence."[16]

It was in this period that Robinson was introduced to Mrs. Eddy's *Science and Health* and concluded that though it was a "remarkable" book, he could not "accept it in detail." He had, he wrote his friend Gledhill, been slowly getting rid of materialism, but, "I am afraid I haven't the stamina to be a Christian."[17] It was at this time too that after a discussion of materialism and idealism he wrote "Two Sonnets" (published in *The Children of the Night*) contrasting the two points of view.

The struggle to find a philosophy continued:

The family was his base, the tie that bound him to the human race, giving him, above all, spiritual support, the assurance that, in a terrifying world, the individual was not alone and detached, an atom in a Lucretian chaos....[John Hays] Gardiner and Robinson took to each other instantly and undemonstratively. The scholar . . . had, like the poet, liberated himself from the religious and philosophical conventions of his background. . . . Burnham [a friend of Robinson in his early New York days] helped Robinson cut the last of the hawsers that bound his spirit to "the crumbled wharves" of accepted theology. . . . Night after night, at some cafe off Columbus Circle, they discussed the Absolute, over beers.[18]

One more friend may be mentioned as having helped to keep Robinson constantly aware of the threatening triumph of scientific naturalism. Professor Lawrence J. Henderson, then a young man at Harvard, forced Robinson to keep on thinking out his position:

Robinson and he liked each other without liking each other's point of view. To the poet, the scientist seemed too skeptical; to the scientist, the poet seemed not to know himself, or to have a clear comprehension of his fellowmen, being inclined to universalize emotions peculiar to his own hypersensitive nature. Robinson, it seemed to Henderson, clearly wanted to see man and his world as it was; he was scornful of sentimentalism, yet his realism had its blind spots, and its limits. Henderson . . . noted that though the poet believed in science and the scientific approach to phenomena, he was inclined to protect certain areas of thought and emotion from the dissection of the scalpel.[19]

Only a few more lines need be drawn to fill out a brief sketch of Robinson's search for a philosophy under the stimulus of the scientific picture of an alien universe. In the later years of his life he probably found comfort, as so many others have, in the new physics. Rollo Walter Brown has told us how he and Robinson frequently talked, at Peterborough, of "the rising philosophical importance of the physicists," and he has told us, too, of Robinson's reading during this last period:

One might find almost any sort of book on the little table in the studio. . . . But whatever else there might be, there was certain to be some volume that was philosophic in its import. It might not be very directly or very ponderously philosophic—a copy of Havelock Ellis's *Fountain of Life*, a readable book by Eddington, the newest volume by Dean Inge—but it provided commentary on the drift of his thinking.

. . . . And in his conversation he grew readier—in the end rather eager—to discuss matters that seemed to reach out beyond the pale of common experience or common thought. "Well, you had better be coming over to settle this business of the whenceness and whyness."[20]

II

Although he never settled, to his own complete satisfaction, this business of the whenceness and the whyness, Robinson stated and restated the terms of the problem in his poetry; and an examination of the forty-year period between *The Torrent and the Night Before* and *King Jasper* will show how his thought on the nature of the world and of man changed with the years. It is not quite true to say, as Ben Ray Redman has said,[21] that Robinson's mature philosophy may be found in "The Children of the Night." His mind did not harden and remain fixed in the immature solutions of his early twenties.

The original stimulus to his lifelong troubled search for faith is clear enough: it was the impact of science upon religion, the challenge of science to the creeds. In *The Children of the Night* Robinson's outlook was very similar to the compromise position so popular at the time, as voiced, for example, in A. D. White's *History of the Warfare of Science with Theology in Christendom:*[22] science had destroyed theology, but had only strengthened and purified religion by cleansing it of all its irrational elements. With Robinson, as with White, Burroughs, and Fiske, to name no more, the warfare was not between science and religion but between science and theology. Of course, the destruction of the old creeds brought doubt and anxiety, and Robinson went through what he called at the time his period of "Materialism"; but nowhere in his poetry published in the nineties do we find evidence either of any naturalistic despair or of any clear awareness of the full extent of the implications of current science. Henry Adams realized those implications; Mark Twain felt them painfully and adopted them with vehement pessimism. But Robinson's awareness of their full significance was not to come until later. With the old certainties crumbling, he wrote: "I cannot find my way: there is no star"; but though he was confused and troubled by the disintegration of theology, he ended his "credo" on a sure note of faith: "I know the far-sent message of the years. / I feel the coming glory of the Light."[23] Though much might be lost, evolution could be interpreted optimistically; the conception of an alien universe finds no detailed expression in these poems of hope and faith in a troubled age:

> Here by the windy docks I stand alone,
> But yet companioned; there the vessel goes,
> And there my friend goes with it; but the wake
> That melts and ebbs between that friend and me
> Love's earnest is of Life's all-purposeful
> And all-triumphant sailing, when the ships
> Of Wisdom loose their fretful chains and swing
> Forever from the crumbled wharves of time.[24]

It is interesting to speculate as to why Robinson omitted the title poem of the volume from later editions of his poetry. No doubt the didactic tone of the piece later seemed out of keeping with the temper of his maturer works. Yet, in view of the many obliquely didactic passages in all of his poetry, it may be that the certainty here expressed seemed to him later immature and unconsidered. For the poem asserts faith in immortality and evolutionary progress and repudiates agnosticism in a positive way not to be found in the later poems:

For those that never know the Light,
  The darkness is a sullen thing;
And they, the Children of the Night,
  Seem lost in Fortune's winnowing.

But some are strong and some are weak,—
  And there's the story. House and home
Are shut from countless hearts that seek
  World-Refuge that will never come.

And if there be no other life,
  And if there be no other chance
To weigh there sorrow and there strife
  Than in the scales of circumstance,

'Twere better, ere the sun go down
  Upon the first day we embark,
In life's imbittered sea to drown,
  Than toil forever in the dark.

But if there be a soul on earth
  So blinded with its own misuse
Of man's revealed, incessant worth,
  Or worn with anguish, that it views

No light but for a mortal eye,
  No rest but of a mortal sleep,
No God but in a prophet's lie,
  No faith for "honest doubt" to keep;

If there be nothing, good or bad,
  But chaos for a soul to trust,—
God counts it for a soul gone mad,
  And if God be God, He is just.

And if God be God, He is Love;
  And though the dawn be still so dim
It shows us we have played enough
  With creeds that make a friend of Him.

There is one creed, and only one,
  That glorifies God's excellence;
So cherish, that his will be done,
  The common creed of common sense.

It is the crimson, not the gray,
  That charms the twilight of all time;
It is the promise of the day
  That makes the starry sky sublime;

It is the faith within the fear
  That holds us to the life we curse;—

So let us in ourselves revere
  The Self which is the Universe!

Let us, the Children of the Night,
  Put off the cloak that hides the scar!
Let us be Children of the Light,
  And tell the ages what we are![25]

Throughout the volume the opinions expressed on two subjects are ever the same: Robinson rejects accepted Christian views, though the need for doing so troubles him; and he is certain that the proper interpretation of evolution is an idealistic one—materialism will not do. But about another important subject he is less consistent: "Two Sonnets," written to set forth his views on materialism and idealism, definitely disavows the belief in personal immortality; but elsewhere he appears to be uncertain,[26] while in some poems he seems to assert the strength of his belief in it.[27] Such shiftings of opinion are to be expected, for the poet was going through a troubled and uncertain stage, probing his own convictions to determine what he could believe.

In succeeding volumes he showed less indecision. His position on the creeds may be simply stated. He had set forth his troubled freedom from them in *The Children,* and he reaffirmed it at length in "Captain Craig":

You have made
The cement of your churches out of tears
And ashes, and the fabric will not stand:
The shifted walls that you have coaxed and shared
So long with unavailing compromise
Will crumble down to dust and blow away,
And younger dust will follow after them;
Though not the faintest or the farthest whirled
First atom of the least that ever flew
Shall be by man defrauded of the touch
God thrilled it with to make a dream for man
When Science was unborn . . .[28]

And the same view was re-expressed many times in most of the later poems.[29]

But though there was no change throughout the years in his reference to the "obsolescent creeds,"[30] there was a change in his views on God and immortality. In the passage just quoted, the reference to God may indicate a living belief in a personal deity, but if so, the belief in its pristine certainty did not survive the years. Again and again in the later poems Robinson referred to or explained the inconclusiveness of faith. One passage will serve as an example. In *The Glory of the Nightingales* the poet himself speaks and says Malory is

like so many of us
Whose knowing is belief, and whose belief
Is a determination to believe,

> Whether in God or in deflated friends,
> Or in ourselves.[31]

There is a divinity in the universe, but one

> so different
> From any man has drafted from the sun
> Or from the seasons, or from the profound
> And healing wisdom of his desperation,
> That you need sigh no longer for a shadow
> That has no substance.[32]

Robinson gave his last word on the subject when, speaking through Zoë in *King Jasper,* he said:

> I don't say what God is, but it's a name
> That somehow answers us when we are driven
> To feel and think how little we have to do
> With what we are.[33]

A similar attenuation of belief happened also to his faith in immortality. Complete agnosticism with regard to all that the traditional religions have to say about the universe gradually replaced a wavering half-faith in the "essence" if not in the "creeds." Writing in *The Town Down the River* of the death of Leffingwell, he could only say,

> And we who leave him say we do not know
> How much is ended or how much begun.[34]

The position expressed later in "The Man Against the Sky" is agnostic; and finally, in *The Glory of the Nightingales,* the question is considered objectively, and no answer is given.[35] Again we may look for Robinson's final view of the matter in his last poem; and again we find that the question of personal survival posed in doubt and fear by Jasper himself is answered by Zoë, the symbolic character through whom the poet speaks, only indirectly, through an assertion of faith in a purposive universe:

> No God,
> No Law, No purpose, could have hatched for sport
> Out of warm water and slime, a war for life
> That was unnecessary, and far better
> Never had been—if man, as we behold him
> Is all it means.[36]

Though in his first volume we find that it was the challenge of science to orthodox beliefs that troubled the poet, there is in the later volumes clear evidence that he outgrew his preoccupation with this early concern. From the time of "The Man Against the Sky" on to the end of his life, what necessitated his troubled search for faith was not so much the plight of orthodoxy as the plight of value. For no sooner had Robinson become reconciled to the loss of the creeds than he became aware of a far more tangible threat to his peace of mind. Thereafter he was concerned chiefly with what he called, in *Matthias at the Door,* the scientific

> news of an ingenious mechanism
> That must have built itself mysteriously
> And infinitely out of infinite nothing.

In such a universe, it was clear, life could be only what he made Garth call it, "a riot of cells and chemistry." If life were only that, as it could only be in such a universe, Robinson knew that *value, purpose, achievement* are empty words. But he did not think that life or the universe could be thus described. What he did think, what his cosmic philosophy was (he would, of course, never have dignified his views with such a phrase) can best be seen by an examination of his thought on two topics, determinism and the authority of science.

On the problem of free will *versus* fate, Robinson, characteristically, never gave a dogmatic answer. But that the temper of his mind and so of his poetry was influenced by deterministic doctrine there can be no doubt. Though he has often been called a fatalist,[37] and with some reason, since the word *fate* and the concept of fate are important in a large proportion of his poems, Robinson never confessed to a belief in determinism. What he did admit many times in his poetry was that he was depressed by a consideration of "how little we have to do with what we are." There was always the "problematical free will"[38] to be considered, and problematical though it might be, it was a possibility, he thought, which man could hardly help believing in.

One cannot allow to free will even a problematical existence if one adopts without reservation the world-view which until recently science seemed to be presenting with such positiveness. Robinson, though he valued science and scientific method, did so with reservations. He denied that science is capable of finding and expressing the whole truth. Had he not done so, he would have been unable, logically, to deny that life is "an accident of nameless energies."[39] He had to deny it and, for his own peace of mind, to deny it logically and consistently. Emerson, as Mr. Carpenter has suggested in his discussion of *Tristram,* contributed much to Robinson's philosophy. Robinson's criticism of science is that of a transcendentalist. But Alfred Kreymborg has said of Robinson that "He is simply, more than any poet of his era, an offspring of the scientific urge"; and the statement, while perhaps debatable because of the area covered by the generalization, does account for the unorthodox temper of the poet's transcendentalism, created as an escape from the unendurable position which many thought imposed by a complete acceptance of science. Instead of escaping from futility in the present by turning back to the past, as Henry Adams did, or accepting futility with lugubrious resignation, as Theodore Dreiser did, Robinson escaped through mysticism. There are, he held, two ways of knowing: intuition, or the Light, and reason, or science.

> I cannot know,
> For certain, that your way, dark as it was,
> Was not the necessary way, of life.
> There was in yours at least a buried light
> For time and man; and science, living in time
> May find at last a gleam nearer than yours,
> For those who are not born to follow it
> Before it has been found. There is, meanwhile
> A native light for others, but none born
> Of penitence, or of man's fear to die.[40]

Once this transcendental division in the knowing process is granted, it is possible to question whether scientific reality is the only reality. Scientific books are no help to Matthias when he is searching for the truth:

> He sought for it in books
> That were like heavy keys for doors not his
> To open, and doubted if they fitted even
> The doors of those who had invented them. . . .
> And there was nothing in any of them for him.
> The best of them were moonshine without light,
> Or news of an ingenious mechanism
> That must have built itself mysteriously
> And infinitely out of infinite nothing.[41]

Now and again the poet expressed in his poetry his reasons for this lack of complete confidence in science. One of these reasons was that the scientific theory of today is discarded tomorrow:

> Small knowledge have we that by knowledge met
> May not some day be quaint as any told
> In almagest or chronicle of old.[42]

More important, science simply cannot answer the truly important questions, for, he says, the infinite cannot be imprisoned in ". . . . a few finite and unfinished words / That are the chips of brief experience."[43] Because of these considerations, then, Robinson felt justified in refusing to admit the necessity of such despair as characterizes what Mr. Krutch has called "the modern temper." The woman in "The March of the Cameron Men" was speaking for Robinson when she said,

> There is more of me,
> I hope, than a pathetic mechanism
> Grinding itself to nothing. Possibly not,
> But let me say there is. . . .[44]

Significant are the words "I hope" and "possibly not." Robinson's was not an easy faith, complacently held. He was too sensitive to the several aspects of "the modern temper" for that. After all, as he often admitted, free will *may* be only an illusion;[45] and man's physical insignificance in the terrifying immensity of the cosmos is undeniable; and he was well aware of, though he did not accept, the consequences for the status of values of certain aspects of science.

> Have you not heard, yet, anywhere, death-bells ringing
> For love and poor Romance? Biologists
> And bolshevists are ringing them like mad—
> So loud that Love, we're told will soon be lost
> With dodos, dinosaurs, and pterodactyls.[46]

III

It was perhaps inevitable that such a philosophy, propounded by a man so averse to dogmatism, should often have been misinterpreted as pessimism, fatalism, or naturalism. Robinson was more sensitive than many of his critics to the intellectual climate of his times, and so more troubled than they by considerations which, it seemed to him, men of intellectual integrity must ponder, if not accept. He never did settle to his complete satisfaction the ultimate questions which, as Rollo Walter Brown has told us, he grew more and more ready to discuss in the last years. "Is there a God? Is there a purpose, or a Law?" he made Cavender cry out at the height of his wretchedness. Robinson knew that man, small, childish, lonely, is not an impressive figure.

> Two insects on a leaf
> Would fill about as much of nature's eye,
> No doubt, as would a woman and a man
> At odds with heritage.[47]

If the sun were "only a spark among superior stars," might not the "chemistry of fate"[48] be the fact behind man's illusion of purpose and achievement?

Robinson did not know. But he did not think so. He never believed that "myopic science" with its "inch-ruling of the infinite"[49] should have the final word on whether or not the stars are more than fire. Though, intellectually honest as he was, he was forced to doubt the conventional triad, God, freedom, and immortality, and though he held no illusions about man's importance in the cosmos, there was one faith which he never surrendered: he never lost his conviction that science cannot know or tell all—that, in other words, there are two ways of knowing, and that both have some validity, though they may seem at times to offer conflicting reports on the nature of reality. Ludwig Lewisohn was wrong when he said that Robinson "has not moved from the philosophic nihilism of his generation, the generation of Bertrand Russell."[50] Robinson was, truly enough, a product of the intellectual revolution effected by science; but he was not a passive product. He reacted vigorously to the cosmic chill, and turned, though hesitantly, to an older and more cheerful American tradition as an alternative to despair. He lost his religion but he kept his faith.

---

1 *The Light of Day: Religious Discussions and Criticism from the Naturalist's Point of View* (Boston, 1900), 119.
2 "A Free Man's Worship," *Mysticism and Logic* (London, 1921), 47-48. The essay was first published in *The Independent Review* in 1903. Possibly the best general discussion of the philosophic reactions to the mechanistic world-view is that in J. H. Randall's *The Making of the Modern Mind* (Boston, 1926), Chapter XXI. See especially the part of the chapter called "Escape from the Alien World into Philosophic Idealism," 574 ff.
3 "Robinson's Later Poems," *New England Quarterly*, X (September 1937), 487-502.
4 "The Optimism Behind Robinson's Tragedies," *American Literature*, X (March 1938), 1-23.
5 "Tristram the Transcendent," *New England Quarterly*, XI, 501-523.
6 Hermann Hagedorn, *Edwin Arlington Robinson, A Biography* (New York, 1938), 18.
7 *Ibid.*, 18.
8 Only one attempt seems to have been made to trace the possible influence of James and Royce on Robinson's philosophy: L. S. Morris, in *The Poetry of Edwin Arlington Robinson* (New York, 1923), sets forth the thesis that Robinson's thought may be described as absolute idealism and may be traced back to Royce. For more recent analyses of Robinson's thought, see David Brown, "Robinson's Later Poems," *New England Querterly*, X (September 1937), 487-502; Floyd Stovall, "The Optimism behind Robinson's Tragedies," *American Literature*, X (March 1938). 1-23; and Frederic I. Carpenter, "Tristram the Transcendent."
9 Hagedorn, 71.
10 *Ibid.*, 65, 74-75.
11 *Ibid.*, 72.
12 *Ibid.*, 91; cf. the title poem in *The Children of the Night* (quoted below) for his faith in the core, if not the creeds, of Christianity.
13 *Ibid.*, 194.
14 *Ibid.*, 90.
15 *Ibid.*, 92-93.
16 *Ibid.*, 94. Exactly when Robinson went through the period of "materialism" is not made clear by Hagedorn. Probably Robinson used the word to indicate merely agnosticism, the disturbing character of which he mitigated with the transcendental philosophy of the "Light" which he was developing.
17 *Ibid.*, 95.
18 *Ibid.*, 125, 126, 131.
19 *Ibid.*, 287-288.
20 Rollo W. Brown, *Next Door to a Poet* (New York, 1937), 7.
21 *Edwin Arlington Robinson* (New York, 1926), 17.
22 New York, 1896. See especially the preface to Volume I.
23 "Credo," *Collected Poems* (New York, 1937), 94.
24 "Octaves," *Ibid.*, 107.
25 *The Children of the Night* (New York, 1914), 11-12. Cf., in the same volume, other poems omitted from the *Collected Poems*, especially "For Some Poems by Matthew Arnold," "Kosmos," and "The Night Before"; also *Collected Poems*, 89, 102, 103.
26 *E.g.*, "The Night Before."
27 *E.g.*, "The Children of the Night" and "Kosmos."
28 *Collected Poems*, 118. Cf. also, in "Captain Craig," 119, 120, 132, 142, 146, 147, 150.
29 See *Collected Poems*, 465, 1082, 1206, 1388.
30 "Captain Craig," *Ibid.*, 132.
31 *Ibid.*, 1012.
32 "Amaranth," *Ibid.*, 1335.
33 *Ibid.*, 1472.
34 *Ibid.*, 332.
35 *Ibid.*, 1471.
36 *Ibid.*, 1471.
37 *E.g.*, Russell Blankenship, *American Literature as an Expression of the National Mind* (New York, 1931), 583-588; Stanley Williams, *American Literature* (Philadelphia, 1933), 154-155; Ludwig Lewisohn, *Expression in America* (New York, 1932), 553-556; Alfred Kreymborg, *Our Singing Strength* (New York, 1934), 297-316; Walter Taylor, *History of American Letters* (New York, 1936), 342-343; and William Braithwaite, "The Year in Poetry: The Man Against the Sky." *Bookman*, XLV (June 1917), 429-430.
38 *Collected Poems*, 1089. Cf. especially "The Man Against the Sky."
39 "Matthias at the Door," *Collected Poems*, 1127.
40 "The Glory of the Nightingales," *Ibid.*, 1072. Cf. Carpenter; also Matthias at the Door" and "Nicodemus," *passim.*
41 *Ibid.*, 1142; cf. also, 129, 1150, and 1284, and the criticism in "Nicodemus" that science endows matter with so many qualities that it is no longer matter, 1203.
42 "Modernities," *Ibid.*, 578.
43 "Matthias at the Door," *Ibid.*, 1151.
44 *Ibid.*, 1222.
45 See *Collected Poems*, 60-69, 500-501, 538, 962, 984, 1205, 1377, 1387, 1410,

1472. Cf. "Man, even if divine, is mechanism while he is here," 1012.
46 "Cavender's House," *Ibid.,* 992-993. Cf., however, the other side of this matter as seen, for example, on page 1222: "And you would soon see in my care for you / How much there is in a man's love / When it is love—which is a little more / Than myopic science isolates / With so much carnal pride."
47 "Mortmain," *Ibid.*, 894.
48 "Cavender's House," *Ibid.*, 962.
49 *Ibid.*, 975.
50 *Expression in America* (New York, 1932), 556.

THE SHORTER POEMS OF E. A. ROBINSON

JOHN R. DOYLE

I

EARLY in the nineteenth century Maine gave American poetry a Longfellow, but later in the century—she balanced the scales. In 1882 Longfellow died, but at that time, not many miles up the Kennebec from Portland, in the town of Gardiner, there was a thirteen-year-old boy almost ready to begin the fight that was to bring him fame as a poet. What position Edwin Arlington Robinson will take in American literature is difficult to say less than ten years after his death, but I dare predict that after the sifting has been completed he will hold a secure place among our true poets.

When in the 1890s Robinson published *The Children of the Night*, he was not giving readers of American poetry what they had been accustomed to in that other son of Maine, who had first wooed their affections with *Voices of the Night*. Nor was Longfellow alone in his poetic practice, as an examination of nineteenth century American poetry will show. Much of the verse being written performed successively rather than simultaneously the various operations in poem building. The poet selected a subject about which it was well to speak; then he added to his argument (which might have been expressed in the language of prose) the beauties of poetry. A diction that was felt to be inherently poetic was diligently sought. The "beautiful" language together with meter, rhythm, and rhyme were their own excuse for being, elegant additions rather than a fundamental part of the total poetic statement. Images were mere decoration, or at most they offered an explanation or perhaps made clearer a relation. Poets made little attempt to force an unassisted image to state a meaning while in the act of presenting an emotion. Meanings were delivered separately in purely conceptual language. Which is to say that seldom were image and concept united,

Reprinted by permission, *Bulletin of the Citadel*, VI (1942), 3-18.

each being carefully tucked in its own little corner. This type of poetry had, and has a wide appeal because its intent is quickly apparent, because it names things worthy of contemplation, because its ideas are correct and capable of formulation, and because its rhythms are easy to grasp at once.

The poets who have followed the practice just described have rather consistently written a poetry of exclusion rather than of inclusion. This tradition, it should be remarked, has had a long and respectable life, and the practitioners have had more than ample support from the critics. To go back only a part of the way into the tradition: Addison postulated that a beautiful object artistically treated must be more desirable than an ugly object treated in the most perfect artistic manner. Dr. Jonson was arguing for exclusion when he demanded a poetry of "positions not limited by exceptions and in descriptions not descending to minuteness." Likewise Wordsworth, in saying that the *imagination* "recoils from everything but the plastic, the pliant, and the indefinite." He believed in the "wisdom of the heart." And Matthew Arnold held that "genuine poetry is conceived . . . in the soul." So runs one tradition in English poetry. Another will be found embedded in English poems spread over five centuries. From Chaucer to Shakespeare and Donne and on through to the present, writers have made all parts of the world's body, the jagged edges and refractory elements of human experience, into poetic subject matter.

It would be foolish, of course, to suggest that either of the above traditions is pure; but certainly it can be said that in general there have been poets and readers who for some reason did not choose to come to grips with the rough surfaces of actual existence, and there have been those who did choose. Longfellow, spoken of here and elsewhere as the symbol of a practice, only talked about life's being "real" and "earnest" but left it for others to make the actual encounters.

Even when actual contact is made with life, different minds bring away vastly different things. One mind recoils from the unlovely. Such a poet may be able to document his lines from the real world, but, according to Aristotle, he is effeminate because he has not been strong enough to stand pain. Another mind sees only the ugly and base. This is not an advance over the first; it is merely the other extreme. Such minds see only the particular, at most the particular and a glimpse of the individual. A great stride forward is made in the mind, the second type, that can look steadily at a chosen material and see not only its particularity but also its individuality and universality. Beyond this point there is the rare mind that can act simultaneously on opposing types of material and see in the opposition the particular, the individual, and the universal.

Edwin Arlington Robinson's mind was of the second type. The material he chose to examine was seldom bathed in a rose-colored glow from the romantic spotlight; more often than not his probing brought up a sample of life that surely must have made the coat tails of gentility assume a rather horizontal attitude in Cambridge and Boston—if they got around to reading such things. For from the very beginning Robinson identified himself with the seamy side of life:

> And with Eutychides in Hell,
> Where's a poor tortured soul to dwell?[1]

> Of all authoritative liars, too,
> I crown him loveliest.[2]

> He sinned enough to make the day sublime![3]

> The laurel of a proved iniquity[4]

The Children of the Night are a battered crew who struggle and fail. Over a death bed the poet remarks, "Liar, physician, hypocrite, and friend." To them with all their faults and scars Robinson pays tribute. It is failure that keeps them human, and so the poet's lines often drink "to the splendor of the unfulfilled." Yet here lies one of Robinson's chief deficiencies: there is not enough good (right strength) to raise, quite successfully, his characters above the pathetic to the realms of tragedy.

Despite this limitation, Robinson is worthy of serious consideration because he is ever trying to extract from his particulars the individual and the universal, even though the particulars represent less of life than we might wish. Often, far too often, his poems are nothing more than commentaries from the poet as he sits in his chair and looks at life. But he does actually look, though frequently his poems, always serious observations on some particular bit of human reality, technically finished, are without distinction. Once in a while, however, he strikes fire, and then his lines throw off the heat of real poetry. While his contemporaries were writing

> Bowed by the weight of centuries he leans
> Upon his hoe and gazes on the ground,
> The emptiness of ages in his face,
> And on his back the burden of the world.[5]

Robinson was writing, in his first volume,

> Out of a grave I come to tell you this,
> Out of a grave I come to quench the kiss
> That flames upon your forehead with a glow
> That blinds you to the way that you must go.[6]

The "weight of centuries," "emptiness of ages," and "burden of the world" are rather immense doses to ask the human mind to grasp. But no careful reader is going to miss the power of the blinding-kiss image because the act is one that can come within the common experience of the whole human family. Thus the immediacy of what is being said leaps out at the reader. Having mastered the image we have mastered the idea the poet wished to convey because the idea is within the image. This is impossible with the too inclusive and the too general statement. There is, however, something here more important than the particular versus the general. Robinson gains intensity because his particulars become personal and individual. Even when he uses the general, he gives it an individuality that creates for it a personality. For example, nothing is more general, and more usual in cheap verse, than moonlight, yet Robinson uses it—in his own way:

> the ruinous moonlight
> That sheds a lying glory on old stones
> Befriends us with a wizard's enmity.[7]

The moonlight is "ruinous"; the glory it sheds "lies" to us; and it befriends us not with the wizard's magic we have expected, but his "enmity." Here the moonlight becomes at once individual and immediate. Always the really genuine poem must become immediate. Yet we have to read much nineteenth century poetry to find stanzas like,

> And maidens with such eyes as would grow dim
> Over a bleeding hound
> Seem each to have caught the strength of him
> Whose sword she sadly bound.[8]

The man who wrote these lines lived a thousand miles south of the Kennebec and died before Robinson was born; but it was this current rather than the one that might have come from Portland, or Cambridge, which this later son of Maine found it in him to follow.

II

From the beginning it is quite clear that Robinson is not using language in quite the same way as his contemporaries or immediate predecessors. He was demanding of himself a new kind of precision, demanding that language carry more weight than the writers around him expected. To begin with, his diction was a far cry from the "poetic" phrasing so dear to the century into which he was born. His first volume produced such lines as

> And when I asked him what the deuce he meant[9]

> We gibed him, as he went, with houndish glee,[10]

> And cried like a great baby half that night,
> And made the women cry to see him cry.[11]

Here the percentage of monosyllables is great, but more important is the matter-of-fact tone and prose sequence, obviously conscious, because Robinson from the very first created the flowing and haunting melodies which many in most ages have desired. Yet the mere fact of the existence of this type of language is much less significant than the work the poet is attempting to make it perform. What this work is can only be seen by a careful examination of the lines themselves:

> Why do you dig like long-clawed scavengers
> To touch the covered corpse of him that fled
> The uplands for the fens, and rioted
> Like a sick satyr with doom's worshipers?
> . . . let the dead flesh be dead,
> And let the worms be its biographers.
>
> Song sloughs away the sin to find redress
> In art's complete remembrance . . .[12]

The language here has sufficient particularity to create an intensely realized if inelegant scene, but the revolting material is not used for its own sake: the particulars present in images Verlaine, his enemies, and the relation between the two. For this reason the particulars become individualized. Further, the lines attempt to indicate the universal in the situation: it is not what the world thinks of a man that counts, but what he has actually accomplished, with specific reference here to artistic creation. Both image and concept are present, but the brush stroke that gives one gives at the same time the other.

The succeeding two and a half lines reveal another demand Robinson was making upon language:

> in His hand was weighed
> Your squeamish and emasculate crusade
> Against the grim dominion of his art.[13]

Here, just as above, the concept is presented in terms of the images; and in addition, which was also true in the sonnet on Verlaine, the language receives an added significance because of its relation to the subject, in this instance Zola. The doom of the attack on Zola is pronounced by harsh and ugly words that the attackers would not have used but which would in no way have disturbed the attacked. Moreover, the whole situation is gathered up in the words "squeamish" and "emasculate." The crusade has grown out of the squeamishness of Zola's opponents, their inability to contemplate the ugly, their insistence on going through life with an averted gaze. Much of their objection was to Zola's use of sex; therefore they were arguing for a sexless or emasculate art. Thus "emasculate" at one stroke shows what Zola had, what his opponents hated in him and were without, and pronounces defeat upon the crusade because it lacks the needed virility.

At this point the question arises, could Robinson achieve this much concentration when there was no reference into the known historical world of the reader? The answer can be found in the following passage:

> Like a white wall whereon forever breaks
> Unsatisfied the tumult of green seas,
> Man's unconjectured godliness rebukes
> With its imperial silence the lost waves
> Of insufficient grief. This mortal surge
> That beats against us now is nothing else
> Than plangent ignorance. Truth neither shakes
> Nor wavers; but the world shakes, and we shriek.[14]

The most interesting word here is "plangent," by no means the first—or fourth—adjective thought of in connection with ignorance. Nor is it the first even if we wish to say recurring ignorance, which it contains; nor pounding ignorance, which it likewise contains. To itself it gathers the entire preceding figure of the restless waves and shows that the mortal surge we fight is an immense force pounding against us without ceasing, all pervasive, sounding near and far with deep and loud reverberations, as breaking waves or tolling bells. The word is so used that it is supported by and in turn supports the context.

Lastly, I wish to examine a small group of words so chosen and arranged that they produce a chain of implications. Though only one clause of seven words will be considered, it is well to have the entire sonnet available.

> When he protested, not too solemnly,
> That for the world's achieving maintenance
> The crust of overdone divinity
> Lacked aliment, they called it recreance;
> And when he chose through his own glass to scan
> Sick Europe, and reduced, unyieldingly,
> The monk within the cassock to the man
> Within the monk, they called it heresy.
>
> And when he made so perilously bold
> As to be scattered forth in black and white,
> Good fathers looked askance at him and rolled
> Their inward eyes in anguish and affright;
> There were some of them did shake at what was told,
> And they shook best who knew that he was right.[15]

I wish to analyze the clause, "The crust of overdone divinity / Lacked aliment." Both "crust" and "overdone" attack the clergy from several points at once. To begin with, "crust" can mean the "upper crust," the very top of things; this is what the clergy should have been but were not. Further study will show why. We approach the word again and observe that "crust" is a hard outer shell, a thin surface, frequently with little or nothing immediately beneath (a monk's shining pate?). The "crust" may be of various materials: earth or snow, for example, suggesting the earthy rather than the divine and cold rather than the warm fellowship of the true Christian. Or the "crust" may be the interior surface of wine bottles, again giving the clergy the undesirable element. Worse still, a "crust" may be a mass of dried secretions, blood or pus; so instead of the blood of life we have a dry, useless surface—not even corruption that is alive, to follow out the other meaning. Then "crust" has a slang overtone, which certainly is not irrelevant here: the nerve, the brass of such a poor, undernourished thing to set itself up to offer the bread of Life. This reading supports and is supported by the rest of the poem. Now we come to the last reading of "crust," as the hardened exterior part of bread, grown dry, or burned. When we reach "overdone," we are inclined to settle on this last meaning, though "overdone" is grammatically attached to "divinity." If we accept this last meaning, we have definitely made the bread of Life a "crust" without nourishment, which is certainly supported by the use of "aliment." But to return to "divinity" modified by "overdone": thus "divinity" which is carried too far, exaggerated, and overtaxed. So the divine, which should be rich and nourishing, has become a worthless surface, a sham; it has been allowed to dry until it has become a "crust" instead of the bread of Life. Certainly the poet has succeeded in saying a number of things in seven words.

All of this leads to the conclusion that Robinson disdained "poetic" diction because he was in search of a language which would agree in tone with what he had to say. Sometimes he needed monosyllables, a matter-of-fact manner, a prose sequence; but no polysyllable was too recalcitrant for use when the occasion demanded, no movements barred if they contributed to the total intention. A search was made for words that cut in more than one direction and for words that could gather up meanings, from the context to gain for themselves an added richness which they in turn gave back. In these aims Robinson was not always successful, far from it; but sometimes he did succeed, as poets before him had, as they have since, and as they will in the future.

III

As has been seen in the preceding section, Edwin Arlington Robinson, like any good poet, used images to give a dimension to his work. Many of his images, naturally, are very simple, as

> the dark wet mooring pointed home
> Like a finger from the sea.[16]

The pointing finger is an addition from the real world, which contributes to the world of the poem. No improvement is made in the logic of the lines by the addition of the figure, nor does it increase the clarity of the statement being made; yet the reader likes the addition because it gives texture to the lines. Some figures, however, offer more than others:

> punch,
> More shrewd than Satan's tears:[17]

Here the reader will want to explore the possibilities for more than a moment, to consider the shrewdness of punch as compared with the shrewdness of Satan's tears. This examination will develop the various implications of each. Again, a simple figure will enable the author to make his statement without remaining always on one plane:

> There was a road
> Through beeches; and I said their smooth feet showed
> Like yours. Truth must have heard me from afar,
> For I shall never have to learn again
> That yours are cloven as no beech's are.[18]

The reader is pleased as his mind presents the meaning. This is only a minor felicity, but much preferred to, "I have learned that you are a devil."

When a poet is at his best, his images should completely control the context and should carry the major share of the poetic statement:

> Whether or not we read him, we can feel
> From time to time the vigor of his name
> Against us like a finger for the shame
> And emptiness of what our souls reveal
> In books that are as altars where we kneel
> To consecrate the flicker, not the flame.[19]

Here again is the image of the pointing finger, but now it is doing more work than in the previously quoted lines. Instead of being presented as one "thing" that resembles another "thing," it is now a symbol for an abstraction. Thus, through the image the idea comes to life. This accomplishment is extended by the use of "shame," which makes the finger an accusing one, which meets exactly the demands. Likewise, in the last two lines the concept is presented through the image, one of Robinson's most successful.

A slightly different type of image control from those just cited is found in

> So the clouds may come and the rain may fall,
> The shadows may creep and the dead men crawl,—[20]

which is quite undistinguished until we reach "dead men crawl" (prepared for by "creep"), which along with death brings worms, decay, and everything that the ugliness of putrefaction can suggest. The atmosphere created at the end of the second line reflects its own color upon the rest of the passage.

Not even a six-year-old child would mistake for typical nineteenth century poetry the dozen passages from Robinson's poems examined in this paper. Everywhere are signs of an attempt at a complexity and a type of struggle with language that had not been approved by most English poets from the seventeenth to the twentieth century. To say this is not to suggest an absence of great poets or great poems during the period: it merely indicates a different outlook on life and on the nature and function of poetry.

IV

One way to measure the calibre of a poet is to watch him at work on old and well-worn material. "The Old Story" is a poem of twelve lines, ten of which tell the old story—when the money gives out, so do the friends. But the last two lines seem to have a slight contribution to make.

> Must you find only at the end
> That who has nothing has no friend?[21]

Surely "who has nothing has no friend," with the nothing referring to gold, is "old stuff," but as written the lines allude to more than gold. As the mind plays back and forth over the idea of giving gold and giving character, we realize that we are getting just what we give when we fail to give ourselves as we get what we give when we give no gold. The two are the same. This is the author's contribution, itself not original, but compactly and neatly put for some reader to discover. In much the same way "Mr. Flood's Party" brings to life through dramatic representation ideas which are not new and about which the author says nothing new. Yet the old realities are given new life for another generation. It is, interestingly enough, the use of alcohol that makes possible the focus achieved in the poem. To have to drink alone is within itself a complete expression of the last extremity. Also, Mr. Flood's utter aloneness is emphasized when the whiskey brings the "salutation" of friends who in "other days had honored him." The past and present are revealed at one instant. Now Mr. Flood travels away from the phantoms of the past to the upland barrenness before him, taken doubly. And all along the way the lines are filled with neatly done particularity, which imparts life to the poem.

Another way to evaluate a poet is to observe what he does with contemporary problems. A sonnet, "Amaryllis," will illustrate the point.

Once, when I wandered in the woods alone,
An old man tottered up to me and said,
"Come, friend, and see the grave that I have made
For Amaryllis." There was in the tone
Of his complaint such quaver and such moan
That I took pity on him and obeyed,
And long stood looking where his hands had laid
An ancient woman, shrunk to skin and bone.

Far out beyond the forest I could hear
The calling of loud progress, and the bold
Incessant scream of commerce ringing clear;
But though the trumpets of the world were glad,
It made me lonely and it made me sad
To think that Amaryllis had grown old.[22]

The tone is perfectly handled. A straightforward conversational manner in the octave contrasts with the trumpet-blare pretentiousness in the sextet, where the "calling of loud progress" and the "incessant scream of commerce" break in, only to be enveloped by the calm of the forest and the grave. The poem's total statement is made possible because of the depth, in time, and breath, in space, secured through the use of Amaryllis in conflict with the world of progress and the impersonal. What the poet has to say is realized through the scene he has created, and the poem's greatest weakness lies in the author's failure to make the modern scene as concrete as he has the opposing force.

"The Town Down the River," written fifteen years after the sonnet just quoted, furnishes another example of Robinson's use of the problems of his day. Here the contemporary references are so well buried that we have to dig them out piece by piece to make sure they are there. Thus the present is not forced upon the reader; its use merely assures that the author is aware of the real world. The present used in this way becomes a strength rather than a weakness.

Among his shorter poems, Robinson's studies of people are perhaps best known. "Richard Cory," first of these to appear, illustrates the strength and weakness of the group. The work is economically and neatly done, and it is clear the poet his understood that often, far too often, men do not see beneath the surface. But because he has given Richard Cory's mere act and nothing more, the author has avoided the really difficult questions: an understanding of the character's action and its relation to society; and the casting of some light on society's failure to grasp the situation. The same can be said of "Cliff Klingenhagen," where the concrete delineation is adequate to the idea presented, but the idea itself falls short of an adequate illumination of a major human problem. Likewise, as far as they go, many others in this group are satisfactory handlings of lesser problems.

Clearly this is censuring Robinson for failing to do that which he never intended, which from most points of view is irrelevant criticism. Yet raising the question may throw some light on the state of modern poetry. When Chaucer wanted to present human portraits, he used a vehicle which offered an opportunity for adequate development. The chance for action and interaction between the characters in the *Canterbury Tales* makes the final work greater than the sum of its parts. Though the comparison as such is unfair, it may suggest that the abandonment of the longer structural forms has made it very difficult, perhaps impossible, to make more than fragmentary observations on the human scene.

There is, of course, a quick reply to all of the above: Robinson did write the long poem—more than any other modern, except Robinson Jeffers, that is just what he has done. Though the discussion of those longer poems is the work of the second part of this paper, it may be said here that a study of the long poems is not likely to prove irrelevant the question that has been raised. The poems are long, but they are strangely similar to the shorter ones, commentaries on life flowing from the mind of the poet as he sits and watches. The great frames within which Chaucer, and Dante, and Spenser, and Milton, and yes, Shakespeare, worked are gone. Discarding them seems to have left the poet without a point of reference. And there is much more to the question than appears in the casual asking; yet the fuller analysis must rest in abeyance until the next paper.

Then, in summary, what can be said of Robinson's shorter poems? Throughout his writing years he tackled boldly the problems of the unlovely side of life, proclaiming in courageous tones the consideration due all humanity. Again and again he uncovered the hitherto normally unnoticed, and the disclosure pointed the finger of condemnation at the surface observation of most of society. Each problem was approached as an individual life situation rather than as a great abstract question. The words through which he presented his ideas are usually of special interest. Always he attempted to make his language the servant of his thought, and at its best it has more density than that of most of his contemporaries. Whenever he took up his pen, he sought to write into his lines that which was of himself, of his age, and of the heritage of humanity. Despite obvious limitations, he succeeded often enough to insure for himself a place among our true poets.

---

1 "Eutychides," 227. All references are to *Collected Poems of Edwin Arlington Robinson* (New York, 1937).
2 "Uncle Ananias," 337.
3 *Ibid.*, 338.
4 *Ibid.*
5 Edwin Markham. "The Man With the Hoe."
6 "Luke Havergal," 74.
7 "Octaves," No. XV, 105.
8 Henry Timrod, "Charleston."
9 "Cliff Klingenhagen," 87.

10 "Calvary," 83
11 "Reuben Bright," 92
12 "Verlaine," 96
13 "Zola," 85.
14 "Octaves," No. XVIII, 106.
15 "Erasmus," 193.
16 "The Return of Morgan and Fingal," 184.
17 *Ibid.*
18 "Another Dark Lady," 42.
19 "George Crabbe," 94.
20 "John Evereldown," 74.
21 "Variations of Greek Themes" (No. VIII, "The Old Story"), 229.
22 "Amaryllis," 84-85.

THE PERNICIOUS RIB: E. A. ROBINSON'S CONCEPT OF FEMININE CHARACTER

LOUISE DAUNER

I

THE WORDS of the doomed hero of Edwin Arlington Robinson's allegorical poem *King Jasper,* "Why must you women, you pernicious ribs, Make havoc always of awakening man?,"[1] reflect an attitude toward women found in numerous other poems by the same author. Is it reading too much into the "pernicious rib" epithet to suggest that it is fundamental in Robinson's concept of feminine nature?

The problem of feminine characterization and its implications is particularly interesting in Robinson's poetry, both because of its biographical overtones and because of its importance in any attempt at adequate comprehension of his art. It is tempting and sometimes misleading, to seek in biographical data grounds for artistic interpretation. With regard to personal reflections to be deduced from his poetry, Robinson once remarked to a colleague, Winfield Townley Scott, "Don't look for me in my poetry, for you won't find me there." Yet, in this very connection, and in a critical article two years after Robinson's death, Mr. Scott writes: "Of course it is true . . . that Robinson is to be found in his work; in no modern poet is there, from first to last . . . so unmistakable a stamp of personality shaped to style."[2] This is not, however, to imply the poems as biographical treasure-chests. It emphasizes, rather, the paradox of Robinson's powers of analyzing and creating feminine character although he himself seemed to stand upon some personal peak in Darien, from whose cloud-wrapped summit he observed and speculated upon the emotional entanglements of those who breathed a less rarefied atmosphere. Robinson never married—there is a rumor of a college engagement, broken after a few months in favor of a single-minded devotion to Poetry[3]—and the intensity of whatever feminine contacts he had remains as yet severely untouched by his biographer

Reprinted by permission, *American Literature,* XV (May 1943), 139-158.

or others who could add to the records of his personal life. At twenty-one he was already to write, "I was never much of a light in company . . . besides Hippolytus never meddled with females."[4] Yet, austere, aloof, inarticulate except in poetry, and apparently detached from the world whose more fervid passions he observed, analyzed, and poetically defined, perhaps few poets have written of the most complex of human emotions with more restrained radiance, more chaste rapture, more tenderness—or more shrewd, ironic penetration. In fact, the bulk of his work deals with the infinitely complicated patterns of human behavior and destiny, in the emotional relationships through which his men and women move, sometimes quietly triumphant, but more often toward tragedy.

For Robinson, like Rembrandt, has his "golden shadow"— the shadow of frustration, of disillusion, over that which so largely glorifies life, or makes it desperate or, in its absence, drab. All three of these qualities of existence are repeatedly exemplified in his poetry. Further, when they occur, they are most frequently directly traceable to the influence of Love, as it blinds judgment, or molds the imminences of shadows into the shapes of folly, of desperation, or even of death. Two facts, then, should be noted: For Robinson the problem of Woman is also the problem of Man, as both are mutually entangled in an irresistible emotional web, with woman becoming either more or less effective, ideally, according to her fulfilled or thwarted relationship to man, or according to her experience of Love. And since Love, more perhaps than any other emotion, impels personal fate or destiny toward definite individuated form, Robinson's attitude toward Love suggests itself as a significant aspect of his attitude toward Fate.

That Fate is essentially tragic. With the exception of one poem, *Talifer*, all of Robinson's domestic narratives are colored with tragedy. Tragedy is induced and ordered by the characters' limited understanding of the meaning of their emotions and the situations in which they are thereby entangled, and by their early failure to perceive, as Robinson clearly perceived, the sheer dark essence of existence. This is why so many of them must find ultimately in sorrow:

> Only the price Love ruled that we should pay:
> The dark is at the end of every day,
> And silence is the end of every song[5]

To explore the personalities of Robinson's feminine characters and their problems is thus to note that for this artist, as for Thomas Hardy, tragedy in life is intrinsic in the structure of life itself; that tragedy lies in an inherent dualism in existence, which creates men and women to be sensitive, idealistic, aspiring to love and beauty and goodness, but which so often also thwarts or damns them by contriving objectively to deny what they must conceive to be the essence of worth:

> God slays Himself with every leaf that flies
> And hell is more than half of paradise.[6]

For man the tragic-content of life reveals itself in the snarls and frustrations which create, and which *are* human tragedy, but which are seen in, hence *seem* to exist because of, the limitations of the personality. So existence is heard as an eternal antiphony between a basic negative principle and man's indomitable, heroic effort nevertheless to realize positive value.

Love itself, then, an instance of unique worth can, like Beauty, only be individuated and so suggested, can never be completely or ideally realized; which is one reason, perhaps, why Art exists—to conquer the blind, shapeless Insistence by giving formal pattern and completeness and individual awareness to what in life can be known only chaotically and incompletely and always under the wing of the inescapable shadow. Art is man's answer to Life: an attempt to force Form upon the Matter of Negation. So the answer to tragedy is Tragic Art; and the spirit that conceives the art is the heroic spirit of the Comic, that sees the inherent irrationality in existence, recognizes it as inevitable, but attempts to give it significance. That the timeless effort and purpose are actually made valid is evidenced in the institutions of culture and civilization, where the structures of politics, religion, art, stand as monuments to man's indomitable refusal to accede to the tragic insistence, and to his demand for a cosmic pattern or order.[7] This positive tendency—this instinctive comic-artistic response to negation—may largely explain Robinson's characteristic use of irony, his aseptic humor, often most apparent when his perception of the tragic structure is most keen.

Any effort then to clarify Robinson's concept of the Feminine is an attempt to work out his concept of the passion of Love and its ultimate darkened implications for human destiny. For the feminine element in Robinson's poetry, as in life, moves subtly, but as a basic force, toward the accomplishment of an inevitable tragic Purpose, and in answer to undeniable, though not always clearly defined, urgencies.

II

Already it is evident that in spite of the humorous intent of the "pernicious rib" epithet, it bears serious consideration. It implies Robinson's full recognition and acceptance of the interdependent relationships of man and woman in a world where, to argue from the balance of his work, too often the two work together—or apart—for immediate tragedy; though sometimes, mediately, or finally, a positive value for one of them gleams through tragedy like a light through fog. But for

Robinson, too often woman *does* "make havoc" of man, awakening or still unawakened.

Perhaps this is really only a further distilling of the ancient Eve-concept, where woman, with a superior subtlety, plays upon the more overt responses of man for double tragedy. Robinson's female characters are refined in thought and perception, self-analytical, self-expressive, and often given to see themselves finally with a heart-broken clarity which sometimes culminates in suicide. But whether their disillusion and futility make such a last tragic positive admission or not, in their objectification of the tragic negation, the inherent dualism, they usually have a similar desperate effect upon the men whose destinies are linked with and shaped by their own.

If Robinson was capable of presenting feminine character with tremendous tenderness, as in "The Poor Relation," "For a Dead Lady," "Aunt Imogen," "Veteran Sirens," the character of Isolt of the white hands,[8] these are less individual portraits than representations of social types—depicting the pathos of the wistful poor, an idealization of the poet's mother which embraces all motherhood, the aging prostitute, the woman whose spiritual innocence, her clear incapacity to design harm for another, is at once her sublimity and her tragic flaw in a scheming and materialistic universe. In the main, and particularly in narrative, his portrait-pen is gold, but tipped with acid which penetrates to the fundamental qualities of the character, which qualities ultimately become the channels for tragedy.

As previously suggested, the tragic-quality prevails in the bulk of Robinson's narratives. At least eight of the long poems, *Merlin, Lancelot, Tristram, Cavender's House, Roman Bartholow, Matthias at the Door, Talifer,* and *King Jasper,* utilize the emotional relationships of men and women as basic motives for tragedy. Personal tragedy is, moreover, a sub-motif for social catastrophe in the Arthurian poems and in *King Jasper. Talifer* alone, of the domestic poems, skirts the abyss of domestic disaster through the intervention of a not-usual wisdom on the part of a platonic observer. Repeatedly too, the short lyrics of Robinson's earlier days suggest obliquely the tragedy of Love in its disillusion or tyranny, even the tyranny of love which no longer exists, or exists only in the obsessed imagination of one of the lovers. It is none the less significant for action if Robinson fails to see in such passion only ecstasy, and rather sees in it the evanescent, the shadow, the *Weltschmerz* so transcendently personified by Tristram and in lesser degree by Lancelot and others of the less well-known characters.

But Tristram and Lancelot are, after all, heroic figures. How does love affect the ordinary citizen of "Tilbury Town"? How, for Robinson, do most women behave toward most men? Why do so many men and women both reap the whirlwind, more or less dramatically as the case may be? We see facets of experience and feminine character clearly reflected in the attitudes and behavior of the men. There is John Gorham, the disillusioned lover, one of "two that have no longer much of anything to say." His own words reveal something of the manner of his disquietude, and of the woman who has effected it:

> You are what it is that over rose-blown gardens
> Makes a pretty flutter for a season in the sun;
> You are what it is that with a mouse, Jane Wayland
> Catches him and lets him go and eats him up for fun.[9]

Gorham is less obvious, more analytical, than John Evereldown, who knows only that always he must respond to the stark sex urge wherever it may lead him; for

> the women are calling John Evereldown, . . .
> And while they call can a man be free?[10]

Heroic or ordinary, however, all men are brothers. John Evereldown is a friendless old reprobate; yet he is blood-brother to Merlin, once-mighty wizard, nonetheless stricken and buried in a "gay grave in Brittany" where, shorn of his superhuman insight as well as his famous beard, he has abandoned both Arthur and magic for a ten-year dalliance with the enchanting Vivian, a young woman who knows what she wants and knows how to get it. Even Lancelot must join the company of men imprisoned by feminine laughter and the light touch of a hand and quick lips; till he foregoes his Light for the lesser and false light of an amorally beautiful queen; and Arthur the King faces the dissolution of Camelot with less of soul-sickness than is occasioned by the unforgettable fact of Guinevere's infidelity.

The love-damned men, however, are legion in Robinson's poetry. It is in the characters of the women who torment them and blind them and reduce them to a futile fevered ecstasy that we find an urgency which strikes the opening notes of subsequent sorrow as surely as inherent doom is presaged in the "Prelude" to Wagner's *Tristan.* Rare indeed is the man who can save or extricate himself from the almost inescapable snare of the flesh—a snare compounded of beauty and intellect and sex and the inherent gallantry and romanticism that are part of the nature of man. Llewellyn,[11] of course, aided by twenty years of Priscilla's goading him for "what God left out" fled one day, in company with a Scarlet One, and turned up on Broadway years later, unregenerate, and unregretful of anything—except that he did not leave sooner. Priscilla it was who faded and died. But though Llewellyn's eyes held the "shine of his one victory," even he had only exchanged one kind of snare for another; and fate, wearing the later guise of "civet, coral, rouge" contrived his continuing bondage with only a little more subtlety than when he had lived thrall to Priscilla's shrill, domestic implacability. In the main, the story is a dark one, where men and women both must accede to love's tyranny

> like a stairway to the sea
> Where down the blind are driven.[12]

Man is more than apt here to find his wits "foiled" with feminine beauty, and to recognize, too late, in a charming face

> the rending
> Of all his purpose among men.[13]

And the story repeats itself endlessly; for the basic urgency cares nothing for individual purposing, so long as the primal plan for perpetuity is maintained.

To the long gallery of corrosive satiric portraits of women which relate to the sturdy forthrightness of the Elizabethan dramatists and the seventeenth-century writers of the "Character," Robinson makes his own contributions. One, presented appropriately enough by that imperturbable philosopher, Captain Craig, reveals the character of a rich woman, "cursed with happiness":

> The cleverness
> God gave her—or the devil—cautions her
> That she must keep the china cup of life
> Filled somehow, and she fills it—runs it over—
> Claps her white hands while some one does the sopping
> With fingers made, she thinks, for just that purpose,
> Giggles and eats and reads and goes to church,
> Makes pretty little penitential prayers,
> And has an eighteen-carat crucifix
> Wrapped up in chamois-skin. She gives enough,
> You say; but what is giving like hers worth?
> What is a gift without the soul to guide it?
> "Poor dears, and they have cancers?—Oh!" she says;
> And away she works at that new altar-cloth
> For the Reverend Hieronymus Mackintosh—
> Third person, Jerry. "Jerry," she says, "can say
> Such lovely things, and make life seem so sweet!"
> . . . And there she goes,
> Like a whirlwind through an orchard in the springtime—
> Throwing herself away as if she thought
> The world and the whole planetary circus
> Were a flourish of apple-blossoms. Look at her!
> And here is this infernal world of ours—
> And hers, if only she might find it out—
> Starving and shrieking, sickening, suppurating,
> Whirling to God knows where. . . But look at her![14]

But she is only one, and nameless, at that. There are dozens of others, each individualized, each an instrument for the realization of the design of a brooding Fate-force, each a facet of the Universal Woman. Their faults, their virtues, their blindnesses, their perspicacities are the channels through which, for Robinson, so many instances of the fundamental Grotesque or Tragic-in-life work themselves out.

III

Like Annandale, man, the incorrigible romanticist, is constantly pricked by the vision of his ideal face—

> The searching face, the eloquent, strange face—
> That with a sightless beauty looked at him
> And with a speechless promise uttered words
> That were not the world's words, or any kind
> That he had known before . . . .[16]

Occasionally, for a dream-held hour, he congratulates himself on finding and possessing his ideal; though in time, it resolves itself into such simple elements as small hands and soft lips, "a love-fragrance in the house," the "sound of someone singing," the "smoothing of slow fingers on his hair," or even the "shimmer of pink slippers on brown tiles."[16] But time has whips for love as for all else, and the flagellation constitutes a part of the tragedy. So, again, the problem might be stated thus: Human love is an instance of tragedy in existence, if by tragedy we mean the inevitable failure of worthy individual human effort and aspiration to realize itself when pitted against primal urgency, garbed here as the Ideal; but man cannot, by nature, escape the urge to love; so woman becomes the instrument for both his ecstasy and his grief. What then for Robinson is the character of Woman?

Eight women, drawn from six long narratives involving domestic disillusion, will provide basic patterns which, combined, may answer the question. There is Vivian, with her diminished magician, Merlin; Guinevere, whose blue and gold beauty spelled disaster for Lancelot and Arthur; the two Isolts, of Brittany and Ireland, both doomed for love of Tristram; Gabrielle, who released Roman Bartholow to spiritual freedom only through her suicide; Althea, whose "white-bird" innocence lost Talifer, for a time, to the "ice and intellect and indifference" of Karen; Natalie, who found at a dark door the end of futility with Matthias.[17]

It is not particularly necessary here to analyze each of these characters individually. Though they are all definite personalities, they all possess certain basic and inalienable feminine qualities, which, combined, will produce a composite figure, Woman. Then we shall be interested to see how woman becomes the snare for man, and how she thus comes largely to personify fate or destiny as it is shaped by love. If it be conceded that a character's fundamental qualities are implied or summed up in his final destiny, it will be enough here to say that of the eight women above selected to suggest a basic Feminine principle, three, Isolt of Ireland, Natalie, Gabrielle, illustrate in death, self-induced or otherwise, qualities making for the final tragic denouement. Three, Isolt of Brittany, Vivian, Guinevere, are doomed by nature to the kind of living death that sheer hopeless endurance, or dumb acceptance of unvarnished duty, may inflict upon a vital personality. One alone, Althea, is allowed a normal experience in which Robinson ironically suggests happiness, but that only after considerable scarring; and one, Karen, temperamentally carries with her the cold ashes of her domestic disillusion as a bed for whatever future fires may be laid there in an attempted reconstruction of her life. All of them, however, are basically feminine; and a number of them seem more or less "related" in that similar qualities predestine them to somewhat similar fates. So, although Robinson's women are difficult to classify, perhaps a kind of grouping can be found for them, and they may be placed, however superficially, into two main groups.

Remembering always that Robinson sees them all, in the "pernicious rib" phrase, as disturbing, provocative, and both the harbingers and agents of tragedy, we may group them as the "knowing" and the "innocent" women. (Of course all of them, as human beings, are limited in their spiritual perceptions.) The "knowing" women may be considered those who, like Isolt of Ireland, who is "all love," are fundamentally and instinctively instances of almost pure femininity with regard to man and passion. The "innocent" women are those like Isolt of Brittany, who have less an all-pervading feminine quality than a kind of asexual innocence (but not ignorance) tending toward mysticism, a tolerance, and a pure inability to conceive harm to another—even another woman.

The tragedy of each group differs somewhat in nature. For the first group, who comprise the majority, the tragedy may be as sharp as suicide or violent death or the desolation of the woman left behind, as Vivian was left by Merlin, or Guinevere by Lancelot. For the second group, it may be as dull as simple endurance or acquiescence to mere duty unrelieved by love. This is to say that the kind of tragedy that ensues is related to a basic quality of activity or passivity in the woman—the "active" woman being one who, under the insistence of tragic love, makes the ultimate concession, of whatever nature, in spite of time, circumstance, duty, or custom, knowing full well that only greater tragedy can ensue, and willing that it must; the "passive" woman, one who, caught in a web of her own blind spinning, can do nothing but wait and suffer, until increasing soul-sickness ends in oblivion or in a kind of depersonalized, dumb endurance.

In a consideration of basic feminine qualities, it is important to note that Robinson's women are all highly complex characters. Like Hardy, again, he is perhaps at his best in the portrayal of feminine character; his masculine characters are apt to be atypically introspective, more given to speech and thought that to the action which one regards as integral to the masculine personality. But, unlike Hardy, Robinson creates no basically contrasting feminine types: i.e., no instances where subtlety is paired with uninstructed or simple-natured womanhood, and where the individual becomes finally perhaps less an individual than an embodiment of the absorbing universal insistence—a vortex into which man, like Jude, must inescapably be drawn, though constantly resisting. We can expect to find then, no Marty South, no Arabella, no Tess. Woman, as conceived by Robinson, is at a high, a most self-conscious level. She is perhaps woman idealized, but idealized ironically, so that her flaws and the inevitable web which she must spin for both herself and her lover are the more starkly imprinted upon our consciousness to strike a kind of Aristotelian note of tragedy.

Yet another and paradoxical fact must also be noted here. These women are sharply etched. We see them objectively, noting their speech, their gestures and expressions, their carriage and grace of movement; and their emotions are so vivid and convincing that anyone who has been able to read the passages in *Tristram,* for instance, where love is both idealized and partially realized without feeling the touch of remembered lips upon his own must be impervious to the emotion itself. But—and here is the interesting fact—in Robinson's narratives woman always occupies a subordinate position. Except for a few brief lyrics,[18] the subjects of Robinson's character poems are men, and the heroes of the long poems which bear their names are without exception men. Yet this feminine subservience is merely on the surface. Actually, woman's apparent weakness is her strength; for by her quality of "dependence" she ensnares the man, and so becomes a basic factor in his tragic destiny. Queen Morgan, guileful siren who seduces Tristram while his heart is still sore from parting with Isolt of Ireland, states the woman's apparent position clearly:

Not even when we are most in power
Are women else than slaves to men they honor.
Men worthy of their reverence know this well,
And honor them sometimes to humor them.
We are their slaves and their impediments,
And there is much in us to be forgiven.[19]

Morgan does not so openly admit the truth—of which Tristram's destiny is an obvious example—that it is man who must be enslaved by woman. Or so, at least, Robinson sees it. Let us, by analysis of general and individual characteristics, suggest how the process occurs.

IV

We have noted that woman, as Robinson sees her, is physically beautiful, pictorially lovely. She is intelligent always, and intellectual, often; yet, being human also, she is not intelligent or self-conscious enough to forestall tragedy by being able to recognize herself objectively, and in advance, as an instrument for the realization of an obscurely working destiny, or as a positive example of negativity endlessly asserting itself in the patterns of individual human difficulties. She cannot protect herself either by acting differently, or by developing a philosophical attitude which would make life endurable if not ecstatic. She becomes, it is true, an instance of the object tragedy, a satisfying example of the perfectibility of human artistry as revealed in the object of art; but in so becoming, she has again asserted the basic negation: she has lived but to die, physically or spiritually, and dying she has become a tragic object—but she has ceased to exist. But for this she cannot be blamed, and Robinson never censures; for she is as much a victim of the tragedy as an agent of it. He does, however, find, and reveal in her character, qualities which build surely toward the darkening fate.

With her charm, her seductive loveliness, she often possesses a certain feline quality—the adjective is repeatedly applied—which makes her capable of dissimulation, of taking rather than of giving, even of a quiet sadism; and of calculated and schematic action toward a perhaps unadmitted end. Part of her ability, or disability, lies in a superior sensitivity which is apt to render her at last hopelessly futile and cynical, and almost always more penetrating than the attendant man. Often she can diagnose her own spiritual illness and that of her lover; but she cannot heal the disease, hence the cynicism. And always her sensitivity impresses upon her the weight of time, circumstance, duty, and custom, which contrive to force her, either through positive action, or positive inaction, toward the ultimate despair of negation.

It is interesting to note that in these "case histories" of domestic tragedy all of the women but one—Althea—are brought to love and be loved by the wrong men; whether wrong because one of the two, in legality or loyalty, has incurred obligations to another, or wrong because of temperamental incompatibility, or wrong because, in two instances, Gabrielle and Natalie, they have married for comfort and position rather than for love, and in two instances, Guinevere and Isolt of Ireland, for duty rather than for love. This somewhat characteristic tendency on the part of these women suggests that Robinson conceives woman as basically an amoral being; or, to put it less harshly, as a being whose acts originate in impulse or passion rather than in reason; or, in indifference or coldness or apathy toward fate rather even than in passion.

Not that these women, however, escape the penalties of reason—mental conflict, or self-castigation; or not that they cannot and do not see themselves, as Lancelot sees them, making toys of men, but themselves made toys by time. Such anticipation leads them often then to a *carpe diem* philosophy, making them seize the present hour with all its doubts and dangers, in preference to an avoiding or deferring of the issue in favor of a future of which they can believe nothing much except that it is almost bound to barren darkness. So it is that Guinevere and Isolt of Ireland and Vivian fly in the face of time and duty and circumstance for obvious tragedy; and Natalie and Gabrielle and Isolt of Brittany submit to the moment less dramatically, but must find their tragedy in silent suffering until, for the first two, self-contempt brings the final futility of suicide, and for the last, ungarnished duty fills the unfillable vacancy left by vanished love.

This suggests that Robinson is making an ironic implication regarding the apparent perversity of destiny—that the significant attitudes and experiences must so often exist outside of the limitations of man's efforts to coerce and order them by the laws of custom, expediency, or practicality. Or perhaps it implies a basic perversity in human nature itself. In general, and for woman, it suggests action motivated by impulse rather than by reason, though reason may even at the time cast a warning shadow over the act, and conscience may brood long over inevitable consequences; or, again it may suggest that here woman, when she cannot act, will simply wait and endure, till negativity becomes positive in sheer malignancy, and destruction ends a kind of spiritual marathon.

But in any case, woman here is both victimizer and victimized. For her, and for her lover then, there is no escape. Passionate, like Guinevere and Isolt of Ireland, or "ice," like Karen, she is doomed. Humble, like Isolt of Brittany, or proud like Vivian, she is at odds with time, which stays its hand not even before the magic majesty of a Merlin. When, as with Althea, virtue seems at long last to find its reward, in the establishment of a home with Talifer and their young son, we remember that here is perhaps Robinson's most sustained irony with regard to domesticity and the permanence of human love. First, Talifer and Althea are closer to "ordinary" people than any of the other characters in question. They are neither rich like Matthias, psychopathic like Cavender, mighty in magic like Merlin, nor noble and "heroic" like the other Arthurian characters. Second, Talifer, in his judgment has already seriously erred, and must be saved by outside advice; hence, in his peaceful readjustment he is fortunate merely, rather than wiser; he may logically be expected to err again. And if, for Roman Bartholow and Matthias, personal freedom for positive moral action is implied in the suicides of Gabrielle and Natalie, respectively, the tragedy has first occurred, the women involved have paid with their blood, and the men with heartbreak.

It remains only to intensify the preceding generalizations with some specific references. It is a temptation to turn to individuals like Queen Guinevere or Isolt of Ireland who make a lasting impression upon us; but perhaps their force of character owes something, at least, to our long traditional acquaintance with them.[20] Of our group of eight, all but two, Althea and Isolt of Brittany, belong by destiny and temperament with the "knowing" women. Of the "innocent" women, Althea temporarily escapes tragedy, so that Isolt of Brittany is the best example. Then, for as much contrast as possible, a brief study may well be made of Natalie and Vivian, as they represent the "knowing" women in two extreme types of fate—suicide and desolation.

Natalie,[21] the wife of Matthias, is slim, with an "easy stateliness," a firm mouth, large eyes, red hair, and "an edible cleanness of countenance." She has a moody, somewhat poetical, temperament, is given to asking uncomfortable questions, and cherishes a demure impulsiveness which often pricks Matthias's bland self-satisfaction and his proprietary pride in her. With the innate flattery of women, she often calls him her "sovereign," yet her mind is her own; it is, furthermore, of a philosophic quality not eased by the fact that she is aware of a "futility to nourish and conceal." Knowing her own defection, she refuses to judge others as, from his "eminence," Matthias sometimes judges Garth a weakling for his suicide.

The cowardice or bravery of suicide troubles Natalie, who herself finds in it a kind of bravery. Behind her mask of resignation, Natalie realizes her life as "a waste of being." She sees herself in a cage, for Matthias to look at and play with; for she has married him for comfort rather than for love, when in honesty of passion she should have married Timberlake. Now, possessing both passion and temperament in a situation which blunts both, she can assume only the guise of a cynical mirthless mirth. "What has a woman left to do but laugh—unless she cries?"[22]

With a kind of masculine candor ("I'll be direct, and so not like a woman")[23] she confesses to Matthias her fault:

> "I married you, Matthias,
> Because I liked you, and because your love
> Was too real to be tortured, and because
> There was no better thing for me to do."[24]

Her confession lies like a sword between them. With the practicality of women, Natalie appeals to his common sense and regard for appearance. Others, she says, have also adapted themselves to an arid way, and "patches are better than holes."[25] But the situation is not bettered, and now Natalie can give herself only to time, a time embittered by her knowledge of the deceits by which she once made Matthias love her defects. For three barren years they attempt to continue the farce, Natalie's inherent passivity making her unable to leave Matthias, although his sense of betrayal sets up in him a physical and spiritual deterioration. Since she is too sensitive, however, to blunt herself into a mere acceptance of the facts, rage and self-contempt alone are left for her. She sees that her initial error lay in what Matthias calls selling herself for "satisfaction and advantage," and in a distorted loyalty which made her give up Timberlake, whose life Matthias had once saved. The situation is too complex for any solution of which she is capable, and seeing no other end to the impasse, Natalie finds in a river her only answer to the problem of mutual betrayal.

Natalie's tragic flaw is a complexity of personality in which fine qualities of character contrive to be self-contradictory. She tries to rationalize the basically irrational motive of sex, but the irrationality triumphs, after all, and her own late-blooming honesty makes her see both her mistake and the fact that its remedy is beyond her. In her downfall, she precipitates the moral collapse of Matthias. Natalie's is a character in which pride, passion, subtlety, physical beauty, and honesty react fatally upon each other. In the end, both man and woman are doomed—by nature, by sex, and by fates and ways that Natalie sees as "so malignantly mixed up that it's a miracle . . . so few of us die crazy."[26] Natalie represents the "knowing" woman, whose tragic charm culminates, through passivity, in overt personal catastrophe, and in the tightening of the already-spun web of despair for her lover.

Vivian[27] illustrates the knowing woman whose destiny, within limits, is consciously and actively self-designed. With a forthright, level-eyed regard for what she wanted, she chose Merlin for her lover when first she saw him on a youthful visit to Arthur's court. The Robinsonian irony is marked here, for Merlin, with all his perception and foresight, and knowing full well exactly what is happening to him, is still unable to resist Vivian's tragic and fatal charms. In ten years' dalliance, Merlin is "buried alive . . . by love made little and by woman shorn . . ."[28] And the strands of Vivian's emotional net?

They are, of course, woven of the inevitable beauty, combined with a certain recklessness and ruthlessness ("I'm a savage, and I love no man as I have seen him yet")[29] and a hard-headed insistence on personal desires. And there are sides of experience that Vivian will have none of:

> Mortality in all its hues and emblems—
> Black wear, long argument, and all the cold
> And solemn things that appertain to graves.[30]

She will, in fact, acknowledge no obligation except to her own beauty and charm and pleasure; and her one fear is that Merlin will go back to Arthur and leave her alone. So she exerts all of her feminine guile, enchanting him doubly with her wit, and with a certain impudence which his gravity finds unique and refreshing, and coiling herself about him like an insinuating and decorative cat.

Actually, there is much of the feline in Vivian. She is too wise ever patently to insist on her own will. She prefers to suggest and charm and coax until her designs—which she makes Merlin think are his inspirations—are achieved, to drop like ripe fruit into her avid, lovely fingers. "Being woman, I can wait," she says.[31] Like every woman the man she loves, she flatters Merlin outrageously: ". . . I am near to giving all to you / Because you are so great and I so little."[32] Or, "You are the wisest man that ever was."[33] Or, "There is no other Merlin than yourself / And you are never going to be old."[34]

But with all her enchanting raillery and charm, Vivian is too practically clever not to recognize forces which even she cannot conquer. Here the defects in the situation lie both within her and without; for added to her own qualities for tragedy are the forces of Time and Change, which mean as much for her as for any woman. Fate, in the guise of Arthur, wrecked by another woman's infidelity, will bring about the one thing that she fears. Merlin must go back, being himself the creature of Time, which at last calls him home.

The snare, however, is sprung again; for when he leaves, he is a shattered Merlin, unable to help Arthur whom once he had created to be the pattern for all kings. And for Vivian we know that the world ends with the sound of Merlin's departure. There are no dramatics for her—only the closing of a gate so quietly that "Merlin could have heard no sound of it."[35] But it is the noiseless sound of the inexorable —the closing in upon her of Time and Change, and a memory that she will not again be alone without. For one of her insistent, pleasure-loving, and vivid temperament her commitment to loneliness can be only a kind of living death. And we know that she will be lonely; having known Merlin's love, she can hardly hope for satisfaction from a merely mortal lover.

Vivian's tragedy is as intense as Natalie's. Essentially, she is a woman of great emotional potentialities—now thwarted. It is no mitigation of her sorrow and desolation to realize, as she does, with unflinching clarity, that she and Merlin are each other's mutual punishment, he being punished for possessing more than mortal wisdom, she, for being "out of tune with Time." If she is siren to Merlin, she is herself captive of a frustrating fate.

In the character of perhaps the loveliest and most moving of Robinson's feminine creations, Isolt of Brittany,[36] exists the most perfect representation of the "innocent" women. Half-child, half-woman, wide-eyed and golden-haired, Isolt lives in a dream-world dominated always by the figure of one man, Tristram. There is in her "the sick touch of prophecy concealing disillusion,"[37] yet there is also a "poise of sense" which enables her to look her own defection of loyalty and belief in the face. If Tristram, who, in a moment of whim, has left her his agate, and unknowingly taken in exchange her heart, does not return, she will have been, she says,

> "but one poor woman more
> Whose punishment for being born a woman
> Was to believe and wait . . . ."[38]

But believing, she is not deceived. Her purity of character, her fidelity and integrity, are symbolized by a "flame-white loveliness." She is tragic and profound in her candor, artlessness, quaint solemnity, patience, mildness, and mystical wisdom (for she is neither old enough nor experienced enough to be practically wise except from intuition). If she cannot win Tristram's passion, she can, she says, "teach and heal." And so she could—if the memory of the other Isolt did not block for Tristram even such hope of peace. In the end, Isolt can admit with serene sadness,

> "I would have been the world
> And heaven to Tristram, and was nothing to him;
> . . . If he had lived,
> He would have pitied me and smiled at me,
> And he would always have been kind to me."[39]

She can reflect that Tristram had never been there, for her; nor had he died for her, nor, perhaps, even thought of her; yet, in the irony of existence, he would continue to be all for her. With Tristram dead, she knows but one duty—to be "Queen of Here or There," and she does not ask much of life except to have her dreams—if she must live. From them, and from the slow changes that will come, wisdom may sometime grow.

It may be questioned how Isolt can be considered a snare for Tristram. It is a case where her very beauty of character works the mischief for both of them. Isolt is too generous in nature to be able to do anything but try to understand a harsh fate, and endure. Tristram's passion is of a more earthy kind, but like Laramie, Isolt knows that

> "Love is not vengeance, though it may be death,
> Which may be life . . . ."[40]

and her very quietude induces in Tristram a pale pity which he tries to convince himself is love. So marrying her, he unwittingly tightens the net, and complicates his own situation by completing the second of the triangles in which he is involved. His sin of adultery is thus double rather than single, and only tragedy for all four characters can ensue.

Thus, from numerous suggestions, emerges the composite figure, Woman. She is beautiful, intelligent, intuitive. She knows man's nature and can flatter and beguile him. She is sensitive—to her situation, to the shadow of time, to the inevitability of fate which can only work cruelty to her love. So she is often futile, hopeless, cynical. If she is none of these last, she is sad with her own dark wisdom, or serene, under the necessity of a tragic waiting. She may be passionate, or distractingly aloof. But—and this is the final emphasis—for Robinson, she is the tragic instrument for man's fall, his deflection from an individual purposing, which is thus destined to be assimilated into the primal urgency. She is, then, to repeat, an amoral being, seen at last, in all her bewitching complexity, as the creature of impulse or emotion or instinct. And now it must be admitted that, though Robinson frequently turns to the romantic concepts of chivalry for his imagery and characters, there is nothing chivalric in his creation of feminine character. His very expertness in feminine psychology relieves him here of any quality of mysticism or suggestion of woman-worship. He admits woman's dangerous charm—and perhaps in retribution, he makes her proud in her knowledge of her own worth, but ultimately humble in her dominant necessity for Love, and her dependence upon man—who cannot live without her, but who frequently cannot live with her—or for her. We remember that two of the most heroic figures, Lancelot and Merlin, left Guinevere and Vivian, the former for his true Light, the latter for a world which he could not resign even though already it crumbled beneath his returning feet.

These then are for Robinson the larger outlines of the feminine character. They are capable of infinite individual personal shadings, but the basic pattern is consistent, and the larger emotional implications are logical and clear: Love, as one aspect of the Life Tragedy, is itself tragic; although in his insistence upon love, Robinson suggests it as also of paramount value—even a value which must be realized only through an obscuring veil of sorrow. But whatever the overtones, the tragic principle is unmistakable. Woman it is—the "pernicious rib"—

who proffers to man the golden apple plucked from a tree of questionable Knowledge. And the gates of the Eternal Garden are closed thereafter to both.

---

1 "King Jasper," *Collected Poems of Edwin Arlington Robinson* (New York, 1939), 1403.
2 "The Unaccredited Profession," *Poetry Magazine*, L (June 1937), 151.
3 Mabel Dodge Luhan, *Movers and Shakers* (New York, 1936), 127.
4 *Selected Letters of Edwin Arlington Robinson*, ed. Ridgely Torrence (New York, 1940), 4.
5 "The Woman and the Wife, *Collected Poems*, 194.
6 "Luke Havergal," *Ibid.*, 74. Note echo of Emerson's "Brahma" here.
7 For the basic esthetic viewpoint suggested here I am particularly indebted to E. Jordan, *The Aesthetic Object* (Bloomington, Ind.: The Principia Press, 1937), chaps XVIII-XIX, "Tragedy" and "Comedy."
8 *Collected Poems*, 45, 355, 184, 40; "Tristram," 595, respectively.
9 "John Gorham," *Ibid.*, 13.
10 "John Evereldown," *Ibid.*, 73.
11 "Llewellyn and the Tree," *Ibid.*, 50.
12 "Eros Turannos," *Ibid.*, 33.
13 "The Unforgiven," *Ibid.*, 39.
14 "Captain Craig," *Ibid.*, 127-128.
15 "The Book of Annandale," *Ibid.*, 198.
16 *Ibid.*, 199.
17 I have not included in this study Laramie, wife of Cavender, or Honoria and Zoë, wife and daughter of King Jasper. The former emerges through the guilt-darkened mind of Cavender to personify his own conscience, and the two latter are almost pure symbols, given feminine nature in the allegory.
18 See "Aunt Imogen," "The Poor Relation," "The Woman and the Wife," previously cited.
19 "Tristram," *Collected Poems*, 611.
20 The problem of what exactly Robinson added to the traditional characters of the Arthurian women is itself an interesting one; we know that he endowed them with tremendous passion and keen intellect. He himself noted that he tried to make Guinevere "interesting."
21 "Matthias at the Door," *Collected Poems*, 1077.
22 *Ibid.*, 1109.
23 *Ibid.*, 1110.
24 *Ibid.*, 1111.
25 *Ibid.*, 1114.
26 *Ibid.*, 1107.
27 "Merlin," *Collected Poems*, 235.
28 *Ibid.*, 260.
29 *Ibid.*, 264.
30 *Ibid.*, 268.
31 *Ibid.*, 275.
32 *Ibid.*, 276.
33 *Ibid.*, 280.
34 *Ibid.*, 279.
35 *Ibid.*, 298.
36 "Tristram," *Collected Poems*, 595.
37 *Ibid.*, 601.
38 *Ibid.*, 600.
39 *Ibid.*, 727-728.
40 "Cavender's House," *Collected Poems*, 979.

RELIGIOUS AND SOCIAL IDEAS IN THE DIDACTIC WORK OF E. A. ROBINSON

YVOR WINTERS

IT IS WITH some hesitation that I broach the subject of Robinson's religious and social ideas in a separate essay. The ideas are few and vague, and they are embodied in Robinson's weakest poetry, most of which is very weak indeed; but they are a part of the product of a great poet, and they are bound to receive a good deal of attention as time goes on. There is already, in fact, especially in the learned journals and in certain graduate schools, a discernible tendency to look for a philosophy in Robinson, and at all costs to find it and to admire it. It is dangerous to admire a great man for his sins: we may too easily adopt his sins for our own out of admiration for his genius; and when the inevitable reaction occurs, the great man's reputation is likely to suffer unduly.

To understand Robinson's mind, we must recollect the essential outlines of New England religious history.

The early English settlers in New England were a carefully selected group, in the main. Their religious tenets, Calvinism in theology and Congregationalism in church government, were disliked by authority in England to the extent that it was unsafe to profess them; whatever the defects of these tenets, the men who held them in the face of danger were men of moral integrity and intensity; those who risked the desperate venture in New England were even more obviously so. It is not surprising, therefore, to find a certain consistency of character in the New Englanders or to find certain New England strains which produce men of unusual ability with remarkable frequency. The Adamses and Holmeses and Lowells are well-known examples of such families, but if one studies pedigrees one is impressed with many examples likewise of

Reprinted by permission, *Arizona Quarterly*, I (Spring 1945), 70-85. Yvor Winters is the author of *Edwin Arlington Robinson* (Norfolk, Conn., 1946).

descent through the female line, where the relationships are obscured by changes of name. Ann Bradstreet, for example, may be called the mother of American poetry in more senses than one; and Robinson, though not descended from her, was descended from her sister. The original settlers, then, were people who were drawn toward certain religious ideas and who had sufficient moral energy to risk life and wealth for their convictions; they must have had certain characteristics in common, and the characteristics must have been strong ones. But once the settlers were established in New England, these characteristics were strongly reinforced by the ideas themselves and by the isolation in which the ideas and the process of breeding to a type were then able to function.

The most important Calvinistic doctrines were the doctrine of man's utter depravity (as distinct from the Catholic doctrine of man's corruption), the doctrine of God's Decrees, and the doctrine of Predestination. According to the first, man was wholly lost in sin and abominable in the sight of God; according to the second, God had ordained from eternity every detail, no matter how trivial, in the history of the universe; according to the third, God had selected, out of his infinite goodness, a few souls for salvation, the selection having been arbitrary and irrespective of any virtues which those or other souls might appear to have. The last doctrine is merely a subsidiary heading of the second, for if all events are decreed, then the fate of each soul is decreed; and it is closely related to the first, for if man is wholly depraved, he is incapable of true virtue, and if God chooses to save him, it is for inscrutable reasons. These concepts, and others related, tended to encourage a highly allegorical frame of mind in the public at large; it became customary to read all events for their significance as part of the divine plan. They tended also to reinforce the moral nature of the Puritan indirectly; logically, these doctrines should have relieved the Puritan of moral responsibility, but actually there was an assumption that election would show itself in conduct, so that the Puritan studied his own behavior assiduously to discover the signs of his election, and it was only human that he should study his neighbor's behavior even more assiduously than his own. Life was incredibly hard, moreover, in early New England, and only the energetically moral were likely to survive.

There was a central contradiction in the Calvinistic doctrine, however, which over a century and a half led to the gradual abandonment of the doctrine: man's acts were decreed, yet man was damned for his sins. The New Englander's moral sense in the long run proved stronger than his loyalty to Calvin, and little by little the doctrine of Predestination disappeared; what was ultimately left, at least in the more intellectual society, was Unitarianism, a doctrine which emphasized morality and minimized theological dogmas. Robinson appears to have come from Unitarian stock, to have inherited the traditional moral sense and moral curiosity, which are the sources of his better poems, and to have broken easily with the few remnants of theology which Unitarianism retained. Like a good Unitarian, however, he seems to have remained unconvinced of the need for precise definition of general ideas.

But the early Calvinism of Europe contained another element, originally the most important of all. It taught that one might be reasonably sure of one's election by virtue of inner assurance, a more or less mystical communion with God, frequently very violent in its emotional form. The first generation of Calvinists in New England found this doctrine dangerous to society, and substituted for it the concept that one might believe oneself of the elect if one entered the Church and conformed to its principles, a belief which strengthened the allegorizing habit, for it made every act symbolic of man's spiritual state. But the mystical element in Calvinism was not suppressed by this modification; it merely remained more or less beneath the surface; and it was revived in the eighteenth century by Jonathan Edwards, who taught a highly evangelical and emotional kind of religion, whatever the learning and ingenuity with which he expounded it.

The mystical tendency in New England was very strong, and Unitarianism gave it no nourishment; in the nineteenth century, when Calvinism was dead so far as the man of intellect was concerned, Emerson gave a new form and a new impetus to the tendency. Emerson took the essential doctrines of European romanticism and restated them in the terms of Edwardian Calvinism. He taught that God and the universe, mind and matter, are one; that emotion and instinct are not only the true guides to virtue but the voice of God, the operation of Grace; the surrender to this guidance is equivalent to the experience of the mystic. In fact, he went farther than this, for he taught that through this surrender one not only communes with God but becomes God. Emerson himself was a product of New England and a man of strong moral habits. He seems to have mistaken habit, or second nature, for nature; since his habits were good, he believed that his nature was good. He gave to American romanticism, in spite of its irresponsible doctrine, a religious tone which it has not yet lost and which has often proved disastrous. He gave also a kind of moral and religious sanction to mere eccentricity, to self-satisfaction, and to critical laziness. The type of mind which follows its first guesses in matters of opinion and perception, with irritated contempt for opposing arguments, and which finds any kind of careful thinking beneath the dignity of a gentleman, is his legitimate heir and can find explicit justification in his writings. This kind of mind is common in modern New England (and no doubt elsewhere); and commingled with the New England moral sense and moral curiosity, there is a good deal of this intellectual laziness in Robinson; and as a result of the laziness there is a certain admixture of Emersonian doctrine, which runs counter to the principles governing most of his work and the best of it. This tendency does not result in stylistic eccentricity in Robinson, as it does, for example, in much of Emerson and of Frost; but it results in loose thinking and in a good many failures of structure, and it shows itself in nearly all of his openly didactic or philosophic pieces except "Hillcrest," a great poem which states an ethical doctrine which is counter-romantic and counter-Emersonian. His greatest poems, with which I am not at present concerned, are in the moralistic tradition: they deal with individual human dramas; the terms in which he understands the dramas are mainly those of traditional Christian morality, terms which have come down to him as folk wisdom or common sense and which he applies directly to the individual experience as a matter of course.

But it is with the explicitly didactic and expository work that I wish to deal here.

There are a good many poems which treat the subjects of God and immortality, but they are not remarkably clear. The most ambitious of these is "The Man Against the Sky," a fairly long contemplative poem, of which the versification is generally similar to that of "Dover Beach." The poem opens with a description of a solitary man crossing a hilltop into the sunset. This man is symbolic of man in general approaching death. Robinson says that his symbolic man may have progressed through great anguish to a triumphant death; or that he may have proceeded easily in the light of an uncritical faith; or that he may have been disillusioned, a stoical artist or philosopher, passing indifferently to extinction; or that he may have been disappointed in life and fearfully unreconciled to death; or that he may have been a mechanistic philosopher, proud of an intellectual construction which gave him no personal hope; but in any event that he represents all of us in that he approaches death alone, to face it as he is able. Robinson asks, then, whether we may not have some expectation of a future life, even if we doubt the existence of Heaven and Hell; and why, if we believe in Oblivion, we are guilty of perpetuating the race. He replies that we know, "if we know anything," the existence of a Deity, a Word, which we perceive fragmentarily and imperfectly, and this knowledge is our sole justification for not ending ourselves and our kind:

> But this we know, if we know anything,
> That we may laugh and fight and sing
> And of our transience here make offering

> To an orient Word that will not be erased,
> Or, save in incommunicable gleams
> Too permanent for dreams,
> Be found or known.

The nature of this Deity, and the nature of our knowledge, are not defined further than this; the crux of the poem is thus offered vaguely and in a few lines; and the greater part of the concluding section is devoted to describing the desolation which we should experience without this knowledge. Philosophically, the poem is unimpressive; stylistically, it is all quite as weak as the lines I have quoted; and structurally, it seems to defeat its purpose—for while it purports to be an expression of faith, it is devoted in all save the few lines which I have just quoted to the expression of despair.

"Credo," from *Children of the Night,* perhaps expresses a similar concept and in an equally unsatisfactory manner, but the connective *for* which introduces the second half of the sestet is confusing:

> I cannot find my way: there is no star
> In all the shrouded heavens anywhere;
> And there is not a whisper in the air
> Of any living voice but one so far
> That I can hear it only as a bar
> Of lost imperial music, played when fair
> And angel fingers wove, and unaware,
> Dead leaves to garland where no roses are.
>
> No, there is not a glimmer, nor a call,
> For one that welcomes, welcomes when he fears,
> The black and awful chaos of the night;
> For through it all—above, beyond it all—
> I know the far-sent message of the years,
> I feel the coming glory of the Light.

In the following sonnet from the same collection, there is a statement of a belief in God based on the evidence of human love and the beauty of nature that, as far as it goes, might be Christian or Emersonian or neither:

> When we can all so excellently give
> The measure of love's wisdom like a blow,—
> Why can we not in turn receive it so,
> And end this murmur for the life we live?
> And when we do so frantically strive
> To win strange faith, why do we shun to know
> That in love's elemental over-glow
> God's wholeness gleams with light superlative?
>
> Oh, brother men, if you have eyes at all,
> Look at a branch, a bird, a child, a rose,
> Or anything God ever made that grows,—
> Nor let the smallest vision of it slip,
> Till you may read as on Belshazzar's wall,
> The glory of eternal partnership.

I do not quote these poems for their poetic virtue, for they have little; the language is vague and trite, the fifth line of the poem just quoted is rhythmically very flat and is guilty of a needless and clumsy use of the progressive form of the verb, and Belshazzar's wall is a curious place on which to read the glory of eternal partnership. But the poems are characteristic expressions of this phase of Robinson's thought; they are characteristic, in fact, of his efforts to express generalized thought on any subject—thought, that, for its own sake, not for the light it throws on a particular human situation, such as the situation in "Eros Turannos" or "The Wandering Jew"; and they may perhaps serve as some justification of my failure to come to definite conclusions with regard to the precise form of Robinson's theology.

In the "Octaves," from the same collection, we have a sequence of poems for the most part on the experiential evidence for a belief in God; the evidence is defined very vaguely, in spite of the effort to achieve a gnomic style, but the writing in certain lines achieves a strength greater than any in the three poems which I have just been discussing. The ninth of these is clearer than most; it deals with the disappointment which we feel when a person of high character displays weakness, and the disappointment is offered as evidence of the real existence of the impersonal standard:

> When one that you and I had all but sworn
> To be the purest thing God ever made
> Bewilders us until at last it seems
> An angel has come back restigmatized,—
> Faith wavers, and we wonder what there is
> On earth to make us faithful any more,
> But never are quite wise enough to know
> The wisdom that is in our wonderment.

The eleventh octave is one of the best written, but offers no solution to the problem posed; it deals merely with the unsatisfied search for the solution:

> Still through the dusk of dead, blank-legended
> And unremunerative years we search
> To get where life begins, and still we groan
> Because we do not find the living spark
> Where no spark ever was; and thus we die,
> Still searching, like poor old astronomers
> Who totter off to bed and go to sleep,
> To dream of untriangulated stars.

The language applied in these poems to the evidence for a belief in God, language, for example, like "spirit-gleams of wisdom" in the eighth, is likely to be both vague and more or less romantic in its connotations; such a phrase as the one just quoted, in fact, would perhaps appear to indicate a belief in the discovery of God through pure intuition and lend some support to those who find a strong trace of Emerson in Robinson; but there is not sufficient evidence in the poems to prove that the intuition is Emersonian intuition or that the God is Emerson's God. The worst one can say of the poems is that in general they are carelessly thought and carelessly written. Emerson used language reminiscent of Edwards without being a Christian; Robinson could easily have used language reminiscent of Emerson without being an Emersonian. Robinson, especially in his earlier years, might well have resembled a good many learned scholars of my acquaintance who claim to admire Emerson and who quote him by phrases, but who fail to understand or for sentimental reasons refuse to admit the total effect of his work. This kind of thing is fairly common and seems merely to indicate a normal and healthy opacity on the part of superior minds. "The Sage" appears to be a poem in praise of Emerson, but it does not define his doctrine. One could adduce a little more evidence of this kind from the shorter poems, but I believe that all of it would be similarly inconclusive.

The evidence scattered through the longer works is even less conclusive. Captain Craig and his friend Count Pretzel von Würzburger the Obscene both talk as if they were paraphrasing Emerson; but "Captain Craig" is a character sketch, not a philosophic poem, and although these two characters are treated with affection, they are likewise treated with irony, and it seems unlikely that Robinson admired them without reservations. The men are represented as helpless failures, and Pretzel as "a vagabond, a drunkard, and a sponge," and their words are perfectly in character. It might seem the part of wisdom to receive their pronouncements as one receives the pronouncements of Falstaff rather than as one receives those of Dryden in *Religio Laici.* Robinson said to Nancy Evans: "If you want to find out about my 'Transcendentalism,' read 'The Man Against the Sky' and *Matthias at the Door*—it's in those poems." And Nancy Evans adds of the quotation marks around the word "Transcendentalism": "The quotes were in his voice."[1] We have considered "The Man Against the Sky"; the philosophical comment in *Matthias* is found in the last ten or twelve pages, in the long conversation between the protagonist and the dead Garth. The gist of the conversation is simply this: that one must be born—that is, achieve spiritual life—before one has a right to die; but the nature of the spiritual life to be achieved is not even suggested. There is the same difficulty in *Lancelot,* the greatest of the long poems. The main theme of this poem is the birth of understanding through error and suffering. Lancelot and Guinevere sin, become involved in tragedy, and then because they become aware of a better way of life, they renounce their love to achieve wisdom. The drama of sin, disaster, and renunciation is handled with great power; but the nature and virtues of the contemplative life are merely implied and hinted through the use of sentimental terms such as "the Light" and "the Vision."

As against the vagueness and the traces of romantic mysticism which I have been discussing, there is the one great expository poem, "Hillcrest," which does not go into theology but expounds an ethic which is somewhere between the Christian and the stoical and which in its last four stanzas is explicit in its disapproval of romantic optimism and romantic mysticism; and there are many poems on individual experiences which seem to be governed very largely by the principles expressed in "Hillcrest."

One appears to have in Robinson, then, a poet too little equipped for speculation, too much at the mercy of tradition, though less at its mercy than were many of his contemporaries; and the tradition which affects him is a complex one: the tradition of Calvinistic moralism on the one hand, and on the other the tradition of Unitarian aversion from thought, this latter qualified to an uncertain extent by the more positive Emersonian glorification of pure intuition and impulse. These tendencies are not in rational agreement with each other, but they have existed side by side in New England since the time of Emerson or earlier, and frequently in the same mind.

Robinson's poems on social ideas are similar to his other didactic works. Most of them are poor and none are of his best; the best adhere most closely to the case of the individual man, the worst adventure farthest into general theory. "The Master," a poem on Lincoln, and "The Revealer," a poem on Theodore Roosevelt, are primarily poems in praise of their respective subjects; but they indicate, perhaps not very clearly, Robinson's distrust of the common man and his belief in the superior leader as the only hope for democracy.[2] They are the best poems which I shall mention in this connection, "The Master," especially, standing well up among the best of Robinson's secondary poems. "Cassandra" is a poem warning the nation against the naively enthusiastic commercialism of the early part of the century:

> Your Dollar, Dove, and Eagle make
> A Trinity that even you
> Rate higher than you rate yourselves;
> It pays, it flatters, and it's new.

The admirable sharpness of such satirical statements as this is not equaled by his statements in praise of the virtues which he defends:

> Think you to tread forever down
> The merciless old verities?

> And are you never to have eyes
> To see the world for what it is?
>
> Are you to pay for all you have
> With all you are?—No other word
> We caught, but with a laughing crowd
> Moved on. None heeded, and few heard.

He does not tell us what old verities he has in mind nor how old they are—whether, for example, they are the verities of Emerson or those of Aquinas. Nor does he define the nature of the price in the last stanza, and a good many divergent definitions would be possible. He is quite as vague here as in his references to a positive theology; yet the force of a didactic poem depends precisely upon the clarity and validity of the ideas expressed.

"Demos," a double sonnet, warns us that "the few shall save / The many, or the many are to fall"; but Robinson is again too vague. Does he mean, for example, that democracy cannot survive unless it is regularly governed by great men? If so, there is small hope for it, for great men rise to power in a democracy only occasionally and as a result of their being incidentally great politicians or as a result of some other chance. Robinson may mean that the common mass should be improved little by little by the teachings of great men as those teachings after many years reach them and become a part of their tradition. I should place my own modest hopes in this latter formula, and in the belief that for the immediate present the common man is guided in some measure by such traditional wisdom, imperfectly as he may apprehend it and profit by it, and by a fairly acute sense of where the economic and social shoe pinches; this is not the formula for an Utopia, but I think it works reasonably well. But Robinson unfortunately does not say what he means, and he seems at times to be recommending a Carlylean leader-worship, or a doctrine of an elite class, either of which in practice would result in a Hitler or in an oligarchy.

"On the Way" is a dialogue spoken by Hamilton and Burr at a time when they were still superficially friendly with each other. Burr expresses the personal jealousy of a politician for a man greater than himself—that is, Washington—and Hamilton expresses an admiration for Washington similar to that expressed elsewhere by Robinson for Lincoln and for Theodore Roosevelt:

> It was a man, Burr, that was in my mind;
> No god, or ghost, or demon—only a man:
> A man whose occupation is the need
> Of those who would not feel it if it bit them;
> And one who shapes an age while he endures
> The pin-pricks of inferiorities;
> A cautious man, because he is but one;

A lonely man, because he is a thousand.
No marvel you are slow to find in him
The genius that is one spark or is nothing:
His genius is a flame that he must hold
So far above the common heads of men
That they may view him only through the mist
Of their defect, and wonder what he is.
It seems to me the mystery that is in him
That makes him only more to me a man
Than any other I have ever known.

With the admiration for Washington one cannot quarrel, nor can one quarrel with the unkind but essentially true statements about the common man; but again one is at a loss to discern the relationship of Washington to the common man, the way in which he may be said to guide the common man or be of value to him. In the nature of this relationship lies all the difference between barbarism and civilization, however halting; for Washington will be merely a menace to the nation if the common man depends upon him blindly. Unless the influence of Washington can outlast Washington, can teach the common man a few truths and give him a few perceptions, so that he can hope to survive the intervals between Washingtons, then the common man is lost.

"Dionysus in Doubt" deals immediately with the prohibition amendment of the 1920s, but more generally with the impropriety of legislation upon questions which are matters of personal morality rather than public:

Also I marvel at a land like yours
Where predatory love
In freedom's name invades the last alcove;
And I foresee a reckoning, perforce,
That you, not eager to see far
From where your toys and trumpets are,
Make nothing of.

With this as a starting point, he deals sketchily with common personal attitudes which he finds a menace to society; for example:

Wherever the dissension or the danger
Or the distrust may be,
All you that for timidity
Or for expediency capitulate,
Are negative in yourselves and in the state;
Yet there are worse for you to see,
As everywhere you may remark:
Some animals, if you see them in a manger
And do not hear them bark,
Are silent not for any watch they keep,
Nor yet for love of whatso comes to feed,
But pleasantly and ineffectually
Are silent there because they are asleep.
There are too many sleepers in your land,

And in too many places
Defeat, indifference, and forsworn command
Are like a mask upon too many faces.

These attitudes, and others which he attacks, are, as he says, a danger; but they are no more common in democracies than elsewhere. Robinson appears to have confused the voices of humanity with the vices of his country. The writing, moreover, is lax and indolent, whereas satiric and didactic poetry above all other should be compact and sharp; the confusing of the trite figure of the watchdog with the equally trite figure of the dog in a manger is an especially bad example of this laxness. Dionysus goes on to meditate on the dangers of the standardization of the human mind implicit in the kind of legislation to which he is objecting:

"Sometimes I wonder what machine
Your innocence will employ,"
He said at length,
"When all are niched and ticketed and all
Are standardized and unexceptional,
To perpetuate complacency and joy
Of uniform size and strength . . ."

But once more he seems to read into his own age and country a danger common to all times and countries: Socrates, Galileo, Abelard, and Columbus suffered from this vice in human nature no less surely than anyone has done more recently. The tendency for the mediocre norm to impose itself and for the superior individual to combat and escape this norm or to be sacrificed to it have always existed and I imagine always will; and as for the prohibition amendment, we eventually got rid of it. I have no objection to the castigation of vices, and the vices which Robinson castigates are real; but unless they are rightly located, the poem suffers and there is the possibility that society may suffer. The reader may assume, for example, that there was less standardization and more individual freedom under the reigns of Louis XIV of France or Philip II of Spain; the reigns of those monarchs may have been marked by important values which we lack, but freedom was not one of them, and it strikes me as doubtful that the values in question would be recovered by the re-establishment of comparable political systems. Before we blame our spiritual defects on a political system which it has cost blood and centuries to establish, merely because the defects and the system coincide in time, we would do well to make a careful study of historical causes. And this issue is not irrelevant to the issue of poetry; a poem which embodies so careless an outburst is not an adult performance—that is, it is not a good poem. "Demos and Dionysus" develops much the same argument, and with no greater distinction.

King Jasper, a long allegorical narrative, and the last poem Robinson wrote, takes up social themes again. King Jasper, the modern industrialist, has erected wealth, power, and civilization (civilization is represented by his charming but ineffectual son, young Jasper) on treachery to Hebron, who represents the common man. King Jasper's wife, Honoria, loves him for what he has accomplished and for his love for her, but at the crisis of the poem she is forced to abandon him and kill herself; Honoria, in so far as she represents honor, seems to represent it in a limited and conventional sense, except in her final act—she is, throughout, in jealous conflict with Zoë, who, according to Robinson, represents intelligence and who, according to Miss Estelle Kaplan[3] and more plausibly, represents intelligence and vitality or (my own suggestion) vitality mistaken for intelligence in a traditionally Emersonian manner. The reasons, on the allegorical level, for the conflict between Honoria and Zoë, are not wholly clear. Young Hebron, his father's successor, who comes in the role of the avenger, is represented throughout as a hard, grasping, and imperceptive barbarian; he destroys civilization in avenging the wrong on which it was founded. Zoë alone survives; she alone understands and cannot be wholly possessed by anyone. As a social allegory, however, the poem is defective with relation to Zoë. Capitalistic democracy, as represented by King Jasper, fails; the revolutionary democracy, as represented by Hebron, contains no elements of potential success—it is represented as the end of civilization. Now, Zoë, as the allegorical representative of intelligence, cannot exist in a vacuum; she has to be possessed by someone, even though imperfectly, yet the only forms of social activity shown in the poem are incapable of possessing her. Either Zoë should have been destroyed or there should have been a solution. To tell us that there is no hope for civilization and then at the end:

> Nothing alive
> Was left of Jasper's Kingdom. There was only
> Zoë. There was only Zoë—alone.—

This is merely outrageous balderdash; it is the final substitution of irresponsible sentimentality for thought. It is fair to remember that this poem was composed during Robinson's final illness and was finished on his deathbed; yet the thinking is essentially similar to that in his earlier work.

Too much of the writing that has been done on Robinson, especially in the forms of books and of long articles, has been done in the spirit of devotion rather than in the spirit of criticism. It is foolish to speak of the Total Vision of a man who could write the poems that I have been discussing. Robinson was in no sense a philosophical thinker. He was a man with a great gift for writing certain kinds of poetry and with a stubborn common sense which prevented a large number of his poems on themes of the sort which he understood from being corrupted by the weaker side of his nature. His inconsistencies are serious if one is bent on being misled by them; and had he been a better thinker, he would certainly have been a greater poet. But his inconsistencies are no worse, and his bad thinking is no worse, than one can find in Wordsworth or Hardy or Bridges; and his great poems place him in the company of those poets.

---

1 Nancy Evans, *Bookman*, LXXV (November, 1932).

2 Hagedorn, in *Edwin Arlington Robinson, a Biography*, tells us that Robinson early conceived an admiration of Carlyle. The fact should not be pushed too far, but it is worth mentioning.

3 *Philosophy in the Poetry of Edwin Arlington Robinson* (New York: Columbia University Press, 1940).

"HERE ARE THE MEN . . . "; E. A. ROBINSON'S MALE CHARACTER TYPES

RICHARD CROWDER

ROBINSON'S critics have been quite generally agreed on his abilities as a psychological explorer of some kinds of human experience. His method in general is to seize upon a situation, usually at its most telling moment, and to subject to minute examination the characters therein enmeshed. Such a system of exposition parallels the classical *in medias res,* except that the reader is not so often plunged into a whirlpool of action as into a well of careful, sometimes virtually picayune analysis. From his first Tilbury Town sonnets to his allegorical *King Jasper,* the number of his portrait studies is large enough to satisfy a very exacting scientist. The critics' numerous comparisons of Robinson with Henry James as a psychological novelist suggest that a typological review of Robinson's characters may be one means of approaching the poet's longer works. The fact that he wrote in smooth, though often difficult blank *verse* should not blind readers to his capacities as a writer of the novel (generally considered a *prose* form). To accept his medium of verse as a convention and to proceed to a consideration of his work as one would of a novel by Joyce or Gide, Howells or James, may be one way of reaching an understanding of a very controversial American poet.

Though Robinson, especially in the sonnets and shorter pieces, often confines himself to descriptive analysis of the immediate situation, there are many poems in which a way out is at least intimated, if not actually described. Some of the long narratives—*Roman Bartholow, Talifer, Cavender's House,*[1] *Matthias at the Door, The Glory of the Nightingales* —show that there are at least potential remedies for the ailments of their heroes.[2]

Reprinted by permission, *New England Quarterly,* XVIII (September 1945), 346-367.

Critics have noted the number of failures—spiritual and material, sometimes intellectual—in the pages of Robinson's *Collected Poems.*[3] This study proposes to look at Robinson's characters as representatives of specific psychic attitudes toward life. Eduard Spranger, the German psychologist,[4] postulates six ideal types of individuality; first, the theoretic; second, the economic; third, the aesthetic; fourth, the social; fifth, the political; and sixth, the religious. To this last Gordon W. Allport would add a seventh category, the sensual (hedonist, vital) man.[5] It should be emphasized, of course, that these are *ideal* types and cannot be completely exclusive, but will indicate only predominant tendencies and interests in any one personality. It is conceivable that a man's attitude may be an intricate union, for instance, of the political and the religious elements perhaps in balance. Granted such a man's personality would be highly complex (possibly even to the point of schizophrenia), still, careful testing and study would probably show the ascendancy—however slight—of one trait over the other.

Testing of fictional characters is, of course, an impossibility. A critic can use only so much information as an author has offered. A classification according to types, insofar as is practicable, may, however, be useful in determining the breadth of an author's interests and may provide one means of accomplishing the complex task of clarifying the intricacies of the author's genius. The seven types of men posited by Spranger and Allport offer a basis for the consideration of the principal male characters in Robinson's long narratives.[6] Even if the common trait often be failure, some differentiation may be detected in the following categories.

I

If I read Robinson correctly, his theoretical men are few in number. Spranger describes this type as fundamentally intellectualist. While it is true that most of Robinson's characters exhibit an analytical bent, we must consider such a trait as a Robinsonian convention, not unrelated to the dramatic monologue,[7] a form with which Robinson experimented. Even such sturdy men of battle as Lamorak and Bedivere are given to analytical conversation. Robinson's male characters are sometimes thought of as atypical in their loquacity and introspection, lacking the drive for masculine action.[8] If one recollects Avon, the widely-traveled, money-making lawyer; Bartholow, who takes a robust pleasure in being out-of-doors; Cavender, the successful business man who, on impulse, travels halfway round the world to come home again; Jasper, the power-hungry industrial magnate; Fargo, the twice-born man turned pumpmaker; Nightingale, first citizen of Sharon; Malory, the scientist who returns intending to murder his erstwhile persecutor;

Nash, enthusiastically pounding Salvation Army drums; Tristram, "the loud-accredited strong warrior"; Lancelot, who valiantly rescues Guinevere from the flaming stake; Matthias, who "glowed with honors earned" and once saved Timberlake from death by fire; and many lesser Robinson characters—if one recollects these men, he will see that most of them are active in a very masculine sense. Their apparent introversion and their self-analysis may often simply be means by which Robinson himself seeks to vary his own method of detailing character types. If during the narrative proper there is a preponderance of self-searching — what Harriet Monroe called "X-ray talk"— the reader should consider the entire record and recognize that, even if not so pictured at the moment of the story, Robinson's men are often forthright and active. It is as if the character has simply paused to have his portrait painted. Many of the highly ramified ideas, much of the probing, most of the scalpel operations of the dialogue, should be thought of as Robinson speaking. If his characters seem at first glance to be introverts, their extroversions may have been temporarily disguised through the Robinson device of self-analysis.

Robinson, then, did not always intend that his characters be thought of as analytical or intellectualist. Spranger's theoretic man[9] aims at organizing his knowledge in an effort to get at the truth. He is indifferent to the beauty or usefulness of objects, seeking only through observation and ratiocination to discover points of similarity and difference. The purely theoretic man would be most likely found among scientists or philosophers, though a complex personality combining, say, the aesthetic and the theoretic, is not inconceivable. One might, for example, think of Robinson himself as looking at life partly as a theorist, partly as an aestheticist. He was always interested in peeling away veneers to see the true wood beneath. But, on the other hand, he was also absorbed in the production of poetry—well-formed verse—to which he had early dedicated his life. Hence, there was in the man a professed aesthetic attitude—a feeling for beauty—which a pure intellectualist would lack. In the full-length narratives there are no examples of this type unless one except Umfraville, the loyal friend of Roman Bartholow.[10]

If intellectualists are rare in the *Collected Poems,* the aesthetic men are no more numerous. Spranger assigns form and harmony as the foremost interests of this type;[11] each experience is enjoyed for its own sake: interest in diversity rather than identities differentiates the aesthetic man from the theoretic. Rather than bewilderment, he feels repulsion at economic activity—big business, advertising, stocks and bonds, transportation of goods. His concern with variety and differences makes him more interested in individuals than in the welfare of the people as a whole. His tendency is towards self-sufficiency and development of his own individuality. In the matter of religion he is likely to be moved by beauty of ritual rather than by genuine religious experience.

Robinson applied himself to examining numerous species of failure—and insofar paralleled the ideal intellectualist. But he made no attempt to relate his pieces of knowledge: he was interested in each case as a thing in itself—and insofar displayed the aesthetic attitude. Robinson's determination to be self-sufficient, to know and to be himself, would also mark him as an aesthetic man. The predominantly aesthetic characters in his poems are hard to find. Pink the poet, one of the dream characters in *Amaranth,*[12] should probably be considered an aesthetic man, though as a poet he is a failure. He continues to give artistic expression to his ideas and emotions—to mold them harmoniously, despite the scorn of the world.

The sensual man is the man for whom pleasure is the highest value. In Robinson's long narratives, such an attitude may be discerned in two types: the lustful villain (King Mark and young Hebron) and the amorous adventurer (Gawaine, Penn-Raven, and Timberlake).[13] Of these, Mark, Hebron, and Gawaine are made ugly by hate; Penn-Raven is made to seem a scoundrel; Timberlake alone is pictured sympathetically. Physical traits are—except in the case of Gawaine—illustrative of their pleasure-seeking attitude. Mark and young Hebron both have lewd, distorted faces: Mark's bloated by long indulgence, Hebron's frenzied and venomous with selfishness. Penn-Raven's face is square, with a heavy forehead, a large nose, and a soft mouth with lips too full. Timberlake's blue eyes shine with a kindly, though now dimming, sparkle. His brownish, leathery face, wrinkled not with age nor decrepitude, but with living, is softened by gentleness. Though not precisely described, Gawaine's urbane carriage implies his essential love of living.

With the exception of Timberlake, these men are all looked upon askance by Robinson: Mark and Hebron are undisguised in their evil; Gawaine, lightly passing from love to love, is eventually scarred by hatred; Penn-Raven's apparently generous helping hand is revealed as an ugly paw of animal desire. Robinson's kindness toward Timberlake is caused possibly by the man's restraint, his honorable bearing toward Matthias, his self-sacrifice. New England morality would applaud such uprightness.

The religious man, according to Spranger,[14] seeks a unity into which his life will fit. As a mystic, his purpose is to relate himself to the cosmos. He strives constantly to find those values which will yield absolute satisfaction. "Immanent mystics" find religious experience in embracing life itself—through affirmation and participation. "Transcendental mystics" are hermitic and ascetic: for them self-denial and meditation are necessary in the search for unity. It must be borne in mind that these are the ideal types and are rarely found in a pure state.

Again, few of Robinson's chief characters are predominantly religious. Lancelot,[15] though deeply affected by what he saw while questing the Grail, is still interested in earthly love, centered in Arthur's queen, Guinevere. But, all the while, he is living "in two kingdoms." A man of energy and of great renown, he has followed Guinevere instead of the Light. At the fall of Arthur's kingdom, Lancelot sees the ephemerality of the world and leaves it—and Guinevere—for his pursuit of the Gleam. His mysticism has predominated at last.

Among Robinson's modern heroes, the well-to-do Roman Bartholow[16] is at least a partial instance of the "immanent mystic." Having been rescued from a three-year spiritual darkness by the "omphalopsychite," Penn-Raven, he now finds tonic in out-door activity and hearty living. His attitude has been chiefly governed by his search in life and in love for the complete meaning of the world. Spranger explains that the religious man is subject to periods of darkness. So is it hinted that Bartholow will not always be in this present Light, but will return to his void. He has escaped once, however, and with persistence will probably be able to emerge again from the hell of no values.

Lancelot and Bartholow, if sometimes erring, achieve spiritual success which would contradict any opinion that Robinson was wholly absorbed by a study of failure. For Bartholow and for Lancelot there are shown roads of escape from the Valley of the Shadow. Despair and disaster are not permanently theirs.

II

The economic man is the "practical" man, whose interest in the useful frequently conflicts with other values. It is more important to him to have amassed wealth than to have gained power (the political attitude) or to have been of service to the people (the social attitude). In his mind the concept of beauty (the chief concern of the aesthetic man) may be confused with luxury. Not a religious man, he still may hold to the God of tradition, thinking of Him as a general gift-giver.

In Robinson's longer works, Avon and Cavender, Fargo and Atlas[17] represent the economic attitude. Fargo and Atlas, pump-maker and stevedore, are members of the working class. The others have gained wealth, Cavender in business, Avon in the law.

Cavender, before he murdered his wife, Laramie, had always thought of her as "an unmatched possession." While living with her, he had been very successful in business, thinking nothing of crushing a man who might be in his way, then justifying his action by charities. A man who believes in a God, a Purpose, a Law (not atypical of the economic attitude), a man who had done much to keep material promises to Laramie, a man possessed of great strength and will beneath a pleasant, playful surface, a man so cloaked by his own vitality that there was no finding out his soul, he would not brook even a suspicion of infidelity. Though he might treat his wife as a toy (he often bought her costly flowers) and would sometimes look elsewhere for the sake of variety, he killed Laramie in a fog of doubt, which has not left him in twelve years of wandering. He is never to have his doubts allayed: he can only hope that she was faithful. His passion over Laramie had been the result of a possessive instinct: she was like the other things he owned. He did not want to run the risk of sharing anything that was his. His economic drive—his instinct for ownership—had put him in a darkness from which he could not escape into the light of truth and of a sympathetic understanding of his wife.

Fargo has now been free for ten years from the "servitude and error" of following the wrong profession. He was warned of his "wrong ambition" by Amaranth (the allegorical representation of the truth about oneself) and escaped from the "wrong world" to a more congenial occupation. He has been a painter of mediocre rank, actually not having much interest in art. Once he recognized the truth, he did not regret destroying his pictures. Having learned from Amaranth that suicide was not the solution to his problem, he became an excellent pump-maker, a realist, a "practical" man. He is no longer a pseudo-aesthetic man, but an economic man.

The political man, according to Spranger,[18] is not necessarily interested in politics. Rather he wants power in some form—whether personal power, a broader influence, or simply fame. This desire is common to many people, but it is the elemental trait in some, its achievement their *summum bonum*. And these are the men to be classed as political.

In the long narratives Robinson's male characters illustrate various aspects of the political attitude. In *Tristram* King Howel and Andred demonstrate two sides to the desire for actual governmental influence. Nightingale, Matthias, and King Jasper achieve power through wealth. Avon's insulted schoolmate gains power through persistent haunting of Avon's very conscience. One group of characters are the familiar Robinsonian failures, whose desire for power, position, or fame has somehow been thwarted: Figg and Flax—in Fargo's nightmare—have learned that their professions were badly chosen; Garth and old Hebron have been held down by materially stronger men; and Nash's ambition has been defeated by his own impatience.[19]

King Howel is a devoted father, but he is primarily concerned with the perpetuation of power within his own family. Andred, on the other hand, is a snake-like lickspittle, always hoping for power in the court, never accomplishing his objective, constantly despised by his superiors.

Nightingale, Matthias, and Jasper are similar to economic men in that they have been activated by the desire for wealth. All three have wanted money, however, not for its own sake, but for the power which can accompany great fortune. Nightingale and Matthias maintain their material influence to the end; Jasper—unrealistic because symbolic—dies as his kingdom falls.

Nightingale illustrates the type. He recognizes early in life that he is to be

> a part of a small world
> Of traps and lies and fights and compromises

and hates himself for it, but he dares not turn away from success even at such a price. He restores the family "honor," which has been dissipated by the improvidence of his thriftless father; he does material good in the city of Sharon, though always with an eye to the profitable return; he becomes, as a matter of fact, Sharon's leading citizen, the man with the greatest influence. When Malory deprives him of Agatha, whom he needs to make his career complete, he becomes blind with malice, permits, through his own wilful negligence, Malory to suffer total economic privation, and so unwittingly brings about the death of Agatha. He has "healed" his soul by trying to believe that Malory, as a man of science, should be willing to suffer; his own bad advice was really not to blame for Malory's misfortune, for, after all, he had himself to provide for and could not be held responsible for others. More recently he has become cognizant of the falsity of this attitude, but he still maintains control in the crisis: his directing of Malory's scientific ambition toward public service in an endowed hospital constitutes the climax of his life of influence and power.[20]

Another Robinson character—the life-long haunter of the conscience-ridden Avon—is successful in the achievement of a different kind of power: power over a man's soul. When at the age of sixteen he is knocked down by Avon for carrying malicious gossip, he warns him that he will always know where Avon is. At school he has been arrogant, somewhat cringing, and finally a little pitying towards Avon. Indolent, malignant, always too neatly dressed, he gives the appearance of uncleanness, no matter how many washings. At Avon's blow, vengeance and desolation come into his eyes. He has haunted Avon ever since, sending him a yearly card: "I shall know where you are till you are dead." Even after his drowning, his ghost returns one night to Avon, who finally dies of fear. The injured man has been successful: he has kept evil control over Avon's personality to death.

These are men who have succeeded in achieving the influence that has been the chief object of their lives. Power over many through government and capital is on a different level from power over one through insidious and relentless probing of the victim's weakness, but either type is representative of the political attitude carried through with vigor and determination.

Then there are men whose principal desire is fame, position, influence, but whose ambitions are fated to disappointment. In Figg and Flax, Robinson gives a dream version of men who, miscast in roles beyond their ability to play, have missed the position they hoped to gain. Garth and old Hebron have had their potentialities smothered by less scrupulous men.

The cause of Fernando Nash's downfall is his very eagerness for renown. From the first, though constantly haunted by the "drums of death," he knew that he had genius which would blossom if he were patient. He was certain that his first two symphonies showed great promise. He was scornful of those who envied his genius, but he allowed doubts as to his ability to take hold of him until he turned to evil ways. For twenty years he has simply wandered in the Valley of the Shadow. At forty-five he curses himself and decides on starvation as a means of extinction. Hunger clears his brain so that the great symphony which would have been his third, and the fame-bearing masterpiece, comes flooding through his consciousness, but he is too weak to write it out. Later, on regaining strength, he becomes resigned to oblivion and devotes himself to the Salvation Army. Though he feels that God was just in taking away his talent, which he had thrown away by being too impatient, the last of his life, however humble, is colored by regret at not achieving renown, at not being able to take precedence, in the world's opinion, over those who, as young composers, were envious of his original genius.

Robinson's proverbial interest in failures, however, was counterbalanced by his interest in success. In this analysis, for instance, it becomes evident that the number of men who satisfy their ambitions virtually equals the number who, for one reason or another, fail. True, where Jasper, Matthias, and Nightingale have gained in affluence they have acquired also ruthlessness and irresponsibility, but they have been successful in accordance with their attitude of mind—the political. The converse cannot be said to hold. Figg and Flax, failing to achieve, are not spiritually virtuous either, but are mere nonentities. Garth and Hebron, lacking success, develop envious dispositions. Even Fernando

Nash, who is re-born to spiritual salvation cherishes a "grim nostalgic passion" for the unattained. What is Robinson saying? Is there any man who can be a total success? Robinson's "successful" men have paid out in honesty and integrity; his "failures" have not reached total wholesomeness of the soul. For the poet the problem remains unsolved.

III

The remaining attitude—the social—[21] is the most complex in Robinson. It may appear in a variety of forms. For the social man the only type of power is love: he is incompatible with the political man. Love may be directed towards one individual or towards humanity, but if that love dominates a man's life and mind, he is a social man. He is kind, sympathetic, and unselfish. In the extreme, his attitude approaches the religious.

Robinson's social men may be grouped in two large categories: those who think of others in large groups and those who are devoted to individuals. In the first class—the group-minded—come those characters who feel a responsibility to society and those who have a natural gregariousness, who love the company of others. Of these only Merlin, Captain Craig, and Lamorak are characters in the long narratives.[22] The others are subjects of dramatic monologues or short portrait studies. Lamorak himself is only briefly glimpsed in *Merlin* as a man of action whose uppermost interest is the well-being of the state. Merlin and Captain Craig represent two phases of this kind of social attitude—service to the state and service to humanity in general.

In Merlin, Robinson pictures a man whose struggle is finally resolved in his leaving the woman he loves for the performance of duty to the government (his dilemma involving two aspects of the social attitude). He has no political ambition to be king, nor is he religious enough to see the Holy Grail, for, as he says, he has seen too much of life. He has made Arthur king that the world might see itself reflected in him. Once with Vivian in Broceliande, however, Merlin is in his grave, so far as the world goes. When first called back to Camelot by Arthur, he is restive until he can again return to Broceliande. Though he loves Vivian, he cannot avoid giving her the impression that states mean more to him than women. Having warned Arthur time and again of ruin if the state be neglected, after twelve years of love and life with Vivian he feels a compulsion to return to his duty to the world, which he recognizes is on the verge of ruin. Once again at Camelot, however, he knows that it is too late to see Arthur and save the kingdom. Nevertheless, in leaving Vivian, he has demonstrated his predominant life motive—service to the state.

Captain Craig is essentially a social man who has found his most satisfying experience in love of life and the world. Whereas he used to curse the afflictions of the unfortunate, he now feels a responsibility to mankind to be a leader toward the Light. Though poor and hungry, he is not bitter, nor ashamed, nor regretful. He is fundamentally beneficent, outward-looking, rather than dreary, grievous, discontented, or envious. Recognizing that he is a failure in terms of the world, he is nevertheless sure that he has something to bestow on mankind, and feels a "larger kind" of gratitude for what he has to give. In his will he bequeaths the universe to his young friends. In his great affirmation of the humor and wholesomeness of the world he would appear as an "immanent mystic," but his feeling of responsibility for drawing all men after him toward the Light would make his attitude predominantly social.

Merlin and Craig are both men of large vision. Their difference lies in the worldliness of the one and the mysticism of the other. Merlin's social attitude looks toward the political; Craig's toward the religious. In the Arthurian narratives are described men who are social through their service and loyalty to individuals (as opposed to the group attitude of Merlin and Craig).[23] These include Blaise, Gouvernail, and Dagonet.

Despite differences of era and social organization, Talifer's friend Dr. Quick is related to these Arthurian characters, as a man who enjoys serving and advising individuals. He secretly loves Althea, but has treated her much like a daughter. She in turn trusts him and confides in him. Though forty years old, he has never found a woman who would marry him, in spite of his attributes—cheerfulness, conversational ability, attentiveness, kindness to animals, ability to dance, complete amiability, and skill at flattery. On the whole, he is unambitious. He is kind and sincere in time of trouble and is the confidant not only of Althea but of Talifer himself. When, after a season in Wales with a woman he cannot love, he returns to find Talifer and Althea comfortably married, he resumes his old role of loquacious observer-counsellor, enjoying the companionship of his friends.

Finally, Robinson's characters include those men who exercise the social attitude through love of woman. Many of Robinson's male characters are married or are attracted to women, but for the most of them the predominant attitude is not social: their main interests lie in other directions. (It should be understood, however, that the largest single group is that of the social man.) In the group who are shown by Robinson to be chiefly moved by love of a woman two distinct kinds of men are evident: those who are variously ineffectual, and those who exhibit forthright, positive, masculine qualities.

No love at all is part of the general futility in the lives of Evensong and Ipswich, dream characters in *Amaranth,* who regret that they have never known love, but have been sidetracked by fruitless careers. These two miscast individuals are inhabitants of a dream and so are not realistic characters, but their instinctive feeling of need for love and marriage is nonetheless valid. They are obviously spokesmen for Robinson. Other characters are married and are chiefly influenced by the love they hold for their wives, but they are undistinguished. Their mediocrity is a hurdle they cannot leap, even with devoted wives to support them.

In Annandale, Robinson sketches a man who loves two wives in turn. At the death of his first wife, Miriam, he feels no grief, however, despite the fact that he loved her devotedly. During her lifetime he has kept, without knowing why, a journal involving his idea of a rich, large, sure life. With Miriam his life has not been abundant enough for him to know whereof he has written. Exhausted by the details of the death and funeral, he feels the call of someone he does not know. Then he finds Damaris, who proves to be the ideal of his book and dream, and is given promise of a new life with her.

Thirty years later (1902-1932), Robinson, apparently troubled by the situation, reintroduces Annandale, who comes to the narrator—a doctor—to confess that he feels a lack of complete understanding with his wife. He loves Damaris but feels that she is not entirely devoted to him. He is sensitive to a paucity of distinction in his character and fears the day that she will discover his mediocrity—and will not tell him. As he leaves the doctor's he meets with such a serious accident in the street that the doctor performs a mercy killing and so saves Annandale the possible suffering of what he has feared from Damaris.

Another man of mediocre ability is young Jasper. Not ambitious in a worldly way, he wants only to be happy and to live with Zoë, whom he loves and to whom he is married, not in the orthodox manner, but "under the stars and under God." Strong, radiant, confident, and unpredictable, he is called self-assured but aimless by his father. His youthful aspirations would be likely to lead him to the impossible without Zoë to restrain him. He senses great unrest in the capitalistic house of his parents but cannot identify all its causes.

A third character who fails of high accomplishment is Samuel Talifer, who, once an ardent suitor for Althea's hand, is diverted by Karen, with whom he thinks he has found peace. Though of splendid appearance, he is not superhuman—and is sometimes even a little pompous. Despite his urbanity and apparent lack of blemish, he has never done anything of notable value. He is bound by tradition and is watchful of his good name. He is potentially a man of importance but has never been moved to exercise his abilities. After one year of being married to cold, intellectual Karen, he recognizes that he was a fool for not marrying Althea, who, after his divorce, does marry him and shows him what honest love can really mean in a man's life.

Like Talifer potentially distinguished, King Arthur fails at everything because of his love for Guinevere, to whom, instead of to his kingdom, he has devoted his life. He sees too late than he has erred in not following Merlin's wisdom. Never loved by Guinevere, he nevertheless feels deserted and lonely when she leaves him for love of Lancelot. He suffers a physical shock when Lancelot and Guinevere are found together, and nearly loses his mind when, forced by law, he condemns Guinevere to the stake. He feels an "unwilling gratitude" at Lancelot's rescuing her and would indeed be willing to leave them together except that Gawaine urges war against Lancelot. Naturally, his pride and heart are wounded by the loss of Guinevere, and he is bitter about the way his friendship with Lancelot has terminated, but he also hates himself for his own infirmities. He is killed in combat by his bastard son, Modred, whom he also kills. He has lost his kingdom because of his love of a woman. He has

> made of love
> More than he made of life and death together.

From Evensong and Ipswich, through Annandale, Jasper, and Talifer to Arthur, there is a progression from complete ineffectualness towards masculine forthrightness and confidence. In Malory and, finally, in Tristram, Robinson pictures the purposive, active man for whom life yields rich harvest because of love for a woman.

Malory, the scientist, like Arthur, is deprived of his wife by another man. His wife, Althea, dies of poverty brought on by the intentional neglect of Nightingale, his financial adviser. His love for Agatha and his determination to avenge her death is the motivation for *The Glory of the Nightingales.* After her funeral he has left Sharon, their city, and stayed away for many years, degenerating in every way. Now he returns with no possession except the gun with which he expects to kill Nightingale and himself. When he discovers Nightingale sickly, he hesitates in his purpose—and never commits the murder. Instead, he becomes Nightingale's heir and lives to serve humanity through his hospital and laboratory—to find life in action. From his original love for Agatha his social vision is magnified until he is living for the benefit of society itself. This attitude of service precludes his being classified as a theoretic man.

Tristram is the great lover of Robinson's poetry. Well-mannered, glamorous, famous as a warrior, an accomplished musician, and a skillful hunter, he has had a

crowded youth,
With a sight error-flecked and pleasure-flawed.

At first blinded to Isolt of Ireland by her anger at his killing her kinsman, Morhaus, or at least by his loyalty to King Mark, for whom Isolt is intended as bride, he sees desperately, on the night of the wedding, that he and Isolt have been fated for each other. Though he has done loyal service for his uncle Mark, he now is enraged and wretched at the thought of giving up Isolt to him. When he is banished from Cornwall for drawing his sword against Mark, he wanders in rage, shame and madness until exposure brings him serious illness. Recovered at the house of Morgan, he is scornful of her, but takes her to bed in lust, all the while remaining indifferent to her. He goes to Brittany, where he successfully rids the country of its oppressor, Griffon. Out of pity which turns to a sort of love he marries Isolt of Brittany, but can never bring himself to take her into his complete confidence. He is enterprising enough in making Brittany a prosperous kingdom, but is glad to return to England, where he soon forgets all other women in the arms of Isolt of Ireland. When she is taken away again, he is overcome. He is killed by the envious Andred at the bedside of his mistress, with whom he has a brief tragic reunion in Cornwall. Energetic, brave, and worldly, he has lived his life under the spell of his love for the Irish Isolt.

If Malory's love was itself early frustrated by poverty and death, it nevertheless led him to an eventual life of service. Tristram's realization of his love ended rather than began his life. Where Malory lived with the memory of his love, Tristram lived in the prospect and hope of love's consummation. At its fulfillment his career was ended, whereas Malory's was only begun in his life with Agatha.

IV

This analysis of male character in Robinson's narrative poetry points to several conclusions. In the first place, his treatment of economic man is often either pitying or acid in quality. In his letters he speaks of his "total lack of all commercial instinct" and his feeling of "the futility of materialism as a thing to live by."[24] This attitude explains his unsympathetic manner of dealing with men whose principal goal is the amassing of fortune. Much the same may be said for his attitude towards sensual men: for the most part, his New England conscience must look with disapproval on the man whose chief aim is pleasure.

With only one or two exceptions, Robinson's religious men are either tramps or figures from the past—sketched in the shorter poems—a fact which leads to the conclusion that the poet reflected his age, in which the religious man was replaced in prevalence by the social, the political, and the economic man. That Robinson, further, should pay so little heed to the aesthetic man might find explanation in his conviction of the rarity of genius:

> Only at unconjectured intervals . . .
> A questing light may rift the sullen walls . . .[25]

The predominance of studies in the social and political attitudes shows where the poet's chief interest lay. His frequent return to the investigation of social character would indicate possibly a sublimation of his own seeming diffidence. Never a "mixer," Robinson sometimes gave the impression of being haughty and unapproachable, where actually he enjoyed people and was a pleasant, witty companion.[26] All his social men in the long narratives are uninhibited talkers; they may be so for the very reason that Robinson himself was generally laconic. The recurrence of the political attitude in his poetry, further more, may be interpreted as the probing of his own conscience, for he was constantly driven—like his Shakespeare—by the urge for attention from the people of his home town.[27]

It is quite commonly agreed that the texture and tone of Robinson's later verse differ considerably from the quality of his early work. His last poems are more qualifying, less lyrical, more circumlocutory, somehow more cautious. The elements of comedy are maintained to the end—the elegance, the suavity, the turn of phrase,[28] but often the poet overplays his hand, is merely wordy.

What relation is there between the quality of the verse and the choice of character type? I can see none. It is true that Robinson drops from his later long narratives the religious character—the types of Lancelot and of Bartholow, but not because of a change in verse quality, for the verse of *Roman Bartholow* (1923) is, in fact, very little different from that of *Cavender's House* (1929) or *The Glory of the Nightingales* (1930). On the other hand, the sensual, economic, political, and especially the social types are found in Robinson's work from beginning to end. It may have been his periphrastic literary habits which led him to the abstractions of his last two poems—*Amaranth* (1934) and *King Jasper* (1935), but the types of character even in these two poems are highly various—ranging through the entire catalogue with the exception of only the intellectualist and the religious types, both of which play only a small part in the whole body of the poetry. So one cannot say that the quality of the verse Robinson used from period to period influenced the types of men he chose to study—at least on the level of the Spranger-Allport categories.

Robinson's own complex attitude was a mixture of the theoretic, the aesthetic, the religious, the political, and the social: that is, he was analytical, sensitive to beauty, mystic, desirous of recognition, and deeply aware of man's relation to society. The men in his poetry no more exhibit pure attitudes than he. Conscious of the tensions in his own inner life, he found in his male characters similar complexities. The ideal type cannot be discovered more frequently in his narratives than in life.

Of the long narratives, eight are concerned with a love triangle, if one counts the story of Annandale, who actually loved only one woman at a time, and *Cavender's House,* in which the "other man" may have been only imagined. The rest of the narratives center on other problems besides those of three-sided love: "Captain Craig" on philosophy and life attitudes; *Merlin* on the tension between love and duty to state;"Avon's Harvest" on persecution and fear; *The Man Who Died Twice* on ambition; *Amaranth* on the concept of resignation; and *King Jasper* on economics. It must be confessed, certainly, that except in "Captain Craig" and *The Man Who Died Twice* love of woman plays some part even in these poems. Merlin is drawn from Vivian by his sense of duty to Arthur's kingdom; Avon is prevented from having a free and normal existence with his wife by the terror which pursues him; two minor characters in *Amaranth*—Evensong and Ipswich— regret that ambition has stood in the way of their loving a woman; and King Jasper's son, wanting only to love Zoë, makes small impression in his world.

Of the "triangle" poems, excluding the Annandale series, all except *Talifer,* the last one, involve two men and a woman. The husbands vary in their attitudes: Arthur and Malory are social, being impelled by love of a woman; Bartholow is mystic; Mark is sensual; Cavender is economic; Matthias is political. The "other men" also are of varying types: Lancelot is mystic; Penn-Raven and Timberlake are sensual; Tristram is social; Nightingale is political. Apparently, Robinson was interested in studying the reaction of dissimilar characters to a similar situation. If there appear to be a unity among the characters of Robinson's longer works, I am inclined to believe that it is only a superficial affinity, suggested by the somewhat uniform continuity of situation throughout the narratives. The foremost problem in the poet's mind for many years was no doubt this problem of complex love; the gallery of diverse portraits he has left us grew from his unachieved desire to find the solution.

If frequency of recurrence has any significance, it may be concluded that for Robinson the most important problems were those of the social man, whereas the theoretic (intellectualist) and the aesthetic, being—with the "transcendental mystic"—farthest removed from the social, invited the least consideration. Robinson's preoccupation with the relationship between men and women testifies to their importance in his mind. The full story of his own experience with love may never be known, but it is evident that the whole problem was fundamental to his thinking. If Robinson was concerned with the plight of contemporary society,[29] it may be added that he was no less concerned with man's part in it, both as public citizen and as private individual. "The elemental dualism of love and duty"[30] is, from another point of view, a problem within the area of social attitude—a problem which must have as many solutions as there are citizens and lovers. To such perplexing complication Robinson bore witness, as he returned again and again to the theme of love, like a restless, questioning stream seeking answer in some far-off, quiet sea.

---

1 Louise Dauner, "Avon and Cavender: Two Children of the Night," *American Literature*, XIV (March 1942), 55-65. Miss Dauner points out that the way of confession to the courts is open to Cavender, though whether he follows it is not disclosed; for Avon, on the other hand, there can be no salvation since his soul has disintegrated in self-betrayal.

2 In his essay on Robinson in *I Hear America* (New York, 1937), 51-60, Vernon Loggins plays Procrustes in fitting Robinson into a bed of despair. He says that Robinson is not interested in causes or remedies, but simply in the portrayal of the current state of maladjustment. I cannot agree, for, especially in the long narratives, the poet, through flashbacks, often describes explicitly the cause of the failure, and just as often indicates the means of salvation.

3 Harriet Monroe in "Edwin Arlington Robinson," *Poetry*, XXV (January 1925), 208-213, and "On Foreign Ground," *Poetry*, XXXI (December 1927), 165, and Horace Gregory in "The Weapon of Irony," *Poetry*, XLV (December 1934), 159, call especial attention to this part of Robinson's interest. Miss Dauner's article, "Avon and Cavender," turns on this theme of failure.

4 *Types of Men: The Psychology and Ethics of Personality* (Halle, 1928).

5 *Personality: A Psychological Interpretation* (New York, 1941), 213-231.

6 Louise Dauner in "The Pernicious Rib: Robinson's Concept of Feminine Character," *American Literature*, XV (May, 1943), 139-158, presents one view of the Robinsonian woman — as the ensnarer of man. I should go further and say that, since nearly all of Robinson's heroines are concerned with some phase of love, it would appear that the poet saw the world of action and of public life as belonging to the men, and women's chief function as being the development of their capacity for love, that men may find nourishment there for their duties in the world.

7 David Brown in "E. A. Robinson's Later Poems," *New England Quarterly*, X (September, 1937), 487-502, shows how Robinson followed Browning not too successfully in the use of this form.

8 Dauner, *American Literature*, XV, 148.

9 *Types of Men*, 109-129.

10 *Collected Poems*, 733.

11 *Types of Men*, 147-171.

12 *Collected Poems*, 1311-1393.

13 In *Collected Poems*, see Mark, *Tristram*, 595-729; Hebron, *King Jasper*, 1397-1488; Gawaine, *Merlin*, 235-314, *Lancelot*, 365-449, and *Tristram*; Penn-Raven, *Roman Bartholow*, 733-856; Timberlake, *Matthias at the Door*, 1077-1155.

14 *Types of Men*, 210-246.

15 *Collected Poems*, 365-449.

16 *Ibid.*, 733-856.

17 *Ibid.*, 543-573, 961-1007, 1311-1393.

18 *Types of Men*, 188-209.

19 In *Collected Poems*, see Howel and Andred, *Tristram*, 595-729; Nightingale, *The Glory of the Nightingales*, 1011-1073; Matthias and Garth, *Matthias at the Door*, 1077-1155; Jasper and Hebron, *King Jasper*, 1397-1488; "Avon's Harvest," 543-573; Figg and Flax, *Amaranth*, 1311-1393; Nash, *The Man Who Died Twice*, 921-957.

20 In this interpretation I agree with that of Estelle Kaplan in *Philosophy in the Poetry of Edwin Arlington Robinson* (New York, 1940), 109-110. See also the discussion of Malory, below.

21 *Types of Men*, 172-187.

22 In *Collected Poems*, see *Merlin*, 253-314; and "Captain Craig," 113-169.

23 In *Collected Poems*, see Blaise and Dagonet, *Merlin*, 235-314; Gouvernail and Tristram, *Tristram*, 595-729; Arthur, *Lancelot*, 365-449, and *Merlin*; Quick and Talifer, *Talifer*, 1231-1307; Annandale, "The Book of Annandale," 195-211, and "Annandale Again," 1200-1206; Evensong and Ipswich, *Amaranth*, 1311-1393; Malory, *The Glory of the Nightingales*, 1011-1073; young Jasper, *King Jasper*, 1397-1488.

24 Ridgely Torrence, editor, *Selected Letters of Edwin Arlington Robinson* (New York, 1940), 41, 92.
25 "Many Are Called," *Collected Poems*, 581-582.
26 See, for instance, Rollo Walter Brown, *Next Door to a Poet* (New York, 1937), and Frederika Beatty, "Edwin Arlington Robinson as I Knew Him," *South Atlantic Quarterly*, XLIII (October, 1944), 375-381.
27 Hermann Hagedorn, *Edwin Arlington Robinson* (New York, 1938), 187.
28 Horace Gregory and Marya Zaturenska, "The Vein of Comedy," *American Bookman*, I (Fall, 1944), 43-64.
29 Louise Dauner, "Vox Clamantis: Edwin Arlington Robinson as a Critic of American Democracy," *New England Quarterly*, XV (September, 1942), 401-426.
30 Kaplan, 37.

E. A. ROBINSON: THE LOST TRADITION

Louis O. Coxe

To the contemporary reader is seems strange that Allen Tate, in 1933, should have referred to E. A. Robinson as the "most famous of living poets" and again as the writer of "some of the finest lyrics of modern times." As far as most of us are concerned, nowadays Robinson ekes out a survival in "anthological pickle," as he called it, and few readers try to go beyond, for if any poet has been damned by the anthologists it is Robinson. Why the decline in his reputation? Did critics puff him far beyond his deserts? Can a critic today judge him on the basis of the old chestnuts, "Miniver Cheevy," "Flammonde," "Richard Cory"? Should criticism reiterate that he ruined himself writing those interminable narratives and dismiss him as a "transition figure" between somebody and somebody else, both presumably more "important"? Yvor Winters, in his recent book, has gone far to disestablish the transitional, and place the essential, Robinson, yet neither he nor Mr. Tate has told why he considers the poems he praises praiseworthy. Mr. Winters has in his brief study given an excellent analysis of Robinson's failings and failures, but there is still the problem of the kind of excellence readers who come to Robinson these days should expect. Vicissitudes of temper and fashion apart, I think much of the neglect of Robinson's work has derived from the deceptively old-fashioned appearance it presents and from the very stern cosmology out of which the poetry arises. The texture of the poetry is of a sort we are not used to; the subject-matter can be misunderstood. Above all, Robinson's technique lends itself to abuse (and he abused it frequently) so that very often the reader may not detect that under an apparently calm surface many forms are in motion.

Robinson is a poet with a prose in view. Read "Eros Turannos" or "For A Dead Lady" or "The Gift of God" and you will feel that the scope of a long naturalistic novel has emerged from a few stanzas. Yet

Reprinted by permission, *Sewanee Review*, LXII (Spring 1954), 247-266.

Mr. Tate, in his brief essay, says that Robinson's lyrics are "dramatic" and that T. S. Eliot observes this to be a characteristic of the best modern verse. I really do not know what the word "dramatic" means in this regard; Robinson's poetry is not dramatic in any sense of the word commonly accepted, unless it be that Robinson, like James, likes to unfold a scene. To look for anything like drama in the poems is idle, in that the excitement they convey is of a muted sort, akin to that which James himself generates. This poet wears no masks; he is simply at a distance from his poem, unfolding the "plot," letting us see and letting us make what applications we will. This directness, this prose element, in Robinson's verse is easy enough to find; less so to define or characterize. One can say this, however: just as Pope was at his best in a poetry that had morality and man in society as its subject matter and its criterion, so Robinson is happiest as a poet when he starts with a specific human situation or relationship, with a "story." By the same token, he fails most notably when he engages in philosophic speculation, when he writes poems, such as the "Octaves," or many of the sonnets, that have no real subject matter, no focus of events or crisis seen objectively. The parallel between his method and that of Pope is patently incomplete, yet each poet, basing his whole scheme on certain immutable moral convictions and concerning himself primarily with man as a social creature, strove for a poetry that would be external, transparent, unified. Neither made elaborate experiments with form but each was content to exploit with dexterity a few common meters, because for both Pope and Robinson the real business was what was finally said and communicated. Both used their individual idioms, each far removed from anything we find today: spare where we are lush, general where we are specific, detailed where we are reticent or silent. The twentieth century has learned to dislike abstractions as the result of being badly cheated by them, yet the fear should perhaps be of the susceptibility to fraud, however pious.

Whatever Robinson's weaknesses, his frauds are few and those few easy to expose. The best poems work toward a condition of total communication by means of suggestion and statement, with no regard for the poet as speaker; that is, the attitudes out of which the poems emerge we take as our own, and there is no need to ascertain those of the speaker since Robinson is everywhere the same. His irony is not "in" the poem but external, one constituent of a cosmology that sees the human condition as comic in the largest sense—sees life as a desperate business but essentially, immutably unalterable. This is not childish disillusionment; it works out in the poetry as a cosmology that seems to us, scions of the liberal-romantic stock, bitter, profitless, perhaps old-fashioned. And because Robinson so early in his career found and grasped his ultimate beliefs, the modern reader does not find what he must naturally look for: progress, novelty, enlightenment. This poetry does not intend certain things, and discussion of the kind of verse Robinson wrote may clear the ground and allow the reader to go to the poetry with some idea of what not to expect or look for.

Many critics have spent too much time saying that Robinson was obsessed with failure, thereby accounting for his lapse into the profitless slough of the long narratives. Yet none has shown how vital a force the failure is as theme, how it contains within itself a possibility of vision and maturity, as well as of pathos. For to Robinson life and humanity were failures inasmuch as they consistently, unalterably fall short of, not the ideal, but their own proper natures. Robinson was never so romantically disillusioned that he could be for long disturbed over the discrepancy between actual and ideal, illusion and reality; for him the real irony, the comedy, lay in man's wilful misconception of life and his role in it. The very wilfulness may have a magnificence of its own, as in "The Gift of God," and the people in his poems who come through to an awareness of the true proportion do not simply rest there in smug knowledge, but rather for the first time see that it is from such vision of things as they are that a man starts:

> He may by contemplation learn
> A little more than what he knew,
> And even see great oaks return
> To acorns out of which they grew.

What may be irony from one point of view may be comedy or pathos, perhaps a kind of muted tragedy, from another. At all events, the point of view is essentially the same, with only a pace back, forward or to one side that gives the particular vision its specific color and shape.

The attitudes which have dominated the writing of our century have been rather different from Robinson's. We seem for the most part willing to contemplate life as a tragic affair, to command the ironic tone in our writing in order to express successfully the tragic division we see gaping between what we are and what we would be. Yet one wonders at times if we actually do *believe* this or whether it is another kind of myth-making, a device for getting poetry written and read, like Yeats's visions. If we really do believe, then we must accept the consequences of our faith, for in a world that is ultimately tragic, happiness is irrelevant, despair the resort of the thin-skinned, and total acceptance the only *modus vivendi.* The acceptance itself must entail a kind of transubstantiation: the Aristotelian essence of life turns to something else while the "accidents" of evil and death remain. This is the realm of miracle; the poetry of Robinson has nothing to do with it, for his work merely tries to come to a naked vision of the human condition without lusting after schemes of revision, without trying to discover something that is not, can not in nature be, there. In "Veteran Sirens" all the terrible irony of mankind's wilful refusal to face facts emerges in the pitying portrait of superannuated whores:

> The burning hope, the worn expectancy,
> The martyred humor and the maimed allure,
> Cry out for time to end his levity,
> And age to soften his investiture.

And we are all life's whores. What strikes Robinson as ironic is not the old discrepancy between illusion and reality, not the wastage of time, but the supreme dissipation of the expense of spirit in a waste of shame, folly and deceit. The stern, still-Calvinist view of carnal sin here has become a trope for life, for the way we all bargain with life for a living and are finally cheated.

The best of Robinson's poems have to do with such plots, such expense of the soul's life, and usually have as their center the single, crucial failure of a man or woman to commit that destruction of the beloved self, to make that complete disavowal of a precious image which alone and finally leaves the individual free. The price of such freedom comes high, "costing not less than everything," and is paid for by a crucial failure in which the image referred to is destroyed, in many such cases along with the life itself; in *Amaranth,* for instance, Atlas and Miss Watchman, both self-deluding artists, are destroyed along with their work, although Fargo, who sees the truth, manages to alter his whole nature and his way of life. The variations on the theme are many; the tone can be somber and tragic, or it can be pastoral and elegiac as in "Isaac and Archibald," or angry and bitter as in "For a Dead Lady." Yet all tones, all attitudes, are part of the one dominating view as the language, however bald or rich by turns it may be, serves the one narrative and ratiocinative end.

If Robinson's attitudes are not common ones, similarly his idiom finds little immediate sympathy in modern readers. Unfortunately we have been accustomed to read Robinson as though he were Edgar Lee Masters from Maine, a crabbed New Englander who should have read Walt Whitman, and unconsciously we judge him by a standard we would reject were it applied to Eliot or Ransom. Here is an old language, reborn, sometimes abstract and involved, unusually sparing of metaphor, though the imagery when it occurs is crucial, perhaps the more so because of its very compression and sparseness. Above all, Robinson organizes his poems to a disarming extent, often building a structure that is so symmetrically proportioned that only the closest reading discovers the articulation. Such a reading I shall attempt here in the hope that the effort will supply an insight into the poems themselves as well as a justification of the foregoing remarks.

"Eros Turannos" emerges to the mind as a narrative, compressed and suggestive yet without the trickery that occasionally irritates us, as in the case of "The Whip" or "How Annandale Went Out." Most noticeably, the language is general, the tone expository, the purpose of the poem communication rather than expression. Adumbrated in the first stanza, certain images, whose latent power and meanings are reserved until the final lines, have the function of motifs, repeated constantly and expanded as the poem opens out into suggestion. There are three such images or symbols: waves, tree, stairs leading down. Throughout, these symbols control and provide a center for the meanings possible to the poem, and from the mention of "downward years" and "foamless weirs" in the first stanza to the triple vision of the last four lines these elements recur, the same but altered. As is the case with so many Robinson poems, the reader must supply, from the general materials provided, his own construction, yet the poet has seen to it that there can be only one possible final product. The poem contains two complementary parts: the abstract, generalized statement and the symbolic counterpart of that statement, each constituting a kind of gloss upon the other; each moves through the poem parallel to the other, until at the end they become fused in the concrete images. In addition to the three symbols mentioned, we find also that of blindness and dimness, summed up in the single word "veil" yet continually present in the words mask, blurred, dimmed, fades, illusion. All this culminates in the sweeping final image: "Or like a stairway to the sea / Where down the blind are driven." Yet such inner orders, such tight articulation as these examples may indicate derives no more from the concrete than from the generalized; contrary to Marianne Moore's professed belief, not all imaginary gardens need have actual toads in them, nor, conversely, do we have to bother with the toad at all if our garden is imagined truly enough. What we must have is room—for toads or non-toads, but room anyhow, and Robinson seems to say that there will be more room if we don't clutter the garden with too many particular sorts of fauna and flora. For in "Eros Turannos" we are not told the where or the wherefore; only, and it is everything, the how and the just so. In the hinted-at complexity of the woman's emotion, in the suggested vagueness of the man's worthlessness, lies the whole history of human trust and self-deception: none shall see this incident for what it really is, and the woman who hides her trouble has as much of the truth as "we" who guess and guess, yet, the poem implies, coming no nearer to the truth than men usually do.

"Eros Turannos" is the Robinsonian archetype, for in it we can find the basic elements, the structural pattern, that he was to use frequently and with large success. The most cursory reading affords a glimpse into the potential power as well as the dangers of such a form; Robinson's use of it provides examples of both. In the poem in question he reaches an ultimate kind of equipoise of statement and suggestion, generalization and concretion. The first three words of the poem set the tone, provide the key to a "plot" which the rest will set before us. "She fears him": simple statement; what follows will explore the statement, and we shall try to observe the method and evaluate its effect.

She fears him, and will always ask
   What fated her to choose him;
She meets in his engaging mask
   All reasons to refuse him;
But what she meets and what she fears
Are less than are the downward years
Drawn slowly to the foamless weirs,
   Of age, were she to lose him.

The epigrammatic tone of the verse strikes one immediately; we are aware that here is a kind of expository writing, capable in its generality of evoking a good deal more than the words state. Important though unobtrusive imagery not only reinforces and enriches the exposition but by calculated ambiguity as well sets a tone of suspense and fatality. The man wears a mask: he conceals something that at once repels and attracts her; notice the play on "engaging" and the implications that involves. The motif is an important one for the poem, as is that contained in the metaphor of "weirs," since these two suggestions of deception, distrust, entrapment, blindness, and decline will be continually alluded to throughout the poem, to find an ultimate range of meaning in the final lines. The second stanza will in such expressions as "blurred" and "to sound" keep us in mind of the motifs mentioned, without actually requiring new imagistic material nor forcing us to re-imagine the earlier metaphors. The intent here is not to be vague but to retain in the reader's consciousness what has gone before as that consciousness acquires new impressions. Hence, in stanza three, Robinson can now introduce a suggestive sketch of the man's nature while he reminds of the woman's and continues to explore it:

A sense of ocean and old trees
   Envelops and allures him,
Tradition, touching all he sees,
   Beguiles and reassures him;

That engaging mask of his becomes apparent to us here in this man who finds a solace and security in the love of his wife and in her solid place in the community, and yet the sinister note first sounded in the image of "weirs" is lightly alluded to in the phrase "a sense of ocean."

Moreover, that he too is "beguiled" presents a possibility of irony beyond what has yet been exploited. The stanza extends the narrative beyond what I have indicated:

> And all her doubts of what he says
> Are dimmed with what she knows of days—
> Till even prejudice delays
>   And fades and she secures him.

The possibilities are many. We grasp readily enough the pathos of her situation: a woman with a worthless husband, proud and sensitive to what the town is whispering yet ready to submit to any indignity, to close her eyes and ears, rather than live alone. Surely a common enough theme in American writing and one that allows the poet to suggest rather than dramatize. Again, in "dimmed" we catch an echo of what has gone before, and in the last two lines the abstract noun "prejudice" with its deliberately general verbs "delays" and "fades" presents no image but rather provokes the imagination to a vision of domestic unhappiness familiar to us all, either in fiction or empirically. And of course the finality of "secures," ironic neither in itself nor in its position in the stanza, takes on irony when we see what such security must be: the woman finds peace only by blinding herself and by seeing the man as she wishes to see him.

Stanza four once again recapitulates and explores. Statement alternates with image, the inner suffering with the world's vision of it:

> And home, where passion lived and died,
> Becomes a place where she can hide,
> While all the town and harbor-side
>   Vibrate with her seclusion.

If this stanza forms the climax of the plot, so to speak, the next comes to a kind of stasis, the complication of events and motives and themes we see so often in Henry James. The outside world of critical townspeople, hinted at before, now comes to the foreground, and we get a complication of attitudes and views—the world's, the woman's, the man's, our own—and the poet's is ours too. Yet even in a passage as seemingly prosaic and bare as this Robinson keeps us mindful of what has gone before. In stanza four such words as "falling," "wave," "illusion," "hide" and "harbor" have served to keep us in mind of the various themes as well as to advance the plot, and in the fifth stanza Robinson presents us with a series of possible views of the matter, tells us twice that this is a "story," reiterates that deception and hiding are the main themes, as in the metaphorical expression "veil" as well as in the simple statement, "As if the story of a house / Were told or ever could be." And at last, in the final lines, thematic, narrative and symbolic materials merge in the three images that accumulate power as they move from the simple to the complex, from the active to the passive, from the less to the more terrible:

> Though like waves breaking it may be,
> Or like a changed familiar tree,
> Or like a stairway to the sea
> Where down the blind are driven.

For the attentive reader the narrative can not fail; Robinson has given us the suggestive outline we need and told us how, in general, to think about this story. He has kept us constantly aware of place, time, actors and action even though such awareness is only lightly provoked and not insisted on. In the last stanza the curious downward flow of the poem, the flow of the speculation, reaches an ultimate debouchment—"where down the blind are driven." Apart from the metrical power, the movement of the poem is significant; Robinson has packed it with words that suggest descent, depth and removal from sight, so that the terrible acceptance of the notion that we must "take what the god has given" becomes more terrible, more final as it issues out in the logic of statement and imagery and in the logic of the plot.

If much of the poem's power depends upon the interaction of statement and suggestion, still another source of energy is the metric. Robinson here uses a favorite device of his, feminine rhymes, in alternating tetrameter and trimeter lines, and gives to soft-sounding, polysyllabic words important metrical functions; as a result, when he does invert a foot or wrench the rhythm or use a monosyllable, the effect is striking out of all proportion to its apparent surface value. Surely the plucking, sounding quality of the word "vibrate" in the last line of the fourth stanza is proof of this, though equally effective is the position of "down" and "blind" in the final line of the poem.

Contemporary verse has experimented with meters, rhyme and rhythm to such an extent that one has to attune the ear to Robinson's verse; at first it sounds jingly and mechanical, perhaps inept, but after we make a trial of them, the skill, the calculation, have their way and the occasional deviations from the set pattern take on the greater power because they are deviations:

> Pity, I learned, was not the least
> Of time's offending benefits
> That had now for so long impugned
> The conservation of his wits:
> Rather it was that I should yield,
> Alone, the fealty that presents
> The tribute of a tempered ear
> To an untempered eloquence.

This stanza from "The Wandering Jew" shows the style. This is mastery of prosody—old-fashioned command of the medium. The reversing of feet, use of alternately polysyllabic and monosyllabic words, of syncopation ("To an untempered eloquence") are devices subtly and sparingly used. The last stanza of the same poem gives another instance, and here the running-on of the sense through three-and-a-half lines adds to the effect:

> Whether he still defies or not
> The failure of an angry task
> That relegates him out of time
> To chaos, I can only ask.
> But as I knew him, so he was;
> And somewhere among men today
> Those old, unyielding eyes may flash,
> And flinch,—and look the other way.

Deviation implies a basic pattern, and although in many cases, particularly in the blank verse narratives, syllable-counting mars the prosody, nonetheless the best poems subtly attune themselves to the "tempered ear," syncopate on occasions, and jingle to good effect.

This analysis is technical and only partial; it seems to presuppose that we must lapse into Mr. Brooks's "heresy of paraphrase." Granted Yet this but begs a question, inasmuch as all of Robinson's poetry assumes that one will want to find the paraphrasable element the poet has carefully provided. These are poems *about* something, and what the something is we must discover. That is why we should consider Robinson as a poet with a prose in view, according to the description of "prose" earlier suggested. "Eros Turannos" is *about* the marriage of untrue minds, but specifically it is not about just untrueness and minds; it is about untrue man A and suffering, self-deluding woman B, as well as about those worldly wisemen who conjecture and have all the dope. Notably unsuccessful in speculative verse, Robinson excels in just this naturalistic case-history, this story of a Maine Emma Bovary. If the theme is still failure, Robinson rings a peculiar change upon it, since at last, the poem forces us to accept the implication that there *is* and must be a "kindly veil between / Her visions and those we have seen"; that all of us must "take what the god has given," for failure is, in Robinson's world, the condition of man and human life. We do the best we can. In "Old Trails," the best one can is not often good, and what is indeed success in the world's eyes has a very shoddy look to those who recognize the success as merely "a safer way / Than growing old alone among the ghosts." It is the success of Chad in *The Ambassadors,* who will go home to the prosperous mills and Mamie and Mom, not that of Strether, who could have had the money and the ease but took the way of "growing old among the ghosts." But a briefer, more compact poem than "Old Trails," one that deals with another aspect of the theme, is the sonnet "The Clerks," which for all its seeming spareness is a very rich, very deft performance.

The octave opens colloquially, gives us a general location and an unspecified number of clerks; the speaker is the poet, as poet and as man. Robinson draws an evocative, generalized sketch of the clerks' past, of their prime as well as of the slow attrition of time and labor, and affirms that despite the wear they have sustained these men are still good and human. It is in the sestet that the poem moves out into suggestion, that it implies a conceit by which we can see how all men are clerks, time-servers, who are subject to fears and visions, who are high and low, and who as they tier up also cut down and trim away. To call the poem a conceit is no mere exercise of wit, for Robinson has clearly punned on many unobtrusive words in the sonnet. What is the clerks' "ancient air"? Does it mean simply that the men are old and tired? or that their manner is one of recalling grand old times of companionship that never really existed? or that one must take "air" literally to mean their musty smell of the store? These possibilities are rendered the more complex by the phrase "shopworn brotherhood" immediately following, for then the visual element is reinforced, the atmosphere of shoddiness and shabbiness, of Rotary club good-fellowship, and the simple language has invested itself with imagistic material that is both olfactory and visual. And of course, one may well suspect sarcasm in the assertion that "the men were just as good, / And just as human as they ever were." How good were they? Yet lest anyone feel this is too cynical, Robinson carefully equates the clerks with "poets and kings."

As is the case with "Eros Turannos," this poem proceeds from the general to the specific and back to the general again, a generality now enlarged to include comment on and a kind of definition of the human condition. Throughout there have been ironic overtones, ironic according to the irony we have seen as peculiarly Robinsonian in that it forms one quadrant of the total view. It has to do here with the discrepancy between the vision men have of their lives and the actuality they have lived. The poet here implies that such discrepancy, such imperfection of vision is immutably "human" and perhaps therefore and ironically, "good." That the clerks (and we are all clerks) see themselves as at once changed and the same, "fair" yet only called so, serves as the kind of lie men exist by, a lie that becomes an "ache" on the one hand and the very nutriment that supports life on the other. You, all you who secretly cherish some irrational hope or comfort, you merely "feed yourselves with your descent," your ancestry, your career, your abject position miscalled a progress. For all of us there can be only the wastage, the building up to the point of dissatisfaction, the clipping away to the point of despair.

Despite the almost unsupportable dures of Robinson's attitude, we can hardly accuse him of cynicism or of hopelessness. In every instance his view of people is warm and understanding, not as the patronizing seer but as the fellow-sufferer. Such feeling informs the poems we have discussed and fills "The Gift of God" with humanity no cynic could imagine, no despair encompass. For in this poem the theme of failure turns once more, this time in an unexpected way so that we see Robinson affirming self-deception of this specific kind as more human, more the gauge of true love than all the snide fact-finding the rest of the world would recommend. The poem is about a mother's stubborn, blind love for a worthless (or perhaps merely ordinary) son, and this in the teeth of all the evidence her neighbors would be delighted to retail. Again, the poem is a compact narrative; again the irony exists outside the poem, not in its expression. As in so many of the best poems, Robinson says in effect: here is the reality, here is the illusion. *You* compare them and say which is which and if possible which is the correct moral choice.

The metaphorical material we can roughly classify as made up of imagery relating to royalty, apotheosis, sacrifice, and love. From the first few lines we are aware of a quality which, by allusion to the Annunciation and the anointing of kings, establishes the mother's cherished illusion and thereby makes acceptance of the emergent irony inescapably the reader's duty; he must compare the fact and the fiction for and by himself; Robinson will not say anything in such a way as to make the responsibility for choice his own rather than the reader's. He will simply render the situation and leave us to judge it, for all of Robinson's poems presuppose an outside world of critics and judges, of ourselves, people who see and observe more or less clearly. His irony is external; it lies in the always hinted-at conflict between the public life and the private, between the thing seen from the inside and from the outside, with the poet, the speaker presenting a third vision, not one that reconciles or cancels the other two, but one which simply adds a dimension and shows us that "everything is true in a different sense."

If the dominant motifs in "The Gift of God" are as indicated above, the progression of the poem follows undeviatingly the pattern suggested. In the first stanza Annunciation; the second, Nativity; the third, vision; the fouth, a stasis in which the mother seems to accept her son's unusual merit and her own vision of him as real; the fifth, a further extension of vision beyond anything actual; the sixth, the culmination of this calculated vision in the apotheosis. More than a schematized structure, the poem depends not only on the articulation of motifs and a plot, but equally on symbolic material that interacts with the stated or implied events in the "plot." Thus, from the outset the poet has juxtaposed the illusory vision and the "firmness" of the mother's faith in it; the language has a flavor of vague association with kingship, Biblical story, and legend, notably conveyed by such words as "shining," "degree," "anointed," "sacrilege," "transmutes," and "crowns." Yet in the careful arrangement of his poem Robinson has not oversimplified the mother's attitude. She maintains her "innocence unwrung" (and the irony of the allusion is not insisted on) despite the common knowledge of people who know, of course, better, and Robinson more than implies the innocence of her love in the elevated yet unmetaphorical diction he uses. Not until the final stanza does he open the poem out, suddenly show the apotheosis in the image of "roses thrown on marble stairs," subtly compressing into the last three lines the total pathos of the poem, for the son ascending in the mother's dream is "clouded" by a "fall"; the greatness his mother envisions is belied by what we see. And who is in the right? For in the final turn of the "plot," is it not the mother who gives the roses of love and the marble of enduring faith? Is the dream not as solid and as real as human love can make it? If we doubt this notion, we need only observe the value Robinson places on the verb "transmutes" in stanza five: "*Transmutes* him with her faith and praise." She has, by an absolute miracle of alchemy, transmuted base material into precious; by an act of faith, however misplaced, found the philosopher's stone, which is love wholly purged of self. What we have come to realize is that in these poems we have been considering we are concerned with narrative—narrative of a peculiar kind in which the story is not just about the events, people and relationships but about the very poetic devices which are the vehicle of the narration and its insights. In "The Gift of God" symbol and theme have a narrative function; they must do in brief and without obtrusiveness what long passages of dialogue, exposition and description would effect in a novel. As a result, the reader is compelled to take the entire poem in at once; he either "understands" it or he does not. Naturally, there are subtleties which emerge only after many readings; yet because these poems are narratives, Robinson must concentrate upon communication, upon giving us a surface that is at once dense yet readily available to the understanding.

> As one apart, immune, alone,
> Or featured for the shining ones,
> And like to none that she has known
> Of other women's other sons,—
> The firm fruition of her need,
> He shines anointed; and he blurs
> Her vision, till it seems indeed
> A sacrilege to call him hers.

This is on one hand simple telling of plot: the mother sees her son as unique and feels unworthy to be his mother. Simple enough. But the story is more than this, more than a cold telling of the facts about the mother's vision of her son. We see on the other hand that it is her need of the son, and of the vision of him, which complicates the story, while the suggestion of kingship, ritual, and sacrifice in the diction, the implication of self-immolation and deception, further extends the possibilities of meaning. All this we grasp more readily than we may realize, for Robinson prepares for his effects very early and while he extends meaning is careful to recapitulate, to restate and reemphasize the while he varies and complicates:

> She sees him rather at the goal,
> Still shining, and her dream foretells
> The proper shining of a soul
> Where nothing ordinary dwells.

In these lines Robinson affirms the mother's illusion: it is a "dream" that "foretells," and recapitulates the theme of kingship, of near-divinity in the repetition of "shining." The stanza that follows gives the poem its turn, states specifically that the son is merely ordinary, that the mother deludes herself, that her motive in so doing is "innocent," and in stanza five the poem, as we have seen, turns once more, pivots on the verb "transmute," turns away from the simple ironical comparison we have been experiencing and reveals a transmuted relationship: son to mother, vision to fact, and an ultimate apotheosis of the mother under the guise of a mistaken view of the son. The poem is about all these things and is equally about the means of their accomplishment within the poem. This is a poetry of surfaces, dense and deceptive surfaces to be sure but none the less a poetry that insists upon the communication of a whole meaning, totally and at once:

> She crowns him with her gratefulness,
> And says again that life is good;
> And should the gift of God be less
> In him than in her motherhood,
> His fame, though vague, will not be small,
> As upward through her dream he fares,
> Half clouded with a crimson fall
> Of roses thrown on marble stairs.

The recapitulation, the tying together, of the symbolic and thematic materials serves in this, the last stanza, a narrative as well as an expressive purpose. The tone is epigrammatic rather than prosaic and must shift delicately, come to the edge of banality, then turn off and finally achieve a muted sublimity that runs every risk of sentimentality and rhetoric yet never falters. The verse requires of us what it requires of itself: a toughness that can encompass the trite and mawkish without on the one hand turning sentimental itself or on the other resorting to an easy irony. The technique is the opposite of dramatic in that Robinson leaves as much to the reader as he possibly can; he uses no persona; the conflict is given not so much as conflict-in-action before our eyes as it unfolds itself at once, passes through complications, and returns to the starting point, the same yet altered and, to some degree, understood. To this extent Robinson is ratiocinative rather than dramatic; what we and the characters themselves think about the "plot" is as important as the plot, becomes indeed the full meaning of the plot.

Observably this ratiocinative and narrative strain tends towards a kind of self-parody, towards a formula. Robinson resorted to trickery too often in default of a really felt subject-matter, as in "The Whip." Yet we must not feel that between the excellence of such poems as "For a Dead Lady" and the dullness of *King Jasper* there lies only a horde of mediocre poems; on the contrary, there is no American poet who has approached Robinson in the number of finished poems of high merit. Mr. Winters' list seems to me an excellent one, though it may seem overly strict to some. In any case, it clearly indicates that Robinson is *the* major American poet of our era, with only T. S. Eliot as a peer. Of possible rivals, there is none whose claim rests on the number of *finished* poems nor on wholly achieved effects nor on the range and viability of subject. Of course, this is a controversial statement in many quarters and odious comparisons are far from the purpose; nevertheless, until such time as serious readers of serious poetry make an attempt to read and evaluate Robinson's poetry, they must take somebody else's word for it. The poetry is there—a fat volume with all the arid narratives at the end for convenience, the better poems scattered throughout. It may be that the time has come for readers of poetry to place Robinson where he belongs, to read him at any rate. This discussion has attempted to get at some of the more striking virtues of the poetry and to dispel some misconceptions, and while I suppose there are readers who do not like Robinson's *kind* of poetry, I have tried to show what we must not look for in it. It is to me important to get beyond fashion if we can and take stock of our best writers, not being deterred by what we have been trained to think about them nor discouraged by faults that loom large to us because they are not our own. If we can understand if not believe in his external irony, his cosmology, then we shall be equipped to recognize his worth in the same way that we recognize that of Swift, for example, or Mauriac. Time and fashion will have their effects, true enough, but unless we can rise above the predilections of the moment in our reading, there is little possibility of our understanding what we read.

DOES IT MATTER HOW ANNANDALE WENT OUT?

DAVID S. NIVISON

I

It is a critic's business to criticize a poet's work, not his intentions. What the poet intends, or has in mind, or is prompted by, is not only distinct in being from his poem—it is even in a sense irrelevant to it. The poet has his own emotion or experience, but in the poem, if he does well, he communicates it in such a way that it ceases to be distinctly his. He universalizes it, so that any sensitive reader may grasp the poem's meaning and appreciate its value without privy knowledge of the poet's personal history.

This view seems to me to present a paradox: it is both compelling and perplexing. It is compelling because in a way it restates our common conception of what language itself is for. And it is perplexing, not only because one occasionally stumbles over counterexamples which make one blush, but also because it seems perfectly natural, when we are trying to understand a poem or judge its effect, to ask at once what personal problem the poet was mulling over, what he was trying to say, and why.

To anyone unable to stop worrying about this puzzle the poetry of Edwin Arlington Robinson must be especially disquieting. Robinson sometimes assumes the role of narrator, and it is impossible to read such a poem as "Isaac and Archibald" and remain persuaded that the use of the first person is merely a formal device. Our impression is strong and persistent that his Tilbury Town is his home, Gardiner, Maine. He writes constantly of people. And, especially in the shorter poems, the people sometimes seem to us to be unusually real ones, not just successful characterizations but people the poet has known. Yet these characters stand on their own feet; the poems carry their own weight without any explanation of their background. It is difficult to

Reprinted by permission, *Colby Library Quarterly*, V (December 1960), 170-185.

see what would be accomplished by identfying the "real" Llewellyn or Mr. Flood, either for our understanding of these poems or for our evaluation of them.

And Robinson may well enough be talking about Gardiner when writing of Tilbury Town, in the sense of allowing his memories to enrich or even to displace his imagination, without in any sense *referring* to Gardiner when he does this. If report be true, the poet himself has had his say about this matter. James Barstow, close friend of Robinson in Gardiner and later in New York, cites George Burnham, another Robinson intimate, as follows:

> . . . . Mr. George Burnham has just recently told me—and I quote him literally—that Robinson said to him with emphasis "that neither Tilbury Town, nor any of the portrait sketches, nor the 'Town Down the River' referred to any particular place. In no instance whatever in any of his writings did he refer to anyone or any place. Tilbury Town might be any small New England . . . town."[1]

Mr. Barstow and Mr. Burnham were men I knew well and respected highly. I do not doubt them; nor need we question Robinson's disclaimer. But the matter is not quite as simple as this. The interesting question is not whether or not Robinson dealt with actual places and persons. For Robinson did not create his characters and scenes *ex nihilo*. A poet is a "maker"; but he is not this kind of maker.

A more meaningful question is this: must we, if we are to understand parts of Robinson's work, know certain things about Robinson himself—the memories, friendships, regrets, experiences, which were part of his history and so part of himself—as he brings himself to the task of writing? And if understanding a poem requires this knowledge, must we count this a defect in the poem? Many would stand on doctrine and answer that we must. Nevertheless I think I can point to cases where having additional information about a poem not only enables us to understand it better but also shows us values in it we would otherwise have missed.

"Miniver Cheevy" is one of the most familiar of Robinson's poems, familiar enough so that perhaps I need not quote it in full. Its popularity is puzzling, for I think very few understand it completely (although what I shall say is really quite obvious, and may have occurred to some; I myself owe the idea to my mother, Ruth Nivison). A pair of stanzas will start us:

> Miniver sighed for what was not,
> And dreamed, and rested from his labors;
> He dreamed of Thebes and Camelot,
> And Priam's neighbors.
>
> Miniver mourned the ripe renown
> That made so many a name so fragrant;

He mourned Romance, now on the town,
And Art, a vagrant.

The poem is said to be one of Robinson's "character sketches." But Robinson's attitude toward this character cannot be matched elsewhere in his poems. Elsewhere we find deep sympathy and withheld judgment, as in "Bewick Finzer"; a constant sense that the human psyche conceals far more than we can ever have knowledge of, as in "Richard Cory"; a deep awareness of worth in apparent failure, as in "Flammonde"; and endless unanswered questioning, as we find even in "Llewellyn and the Tree," a poem Robinson manifestly enjoyed writing.

"When were thoughts or wonderings to ferret out the man within?" he asks in "Clavering." Still, Robinson is incurably thinking and wondering, and always asking us to do likewise. It is his way with his characters, and it must have been his way with his fellow men and with the world. But in "Miniver Cheevy" this trait of endless pondering is assigned to Miniver himself, and Robinson makes fun of him for it. Indeed, instead of sympathizing with his character and wanting us to ask what more there might be to say of him, Robinson laughs at him without reserve in every line, and leaves us with no compulsion to take him seriously or to go deeper into his make-up. His faults are lampooned with what we suspect is outrageous exaggeration. Even his harmless qualities and virtues, if he has them, are presented as absurdities. The poem is on the surface at least the opposite of serious; repeatedly we are entertained with what an unkind critic would call parlor-trickery (thus, "He missed the medieval grace / Of iron clothing").

In short, Robinson talks about Miniver as he could bring himself to talk about no other man, real or imaginary—except himself. And not even about himself, I think, except in the secure company of a group of intimate friends, and then only with a guarded wry remark or sly word. If we now reread the poem, we will see that if we make due allowance for exaggeration, what is said of Miniver is applicable to Robinson himself—even (for a season) the drinking part of it.

I do not mean that Miniver is, literally, E. A. Robinson. I do mean that before we can understand the poem adequately we have to ask who it was Robinson was thinking of, and how. The "how" is important. For Robinson very often projects himself into his poems, in various ways and in varying degrees. "Mr. Robinson . . . withholds himself and studies his fellows" wrote Robert Hillyer.[2] But, of course, one can't "withhold himself" completely if one is to study his fellows sympathetically. In "Aunt Imogen," for example, after assembling his character he had to imagine what it would be like to be such a person. And he found that to a surprising degree he *was* such a person. To this extent the method of the poem is self-explorative. But if there is self-exploration in "Miniver Cheevy" it is of a very different kind. Here, Robinson is not exploring the unknown in a human individual by turning inward. On the contrary, he has set up a fiction and has developed this fiction by talking about him as he sometimes feels like talking about himself. And, of course, he is having fun—but serious fun. It is almost as if he wanted to see how the total composition would turn out if he gave this impulse free run.

Miniver, in a word, is not a character but a travesty, and "Miniver Cheevy" is not a character sketch and was never intended to be. How was this understanding of the poem reached? No esoteric information about the poem was needed (for there isn't any to be had). Close reading was all that was needed—or almost all. We also needed some knowledge of the poet's personality, and of his typical method (in order to notice that it is *not* exemplified here) of dealing with human character. The needed knowledge can be gained by anyone from a reading of Robinson's published work, taking together both poems and letters. But it is knowledge about the poet nonetheless, and is something more than a reading of this poem alone can give.

If this much be true of "Miniver," we can well imagine that Robinson may have other poems which yield their meaning less readily, requiring of us information harder to come by. We might want to complain in such cases that the poet is playing a private game, that he is not playing fair. But it is best and fairest to leave this question until the cases come up. Meanwhile, what of "Miniver Cheevy" itself? Robinson is not exactly obvious about what he is doing in this poem. Does the poem, for all we have said about it, still merit censure for making unfair demands upon the reader?

It seems to me at least arguable that Robinson's privacy in what he is about in this poem is as much a virtue as a fault. Suppose he had let us in on the game at once, by entitling his poem not "Miniver Cheevy" but, say, "Self-Portrait." I think anyone will admit that this would have been grotesque (as well as not wholly accurate)[3]—and worse, would have displayed a gross lack of modesty. Robinson does talk in this way about himself in letters to close personal friends (letters he usually asked them to burn). Here he has done the same thing in a published work of art, and the same need for privacy exists. Perhaps we should say that if he were consistent he should have burned his own poem. But I for one am grateful that he didn't.

II

I turn briefly to another example, less familiar and of a different kind. "Cortège," a poem of six four-line stanzas, is included in *Cap-*

tain Craig (1902). I do not know when it was written, but the extraordinary state of mind that produced it has a precise date. The poem has a surface meaning which is hardly difficult: two friends have died, their funeral is at hand, and the poem tells us how the poet feels about it.

But this much will satisfy scarcely anyone. And this time the widest reading of Robinson, coupled with the closest rereading of the poem, will not remove all difficulty. It might be that more information about the poem would sustain what we see simply from careful reading. And it would still be possible to treat the poem as fictional—indeed if we take it literally it is necessary to do so.

Nonetheless the impact of the poem would be greatly augmented, for we would see that Robinson was impelled to write it by the extraordinarily intense emotion of a permanent quality, rooted in an indelible chapter in his personal history. So intense is this emotion that fragments of the actual incident, irrelevant to the poem "itself"—or at least inexplicable except through an exercise of pure fancy by the reader—are still in place: "four o'clock this afternoon," "fifteen hundred miles away." These shattered pieces do, however, support the almost explicit suggestion of a despair close to distraction, at war in each stanza with reiterated and unconvincing philosophizing of the kind we find in "Leonora": "Best for them the grave today." We may view the poem as fiction if we prefer, but as a release of personal feeling it is not play-acting.

It would be a mistake, perhaps, to say that the situation which moved him to write a given poem is even a part of what Robinson *intended* the reader to think of. Nonetheless "Cortège" shows that this situation and Robinson's involvement in it is sometimes so important to him as to overshadow anything apparent on the surface in the poem itself. It must be granted that Robinson could scarcely have hoped that a poem like "Cortège" would be fully understood by anyone except a few members of his family. He surely didn't care. Such poems are in his collected works because they are a part of himself, which he might let time destroy, but which he had to preserve as long as he could. They are like personal memories, so intimately a part of what one is that one must concentrate on holding on to them yet strive to conceal them. We must grant also the unlikelihood that Robinson would have acquired the stature he has if this kind of poem were all he produced. Still, some of this poetry is very moving, and many poems which are independently quite excellent can only gain in value, it seems to me, if we know more about them. I must apologize for saying no more of "Cortège" at this time except that it was conceived one black afternoon in late winter of 1890, when Robinson's brother and sister-in-law left

Gardiner after their recent marriage (figurative death?) on the four o'clock train for St. Louis—fifteen hundred miles away.

III

The sonnet "How Annandale Went Out" presents us with all of these complexities together and an additional one: in this case, other parts of Robinson's writing may actually *mis*lead us.

To begin with, this poem is a fascinating example of a familiar problem in critical theory. Some (*e.g.*, I. A. Richards) have tried to patch up the idea that a poem "is" what the reader makes out of it (regardless of what the poet's intentions were) by admitting that not just any reader, or just any reading, will do. The importance of the poet's connection with his poem is brought back into the picture by suggesting that the poet himself is one of its readers, and that for the authoritative reading of his poem we should take the poet's own review of it at the moment creation is finished, when, God-like, he looks upon his work and sees that it is good. One trouble with this theory is that the moment of review is, of course, a "specious present." And in Robinson's case, never in the folklore of metaphysics was the specious present more specious. Not only did Robinson in this instance reread and mull over his own work; he did so over many years, and he kept on creating as he reread.

He has given us not one but three "Annandale" poems, written in different forms, in different moods and at widely different times. "The Book of Annandale" is in blank verse, and takes up more than sixteen pages of the *Collected Poems.* It first appeared in *Captain Craig* in 1902, but it was begun earlier, and is in two parts surely not written at one sitting.[4] "How Annandale Went Out," a sonnet, was included in *The Town Down the River* in 1910. "Annandale Again," a poem of forty-seven quatrains, was first published in 1929, and was probably completed within a few years of that date.[5]

The first of these poems tells of George Annandale, of a book he wrote for his first wife without being able to show it to her before she died, and of the inner self-struggle of the woman who was to become his second wife. I believe (though I shall not press the matter here) that it is related to Robinson's personal history in the same way as is "Cortège" — nonreferentially but as an intense emotional expression.

The sonnet is a monologue: a physician tells of attending a man named Annandale who is in some way fatally stricken and of ending his suffering, perhaps with a lethal injection.

HOW ANNANDALE WENT OUT

"They called it Annandale—and I was there
To flourish, to find words, and to attend:
Liar, physician, hypocrite, and friend,
I watched him; and the sight was not so fair
As one or two that I have seen elsewhere:
An apparatus not for me to mend—
A wreck, with hell between him and the end,
Remained of Annandale; and I was there.

"I knew the ruin as I knew the man;
So put the two together, if you can,
Remembering the worst you know of me.
Now view yourself as I was, on the spot—
With a slight kind of engine. Do you see?
Like this . . . You wouldn't hang me? I thought not."

I see no indication other than sameness of surname that George Annandale and Annandale are the same person. The sonnet is a strange one. There is intensity here as well perhaps, but not the sustained psychological pressure of the earlier poem.

Robinson brings the two Annandales together as a single character in "Annandale Again." Clearly he was writing long after the composition even of the Annandale sonnet. The intense tone is now gone. The speaker is again the physician. Annandale appears at his door—"Almost as if my thought of him / Had called him from he said not where"—he might indeed, be an image arising in memory. The image speaks, however, recounting as his own story the story of George Annandale in "The Book," and dwelling affectionately on the character of his present wife. Then he leaves, and is at once struck down in the street by a moving vehicle. The physician goes to his aid and is present "to watch while Annandale went out." He then repeats his justification of his act in the sonnet: "mine was the one light I had / To show me the one thing to do."

In "Annandale Again" we at last have the whole story—or so it seems. Robinson has taken the earlier fragments of the Annandale picture, fitted them together, and filled them out for us. But in doing so has he necessarily given us merely what was in his mind from the start? I do not see that we have any reason to assume this. What he often does in creating a poem is to present a few pieces of a poetic conception—pieces which could be fitted into a *number* of *different* stories —and then to suggest, cautiously and tentatively, the direction our search for an understanding of them should proceed. This is not a detective-story device. It places us in the situation we are in fact always in when we must appraise people and situations. In "The Whip" we have the method within the confines of a single poem: the speaker sees, ponders, begins to grope toward understanding, then leaves us, with a question, to go on ourselves to whatever end we can reach. In "Annandale Again" the poet takes the earlier Annandale poems and does himself—here it becomes his method of developing his fiction—what elsewhere he invites us to do.

But if this be the case we might do well to look again at "How Annandale Went Out" and ask if other stories can be built out of what it provides. There is one significant difference between the sonnet and the later poem which is on its face so trivial Robinson himself may not have noticed that he left it for us. "Annandale Again" is told directly in the first person. We do not, of course, take the "*I*" here to be in an exact sense the poet himself, though often in this manner of poem it is. "How Annandale Went Out" is also in the first person—but no, not quite! The whole poem is in quotation marks. This in itself might not be significant; for Robinson often has used the monologue device without quotation marks. But here the difference is important. In the later poem, the speaker is doing what Robinson so often does—pondering over the meaning of a story he has told insofar as he is able to tell it. In the earlier one, Robinson is exhibiting another man's self-defense—sympathetically: Robinson has accepted the defense and wants us to also. Nonetheless the tone of self-justification makes the inverted commas a necessary part of the poem. We learn nothing of the ordinary "I" of Robinson's poems save that he is meditative, puzzles over things, is sympathetic, observing, withholding judgment. Even in "Annandale Again," where the "I" is a physician, his physicianhood scarcely intrudes itself. The "I" in "How Annandale Went Out," on the contrary, is a definite character whom Robinson portrays by allowing him to speak. Apparently in twenty years' time our physician has changed his identity.

There are other things about "How Annandale Went Out" which may make us wonder whether Robinson's own extrapolation of it is the best possible one. "A wreck, with hell between him and the end" and "I knew the ruin as I knew the man" might, with a stretch of language, apply to an accident victim, but it would be more natural to imagine the physician's patient as the victim of a wasting malady for which no help could be given. Likewise "I watched him" suggests a long-enduring situation, hardly an accident scene.

I want now to suggest a way of thinking about this poem which I think will be worth trying. Consider again carefully the lines—"I knew the ruin as I knew the man; / So put the two together, if you can, / Remembering the worst you know of me." Let us try making the physical "ruin" ("They called *it* Annandale"—but is this the real Annandale?), the (real) "man," and "me" not three persons, nor even two, but *one*. We would have in the poem the words of a dead man, a physician, who had been fatally ill, justifying his own act of self-destruction. In this poetic apologia, as perhaps psychologically in life also, physician and "wreck" are split apart. Suicide becomes merely treatment of a case; he did the reasonable, if socially unapprovable, thing to do. We may also guess that something else unnamed—perhaps the nature of the malady, which he found himself (*qua* physician and *qua* "man") helpless to control? —constrains him to separate himself as "man," as human character, from himself as powerless in will, as "ruin." Now reread the poem, and notice the Beaudelairian word "hypocrite" in line three.

I am not quite sure whether what I offer here will pass as an *interpretation.* For the words, "there / To flourish, to find words and to attend:" are altogether too easily taken as meaning just what they say: we know well enough how to recognize a doctor doing his job. It is an idea, however, which the poet seems almost to be expressing in spite of himself. Do we have here another case of a poem prompted by an actual incident—an incident developed by Robinson into a conception which on its face is fiction, but an incident which continued to have more of a hold on the poet's thought than the derivative conception he worked with?

Lawrance Thompson includes this poem in his selection of Robinson's verse entitled *Tilbury Town,* published in October 1953. He has a brief note on it, which reads, in part:

> One particular example of "euthanasia" practiced by a doctor occurred in Robinson's own home; but with an ironic twist, in that it was self-inflicted. Robinson's brother Dean, who was a doctor, apparently used a needle to give himself a lethal "shot" of morphine, which was believed to have caused his death.[6]

Professor Thompson, perhaps wisely, refrains from drawing any inferences. However, if the line of thought I have suggested has proved at all tempting, this bit of family history ought to be of no little interest.

Horace Dean Robinson was twelve years older than his youngest brother. There are indications that the poet had a deep admiration and affection for him. In 1930 Robinson made a gift to the Gardiner General Hospital to equip a laboratory in Dean's memory. Details of "Captain Craig" reveal that Dean (along with Alfred Louis, an acquaintance) had much to do with the poet's conception of the "captain."

Dean, educated at Bowdoin Medical School in Portland, had started practicing in Camden. There, as the youngest member of his profession, he took the most arduous work, including frequent night calls to outlying islands. Vexed by excruciating sinus trouble and facial neuralgia, he began to relieve himself by imprudent self-medication. Presently he had become a drug addict. He returned to the family home in Gardiner, and his father bought him a drugstore, which kept him in morphine and deepened his addiction. He repeatedly sought institutional treatment, but nothing could break the habit. He drifted gradually downward. For a time he served as city physician and was well enough to earn praise for his work. He later worked as an ice-cutter on the river. After the panic of 1893 and his brother Herman's business failures in St. Louis the family's financial situation was bleak and was becoming desperate. Dean's condition deteriorated; he was often bedridden and delirious, and from 1896 until his death the family had to engage an attendant to watch him.

Dean was fully aware of the burden he had become, and, both as a doctor and as an individual struggling helplessly with his addiction, he must have known the hopelessness of his case. On September 29, 1899, he died suddenly and from no apparent cause. Edwin was unwelcome at home because of a recent incident with his brother Herman, and had been living away from Gardiner for over half a year. He was quickly called back. My mother, then age 8, has written of this event as follows:

> I remember vividly his sad pinched face lying in the casket, and the family arguing why and how he died. They decided that, realizing his plight, he had saved a little of each portion sent up from the store until he had accumulated a lethal dose. He was a Knight-Templar, and at his funeral the commandery marched in uniform to the "Dead March" in *Saul.*

Robinson left again at once.

The memory of his brother remained with him throughout his life, and with this memory a painful sensitivity about what others in Gardiner may have thought of Dean. When, in 1930, my mother suggested to him a memorial in the hospital, he took up the idea quickly, but expressed apprehension about how the proposal would be received. "I don't know anything about Gardiner now," he wrote, "but . . . it is barely possible that there are some who may not quite realize that Dean's unfortunate infirmities had no relation whatever to the fineness of his character. If he hadn't been so fine, he might be alive now and thriving."[7]

Are we to identify the Annandale of the sonnet with Dean Robinson? Here we must recall the poet's earlier objections: he might well protest that he was not, literally, writing about anyone. We can respect this protest and still ask if Dean's death supplied Robinson with his theme, his attitude toward that event becoming the attitude which we detect in the poet behind the poem.

In the spring of 1953 I was invited by a friend to spend an evening with Dr. Merrill Moore, late Boston psychiatrist and writer of many sonnets. I soon found myself with a group of others in the midst of a lively discussion of sonnetry and psychiatry with Moore at the Boston

Harvard Club. Moore had been an intimate friend of Robinson's and, though this was unknown to me, knew other members of the family.

The evening with Moore I shall never forget. Moore had a genuine light-hearted and unconcerned humility about his own work which would have drawn anyone to him. His enthusiasm for his craft was contagious, and his sympathy for all human beings was irresistible. He read sonnets, he talked about the art of the sonnet, and of the different and unusual tasks to which the sonnet form can be and has been put. In particular he called our attention to the use of the sonnet to tell a story.

At this juncture I spoke up, observed that even dramatic monologue could be found in sonnet literature, and cited, "How Annandale Went Out." Moore looked at me sharply. "That poem is about your Uncle Dean," he said. I was dumbfounded. The "inner" explanation of the poem, and with it the whole story of Dean's end, had been, I thought, a dark family secret. "What do you know about Dean?" I shot back. "Oh, your uncle (*i.e.*, Edwin) told me a lot about Dean," he answered; and that was all he would say. I thought at the moment that in respect for my own feelings he didn't wish to go into the matter before a large gathering.

But at a subsequent meeting alone with Moore a week or so later I was unable to get any more light from him on the matter. Did he have misgivings about having said boldly in so many words that the sonnet was *about* Dean? Had he perhaps once talked with Robinson about the poem, to find the conversation shift abruptly but somehow naturally to Robinson's brother, and then, familiar in his own work with a proximity between poetry and personal problems, made the identification of Annandale with Dean himself? Or did he sense in what Robinson had told him a reticence which, as a professional man accustomed to dealing with confidences, he felt still bound to respect? I shall never know.

I do know that it would not have been surprising for Robinson to have talked with Moore about Dean's case, and perhaps also about the case of his other brother Herman, who became an alcoholic after meeting with financial disaster. Both were "wrecks" in the eyes of the world. Both were men Robinson knew to be admirable. Both were elder brothers he had struggled with himself to analyze and justify. He could count on Moore's native human sympathy. And Moore must have been deeply interested. One of his principal professional interests in later years was the psychology of addiction.

I have one more detail to add, and this one too must end with a question. In 1931 Macmillan brought out a selection of Robinson's poems edited by Bliss Perry, professor at Harvard and for some years editor of the *Atlantic Monthly*, whose acquaintance with the poet went back to

1902 when he had read the manuscript of *Captain Craig* for Houghton Mifflin and Co. Near the close of Perry's preface we find the following passage:

> My function has been simply that of planning the contents of the book, and my pleasure in performing it is all the more keen because of the many sessions in which Mr. Robinson has generously given his approval of the choices made. Perhaps he will allow me to betray the secret that I have included one sonnet—impeccable in its art but *macabre* in theme—which he likes better than I do. But we drove a Yankee bargain over it, with the result that the reader now gets two additional sonnets for which the author's enthusiasm seems less warm than mine. I think that I—and the reader—have the better of this trade, but I wisely refrain from giving the titles of the sonnets under discussion.[8]

Now here is a puzzle! What is this sonnet "impeccable in its art but *macabre* in theme" which the poet would not give up despite his editor's uneasiness?

Of the twenty-six sonnets included in *Selected Poems,* I find not a few which could fitly be judged impeccable in art, but only two, I think, which qualify as *macabre* in theme. These two, I suggest are "Haunted House" (pp. 298-299) and "How Annandale Went Out" (p. 293). "Haunted House" is indeed chilling.[9] Still, I find it difficult to see what there might be in it that would have given Professor Perry such pause. "How Annandale Went Out" is another case entirely. It deals approvingly with euthanasia, and perhaps also with suicide; and Perry, I fear I must recall, was a member of the Boston Watch and Ward Society! And it is extremely—well, realistic. One can almost feel the needle—"Like this . . ."! One can only guess what the offending poem was, but I find it fascinating to speculate that Robinson may have insisted on the presence of the Annandale sonnet in the selection, possibly without being able to bring himself to own his own motives.

For if what I have said of it has any justification, "How Annandale Went Out" is like "Cortège"—so important to the poet that it was almost a part of his being, to be guarded as though it were a piece of himself. It is more accessible than "Cortège." We need no privileged information to make sense of it, indeed, to make sense of it in different ways. And perhaps Robinson intended us to have this multiple possibility of interpretation. He may even have preferred to have us take the obvious choice, of seeing in it simply a doctor's account of his dealing with a patient. The obviousness of this interpretation is perhaps a needed disguise—just as "Miniver Cheevy" needed to be at least thinly disguised—protecting the privacy of the poem's associations for Robinson himself.

Still I do not think we would want to miss the opportunity to consider the alternative I have suggested; psychologically it seems to me to be far richer. And I feel we are poorer if we are unable to consider what this poem meant to Robinson, its intimate connection with a painful memory, a case in his own life and family of that problem which always absorbed him, of worth in apparent failure, of the man enduring through the ruin. For at the level to which criticism must rise in Robinson we deal with more than just the poem; we deal with the poet as well. Criticism is more than just an esthetic-semantic problem having to do with words, and with meanings which are attributes of words —it becomes a moral problem of judging attitudes, which are the attributes of a man.

In a sense, however, it does not matter how Annandale went out. What matters is the kind of question Robinson put to the event. Here in life he was confronted with the problem which is presented in poem after poem, of a human enigma in which we must learn to accept that we must remain in ignorance and doubt. The physician is not telling us what happened—he is saying what Robinson conjectures he might have said could we ask him. For no one knows how Annandale went out, really. Except, perhaps, Annandale himself.

---

1 James S. Barstow, *My Tilbury Town* (Privately printed, 1939), 7.
2 *New England Quarterly*, III (January 1930), 149.
3 A much closer approach to a self-portrait is "Old King Cole, another pseudo-character-sketch.
4 Edwin Arlington Robinson, *Collected Poems* (New York, 1945) 195-211. In a letter to Harry DeForest Smith dated January 13, 1898, Robinson says that he "did 24 lines this afternoon beginning 'George Annandale'—a long thing in blank verse which is either good or bad." Denham Sutcliffe, ed., *Untriangulated Stars* (Cambridge, Mass., 1947), 294.
5 *Scribner's Magazine*, LXXXVI (August 1929), 129-134. One stanza seems to allude to an incident which must have occurred in Boston in 1922 or 1923.
6 Lawrance Thompson, editor, *Tilbury Town* (New York, 1953), 140.
7 Quoted from an unpublished letter to Ruth Nivison, dated September 4, 1930, now at the Colby College Library.
8 Bliss Perry, editor, *Selected Poems* (New York, 1931), VII-VIII.
9 But I will not force upon the reader the experience it will give him; it is found in *Collected Poems*, p. 870.

IMAGE PATTERNS IN THE POETRY OF EDWIN ARLINGTON ROBINSON

CHARLES T. DAVIS

E. A. ROBINSON'S imagery[1] has been the subject of much critical comment, but it is comment which fails finally to do justice to Robinson's poetic practice. For one thing, the discussion is often restricted to the light and dark figures in Robinson's verse—and these are important, certainly, though they represent only one pattern of references which the poet found useful. For another, the approach to Robinson's imagery has been too rigid; it has tended to be philosophical rather than literary and to stress, as a consequence, the poet's intellectual growth or his attitude toward life.[2] These are valid interests, of course, but they do not lead to a full or accurate description of the contribution of the image to Robinson's art.

Robinson is not, obviously, a "symbolist" poet after the pattern of T. S. Eliot, Hart Crane, or Wallace Stevens. He is not "modern," if we equate modernity with that intense preoccupation with the image which stems from Baudelaire, Rimbaud, and Mallarmé. He is "modern," if we approach poetic technique more broadly and give Robinson credit for developing a rich and personal idiom, though one which is less allusive and more formal than that of the major poets of our time. Robinson, from the beginning of his career, relied heavily upon a few carefully chosen figures, perhaps because he realized that they retarded his natural drift towards an abstract and somewhat arid speech. These, though limited in range, have great importance, because they give concreteness to Robinson's explorations of psychological states and permit commentary upon such shifting variables as success, failure; salvation, damnation; love, hate—the variables which were so often the themes for his poems.

References to light are everywhere in Robinson's verse; they are

Reprinted by permission, *College English*, XXII (March 1961), 380-386.

present in his earliest volumes, *The Torrent and The Night Before* (1896) and *The Children of the Night* (1897), and in his last, *King Jasper* (1935). In the early poems light stands invariably for the perception of spiritual truth: "a shaft of God's eternal day" (in "Supremacy," *Collected Poems,* 97)[3] or "coming glory of the Light" (in "Credo," *CP,* 94), and it is used still for this purpose in the Arthurian narratives,[4] *The Man Who Died Twice* (1924) and many pieces of moderate length like "The Three Taverns" (1920). Often in the late dramatic narratives, light comes to mean understanding or truth in human relationships, and we find it used in this way in *Roman Bartholow* (1923). Here, Penn-Raven, apparently a false friend, advises Bartholow against acting from impulse by saying: ". . . tonight a cloud is hiding you / From your soul's eye" (*CP,* 830).

Light in Robinson's verse has a multiple form and is rich and complex in its associations; it is not a simple, unvaried reference. There is, first, the whole range of specific and concrete images which define and qualify the light—"living spark" (XI of "Octaves," *CP,* 103), "spirit-gleams" and "scattered lamps" (VIII of "Octaves," *CP,* 103), "love's elemental over-glow" ("Sonnet," *CP,* 96), "sun" ("Captain Craig," *CP,* 166).[5] They are too numerous to list, especially in the early poems; there is a decided falling off in the number of direct references in the later poetry.

Nearly as important as these varied descriptions of light are certain other references so intimately associated with the primary light imagery as to be used in place of it or to reinforce it. One common extension is to music; and harmonious sound, like light, stands for the intimation of spiritual truth. Again the references are too abundant to list, but we should recall, for purposes of illustration, the "imperial music" of "Credo" (*CP,* 94), the "sure music" of "The Man Against the Sky" (1916) (*CP,* 60), the "gold-throated forward call" of "Captain Craig" (*CP,* 157), and the "infinite plain-song" and "chime primordial" of "Octave XIX" (*CP,* 106). A most effective fusion occurs in *The Man Who Died Twice,* in which music is used extensively to complement the light references. We find here "one shaft / Of singing fire" (*CP,* 947), "singing light" (*CP,* 951), and "choral golden overflow" (*CP,* 952).

Another, less common extension is to equate light with the "word," spoken or written, and the consequence is a more abstract pattern of references to "Wisdom" ("Octave XXIII," *CP,* 107), "Thought" (II of "Two Sonnets," *CP,* 89), "orient Word" ("The Man Against the Sky," *CP,* 66), and the "living Voice" in *Lancelot* (CP, 448).

The light figures have their opposites, the dark images representing the absence of truth or perception. The reference is frequent in these to night, blindness, discord, chaos, and they culminate in the conception of "The Valley of the Shadow," inhabited by the "children of the dark" (*CP*, 456). There exist also for these sets of opposites appropriate effects or emotional responses. The light images point to freedom, joy, health, and honor; the dark world is a background for imprisonment, sorrow, disease, obsession, and shame. Captain Craig, the garrulous derelict, who has been rescued by a group of friends, all regular customers of the Chrysalis tavern, puts the case succinctly at the very end of his final lecture to his benefactors:

> "There is no servitude so fraudulent
> As of a sun-shut mind; for 'tis the mind
> That makes you craven or invincible,
> Diseased or puissant" (*CP*, 166).

Though light in its various forms is to be discovered all through the Robinson canon, there are other patterns of images which acquire importance. We must understand the frequent allusion to "house" (or "tower" or "castle") and "garden" if we hope to achieve a complete appreciation of the narratives of Robinson's middle and late periods. "House" means for Robinson the form of a man's material and worldly accomplishment—in short, the design of a successful life in terms of man's limited and inadequate values. The unfeeling Matthias (in *Matthias at the Door*, 1931), rich in reputation and worldly goods, is shocked at the real state of his house, which had appeared to be sound, even eminent:

> He must be the same man,
> For he was still Matthias. If he had built
> His life like a tall tower to see it fall,
> There were no failures in his masonry,
> Nor in the safe precision of his plan;
> He had built, with all his foresight and selection,
> On undivined and insecure foundations
> Deeper than all security and precaution
> Had whispered there was reason to explore.
> He saw it lying about him, shafts and arches,
> And shattered walls, in fragments on the ground,
> And for no fault of his (*CP*, 1142).

Roman Bartholow, just recovered from a long illness, cannot build a "new" house, because, in his preoccupation with himself, he has failed to retain his wife's love and sympathy. It would be, as the wife Gabrielle remarks, a "queer new house" made of "timber out of trees that never grew" (*CP*, 757). Cavender (in *Cavender's House*, 1929), who has murdered his wife, learns from her spirit that he must come to terms with the "dark house" in which he lives and discover, if he can, new possibilities for it. Flax, the clergyman in *Amaranth* (1934), talks of his failure to find satisfying the forms of the church: "All I can tell you is, that when I found / My house was falling, I fled out of it"

(*CP*, 1388). Nightingale's large and lonely house (in *The Glory of the Nightingales*, 1930) finally achieves "glory" when it is deeded to Malory as "A pleasant home for microbes" (*CP*, 1069).

Robinson's interest in the figure of the "garden" goes back to an early sonnet, "The Garden,"[6] which is almost a pure statement of Emersonian transcendentalism. In it the poet sees his life as a wild growth surrounded by a riot of weeds, and he is struck with dismay and awe at the economy in the life process, in which "every leaf, miraculously signed," has "Outrolled itself from Thought's eternal seed" (*CP*, 87). The garden is the world, and the world rests ultimately upon spirit or God. In later works Robinson uses the garden image for the completed growth of the individual, for man's mature nature, and the poet talks less about an origin in Thought. What is emphasized, in the secular versions of the image, is the importance of roots, the dependence of the present upon the past, and the power of the most trivial action to influence the course of life.

Avon's Harvest (1921) is a perverse elaboration upon the basic garden figure. Avon's harvest is hate, the enduring enmity of a former school acquaintance whom Avon has insulted. The situation is stated fully by this organic reference:

> "and if you scent remorse,
> There may be growing such a flower as that
> In the unsightly garden where I planted,
> Not knowing the seed or what was coming of it" (*CP*, 551).

The confused and tortured life in the house of Roman Bartholow is attributed to:

> The weird existence of a tangled vine
> Too vaguely intertwisted and involved
> For sanguine gardeners . . . (*CP*, 856).

But there is hope for Matthias in the bleak prospect which life holds for him since he does not know "that in his garden / There were some perilous seeds of sympathy" (*CP*, 1144).

Another continuity of references of significance to Robinson is that involving the "flame" and the "ashes." The line of images had its beginnings also in an early poem, "The Story of the Ashes and the Flame,"[7] which suggests that "flame" is blind, shameless passion and the "ashes," perhaps, the fruitless, sterile consequence (*CP*, 84). Old King Cole, cursed with worthless sons who will come to a "bad end," advises a critical Tilbury Town: "There may be room for ruin yet, / And ashes for a wasted love. . . " (*CP*, 20). It is in the Arthurian narratives that we have a large development of the pattern. Merlin cannot forget the vision of Camelot set afire by the uncontrolled passions, hates, ambitions in Arthur's world (*CP*, 266). Lancelot describes in these striking lines the tasteless life which he cannot escape:

> "God, what a rain of ashes falls on him
> Who sees the new and cannot leave the old!" (*CP*, 385).

Guinevere pleads with the Lancelot who is returning her to Arthur for a "few crumbs of love" before these too become "a few last ashes on a fire" (*CP*, 419).

Tristram has an even weightier reliance upon the system of figures, since the references to flame and fire convey much of the overpowering strength of the love between Tristram and Isolt of Ireland. This is evident in Isolt's lament early in the narrative: "What have we done / So false or foul as to be burned alive / . . ." (*CP*, 614). The lovers' kiss is a "Blending in their catastrophe two fires / That made one fire" (*CP*, 616). Tristram's eager anticipation of a reunion with his beloved is recorded in an ambitious design in color and heat. Very nearly the last thought which the dark Isolt has of Tristram identifies him "as a thunder-stricken tower of life / Brought down by fire . . ." (*CP*, 717).

Flame or fire is the leading image in Robinson's last verse narrative, *King Jasper*. It is the fire in the factory "chimneys" which sustains Jasper's kingdom and creates his nation's industrial strength. If we view this as a controlled flame, the "miracle" which the King's wife, Honoria, says is the "landmark" of his power (*CP*, 1400), we have an uncontrolled flame too, one which means the downfall of Jasper and the death of his industrial society. The menace emerges from Jasper's past, "the dark way behind him" (*CP*, 1419), because the King has been unscrupulous and ruthless in his rise to power. It is the "demon of ambition" (*CP*, 1425) which lives in the King which has created an implacable and merciless foe in young Hebron, the son of a former associate whom Jasper has betrayed. When catastrophe does come and when the chimneys begin to topple, neither the privileged exploiter nor the coldly righteous revolutionary is permitted to survive, since young Hebron has become dehumanized and brutalized by hate, by "his inflamed / Assurance of his power to serve the world / When he is doing his ruinous worst in it" (*CP*, 1451). The King's son, young Jasper, calls the nation's industrial power the "dragon"—perhaps, because it is the monstrous creation of burning ambition, or because it is responsible for the reduction of man, making him more animal than man. Flame, though it assumes various forms in *King Jasper*—ambition at one time, hate at another, and lust finally— becomes the general detructive element which puts an end to king and kingdom. It is young Jasper's wife, Zoë, symbol of the human spirit, who alone survives the grand holocaust.

A final pattern of references which Robinson used extensively and effectively in some of his long narratives is the "sea" imagery. We have a record of the poet's fascination with the sea as early as 1910, in "Pasa Thalassa Thalassa."[8] Here, "the cold work of the sea" has accounted for the disappearance of "the sea-faring friend" who has been "Gone for a decade" (*CP*, 335). The sea seems to be in the poem an element vaguely hostile to man, indifferent to his identity, obliterating even his memory. This foreshadows one of the functions of the sea figures in the later narratives *Tristram* (1927) and *The Glory of the Nightingales* (1930).

The first image which meets our eyes in *Tristram* is that of "a blank ocean and the same white birds / Flying, and always flying, and still flying" (*CP*, 595), and Isolt of Brittany feels the indifference to her of the unfathomable force of the sea, of even the white birds:

> Not one of them,
> For all their flying, she thought, had heard the name
> Of Tristram . . . (*CP*, 595).

The concluding image in *Tristram* is of the sea too, and we discover the white Isolt once more watching the white birds. The birds still fly, but there is a change in Isolt:

> Alone, with her white face and her gray eyes,
> She watched them there till even her thoughts were white,
> And there was nothing alive but white birds flying,
> Flying, and always flying, and still flying,
> And the white sunlight flashing on the sea (*CP*, 729).

Isolt has become identified with a scene which seemed before indifferent and unsympathetic, and that identification suggests, not the restless dissatisfaction which is the earlier emotion, but resignation and peace.

The two sea images seem to be symbols of the continuum of life, of the inevitable course of an existence which is unchanged by human will or human aspiration. Moreover, the sea, in its ceaseless movement, tends to mirror the emotional condition of the actors of the drama. To a Tristram, tortured by the prospect of the loss of Isolt of Ireland to his uncle, King Mark, the sea is

> the changeless moan below
> Of an insensate ocean on those rocks
> Whereon he had a mind to throw himself (*CP*, 608),

but realization of a happier fate comes over him in

> a bright summer sea
> That like a field of heaving steel and silver
> Flashed there below him, . . . (*CP*, 690).

Here the sea provides a sympathetic background, but it retains its mystery and its distance too, and with these the promise that life has more than love and joy.

While the sea torments, then delights Tristram, and while it educates "that other Isolt" (*CP*, 695), it baffles Mark. He witnesses the shocking consequence of the concluding action of *Tristram,* the dead bodies of the lovers and the helpless form of their murderer, pleading for royal approval, and he feels the strangeness of the scene, filled with "unreal creatures of the sea / Thrown ashore dead by storms" (*CP*, 720). The sea has no answer for the king who turns and gazes into it. Mark is not graced with the ultimate perception of the Robinson hero, as is Isolt of Brittany. His lot is peace, at last, but accompanied by no understanding of the completed drama.

The Glory of the Nightingales is another impressive demonstration of facility in handling sea images. The sea for the successful Nightingale is originally an indispensable part of the background for his new home, "his impressive mansion" (*CP*, 1015). But Nightingale's belated vision reduces sadly this monument to his vanity: "Now he had sea and mansion, / And having them had nothing" (*CP*, 1015). Malory, who has come back to the town of Sharon to pay his respects at his wife's grave and to go on to kill Nightingale, can see the ocean only as death. It is comforting to him to exist in a world now so direct, so purposeful and so limited.

The discovery of a dying penitent Nightingale wrecks Malory's rigid design. Malory hesitates, and the turning of his purpose is reflected in a new meaning for the moving sea, a stirring of new possibilities:

> Those flashing waves were life; they were not death,
> Or sleep. The power that made them flash was power,
> It was not nothing. It was like a wish
> To live, and an awakening wish to serve (*CP*, 1060).

It is the sea, also, which conveys to us the preparation in Malory's mind to accept Nightingale's proposal to begin a career of medical service. There is in this reference something of the new humility which Malory is acquiring:

> they were not his waves.
> Yet surely they were flashing with a language
> That was important and inevitable;
> There were too many of them to be dismissed
> By one whose life was only a little more
> Of time than one of theirs. (*CP*, 1065).

Malory heeds Nightingale's call to help the "unhappy millions" (*CP*, 1068) of the afflicted and accepts the gift of the mansion as a hospital and a research center. Malory's awakened sympathy is recorded most fully in his reaction to the waves, as he comes finally to identify them with "toiling, weary people" (*CP*, 1071), and his resolve now is to work against pain with only "the lonely joy of being alive / In a good servitude, . . ." (*CP*, 1069).

The sea references in *The Glory of the Nightingales* serve much the same purpose that they do in *Tristram.* They are used to mirror the emotional state of the characters and to suggest that life has an inevitable movement and a grand scope extending far beyond the restricted vision and limited aspiration of the individual. In general, the sea image in Robinson's hands is a tool of rare flexibility, employed with great skill to indicate subtle shifts in attitude and dramatic tone. It manages to retain great emotional power too, despite the delicacy in gradation and shading.

There are other image patterns, though their use is more local and restricted. We can cite, indeed, the abundant animal images in *Tristram* (suggesting passion more ignoble than that indicated by the "flame"), the drums in *The Man Who Died Twice* (at first announcing death, then life), and the doors in *Matthias at the Door* and in *Cavender's House* (really part of the "house" figure and used to represent new possibilities and new discoveries for characters confined by "houses").

One of Robinson's important claims to being a modern poet rests upon his imagery. What is modern is his emphasis: the tendency to organize the references into systems, the ability to use the image at depth—with a sense of discrimination and nuance, and the incorporation of the image into a poetic idiom which is essentially personal and emotional, not general and intellectual. And this emphasis is Robinson's, even before the work of Eliot and Pound. It is Yeats who is Robinson's real contemporary and who shares his concern for the flexible figure, though to a degree which is far more intense. Both were alike in being forced to sever strong ties with nineteenth century verse and in relying partly upon a fresh approach to the image to effect the break. The liberation from earlier precedents went farther in Yeats, it is true, since Robinson never permitted an object, a picture, or a form, natural or synthetic, to carry the whole burden of a poem, as it does in many early Yeats pieces. In short, Robinson's image, for all its precision and effectiveness, seldom approaches the formal symbol, full-bodied, sufficient, and pregnant with multiple meanings. Robinson was always too conscious of values which were dramatic and moral. With him the image remained a contributing device, to be used with originality and resourcefulness to reinforce other, more basic poetic techniques.

---

1 I must thank the Macmillan Company for permission to quote from *Collected Poems* and Charles Scribner's Sons for permission to quote from *The Children of the Night* and *The Town Down the River*.

2 I have in mind Miss Estelle Kaplan's study, *Philosophy in the Poetry of Edwin Arlington Robinson* (New York, 1940).

3 All quotations from Robinson's poems come from *Collected Poems of Edwin Arlington Robinson* (New York, 1946), hereafter referred to as *CP*.

4 *Merlin; A Poem* (New York, 1917); *Lancelot; A Poem* (New York, 1920); *Tristram* (New York, 1927).

5 The first printing for the "Octaves" was in *The Children of the Night; A Book of Poems* (Boston, 1897); for "Sonnet" in *The Torrent*, 8; and for "Captain Craig" in *Captain Craig; A Book of Poems* (Boston and New York, 1902).

6 *The Torrent*, 30.

7 *The Children*, 40.

8 *The Town Down the River; A Book of Poems* (New York, 1910), 59-63.

E. A. ROBINSON AS SOOTHSAYER

RICHARD CARY

IN COMMON with most time-bound earthlings, Edwin Arlington Robinson often yearned to cut through the veils of the future and preview the "mintage of Eternity." There is no record, however, that he subscribed to astrology, phrenology, or palmistry. He is not known to have consulted gypsies, crystal balls, tea leaves, conches, Ouija boards, animal entrails, or footprints in ashes. Nor did he practice automatic writing or *sortes virgilianae*.

While he never pretended to Delphic wisdom, there was a touch of the mystical in his early claims to divination. "I have presentiments, and have always had them," he confided to his former high school mate, Arthur R. Gledhill, on August 20, 1895.[1] These intuitive flashes accord with Emerson's concept of the poet as seer, which Robinson poignantly expressed in his 1894 sonnet—a cry for a poet who would "rift this changeless glimmer of dead gray." Robinson's faith in occult cognition seems to have remained steady until the end of the nineteenth century. As late as April 18, 1900, he could say to comrade Daniel Gregory Mason, "I have a prophetic feeling. . ."[2]

The irruption of a new century had unquestionably less influence upon Robinson's shift of attitude than did his own maturing emotions and intellect. Thereafter he speaks with smaller confidence to Hermann Hagedorn about "my cloudy prognostications,"[3] and comes close to disclaiming all fatidic vision on his part in an unpublished letter to Edith Brower. Contemplating public reception of shorter poems years hence, he wrote: "It is contrary to my nature to consider these contingencies, and you will have observed that no great amount of my time heretofore has been spent in considering them" (September 24, 1925).[4]

In his poems after 1900, the flow of the future takes on a cyclic appearance. Time is represented as a continuous holocaust in which old ways dissolve in flames as the new rise from among the ashes.

Reprinted by permission, *Colby Library Quarterly*, VI (June 1963), 233-245.

Inherent in this endlessly repetitive scheme is man's tragic inability to alter his destiny. In so purposive a universe the wellsprings of prophecy are fed from more determinable areas than the purely visionary.

Merlin (1917), with its theme of inexorable futurity and a protagonist whose foresight "made other men / As ordinary as arithmetic," is perhaps the best illustration of Robinson's conclusive views on augury. Merlin is not a medieval wizard with wand, whiskers, and conical cap. He is a world-weary realist privy to time's grinding effect on human ideals. His clairvoyance comes of deep experience and a judgment made acute by knowledge of man's proneness to self-indulgence. He foresees, but he does not have the ubiquitous powers of a god or devil to manipulate events. Perceiving Camelot's coming collapse "as through a cracked and cloudy glass," he exclaims with impotent sadness: "I saw; but I was neither Fate nor God." Robinson thus reduces prophecy to modern, mundane levels—a reliable extrapolation of the known, announced without sham or passion.

Irresistibly, but with increasing caution, Robinson indulged in speculation on the probable shape of things to come. His published letters yield a plenitude of predictions within a narrow range of topics: his development as man and writer, the success or failure of other writers, the direction of world events, and—most rarely—afterlife, about which he preferred to be agnostically vague. The cast of his recipient's mind apparently governed Robinson's predictive tendency. He was in general more apt to venture into the unknown with his artistic acquaintances than with those in the prosaic professions. Compare, if you will, the correspondence with Laura E. Richards, who had an affinity for whimsy, and that with Harry de Forest Smith, a friend of his youth who became a professor of classical literature.[5] The first is lavish with annunciations; the second is almost devoid of them.

Perhaps because Edith Brower—who discovered genius in his first, self-published book, *The Torrent and the Night Before*—shared his fervor for poetry and for music, he could unbosom himself of numerous forebodings while writing to her. It may be that, as in Mrs. Richards' case, he felt the feminine temperament more receptive to unverifiable utterance and less inclined to scour him for demonstrated error. Whatever his motivation, Robinson sprinkled his long series of letters (1897-1930) to Miss Brower with forecasts, sometimes solemn, sometimes sportive, but always founded on the same brand of experience and judgment he attributed to Merlin. The following extracts from these hitherto restricted letters reveal Robinson's habitual resort to prevision and, a generation later, make for indicative comparisons between his anticipation and the actual outcome.

In the first two troublous years after the appearance of *The Torrent*

(1896), his letters to Miss Brower are most heavily punctuated with assertions about his dubious prospect as a poet. He showed remarkable insight into his own personality, made some shrewd assumptions about particular poems, but depreciated his eventual emergence as a public success. Keenly conscious of his ingrained reticence, he had told Smith in May 1894: "When I look far into the future, I see myself—sometimes in the light of a partial success—living alone in some city—Boston, most likely—with a friend or two to drop in upon me once in a while, and a few faithful correspondents."[6] With similar surety he had declared to Gledhill in August 1895 that he would "never be a Prominent Citizen."[7] Out of this firm self-knowledge he disclosed to Miss Brower (undated letter, March-April 1897) that "if ever I achieve worldly success, I'm half afraid it will finish me." He was to achieve worldly success but it did not finish him, for he never deviated from the design for living which he had outlined to Smith—mostly in New York City and Peterborough, New Hampshire, with charily selected friends and some excellent correspondents.

An amusing sidelight along these lines is Robinson's accuracy in predicting the behavior of Miss Brower's cat on his visit to her home in Wilkes-Barre in 1898. Miss Brower evidently warned him that her fifteen-year-old tom had all its life fled from anything wearing trousers and having a deep voice. Robinson, who in his time had consorted with a cat or two, wrote back evenly: "The cat and I are going to get along first rate" (January 6, 1898). Miss Brower later described the confrontation in "Memories," an unpublished reminiscence of her friendship with EAR. "The moment he laid eyes on Robinson, he went straight to him [and] jumped upon his knees." Miss Brower took this to mean that the poet was "all right."

His earliest conjectures on his ultimate evolution as a poet took on the darkling tone of this remark to Gledhill (October 28, 1896) in respect to *The Torrent:* "This book will probably mark the end of my poetical career."[8] On April 10, 1897, Robinson ruminated moodily to Miss Brower: "I don't feel that I have done very much as it is, and I doubt very much, sometimes, if ever I shall do anything better." A fortnight later he rated her for calling him "a poet, a real one," and witlessly admonished her that "those words will embarrass you some day." The publication of *The Children of the Night* (1897) bolstered his belief that he was "going in the right direction," but did not dispel his low estimate of future growth. "I realize now [December 10, 1898] more than ever my one-sidedness. This need not prevent me from doing good work but one-sidedness doesn't often go with the production of anything great. . . . The thought that I shall ever do anything even approaching it sometimes makes me laugh." Public apathy and his impregnable modesty contributed more to this unprepossessing picture than any prescience on his part. All of these dismal monitions were to prove baseless.

Because taste and self-criticism were involved in his appraisal of individual poems, he more consistently forecast their probable status. "I have done forty Octaves," he told Miss Brower in April 1897, "but I do not think they will be very well received." He was right. His Octaves are rather formidable exercises in eight-line blank verse which now and again catch the eye of a scrupulous critic but have never registered with his larger reading audience. In July of the same year he called the turn correctly on "Richard Cory." To Miss Brower he said, "There isn't any idealism in it, but there's lots of something else—humanity, maybe. I opine that it will go." In company with "Miniver Cheevy" and "Mr. Flood's Party," it is one of Robinson's most widely known and anthologized poems.

The familiar axiom that every comedian wants to play Hamlet finds its counterpart in the heart of many a poet and novelist who longs to be a playwright. Flaubert and Henry James, among countless others, broke their lances in futile efforts to create dramas acceptable to theatre-goers of their day. And so it was with Robinson. He embroiled himself for at least a decade in writing, revising, and trying to market *Van Zorn* and *The Porcupine.* They were unanimously rejected by producers who squirmed uneasily under the heavy weight of their psychological themes. Pride and frustration must have clouded Robinson's prognostic faculty when, after admitting to Miss Brower on January 17, 1916, that both plays had "fallen utterly flat," he persisted: "I nourish a more or less idiotic faith in their coming to life some day." His faith was misplaced. Macmillan had published the plays in 1914 and 1915, respectively, but neither has kindled any coteries in the intervening half-century. *Van Zorn* was performed briefly by a community theatre group at the Brooklyn YMCA in 1917; *The Porcupine* never reached the boards.

Prompt to assess his own future, Robinson was no less loath to gauge the prospects of other authors and their works. Scores of such instances are to be met in his published letters and comments. After reading only three pages of A. E. Housman, he boldly asserted that this new bard "had come to stay." Robinson was quite as sharp about Nietzsche's continuing eminence, but he miscalculated G. B. Shaw as merely an "illogical composite of red rags and white corpuscles." About Thomas Hardy he vacillated wildly. At first laudatory (he wrote a eulogistic sonnet "For a Book by Thomas Hardy"), then dour ("Nearly all of Hardy will die"), later he foretold that Hardy would "take his place among the solid poets of England."[9] While several of Hardy's novels are still at their peak of renown, the recent trend has been toward re-evaluation of his power as a poet; *vide* J. O. Bailey's *Thomas Hardy and the Cosmic Mind* (Chapel Hill, 1956), and Samuel Hynes's *The Pattern of Hardy's Poetry* (Chapel Hill, 1961).

Writing to Miss Brower, Robinson exhibited resources of strength and assurance he was not ready to unleash on the world at large. As yet a tyro (March 14, 1897), he slid from generalization to particularity with the ease of a vested pundit.

> As for the popular American story writers, who command such prices and are so ridiculously overrated, — I advise you to steer clear of them. As long as they are well advertised they will make an impression on the public, but when they die, their work will die with them. Two or three stories by Miss Jewett, two or three by Miss Wilkins, one by F. J. Stimson ("Mrs. Knollys") and a few other scattered sketches will live; but they will only live for the spirit that is in them. None of them can live for the sheer art of their making.
>
> . . . .
>
> Art for art's sake is a confession of moral weakness. Art for the real *Art's* sake is the meaning and the truth of life. This is just beginning to be understood, and it is on this understanding that the greatness of future literature depends. If Mr. Howells could realize this, he might write novels that would shake the world. . . Zola is a parallel case, but his objective power is so enormous that his work must eventually have a purifying effect.

Robinson's inability to sell his poems at this time doubtlessly darkened his animus, but it is honest to say that throughout his life he contemned the glibly commercial writer. While he was sparse as to the number, he properly foretold longevity for the stories of Sarah Orne Jewett and Mary E. Wilkins Freeman, the sturdiest pair in the New England local-color school. F. J. Stimson has sunk from the memory of all but the more zealous graduate students of regional American fiction. Howells' congenital *bienséance* never permitted him to grasp the gist of Robinson's observation, and so his novels are still read without palpitations. On Zola, Robinson was unvaryingly right: here, in his 1896 sonnet, and in his letter (April 4, 1897) to Harry Smith: "Zola is the greatest worker in the objective that the world has ever seen, and someday he will be recognized for what he is."[10]

Another of Robinson's prophecies which missed its mark was based rather in his disaffection than on any visible omens. In a moment of weariness after "doing" twenty-eight hundred lines of *Tristram,* he wrote to Miss Brower on September 24, 1925: "A long poem nowadays is at best a getting down on one's knees to invite disaster, and . . . it is quite possible that even short poems in the future will have about all they can do to survive." Since 1915 he had been turning to the longer and longer poem as his vehicle. Of the briefer pieces he had formerly proliferated, he told friends: "They just don't come anymore." Almost four decades after his doomsaying, the short poem thrives and is likely to as long as poems are written and read.

Time and again he reverted to the prodigious name of Robert Browning, most often in the vein of "Not that I dislike Browning. . ." Onerous upon his shoulders lay the mantle of "American Browning," an epithet foisted on him by his first critics and perpetuated *ad nauseum* to this day. Barring their common penchant to psychologize in depth, Robinson could not "quite see the relation between" himself and the man from Asolo. *The Ring and the Book* provoked Robinson's most frequent commentary but adduced only one prognostication (to Miss Brower, August 17, 1899). "If the poem holds its present place in nineteen hundred and fifty—for a round number—I shall be all wrong in my judgment." It has, if anything, increased in stature. In this half of the 20th century Browning, more cordially than his Victorian peers, is received as a poet of significance. Formalistic and semantic critics, particularly, uncover surpassing values in his tortuous themes and obscurant locutions. Upon Robinson, the unrelenting reiteration of the critics became more than he could bear. With jocosity born of exhausted repugnance, he finally capitulated on November 4, 1928: "I'm altogether too lazy to kill anyone—even a critic who calls me the American Browning, meaning apparently to give pleasure."

He said a good deal, too, to Miss Brower about his midwestern friend, William Vaughn Moody.[11] Despite some unconscious agitations roused in his breast by Moody's instant public acceptance, Robinson designated the approximate position now held by Moody in the hierarchy of American poets and dramatists. "I have convinced myself that he is one of the fellows whom the future will have to deal with," he wrote (December 16, 1900). On January 7, 1901, he energized this inert projection: "Moody is beyond doubt the coming man." Upon Moody's death: "He did enough as it was to give him his high place in English poetry—probably much higher than most of us realize today." This last is too generous. Moody's "Ode in Time of Hesitation," "The Menagerie," and "Gloucester Moors" are still staple fare in representative anthologies of American poetry, and *The Great Divide* must be taken into account in any history of the development of American drama. But Moody today is relegated to the echelon of minor giants, distinctly lower than Robinson himself.

In other cases where the work of his friends was involved, Robinson tended to exaggerate its potential durability. The fame of Josephine Preston Peabody, though not negligible in the first twenty years of this century, is undeniably quiescent today. Probably misled by her inspiriting companionship and her valiant efforts to get *Captain Craig* published, he overrated her tenuous verse and poetic dramas on three occasions to Miss Brower. April 28, 1901: "Miss Peabody is here with a five act drama called *Marlow*. Two acts of it gave me an impression that it may take a pretty high place." November 4, 1928: "Her place is safe enough in American literature." February 18, 1930: "She has written several things that cannot easily die."

With even less justification he bespoke a future for Henry A. Wise Wood, a superlative engineer and inventor but assuredly no poet. Robinson may have been overly solicitous because Miss Bower had introduced them to each other. "Wood brought his book the other day," wrote Robinson on April 1, 1901. "I honestly believe that he will surprise people, including himself, in the course of two or three years." And on the 28th day of the same month: "I am more than half ready to believe that that single poem will give him a place, though I don't say it to him." The poem he refers to is "The Building of the Rose," which appears in the only volume of verse Wood published, *Fancies* (New York, 1903). Neither the poem nor the book has ever attracted more than bibliographic attention.

Miss Brower's exhilarating interest in his poems during his bleakest early era must have fostered Robinson's undue enthusiasm for her own writings. In February and March of 1897 he told her, "You are going to do something infinitely finer and stronger," and "[My] faith in your ability to do remarkable work is not weakened in the least . . . it is strengthened." Robinson had rushed to read all the essays and stories Miss Brower had contributed since 1888 to such periodicals as the *Atlantic Monthly*, *Lippincott's*, *Harper's Weekly*, and *Catholic World*. Although competent in their way, they induce no spontaneous expectations of "remarkable work" to come. It was simply another example of Robinson's personal sympathies impairing the acuity of his vision.

When Robinson turned his eyes toward the world at large, however, he allowed no such considerations to befog his view. It was to him clearly a matter of whether the world had succumbed to materialism or was to be sundered by moral obtuseness (themes he brought to fruition by 1917 in "Cassandra" and *Merlin*). Or, in his lowest moments, whether the mismanaged world was hellbent on *both* those wheels. He shied at international pacts and was skeptical about any parliament of nations. He was uncannily precise about Hitler (whom he called a "neurotic fanatic") and unholy alliances between Germany and Russia.[12] He heard, on the underside of the horizon, the portentous tread of dark-skinned peoples on the march toward domination of the planet.

War troubled Robinson in a different way than it does most; he pondered its deeper consequences on human morality rather than its immediate shocks and splendors. When, sixty-five years ago, the presence of an unfriendly foreign power in Cuba caused another American president to take drastic measures, Robinson decried the impending carnage but foresaw one boon to the United States: possible purgation of tawdry standards. On April 14, 1898—three days after McKinley sent a war message to Congress—Miss Brower received Robinson's condemnation of America's "crudeness and general cussedness" which made him "sorry, and finally glad." "There will be a collapse before long," he avowed, "but it will be to get a new start." It was a dogma of his somber optimism that conscience could benefit from catastrophe, but it is a rare historian who will claim for American society any momentous gains from the experience of the Spanish-American War. Nevertheless, Robinson did recognize that this involvement might indelibly affect the U. S. attitude toward isolationism. "It is a war that will, I believe, be of tremendous historical importance," he said after the shooting started. "Cuba is a very small part of it."

In his forecasts of global events, he could be grim or gay, sometimes both in the same breath. Although accepting subjugation as a transitory condition, he reaffirmed his romantic reliance in the freedom and primacy of the individual. "The socialistic dark ages are coming, and the individual is going to 'wither' as Tennyson foresaw, but he'll swell up again after a few hundred years, and knock down the whole damned business—which is description, not profanity" (August 26, 1928).

On November 10th of the following year Robinson was far less sanguine as he surveyed the current state of world brotherhood and re-echoed his obsessive dread of the darker-hued races.

I have to bristle and spit at any League of Nations that would include this mishandled republic of ours. We would get into all sorts of a mess if anything really happened. So I believe in a League of Europe and let it go at that — though I don't see how such a thing can be with Russia and Mussolini in the way. Sooner or later the yellow men will come over and get us, and in about five thousand years there may not be any white folks left. It looks sometimes as if our part in the business will have been to make the world ready for the tinted and colored races to use. They can't do much worse with it than we have done. Meanwhile time means nothing to them — no more than life or death — and they are in no hurry — except just now in India. But that is more or less a local issue, though of course it might develop into something else. England will have to fight or get out before long — and either way will be bad for all concerned.

Passage of years has borne out Robinson's prudence in regard to international tribunals, Russia, fascist Italy, and liberated India. Jeremiahs of our day detect the yellow man's urge for world possession in Communist China's crass willingness to sacrifice one or two hundred millions of her population in a nuclear exchange with the West—confident that her remaining millions will then overrun the earth.

Conversely, Robinson could disguise prophecy as gently satiric paradox:

A few ultra-radicals don't like [*Cavender's House*] because it makes too much of love and marriage. But romance, judging from all the murders and suicides in the newspapers, isn't quite dead yet, and I shouldn't wonder if it outlived some of the ultra-radicals (June 24, 1929).

Or as burlesque:

What is New York going to look like in a thousand years, and what are people going to do with themselves? Maybe they are going to read sonnets, but there is just a possibility that the sonnets won't be mine. Perhaps by that time people won't read at all, but will just "listen in" and fly around the moon and chase after one another's wives — as they do now. Only by that time there won't be any wives, from present indications — which may simplify matters. Speaking of progress, some one with a far-seeing eye for trouble has prophesied that some generations of bobbed hair will result in whiskers on the faces of all the fairest women. It doesn't sound good, but the barbers may like it. Only there won't be any barbers, perhaps, by that time. God only knows what there will be, but one thing is certain, all sorts of people will be trying to do things that the Lord — if there is any Lord left — never meant them to do, and will make just as bad a mess of it as they are making now (September 9, 1924).

Droll about sonnets and wives and barbers, indeed, but what of only listening in and flying around the moon?

Life hereafter was a thesis Robinson chose not to joke about, nor to define too positively. In "Luke Havergal" he postulates a western gate where "the dark will end the dark" and the mysteries of afterlife unfold. In other poems he fixes his hope in a sourceless Light or a similarly vague orient Word. These were the eyes and voice of his inchoate God intimating—in the midst of this acrid existence—a far better one in the offing. With instinct his only weapon, Robinson took a brave stance at the side of teleology. On June 1, 1919, he revealed this version of the universal plan to Miss Brower: "The world, meanwhile is undoubtedly a hell of a place; and I cannot see that there would be any logical reason for its existence if it were otherwise. For if we aren't continuous," he went on irritably, "what the deuce are we anyhow, and why?"

Less than five years later he promised Mrs. Richards that "If there shouldn't happen to be any next world . . . we shall go on somehow or other."[13] Whether or not these maximal predictions of his were well-founded, no Light nor Word has yet divulged.

In the opening scene of *Merlin,* Gawaine stares broodingly into space from a height over Camelot as Dagonet asks:

Gawaine, Gawaine, what look ye for to see,
So far beyond the faint edge of the world?

Some seventy lines later Gawaine rouses himself from forebodings of disaster and answers: "I look through Time, / For sight of what it is that is to be." Throughout his life Robinson strove to pierce the temporal mists that enveloped him. The past, with its haggard memories, was better forgotten. (A gift of apples from his sister-in-law "took me back into the past—where as a rule I don't go.")[14] He preferred to think that the value of history lies in its expositions of man's weakness and folly, that man is capable of using the sad lessons of the past as rungs toward a glorious summit.

He derived patent satisfaction from thrusting outward beyond mortal range. He would have enjoyed knowing how close he came to foretelling atomic warfare,[15] the imminent moon shot, the fragility of the United Nations, and the ominous population explosion in the so-called underdeveloped countries. He may right now, in fact, be chuckling softly somewhere over the sagacity of his last line in "John Brown": "I shall have more to say when I am dead."

---

1 Ridgely Torrence, editor, *Selected Letters of Edwin Arlington Robinson* (New York, 1940), 11.
2 *Ibid.*, 29.
3 *Ibid.*, 94. June 1, 1916.
4 This is from one of 189 letters by Robinson to Miss Brower now in Colby College Library. They have since been edited by Richard Cary and published in entirety by Harvard University Press (1968).
5 Thirty-five of Robinson's letters to Mrs. Richards are included in Torrence's *Selected Letters*; his letters to Smith are presented in Denham Sutcliffe's *Untriangulated Stars* (Cambridge, Mass., 1947).
6 *Untriangulated Stars*, 156-157.
7 *Selected Letters*, 11.
8 *Ibid.*, 13.
9 References to Housman, Nietzsche, Shaw, and Hardy are from *Selected Letters*, 130, 136, 55, 45, 129.
10 *Untriangulated Stars*, 282.
11 For a full account, see Richard Cary, "Robinson on Moody," *Colby Library Quarterly*, VI (December 1962), 176-183.
12 *Selected Letters*, 175, 115.
13 *Ibid.*, 142.
14 Richard Cary, "Robinson's Notes to His Nieces," *Colby Library Quarterly*, V (December 1960), 200.
15 To Mrs. Louis V. Ledoux, February 2, 1921: "The whole western world is going to be blown to pieces, asphyxiated and starved, and then, for a few centuries we poor artists are going to have a hard time." *Selected Letters*, 124.

E. A. ROBINSON'S SYSTEM OF OPPOSITES

JAMES G. HEPBURN

IN A LETTER to Harry de Forest Smith of 3 June 1894, E. A. Robinson says of his poem "The Night Before":

> The story is unpleasant, founded upon my system of "opposites" that is, creating a fictitious life in direct opposition to a real life which I know. My recent mental disturbances have rendered some kind of more or less literary expression an absolute necessity; and this story, which by the way, comes dangerously near to being what the world calls "hot stuff" is doing me a good service in working off my general discontent. It reflects, in a measure, my present mood in the narration of things of which I know nothing except by instinctive fancy.[1]

What Robinson meant by his system of opposites, the varying extent to which the term can be properly applied to some of his early poems, and its importance in the emergence of his poetic voice and vision are the subjects of the present article. Robinson seems not to have had a clear perception of what constituted his voice and vision; but when his confusion is laid bare, one sees how it served him poetically.

The phrase "system of opposites" does not occur elsewhere in Robinson's published writings; and the absence of critical comment upon it is perhaps tribute to Robinson's general indifference to poetic theory. But the passage above and a few remarks in other letters throw adequate light upon the term. When *The Torrent and the Night Before* was printed, Robinson wrote again to Smith:

> I don't exactly understand what you mean when you say I have put too much of myself into my work. With the exception of an occasional sonnet and the obviously didactic—"damned didactic," if you prefer it so—pieces, I intended the book to be entirely impersonal. I fear you are inclined to make too much of my frequent use of the first person singular (17 January 1897).

In a letter of February 3rd of the same year he remarks that " 'The Night Before' is purely objective, and may be called anything from pessimism to rot." On April 4th he says that "Zola is the greatest

Reprinted by permission, *Publications of the Modern Language Association*, LXXX (June 1965), 266-274.

worker in the objective that the world has ever seen." Later in the year he remarks:

> If anything is worthy of a man's best and hardest effort, that thing is the utterance of what he believes to be the truth. Of course I like a joke, and I like art for its own sake; but those things in themselves are not enough. Just as deliberate pathos in literature . . . is almost always a mistake, so, I think, is mere objectivity . . . at the best unsatisfactory. So I hope you will like my "Octaves," "Calvary," "L'Envoi," etc. better than "The Night Before" (1 November 1897).

In sum, then, Robinson associates his poetry of opposites with objectivity and realism; he sees such poetry to be divorced from his own voice and vision; and he seems generally to regard it as lesser work.

Difficulties begin when one examines the chief exhibition of the system of opposites. To be sure, the situation of "The Night Before"—a man about to be hanged for the murder of his wife reviews his crime—is far removed from anything the celibate and mild-mannered Robinson ever experienced; but the fact that the poem followed as "an absolute necessity" upon Robinson's "recent mental disturbances" suggests that the removal is mere disguise. In presenting a brief account of Robinson's life, Louis Coxe remarks somewhat ironically: "To a Freudian, all things are Oedipal and there is indeed a case for seeing in Robinson's life the familiar pattern of the unwanted third son, rejected . . . by the father and kept at a distance by a too beloved mother."[2] Thus to a Freudian, "The Night Before" is Oedipal, especially in view of the fact that the poem was composed during the interval between the death of Robinson's father and the final illness of his mother. But the case need hardly be pressed so far. If one thinks of Victor Hugo's observation that we are all condemned to death, and thinks then of Robinson's reiterated opinion that he would die early ("there is not enough of me . . . to last a great many years"), one equally sees a personal poem.[3]

Perhaps, though, Robinson means "a fictitious life in direct opposition to a real life which I know" to apply more to the views of the condemned man than to his situation. Thus one might point to the fact that the man observes that "after / The last loved thing in the world has left us, / We know the triumph of hate" (ll. 243-245).[4] And one would note in contrast that Robinson himself says in a letter to Smith of 13 May 1896, "I am inclined to be a trifle solemn in my verses, but I intend that there shall always be at least a suggestion of something wiser than hatred and something better than despair." The difference, however is superficial. The condemned man is himself nothing if not solemn in his speech, and he also suggests something wiser than hatred; for in fact he has moved beyond that attitude: "So I foster / Even tonight for the woman who wronged me, / Nothing of hate . . . " (ll.

112-114), and for all who have fallen— / Even for him [the lover]—I hold no malice . . . " (ll. 364-365). He does not know the opposing triumph of love, but he is moving in the direction of such wisdom rather than against it.

The similarity of vision of Robinson and his condemned man can be inferred from other evidence. In his letter to Smith of 3 June 1894, Robinson remarks of the poem, "Here is a little observation that will come in towards the end:

> I tell you, Domine,
> There are times in the lives of us poor devils
> When heaven and hell get mixed."

The phrase "poor devils" is echoed in a letter to Smith of 13 May 1896, just at the time the poem was printed: "if some poor devil of a man or woman feels any better or any stronger for anything I have said, I shall have no fault to find." In his letter to Smith of 3 February, 1897, Robinson uses the phrase "despairing devil" similarly. One infers that the catharsis which he offers the reader is just what he says he himself experienced in writing the poem. He sees himself, the reader, and the condemned man as all poor devils in the world.

It is apparent that "The Night Before" partly expresses rather than opposes Robinson's own voice and vision. Its position can be seen more clearly by examining another early poem, *Captain Craig*. Although Robinson does not speak of his system of opposites with regard to this work, his comments on it are similar to those on "The Night Before." He writes to Smith on 2 June 1900: "There is not very much of myself [in the poem], but there are pages of what certain people take to be myself. . . . I should never have written it, as it stands, if I had not passed through those six months of hell in the College Office [as private secretary to President C. W. Eliot]." Again the acknowledgment that other people do find him in the poem, and the admission that the poem sprang from personal distress suggest that the assumed objectivity is unreal. Also the material circumstance of Craig's life is close to Robinson's own.[5] In contrast to "The Night Before," in which the similarity of voice and vision to Robinson's needs to be argued, the similarity here seems obvious. From the time of publication to the present day, most critics have taken for granted that the eponymous hero of the poem speaks entirely for Robinson.[6]

A glance at a few details of the poem may nevertheless be useful to clarify the ways in which Robinson and his hero seem similar. The poem comes close to being a monologue like "The Night Before." A narrator introduces himself and then introduces Captain Craig, who by line seventy takes over and who in monologue, letters, and testament speaks the vast bulk of the poem's two thousand lines and virtually all its philosophy. The narrator presents himself as a skeptic who listens to and is won over by Craig; but his opposition to Craig's views amounts to no more than a brief tossing and turning in bed one night, and he is thereupon the Captain's champion. His friends such as Killigrew and Plunkett have little to say, and nothing directly. The other characters who do speak to some purpose in the poem are mere instruments of Craig's viewpoint. In the Captain's first letter are described a man and a girl, the one "the child in absence" (l. 628) and the other the child "in excess" (l. 629). These are the extremes whose union produces the true visionary such as Craig: "The Child that is the Man, the Mystery, / The Phoenix of the World" (ll. 2000-01). In the second letter the Captain describes Count Pretzel von Würzburger, who is a mendicant like the Captain and who is child enough to play cradle songs on the piano. Elsewhere Craig has spoken of "God's music of the soul" (l. 197); because to the idealist death is a triumph, Craig will have a triumphal brass band at his funeral; and Craig's last word at his death, "trombones," implies that he hears "the golden tone / Of that far-singing call you all have heard" (ll. 1627-28). The incarnation of his philosophical outlook is properly a musician such as Count Pretzel. Other figures such as the soldier and Carmichael are comparable.

The views that Craig and his doubles express in the poem seem transparently the same as those expressed by Robinson in his own person in such poems as the "Octaves," "The Children of the Night," and "Credo," and in his letters. Very frequently the imagery is the same. A few illustrations may be appropriate.

> Then shall at last come ringing through the sun,
> Through time, through flesh, God's music of the soul.
> For wisdom is that music, and all joy
> That wisdom.
>
> (*Captain Craig*, ll. 196-199)

> For through it all,—above, beyond it all,—
> I know the far-sent message of the years,
> I feel the coming glory of the Light!
>
> ("Credo")

> Through dusk that hindered it,
> I found the truth, and for the first whole time
> Knew then that we were climbing. . . .
> . . . as a man, a scarred man among men,
> I knew it . . .
> The light that burned above me and within me.
>
> (*Captain Craig*, ll. 1552-54, 1562-63, 1567)

> Let us, the Children of the Night,
> Put off the cloak that hides the scar!

Let us be Children of the Light,
And tell the ages what we are!
("The Children of the Night")

These things [the present age, scientific progress, materialistic philosophy] . . . are damned uninteresting to one who can get a glimpse of the real light through the clouds of time. . . . [Christian Science] is only a stepping stone to the truth. . . .
The great scholars of the world are for the most part spiritual imbeciles, and there is where the trouble lies. The willingness "to be a child again" comes hard.
(Letter to Smith of 15 March 1897)

You see I have come to look on death as a deliverance and an advancement (*vide* "Kosmos," "Two Sonnets," etc.) and I am very glad to be able to stand up and say that I am an idealist.
(Letter to Smith of 7 December 1896)

It is hard to believe that had Robinson written *Captain Craig* by 1897 he would not have included it among such poems as the "Octaves" and "Calvary" (and presumably "The Children of the Night" and "Credo") as the higher personal poetry that he contrasts to "The Night Before" in his letter to Smith of 1 November 1897. And it would seem, then, that he describes this poem as well as "The Night Before" inaccurately. Neither presents a vision opposed to his own. That in "The Night Before" is partial; that in *Captain Craig* is truly his.

But to make such a judgment upon *Captain Craig*—to infer that it wholly expresses Robinson's voice and vision—is equally to rely upon Robinson's word. For although there can be no doubt that Robinson means himself when he uses the first person singular in such poems as the "Octaves" and "Credo," the vision in these poems and in *Captain Craig* is as exaggeratedly exalted as the vision in "The Night Before" is anguished. "The Night Before" and *Captain Craig* present, in fact, the two poles of Robinson's experience. The circumstances of their heroes are identical in the respect that they are men who have been scarred by life and who are now at the point of death; but Craig has won his way to love, truth, and light, whereas the condemned man has sunk too deeply into passion and darkness to attain more than a liberating glimpse of what Craig sees. As man and poet, Robinson had ideas about what he wanted to see and what he ought to see; but actuality—what he did see—was something else again. In the letter of 15 March 1897, in which he speaks of the glimpse of light through the clouds, he adds:

It is that glimpse that makes me wish to live and see it out. If it were not for that glimpse, I should be tempted, as Tennyson used to be, to stick my nose into a rag soaked with chloroform and be done with it—that is, if I could screw up the courage. But now, thank God, that is not the kind of courage I am praying for; what I am after is the courage to see.

Remembering too that the exalted vision of *Captain Craig* followed upon the "six months of hell" in Cambridge, one is brought after due reflection to the opinion that the poem is not one whit more wholly Robinson's voice and vision than "The Night Before." Indeed, it seems less.

It must be concluded that although Robinson was aware that the voice and vision of some of his early poems were only more or less his own, he had an imperfect and inconsistent notion of what in them was "opposite." The situation is fascinating because his best and most personal poetry is often that poetry which he regarded as alien and inferior. At the same time, one of his best poems, "Luke Havergal," is not to be understood without invoking the system of opposites in a significant way.

II

Among the early poems, probably the least successful are those such as the "Octaves" in which Robinson the moralist and seer speaks directly and publicly to his audience without a trace of irony. If anything makes *Captain Craig* a better poem, it is the nominal disguise of person and the occasional irony with which Craig regards himself and is regarded by the narrator's friends. But these things apart, the voice of Craig has the same high moral tone as that of Robinson in his own person in the "Octaves."[7] The voice is pitched slightly less moralistically in such poems as "The Torrent" and "Supremacy," in which Robinson mainly presents an image which contains the moral point. At a still lower pitch are some of the portraits: "Reuben Bright," "Cliff Klingenhagen," and "Richard Cory." How different the voice is can be seen by comparing the ending of "Richard Cory" ("And Richard Cory, one calm summer night, / Went home and put a bullet through his head") with the typical ending of one of the "Octaves" ("That record of All-Soul whereon God writes / In everlasting runes the truth of Him"). But the difference should not obscure the fact that the moral intention in both sorts of poems is the same. Characteristically in the poems of an explicitly high moral tone, the last line or lines provide the final uplift and vision: it is here that we get "untriangulated stars," "the coming glory of the Light!" and "dead men singing in the sun." In the portraits the last lines are no less indispensable, but they leave to the reader a task of interpretation. Uplift and vision follow only upon the reader's success. The obvious irony of "Richard Cory," that the envied and happy man is unenviable and unhappy, is intended to bring the reader to an awareness of the light that both Richard Cory and the people on the pavement fail to see. The greater irony of the poem, then, is its irony of voice: the moralist and seer forswears his characteristic tones and assumes the manner of one of the unenlightened.

In what are probably the two best early poems, "The House on the Hill" and "Luke Havergal," Robinson completes the descent from a high moral tone. The special interest of "The House on the Hill" is that two versions of it show him eliminating the moralistic voice. The poem as it originally appeared in a letter to Smith of 25 February 1894 is as follows.

> They are all gone away,
>   The house is shut and still:
> There is nothing more to say.
>
> Malign them as we may,
>   We cannot do them ill:
> They are all gone away.
>
> Are we more fit than they
>   To meet the Master's will?—
> There is nothing more to say.
>
> What matters it who stray
>   Around the sunken sill?—
> They are all gone away,
>
> And our poor fancy-play
>   For them is wasted skill:
> There is nothing more to say.
>
> There is ruin and decay
>   In the House on the Hill:
> They are all gone away,
> There is nothing more to say. . . .

In the letter, Robinson describes the poem as "a little mystical perhaps" and also as "poetry of the commonplace." Although he does not suggest so, the terms are presumably contradictory, the mystical element pointing to a meeting with the Master in the next world and the commonplace keeping the focus upon the present plain world. The failure of the poem in this first version is that the contradiction does not become a poetic irony comparable to that which sustains "Richard Cory." Instead of commonplace language and imagery whose reverberations are mystical, there is merely a clash of tones. The formal, moralistic diction of the third stanza jars against the plain language of the first stanza, and the return to plain language in the final stanza jars again. Unlike other early poems with a moralistic voice, though, this one does not provide the rising note at the end, and even the voice in the third stanza is softened by the interrogative form.

Robinson's revision is to eliminate the moralistic strain altogether, so that the mystical meaning is entirely to be inferred. Nor does he replace the moralistic strain with the slightly ironical tone of the speaker in "Richard Cory." He gives nothing away: his voice is somber and detached; he relies upon the general simplicity and repetitiveness of his diction to yield the overtone of meaning. In the revision, the second, third, and fourth stanzas read thus:

> Through broken walls and gray
>   The winds blow bleak and shrill:
> They are all gone away.
>
> Nor is there one to-day
>   To speak them good or ill:
> There is nothing more to say.
>
> Why is it then we stray
>   Around that sunken sill?
> They are all gone away,

One might describe the revised poem as an attempt to set voice and vision at a far remove from each other, not through verbal irony (in which distance dissolves as soon as the irony is grasped), but through a neutralization of the resonant voice that is ordinarily to be associated with a moralistic vision.[8]

The question is whether readers of the poem in its final version understand it in the way that Robinson presumably intends it to be understood. The reverberations seem to this reader to be less lightening than darkening, less mystical than materialistic. Robinson seems to have put an almost impossible burden of interpretation and illumination upon his audience, to have defeated his announced intention of always leaving his audience with "at least a suggestion of . . . something better than despair" (letter to Smith of 13 May 1896). One is inclined to say that of all the poems thus far examined, "The House on the Hill" comes closest to being a poem of opposites (though not exactly in the sense that Robinson himself meant): it presents a powerful case for despair by a man who professed to have hope. The ramifications of the situation can best be explored by looking at "Luke Havergal," upon which there exists more comment by both Robinson and the critics.

Not least among the critics of that poem is Theodore Roosevelt, who in his review of *The Children of the Night* confessed that although he liked it he could not understand it. In 1956, Robert David Stevick came to the same conclusion. Reviewing several interpretations of the poem, he took their irreconcilability to be "good evidence for its lack of intelligibility"; but he also asserted that the poem "is a rare example in Robinson's verse in which unintelligibility is not damaging."[9] The situation is perhaps less difficult than Stevick sees it to be, since not all the interpretations are equally legitimate; but the fact remains that most critics have liked the poem in spite of being puzzled by it. The main problems of the poem are the following: (1) is the speaker ("Out of a grave I come to tell you this") to be identified with Luke's presumably dead lover ("Yes, there is yet one way to where she is")? (2) does the speaker recommend death? life? life after death? and is his counsel to be regarded by the reader as wise? and (3) what specific interpretations are to be put upon "western gate," "eastern skies," "night," "dawn," and other symbols? Perhaps the main stumbling block for the critics has been the fact that the imagery of the poem is Robinson's familiar imagery of light and darkness, and the temptation has been to read the poem as one more expression of his quasi-religious outlook. Thus one critic identifies the western gate with Christianity, the eastern skies with Eastern religions, and explains the poem as an exhortation to Luke to choose the former.[10] Other critics connect the western gate merely with faith or the future.[11] But most of them are also uneasily aware of a contrasting implication. Yvor Winters states the dilemma succinctly: "It might be said, I presume, that the poem seems to display a faith in life after death; but if one considers the intense desolation of the tone, it becomes rather an expression of longing for death, of inability to endure more."[12] The way out of the impasse has been pointed to by a few critics, but they do little more than note the comments by Robinson that imply an unusual intention.

The first of the comments appears in a letter to Smith of 14 December 1895: "I also have a piece of deliberate degeneration called 'Luke Havergal,' which is not at all funny." The second is in a letter of 18 May 1900, to Daniel Gregory Mason, in which he refers to the poem as "my uncomfortable abstraction."[13] Both references suggest the unpleasant and alien qualities that are associated with his poetry of opposites in his letter of 3 June 1894; and the first makes an illuminating allusion to Max Nordau.[14] There is no doubt that in some respects Robinson was sympathetic to Nordau's onslaught upon modern art in *Degeneration.* In one of his letters he remarks that the *Yellow Book* was "an elegantly got up fake"; in another he gives reserved approval to Nordau's attack upon Zola; and in *Captain Craig* he has Craig condemn Swinburnian poetry.[15] Nordau's general theory of art requires that it be expressive but not unhealthily so, and expressive rather than objective. Robinson's remarks about the "morally debilitated" art of Gautier (in a letter to Smith of 20 May 1894) and his relegation of his poetry of opposites to an inferior status indicate broad agreement. In the very same years, though, Robinson wrote in praise of Zola, and in the late nineties he was being swept off his feet by Wagner, who for

Nordau was a prime example of degeneration. What perhaps was most likely to put Robinson off was that Nordau's general description of the degenerate man must have struck home at several points. Despondency, an inclination towards reverie, intellectual doubt, and an inability to share in normal human labor are some of the terms of Nordau's indictment, and Robinson could hardly have avoided recognizing their applicability to his own case.[16] But he must have had too much egotism, Puritanism, and good sense in him merely to have pleaded guilty. At any rate, as early as 1894 he wrote "A Poem for Max Nordau," which mocks Nordau's attack on Swinburne by being Swinburnian. The poem is negligible, no more than an exercise. But its very existence, along with Killigrew's *fin de siècle* poem in *Captain Craig*, shows Robinson to have written poetry in a mode that he himself opposed and labelled "mere mellifluous rhyme" in the "Octaves." Here is a poetry of opposites. And "Luke Havergal," by being a piece of deliberate degeneration, presumably belongs in the same category. The poems differ, though; for "Luke Havergal" is Robinson at his best, and its presentation of a degenerate attitude is in truth an expression of profound personal feeling.

To regard the poem as a piece of deliberate degeneration, one must assume that the speaker voices despair in his meaning as well as in his accent. He is addressing Havergal, whose beloved has died, and he is counselling suicide. He is a projection, an objectification, of the voice of despair in Havergal himself. In the first stanza he tells Havergal to pursue death: go to the western gate where the sun dies, where the autumn leaves die, where the wind moans. In the second he denies the possibility of any human recovery from despair: no dawn can rift the fiery night of Havergal's anguish; only the darkness of death can end his darkness. The speaker then presents an image of the whole universe dying ("God slays Himself with every leaf that flies"). In the third stanza he acknowledges that his is the voice of death ("out of a grave I come"), and admits that the enemy to his own counsel is love. He must quench the kiss—the memory of love and the desire for life—that still prevents Havergal from committing suicide and following his beloved into death. The final stanza largely repeats the first, with the speaker emphasizing that Havergal should not try to find an explanation for death: he should abandon all feeling and die.

The difficulties with this interpretation are first of all problems in irony. In the first and fourth stanzas the speaker says, "if you trust her she will call": in the third he says that the way to where she is is "one that faith can never miss." In order for the interpretation to stand, these lines must be understood ironically; but since the speaker of the poem is not being ironical, the reader may be misled. Only from the pervasive gloom of the poem is the reader enabled to see that what the speaker calls trust and faith must be distortions of conventional Christian notions.[17] The other difficulty concerns Robinson's imagery. In a certain respect it merely repeats the imagery of other poems. Darkness is spiritual and literal death, and light is truth. But when the speaker of the poem says, "No, there is not a dawn in eastern skies," he means it entirely, whereas when the speaker of "Credo" says, "No, there is not a glimmer, nor a call," he means it only for the time being, and by the end of the poem he rises out of such despair to say that he feels "the coming glory of the Light!" Similarly the paradox that "the dark will end the dark" employs Robinson's customary symbolic meanings, but it diametrically opposes his belief that the light will end the dark. No other phrase of the poem more plainly sets the speaker at odds with Robinson the moralist and seer. One or two familiar images in the poem present more of a problem. When the speaker says that the remembered kiss "blinds you to the way that you must go," he must be understood ironically, as in the manner of his speaking about trust and faith. In poems such as "The Children of the Night" and "The World" "blind" refers to spiritual blindness; but what "blinds" Havergal is a memory of love and life that may save him from suicide. Only a counsellor of despair could call such a memory blindness.[18]

The problems in interpreting "Luke Havergal" as a piece of deliberate degeneration are incidental ones. At most they suggest minor flaws of composition. But what of the poem as a whole: is not there a general defect in a poem that so consistently confuses its readers? Perhaps not; for in a way the poem has never been confusing. No critic who has commented on the tone of the poem has ever described it as anything but despairing. But instead of listening to that tone, looking steadily at the poem, most critics have turned away to find an interpretation consonant with Robinson's general philosophical outlook. At least two of them have admitted to being defeated by the tone: the interpretations they have arrived at seem to them less important than the melancholy tone.[19] But that melancholy tone itself renders Robinson's intended meaning in a most powerful way.

Looking back now at "The House on the Hill," one might suspect that the bleak tone of the final version of the poem does not defeat Robinson's mystical intention, rather that the mystical intention refers only to the first version, and that in revising the poem Robinson undertook the same sort of task as in "Luke Havergal": to express a viewpoint totally at odds with his professed outlook. Consider such an attempt in the light of the moralistic poems. Broadly speaking, the moralistic poems take two paths: either they begin strongly and continue strongly to the end, as with most of the "Octaves" ("We thrill too strangely at the master's touch" is complemented by "Is always and unfailingly at hand"), or they begin in despair and rise to triumph, as with "Credo" ("I cannot find my way" yields to "I feel the coming glory of the Light!"). "The House on the Hill" and "Luke Havergal" might be described as experiments in writing only the first half of "Credo."

But both poems are too impressive to be regarded merely as experiments. In a letter to Smith of 17 April 1892, Robinson quotes a portion of "Supremacy," a moralistic poem that rises in the manner of "Credo" from a first line that reads, "There is a drear and lonely tract of Hell." Robinson remarks upon the poem: "I don't know how long this Hell business will last, but I may sigh out two or three more. It is a damned cheerful subject and my muse is merry whenever she gets into it." "Merry" must mean "inspired," since Robinson's poetry is never merry; and Robinson must be recognizing the fact that his best poetry speaks of hell rather than of heaven.

III

Although Robinson's critics have not been hesitant about making final pronouncements upon him, there can be little doubt that the past thirty years have provided just the wrong sort of atmosphere for an adequate appraisal. "Verse that is to easie" was R. P. Blackmur's judgment upon *Talifer*, but what has been easier than the critical stance itself? Everyone knows that morality and philosophy are not poetry, and even Robinson's most sympathetic critics invariably make apologies. But the present high critical tone was not always taken, and may not be in the future. One suspects that a preoccupation with symbolic meanings is not so far removed from an interest in explicit meanings as is often assumed. Suppose, though, that Robinson's poetry is indeed defective to the extent that it is philosophical and moral. Will the judgment have to be modified if the voice of the poetry is an opposing voice?

"The Man Against the Sky" offers such a problem. As Robinson wrote to one of his friends, the purpose of the poem was "to cheer people up";[20] and the poem is a straightforward enough review of various philosophical attitudes available to man, with Robinson pointing out the sole satisfactory one. Ask, though, where the elevated moralistic voice is, and the answer is that it evidences itself in the seven lines (out of three hundred and fourteen) that describe the way to salvation: "But this we know . . . " (ll. 226-232). Nothing more remains of the confident moralist of "The Children of the Night"; the rest belongs, in a muted way, to the mood of "Luke Havergal," from the sunset image with which the poem opens to the final darkness of the last lines. Judge the poem to fail in fulfilling the poet's intention, to contradict its meaning in its voice, to be unpoetic insofar as it is philosophical and moralistic. Then imagine a critic who nevertheless regards the poem as the equal of any other American poem of comparable length: he listens to the discoursing melancholy voice, and is satisfied to hear it; he says that similarly he is unconcerned with the hope that T. S. Eliot constructs in *Ash Wednesday* but is moved by the accents of despair ("Because I do not hope"—"And let my cry come unto Thee").

It is tempting to say that the dilemma of Robinson's career was the struggle between true voice and false belief. The latter induced him to assume the false voice of the prophet; it also led him to see his poetic function in grandiose terms that made the long narrative poems inevitable. The true voice had at first to express itself in the ironical modulations of "Captain Craig" and "Richard Cory," in the opening of such poems as "Credo" and "Supremacy," and in the supposedly false belief of the poetry of opposites.[21] It came ultimately to dominate his poetry, and to provide its richest occasions, not only "Luke Havergal" and "The Man Against the Sky" but other lyric poems such as "For a Dead Lady" and passages such as the opening of *Cavender's House* and the close of *Tristram.*

Inevitably one is led to ask whether the dilemma explains Robinson's failure to be a great poet (for his failure preoccupies his critics). Had he understood himself and his poetry more clearly, he would not have cried, "Oh for a poet—for a beacon bright / To rift this changeless glimmer of dead gray," and he would not have made the mistake that most critics regard the long narratives as being: poems whose large intentions are flawed by a deficiency of energy. But what instead would he have done? He might, for one thing, have seen the uselessness of poetry itself, and been still less of a poet. At best he would have avoided the seven offending lines in *The Man Against the Sky* and would have written several more lovely lyrics of despair in the manner of "Luke Havergal." His position in American letters would not be significantly improved—and there would be readers to regret that he did not write the long poems that for all their defects have unforgettable passages.

R. P. Adams provides the alternative way out of the dilemma: Robinson should have abandoned despair rather than philosophy. As Adams describes his situation, Robinson was susceptible to the chill that late nineteenth-century science laid upon most thinking people, describing for them a universe that was mindless, aimless, dead. Robinson had enough wisdom to recognize the inadequacy of the scientific vision, but he lacked a strong alternative conviction. The consequence was that the access of creative energy that comes to the man of strong positive belief never came to Robinson; he was unable—in contrast, say, to Yeats—to rise out of malaise.[22] Adams' view has much to recommend it, but it does not take into account what for this critic is the central fact of Robinson's poetry: that it is always at its best when it is despairing. To make Robinson a greater poet by eliminating the characteristic quality of whatever greatness he does possess is to transform him into an altogether different poet.

We are left, perhaps, with a poet for whom a significantly different fate was not possible. In any event, his dilemma was not a simple one. In a letter to Smith of 7 December 1896 he writes, "I am an idealist. Perhaps idealism is the philosophy of desperation, but I do not think so." He recognizes here the inescapably twofold vision of the idealist; he denies only that the vision of the actual world need be one of despair. Such a twofold vision implies, for a poet, a double voice. Rephrase Robinson's dilemma as a conflict between two true voices, or between two true visions, and there is no way out of it. The justification for regarding the dilemma as one between true voice and false belief is only that Robinson seems at once to have failed to see how very somber and compelling the one voice and vision were, and to have overestimated the other voice and vision both poetically and philosophically. A poet, of course, is not required to see himself and his poetry clearly. Why should Robinson realize that his poetry of opposites was closest to his heart? Why should T. S. Eliot realize (until three decades later) that the impersonal poetry produced by a catalytic agent was his own demon speaking? Any stratagem is permissible to protect poetic self-confidence from despair or self-consciousness.

---

1 *Untriangulated Stars: Letters of Edwin Arlington Robinson to Harry de Forest Smith, 1890-1905*, edited by Denham Sutcliffe (Cambridge, Mass., 1947). Quotations from this volume are generally identified by the dates of the letters in which they appear.

2 *Edwin Arlington Robinson* (Minneapolis, 1962), 11.

3 Robinson makes the comment in a letter to Arthur R. Gledhill: *Selected Letters of Edwin Arlington Robinson*, edited by Ridgely Torrence (New York, 1940), 11. See also 50. Friends such as William Vaughn Moody regarded his character as "mortuary."

4 Except as noted otherwise, all quotations of Robinson's early poetry follow the texts of the first editions of *The Torrent and the Night Before* and *The Children of the Night; A Book of Poems* as reproduced in *Edwin Arlington Robinson, Selected Early Poems and Letters*, edited by Charles T. Davis (New York, 1960).

5 Craig is poor and an outcast, as was Robinson at the time he wrote the poem. Of course, Craig's material circumstance is of negligible importance except in a symbolic way: he has rejected materialism and is rejected by a materialistic society. Thus one could say that he is as much like Christ (see ll. 1072 ff.) as he is like Robinson or—for that matter—Alfred Louis. With regard to character, Craig seems equally, except for his garrulity, a self-portrait. In "Early Letters of Edwin Arlington Robinson," *Virginia Quarterly Review*, XIII (Winter-Autumn 1937), 57, Daniel Gregory Mason describes Robinson in a way that very aptly applies to Craig: "Admirable, all through this time [when he was distressingly poor"], was his half serene, half humorous detachment from his surroundings." The two articles that deal with Louis—Denham Sutcliffe, "The Original of Robinson's Captain Craig,"

New England Quarterly, XVI (September 1943), 407-431; and Robert W. Hill, "More Light on a Shadowy Figure," *Bulletin of the New York Public Library*, LX (August 1956), 373-377—have nothing to say on the point.

6 See, for example, the early review in the *Nation*, LXXV (1902), 465; Harriet Monroe, *Poets and Their Art* (New York, 1932), 3-5; and Horace Gregory and Marya Zaturenska, *A History of American Poetry (1900-1940)* (New York, 1946), 119-121. Robinson's preoccupation with success-in-failure and failure-in-success has ambiguities connected with those with which this article is concerned, and in *Captain Craig* they have occasionally fostered misunderstanding. Harriet Monroe, writing her discussion of the poem around 1924 and bringing to bear on it her own temporarily pessimistic outlook, thinks that Robinson is rightly arguing that success is impossible in human life; in the same book, pp. 100-105, but six years later, she rejects the validity of the despair that she sees in *The Waste Land*. Louis Coxe, p. 24, refuses to identify Craig with Robinson, but he does not argue the issue. Evidence that suggests their single identity is given in nn. 5 and 7, and in the parallel passages quoted in the discussion below.

7 T. S., Eliot's *The Three Voices of Poetry* (Cambridge, England, 1954) can be usefully applied to *Captain Craig* to show that it is characteristically in the voice of the poet addressing an audience. Robinson's avoidance of dialogue in the poem—perhaps a reflection of a difficulty in writing convincing dialogue (a difficulty that he transforms into an artistic principle in letters to Smith, *Untriangulated Stars*, pp. 205, 210)—precludes, according to Eliot, the creation of voice and character distinct from the poet's own. Robinson's sending the narrator on a trip and having him return only in time for Craig to die are transparent devices that enable the poem to proceed via letters and testament rather than dialogue. There is a nice irony here: the non-stop talker Craig has no more a voice of his own than a latter-day cousin such as the hero of Wallace Stevens' *The Comedian as the Letter C*, who never says a word. Even in Robinson's later poetry, in which there is dialogue aplenty, the situation does not seem to be significantly different. One infers from the tones of these poems that the speaking characters are perhaps always Robinson himself.

8 There are other changes of negligible importance—punctuation and capitalization—in the revised poem. In editions of the *Collected Poems* there is a further change: in line 11 Robinson reverts from *that* to the original *the*.

9 "E. A. Robinson's Principles and Practice of Poetry," diss. (Univ. of Wisconsin, 1956), 124, 126. Stevick's discussion in Ch. II of Robinson's characteristic indirection of statement broadly supports the thesis of the present article.

10 Mathilde M. Parlett, "Robinson's 'Luke Havergal'," *Explicator*, III (June 1945), item 57.

11 Walter Gierasch, "Robinson's 'Luke Havergal'," *Explicator*, III (October 1944), item 8; A. A. Raven, "Robinson's 'Luke Havergal'," *Explicator*, III (December 1944), item 24.

12 *Edwin Arlington Robinson* (Norfolk, Conn., 1946), 35.

13 *Selected Letters*, 30.

14 The following discussion makes some use of the discussions of Nordau by R. P. Adams, "The Failure of Edwin Arlington Robinson," *Tulane Studies in English*, XI (1961), 131-134, and by Edwin S. Fussell, *Edwin Arlington Robinson; The Literary Background of a Traditional Poet* (Berkeley and Los Angeles, 1954), 122-125.

15 *Untriangulated Stars*, 168, 229, and ll. 1153 ff. in *Captain Craig*.

16 On Robinson's intellectual doubts see H. H. Waggoner, "E. A. Robinson and the Cosmic Chill," *New England Quarterly*, XIII (March 1940), 65-84, and R. P. Adams (see n. 14) in his general discussion in his article, 97-151. In the *Virginia Quarterly Review*, 53, Mason notes Robinson's "helplessness in practical affairs," and Robinson himself, in a letter to Smith of 4 February 1894, expresses his unhappy awareness of the fact.

17 In editions of the *Collected Poems* Robinson made a few revisions in the poem, among them a change from "trust her" in the first stanza to "listen." However, he retained "trust her" in the final stanza.

18 The situation may be more complex. Robinson was often concerned with love that is blind; and the suggestion of passion in Havergal's love may be meant to imply its similarity to the "blinded love" of the condemned man in "The Night Before" (l. 203). Had Havergal's love been purer, the death of his beloved would perhaps not have led him into thoughts of suicide. "John Evereldown," a poem remarkably like "Luke Havergal" in both its imagery and idea, portrays a man "pointing away from the light" to "follow the women wherever they call."

19 Raven in *Explicator* and Adams, 130, 135.

20 *Selected Letters*, 92.

21 How common Robinson's predicament must have been in his day can be seen by a glance at Robert Frost's early poems. There are the same extremes, the elevated moral tone in "A Prayer in Spring" and "Revelation" and the melancholy tone in "Ghost House" and "A Dream Pang." The slight impudence in the last lines of the two former poems marks their chief difference from the eighth and final stanzas of "The Children of the Night." Frost also undertook a *fin de siècle* exercise in "A Line-Storm Song."

22 Adams' article is devoted to this argument.

E. A. ROBINSON'S POETICS

LEWIS E. WEEKS, JR.

I

Why a Poet Writes

ALTHOUGH Robinson was content to write poetry without theorizing extensively about it and had a rather low opinion of self-criticism and self-interpretation,[1] it is possible to discover an interesting and illuminating "poetics" in his letters and works. This subject is particularly pertinent in a period when rapid change, automation and nuclear arms bring bewilderment, terror, and inspiration all at the same time and when art responds with a frantic series of experiments that leave the sincere critic groping for standards and questioning the convictions of the artist. In view of the present dehumanization apparent in much of our culture, it is worthwhile to reexamine the compassionate concern of one of America's greatest poets.

For Robinson, the question, Why does a poet write? is of particular importance in view of his long struggle for recognition. It was a struggle darkened by personal tragedy, lack of encouragement, material poverty, self doubts that were strangely compounded with confidence, a long bout with alcohol, and a perhaps over-magnified sensitivity that was frequently expressed in his letters and that spoke in poems such as the sonnet "Dear Friends." In the face of such obstacles, against all apparent reason, confronted by indifference and even hostility, with the bare bones of failure rattling loudly in his ears year after year, why does a man continue to write poetry? Bearing witness to the answer that is no answer but which has been echoed since poets began to write, Robinson's is that a poet writes because he must. In 1893, when he was twenty-four years old, Robinson wrote to a friend: "I will make a clean confession and say that writing has been my dream ever since I was old enough to lay a plan for an air castle. Now for the

Reprinted by permission, *Twentieth Century Literature*, XI (October 1965), 131-145.

first time I seem to have something like a favorable opportunity and this winter I shall make a beginning. If I make a failure of it, and the chances are about ten to one that I shall, my life will be a disappointment and a failure."[2]

Three recurrent themes appear here: first the fact that poetry has been the goal since early youth, second the fear of failure, and third the realization that there is nothing that would bring satisfaction except poetry. It is not surprising that Robinson should have had his moments of doubt and discouragement; the wonder is that they were not more frequent and completely destructive. On another occasion he wrote to a friend, allowing a few more years to prove himself, indicating the possibility that he might have been laboring under a delusion as to his poetic talent for fifteen or sixteen years, and shuddering over the fact that he might have to give up his dream.[3]

One of these periods of doubt, Hagedorn points out, resulted in the decision to take a job and consequently in the haunting sadness of the lovely "Ballade of Broken Flutes" addressed to his friend and mentor, Dr. A. T. Schumann.[4]

> No more by summer breezes fanned,
> The place was desolate and gray;
> But still my dream was to command
> New life into that shrunken clay,
> I tried it. And you scan to-day,
> With uncommiserating glee,
> The songs of one who strove to play
> The broken flutes of Arcady.
>
> Envoy
>
> So, Rock, I join the common fray,
> To fight where Mammon may decree;
> And leave, to crumble, as they may,
> The broken flutes of Arcady.[5]

On this occasion Robinson didn't take a job, didn't become respectable. For him it seems literally to have been quite true that he could do nothing but write poetry.[6]

Moreover there is abundant evidence that, for Robinson, the combination of a job that paid but only left part time for writing was intolerable. His restricted output while working on the New York subway and the same problem—even less accountable on the grounds of fatigue and mental distress—during the period of his sinecure in the Customs Service supports this contention. After less than a year spent as one of President Eliot's secretaries at Harvard, Robinson in a letter to D. G. Mason tells of the profound relief he felt upon giving up the position, "feeling every morning the joy of a liberated idiot for the thought that I am no longer a necessity in University." He goes on to speak movingly of a mutual friend, Philip Henry Savage, who had died a short time before, had been a promising poet, and had faced the same problem Robinson was plagued with:

Do you know that I have wondered sometimes if Savage was not often the victim of what the world has a way of calling a good situation? Very likely this is fancy, but those infernal photographs of him tell me things that it makes me sick to think of. The octopus of superficial self-respect—as opposed to the other, which I grant may be carried too far—he refuses somehow to take hold of me—is worse than anything that Hugo or Jules Verne ever dreamed of, and I cannot but feel half afraid that Savage lost himself in the black water with which this particular beast is said to bewilder his victims.[7]

In another letter to his friend Mason, who had the problem of deciding whether to marry at once and give up his plans to study music in Paris or to postpone the wedding and take advantage of the opportunity, Robinson repeated his own artistic credo, pointing out that the dedicated artist must seem selfish sometimes in the pursuit of his goals but that he has an obligation to himself and to the world to be true to his genius.[8] A similar opinion is expressed in greater detail when Robinson says:

In the great shuffle of transmitted characteristics, traits, abilities, aptitudes, the man who fixes on something definite in life that he must do, at the expense of everything else, if necessary, has presumably got something that, for him, should be recognized as the Inner Fire. For him that is the Gleam, the Vision and the Word! He'd better follow it. The greatest adventure he'll ever have on this side is following where it leads.[9]

This sense of dedication repeats itself again and again. Hagedorn discusses Robinson's own choice made between marriage and the muse.[10] With characteristic contempt for the faddist and the dilettante, Robinson says that he does not devote himself to poetry that does not pay because of a fond belief in "art for art's sake" but because he can do nothing else.[11] And yet again, with typical understatement, he says, "To be born with just one thing to live for, and that thing a relative impossibility, is to be born with certain disadvantages."[12] Finally by 1930, looking backwards, Robinson can write, "It must have been about the year 1889 when I realized finally and not without a justifiable uncertainty as to how the thing was to be done, that I was doomed, or elected, or sentenced for life to the writing of poetry."[13]

It was this sense of election, that must have seemed like a doom or a sentence in the troubled years, which somehow carried him through all difficulties and nagging doubts and back out of the many dead ends he found in his way. Although it is certainly far from the truth, even though excusable as hindsight, for Robinson to say that his incurable belief in what he was doing made him "indifferent alike to hostility or neglect," his faith is plainly expressed in a letter to a friend in 1894, which expressed a rather unusual confidence, qualified by an occasional nightmare vision of his life should his faith in himself prove unfounded.[14]

The fact that he was not indifferent to hostility and neglect is indicated in the painfully flippant dedication to his first volume of poetry, privately printed, and his many letters to his friends, upon whom he leaned gratefully, though with characteristic obliqueness, for appreciation and confidence. It is significant, too, and typical of Robinson's honesty that, when the long hard times were past; when the doubts were laid the rest by acclaim; and when success, recognition, and homage were all his, the first reaction to Edith Isaacs' suggestion of writing his biography was to say that she must make it quite clear that he had given up nothing to be a poet, as poetry was the only thing that meant anything to him.[15]

This note of dedication, of compulsion appears also in the poetry that deals with the artist. In "Ben Jonson Entertains a Man from Stratford," Ben says of Shakespeare, "He treads along through Time's old wilderness / As if the tramp of all the centuries / Had left no roads —and there are none for him."[16] In the sonnet "Dear Friends," already mentioned, the note of doubtful certainty is strong; and in "Rembrandt to Rembrandt" comes the word that the truly inspired artist who has faith in his vision, even though the world disagrees, will finally see the world walk in his light.[17]

Robinson, however, was aware that mere dedication was not enough. The poetic faith, the inner urge, compulsion, and devotion to the muse might be a will-o-the-wisp; but that was the gamble of art. The sonnet "Many Are Called" makes this important qualification clear.

Thus it may be seen that Robinson was early dedicated to poetry, believed a true poet had to submit to his genius and ought to be willing to make whatever sacrifices were necessary to follow his dream; had frequent doubts; found it difficult to combine writing poetry with a paying job; and finally had enough faith somehow to continue doing the only thing that really counted and made life worth while.

II

How a Poet Writes

Although Robinson was convinced that poets were born not made—or if made, made only in the sense expressed in "Many Are Called" —there are a number of other factors that enter into the creation of poetry. Ultimately he believed firmly in inspiration, as is amply illustrated by his many references to it; yet, it is abundantly clear that for Robinson inspiration was a great deal more than automatic writing, and this in spite of a statement made to his friend Walsh, who says, "One day I reminded him that Goethe had had a sense of being dictated to when he wrote his best verse, and asked him if he had ever felt anything of the sort. 'I always do,' said Robinson serenely, 'in everything I write.' "[18] However, on another occasion, in a letter to L. N. Chase, he suggests that both the best and the worst poetry has been written "in the finest frenzy of inspiration."[19]

This sort of statement clearly indicates that, as Robinson uses the term, *inspiration* has different meanings or at least is a two-edged sword. In an interview in 1933, two years before his death, he speaks of the mystery of creative processes, not, I think, with any intent to elevate the craft or to surround it with wonder for the eyes of the uninitiated, but humbly and sincerely. "No one who writes poetry," he said, "can tell why he wrote it. I write these long poems of mine because they come to me and have to be written. . . . 'John Evereldown' and 'Luke Havergal' were young poems. I don't know where they came from. They just came out of the air."[20] This is the power that Apollo gives not frequently. Rembrandt in "Rembrandt to Rembrandt" felt it and was ". . . . a living instrument / Played on by powers that are invisible."[21] Fernando Nash, "The Man Who Died Twice," had been touched by the golden wand; but other qualities were lacking in him; and though he heard his deathless symphony, he did not set it down for others. Almost a paraphrase of the lines from the Rembrandt poem is Robinson's own statement in a letter, "I discovered long ago that an artist is just a sort of living whistle through which something blows."[22]

The vagueness of that "something" seems to be about as close as Robinson will come to a definition of the inmost secret of the poetic inspiration. On another occasion, after confessing that more than inspiration was involved in writing, Robinson's reticence returned with the cryptic remark: "One writes as one paints. There really is no method."[23] Perhaps the final comment on inspiration might be to note that, regardless of the poet's feeling of possession, his inspired poems are invariably typical and characteristic of himself.

Here and there, however, Robinson has left suggestions as to his method and his training as a poet. His interest in books and poetry began when he was very young and never after flagged. Neff points out that at the age of ten Robinson was fascinated by words and collected them as other children collect marbles, bugs, and such like treasures. They were Bible words, long words, those out of Shakespeare, whose melody entranced the child before he could understand the meaning of the words.[24] Winfield T. Scott indicates that Robinson was reading Shakespeare's *Antony and Cleopatra* while writing *Tristram* and that he liked to read Milton's blank verse while using the same form himself.[25]

Hagedorn presents a chapter in his biography called "The Making of a Poet." In it Robinson's reading and particularly the influence of Dr. Schumann are discussed. Of this period of youthful experimentation, Robinson himself writes of his struggles to find adequate words. "In those days time had no special significance for a certain juvenile fisher of words who thought nothing of fishing for two weeks to catch a stanza, or even a line, that he would not throw back into a squirming sea of language where there was every word but the one he wanted. . . . He wanted fish that were smooth and shining and subtle, and very much alive, and not too strange; and presently, after long patience and many rejections, they began to bite."[26]

In the same article, Robinson tells of his newly awakened interest in blank verse when he was seventeen. To learn about it, he made a blank verse translation of Cicero's first oration against Cataline and did the same with a long passage from Virgil. After his period of study at Harvard, he returned to Gardiner and laid plans for a blank verse version of Sophocles' *Antigone.* His friend, Harry de Forest Smith was to turn the play from the original Greek into a literal English translation, which Robinson was to do over into verse. The two were enthusiastic; and Robinson especially had high hopes for the project, which was never to be realized.[27] The following excerpt from a letter to Smith indicates that Robinson's absorption in the task, his painstaking methods, and apparently an almost demonic drive in writing: "I find, though, that I am letting the play run away with me, and must somehow contrive to get rid of it for a time. It chases me day and night, and I am often two or three days in getting a passage into anything like a satisfactory condition."[28] Two years before the preceding letter was written, Robinson speaks of his artistic deficiencies and his recognition of the difficulties of learning his craft.[29] The severity of this apprenticeship is suggested in the effort that was absorbed by the *Antigone,* which seems never to have been published and to have quite disappeared.

There are many references by Robinson himself and by others to the meticulous care he took in revision and to the great amount of time he spent in composition. Speaking of his early years as a poet, he say, "It was no uncommon performance of mine to write a sonnet in twenty minutes or half an hour, and work over it for twenty days." And again, ". . . there was nothing for me to do but go on filing and fitting words."[30]

In referring to the difficulties and incompatibility, already mentioned, of work other than that of writing, Robinson speaks with affectionate gratitude of the friends who aided in installing him as secretary at Harvard, a job that literally seems to have staved off starvation, but he dwells on the virtual impossibility of holding down a regular job when poetry, the only work he cares to live for, involves for him "an unusually slow and complex method."[13]

Almost twenty years later, there seems to have been little change in method nor in his attitude towards "work." He complains of being cooped up in the Custom House when he is in the mood to work and adds pungently, ". . . work with me means studying the ceiling and my navel for four hours and then writing down perhaps four lines—sometimes as many as seven and again none at all." However, this extremely slow method of composition does not worry him, for he goes on to suggest that "a dozen titles are quite enough to string wires on that will reach through ten times as many centuries."[32]

Although the writing itself was generally a slow and painstaking process, revision, too, seems to have been even more carefully done. A comment in an early letter emphasizes this fact and foreshadows the routine that Robinson was to follow in later years, writing during the short summer months spent at the MacDowell Colony in Peterborough, N. H., and revising this output during the long wintertime that preceded the annual return to the Colony. "I am now turning our friend 'Theodore' inside out, completely rewriting him. . . . I do not expect to do any more original work until next winter—nothing now but copying and tinkering. . . ."[33] Indeed, although Robinson more than once claims he is no judge of his own poetry, he seems to set up the amount of effort expended as at least one criterion for determining excellence. "I have written that little marionette thing. . . . I call it 'Lachesis' and do not think it amounts to anything in particular, perhaps because I wrote it so quickly."[34] In a letter to D. G. Mason, he quotes with gusto and hearty approval R. H. Stoddard's compliment to Clarence Stedman, "The public will never know how much of your stuff you strike out."[35] Miss Ester Bates, who typed most of Robinson's work during the last twenty years, bears witness to the extent of his revisions, which, on the final manuscript, consisted chiefly of omissions running from a few to many lines.[36]

The fact that inspiration, whatever it may be, is related to age and intellectual vigor seems to be suggested by Robinson's output towards the later years and his commentary upon the same. Neff reports that, when asked why he was writing no more short poems, he replied, "I am over sixty."[37] W. T. Scott notes that Robinson was saddened at ceasing to do the short poems and reports him as saying, "They don't come any more."[38] The implication is obvious that the shorter poem is in some way a more spontaneous, more concentrated, more power absorbing type of creation and that age affects the inspiration necessary to its production. Is youth for passion and feeling and age for reflection?

Finally Robinson was keenly aware of what so many modern critics and poets have lamented, the fact that the poet is affected by his times. In speaking of this influence, he says that the best poetry is written when poetry and greatness are in the air. A sympathetic, critical, and appreciative audience is more important than an income. Although Robinson was by harsh experience aware of how much poverty takes out of poetry, he felt it was beneficial to an artist to know privation and hardship, but not after twenty-five or thirty, when the vigor and resiliency of youth begins to decline somewhat.[39]

III

What Poetry Is

The question of why and how a poet writes leads to that of the nature of poetry itself; and the following divisions suggest themselves as possible groupings for Robinson's comments: first, the language of poetry; second, the subjects of poetry; third, the form of poetry; and finally, the characteristics that distinguish poetry from other types of writing.

From the very beginning of his interest in poetry, Robinson was bothered by its conventionalized diction. Hagedorn reports Robinson's questions "Why all the thees and thous, the forsooths, the hifalutin solemnities? Must the language of verse be twisted out of reason in order to be poetical? Why not write as the clerks talked in the stores on Water Street?"[40] And that was what Robinson proceeded to do, write poetry in the language of the clerks on Water Street, with the result that rejection after rejection of his verses followed his attempts to interest publishers and editors who were convinced that there was a poetic diction. He says:

> I was still confident that the poems had nothing worse than a new idea to condemn them, the fault must be somewhere else. By degrees I began to realize that these well typed and harmless looking verses of mine might as well be written, so far as possible attention or interest on the part of editors and publishers was concerned, in the language of Senegambians. "I did not think that I should find them there When I came back again." was evidently too much and not only for Mr. Dana but for the traditional sensibilities of editors in general.[41]

I have already mentioned Robinson's reference to himself as an incorrigible fisher for words; and this concern over the choice of words, so important in poetry, recurs frequently. Early in his career an almost despairing note creeps into a letter to a friend, and a half-doubt that is soon suppressed is evident:

> I think I have a little originality, but have I the genius for selection that is the one requisite of a literary man next to an easy flow of language?
> I am too fussy, I have fiddled too much over sonnets and ballades. I demand a certain something in the arrangement of words, and more in their selection, that I find in very few of our writers today. . . . I do not wholly believe in art for art's sake, but I do not think that anything is good literature when art is wholly sacrificed to the subject matter.[42]

In spite of the fact that he has expressed the fear that he may be too meticulous in his search for the right word, Robinson is sure that most of his contemporaries are too careless in this respect, too concerned with getting something said than with saying that something well. He might have added that in poetry, especially, the *how* of the saying is a great part of the *what* that is said. Yet there must be a balance between the two extremes, for words do have meanings and the poet must recognize that fact. Pertinently he suggests, ". . . many poets—Swinburne and Lanier, for example—have gone too far in trying to make words do the work of tones."[43] In connection with the problem of poetic diction, Robinson on several occasions took his friend Moody, whom he admired a great deal, to task. In criticizing "Gloucester Moors," he objects to gratuitous archaisms and considers "Like a gallant, gallant ship" rather "sophomoric."[44] And in another letter to Moody, he austerely and roundly condemns the use of the word *darling*, not without recognizing his subjective feelings and the fact that they were not infallible. At the same time he reveals much of his attitude towards life, poetry, and diction.[45] Again in the matter of diction, he gently criticizes Moody's "An Ode in Time of Hesitation" by saying, "I cannot help thinking that you are still given to what Gardiner calls an 'occasional affectation of vocabulary.' "[46]

Robinson suggests that there is no poetic diction as such. In fact he rejects the traditional conventions of the language of poetry and substitutes a new choice of vocabulary that may be called "realistic" in the sense of average, every day. As he himself put it, it was the language used by the clerks in the stores on Water Street. It should not be inferred for a moment, however, that Robinson saw his poetry as merely clerkly commentary. The vocabulary was simple, it is true, and thus familiar; but the "selection," the "easy flow," and the combinations were what made it poetry.

To turn from poetic diction to poetic subjects or, as Robinson would probably insist on saying, to the subjects of poetry, is but a short step. Here again Robinson is breaking with tradition and blazing new trails, though perhaps it would be more accurate to say retracing somewhat neglected ones. In a letter to Arthur Gledhill, concerning his first book that was soon to be published, by the poet himself, he speaks of the romantic tradition and its subjects:

> You won't find much in the way of natural description. There is very little tinkling water, and there is not a red-bellied robin in the whole collection. When it comes to "nightingales and roses" I am not in it nor have I the smallest desire to be. I sing, in my own particular manner of heaven and hell and now and then of natural things (supposing they exist) of a more prosy connotation than those generally admitted to the domain of metre. In short I write whatever I think is appropriate to the subject and let tradition go to the deuce.[47]

Robinson's friend and fellow poet did not have the same feelings towards the traditional subjects and was devoted to what Robinson called "warm blooded sonnets." Robinson wryly remarked that after two hundred and fifty warm blooded poems, they do become a bit monotonous and continued, "I wish that he could realize a little better than he does that a love poem, to be good, must be very good."[48]

Mrs. Laura Richards, Gardiner friend of the poet's, lamented that he did not produce more lyrical verse:

> How I used to beg him for more lyrics! The long, deep-thoughted, hair-splitting, cobweb-spinning dialogues were wonderful, and again wonderful; but when a man can *sing!*
> "I'll write you a whole volume of lyrics some day!" he promised; and pointed out that meantime "The Klondike" ought to have lilt enough to satisfy me. It had. I wanted more "Klondikes," more "Wildernesses," more "Twilight Songs"; but I never got them.[49]

In a half-serious vein, Robinson refers to his masters, the Greeks, to justify his hardiness as well as his subject matter. "Most of the poetic fellows have curled up before coming to my age—excepting the Greek tragedians, who kept themselves healthy and happy by writing about nothing but murder and worse."[50] And search as you will through Robinson's volumes, you will rarely find music that is not singing of an individual and his relation to himself, to two or three others, or to the world, which often is himself; and almost invariably it is the still sad music of humanity which has fascinated all the greatest poets. Occasionally it is not quite so still, for Captain Craig was buried to the blaring of trombones of the town band.

Having learned this lesson young, either through observation or experience, and probably both, Robinson justifies his choice of failures as subjects by emphasizing the obvious fact that they are more interesting and dramatic than successes.[51]

As suggested in the preceding reference, Robinson's primary concern is with mankind. It is in man and his eternally recurring problems that are essentially a part of his humanity that this poet seeks the universals that will outlive time and the tides of taste. He makes this fact clear when he says of the poem "Ponce de Leon" that in it he "was trying to capture the essential elements of the man himself, not the rich and exciting period of which he was a part."[52] Again, in a letter to Amy Lowell, he shows his belief in humanity as the most worthy subject for poetry when he says, "I find it necessary to remind you now that what seems to me to be the very best of your *vers libre* is almost exclusively 'human' in its subject matter, and therefore substantially old-fashioned."[53] Robinson's sonnet "Supremacy" is important because it reiterates his primary concern with human values as the subject of poetry and makes a distinction between the subject matter and poetry itself.

His comment follows:

There is poetry in all types of humanity—even in lawyers and horse jockeys if we are willing to search it out. . . . I have brought out the idea of the occasional realization of the questionable supremacy of our lives over those we most despise in a moderately new way. If there is a little poetry in it, then all the better.... I will state here that the verses in question must be taken as rather vague generalities: they will not bear, and I never intended them to bear, any definite analysis. To me they suggest a single and quite clear thought; if they do as much to you and to any other person who has seen them, I am satisfied.[54]

The idea alone, not an uncommon one, is expressed poetically, that is, in a "moderately new way," as Robinson characteristically understates it. While it might seem that the reference "if there is a little poetry in it, then all the better" places chief emphasis on the proposition expressed, I think this is another case of Robinsonian understatement, for he goes on to suggest that the verses must be taken as rather vague generalities and that they will not bear definite analysis. Thus the emphasis is thrown away from the idea or proposition and back onto poetry or the suggestive expression of a quality of emotion.

In connection with this matter of the subjects of poetry, Robinson exhibits an interesting example of the way in which personal interests, tastes, and circumstances will influence judgment. It is revealed in two letters concerning the husbandry of the Gardiner household during the period that he was its head. In the first, an old apple tree has apparently been felled, split, and sawed up for stove wood. Robinson says, "There is poetry in reducing a sprawling apple limb but Joe cannot see it."[55] Exactly a year later within a month, Robinson is writing to his friend Smith again. He tells him that the slab wood is all in and that if it weren't for the apples he could shout for joy. Then he continues: "I never could find any poetry in gathering apples. It is the worst work I know except washing dishes and listening to a debate."[56] Although he admired Frost's poetry, I do not know of his opinion of "After Apple Picking." Nor do I think he meant to be taken very seriously.

While Robinson has said, "I do not think much of carrying fact into fiction anyhow,"[57] Hagedorn points out, time after time in his discussion of the poetry, originals of characters and incidents that were the starting points of poems but only starting points; for Robinson himself suggests how the artist's imagination takes a suggestive bit of experience and builds up his imaginative vision. In referring to his sonnet "On the Night of a Friend's Wedding," he indicates that there was no friend at all; the only fact was that of the ringing bells in a church in the village below.[58]

Neff suggests that Bryant's poetic credo, found in the introduction to *The Library of Poetry and Song,* a book which was Robinson's first treasure chest of poetry, became his own. He quotes the following: "The elements of poetry lie in natural objects, in the vicissitudes of human life, in the emotions of the human heart, and in the relation of man to man. He who can present them in the combinations and light which at once affect the mind with a deep sense of their truth and beauty is the poet for his own age and the ages that succeed it. It is no disparagement either to his skill or his power that he finds them near to hand."[59] The only possible suggestion that does not apply in a particularly effective way to Robinson's own ideas is in the reference to natural objects as the subjects of poetry. Robinson, as has already been suggested, rarely used them other than as background to the central figures in his poems or to provide suggestive imagery of a parallel or contrasting nature. Yet this limited use indicates the keenness of his eye.

As far as I could discover, Robinson had little to say about the matter of poetic form. It is obvious, however, that he preferred to abide by the traditional ones, finding variety and freshness in other ways. As Frost said, "Robinson stayed content with the old way to be new." Although Robinson was sure that form was not what made a poem poetry and could say to Amy Lowell, "I don't care a pinfeather what form a poem takes so long as it makes me sit up,"[60] he could also say, "Sinners in art believe there are short roads / To glory without form."[61] And in a letter to Witter Bynner, he says, "I am pretty well convinced that free verse, prohibition, and moving pictures are a triumvirate from hell, . . ."[62] Likewise, in "Ben Jonson Entertains a Man from Stratford," Ben says, "He might have given Aristotle creeps, / But surely would have given him his *katharsis.*"[63] On the other hand, in 1933, two years before his death, he says somewhat testily, "Modern stuff without punctuation or capitals, I do not see how they can expect to go far with it. . . . I think there is a main road in all the arts."[64]

Although there seems to be a contradiction in these comments, I think there is really none. It appears to me that Robinson was sincere in his suggestion that the quality of poetry resides in what he called the ability to make us sit up, regardless of its form. And by the ability to make us sit up, Robinson does not mean to suggest the shocking, as is made clear by his observation that much of the popularity of mediocrity is the result of the violent, the conspicuous in color, and the sensationally odd which makes an immediate appeal. He points out that Kipling's "Gunga Din" is popular because of its oddity; while "There's a Whisper Down the Field," which is one of Kipling's best poems, is sadly neglected.[65]

What he did mean was that too many poets, or would be poets, were trying to make us sit up by means of startling innovations in form or were too lazy and undisciplined to subject themselves to the traditional forms; hence their verse for the most part lacked the electric quality, not because it was written in unconventional forms but because it lacked control and concentration of which the choice of form was but a symptom. In his sonnet "Oh for a Poet," Robinson goes beyond the mere criticism of mechanical form and suggests that greatness, soul, vision, depth is what the true poet's greatness rests upon. It is interesting to note in this sonnet, referring for a moment to an earlier matter, that nature in the sense of flowers, seasons, and sunsets is listed as a perfectly legitimate subject for poetry. As has been pointed out, however, it was not for Robinson's muse.

If there is no inherently poetic language, if there are no subjects that are peculiarly poetic, if even the traditional forms are not absolutely essential to poetry, and if poetry is more than the expression of propositions and thoughts, what is the magic component, the fine essence of poetry?

Robinson offers several suggestions towards a possible answer in a letter to Josephine Peabody, a poet and friend who often sought his advice in connection with her work. Referring to her choice of words, the poet gives the apparently paradoxical advice that "the word that seems to express the required meaning most clearly and concretely is very often the last word that metrical language—particularly song language will tolerate."[66] The obvious implication in this comment is that words in poetry are not primarily or at least entirely important as the vehicles of concrete meanings and explicit ideas. It is the suggestive power of the word, its ability to body forth the quality of an experience that Robinson seems to be pointing out.

In a humorous letter to Mrs. Laura Richards, he includes an imaginary obituary notice of himself; and even allowing for the situation and the fact that he was often annoyed and distressed by critical reference to his intellectuality and difficulty, his suggestion, I feel, is to be taken quite seriously. "Many seemed to think that he should have fussed and cussed more than he did for having been born to such an ornery lot as that of an 'intellectual poet'—when, as a matter of fact, anything like a proper comprehension of his product was, and is—so far as it is at all—a matter of feeling, not of cerebration."[67] The important point to notice is that the understanding of poetry is not merely of the intellectual or paraphrasable part but consists of a "matter of feeling, not of cerebration" insofar as poetry is comprehensible at all. The implication of this last suggestion appears to be that there is something, some part, some element of poetry that is beyond the logical comprehension.

In a similar connection, Robinson objects to criticism of his poetry as vague and suggests that by its nature poetry should not be entirely "understood." "I have encountered so much rotten imbecility in the way of failure to get my meaning that I am beginning to wonder myself if it may not be vague. But I won't have it any worse than obscure, which I meant it to be—to a certain extent."[68]

If obscurity is a virtue, what is its purpose? I would suggest two possible answers to this question. First because, by its very nature, poetry uses metaphor and figures to express its meaning, it cannot and does not pretend to be scientifically precise. Secondly poetry that is great has a quality of depth that leads through layer after layer of meaning. This depth conveys an *impression* of obscurity.

Finally, having discussed language, subjects, form, emotion, and thought, and having concluded that they contribute to but are not poetry, Robinson essays the following paradoxical definition that can hardly be said to unlock the door of revelation. "Poetry is a language that tells us through a more or less emotional reaction, something that cannot be said. It is eventually unmistakable, and indefinable."[69]

Although I may be reading what is not there, it seems to me that Robinson, in his reluctance to discuss poetry, in his insistence upon inspiration or genius, and his ultimate failure to define poetry logically is not denying that various components of poetry can be isolated, discussed, even taught. What he is suggesting is that the quality of poetry, the essence, the "nimble element" that "makes me sit up" is the result of a combination of the parts enumerated above that works in such a way as to convey, not facts, not feelings alone, but a quality that can only be described in metaphor or by writing a poem, which is but an expanded figure.

On one occasion Robinson likens poetry to gold and suggests that some poets can dig up more than others. Housman's poetry he considers pure gold and laments that there is so little.[70] At another time, upon receiving a volume of Archibald MacLeish's poems, Robinson wrote thanking the author; and among his comments was a reference to one of MacLeish's best poems, "You, Andrew Marvell," as "Poetic magic." One final example from "Ben Jonson Entertains a Man from Stratford" suggests the impossibility of defining poetry in any other way than by writing a poem.

> To-day the clouds are with him, but anon
> He'll out of 'em enough to shake the tree
> Of life itself and bring down fruit unheard-of,
> And throwing in the bruised and whole together,
> Prepare a wine to make us drunk with wonder.[71]

IV

What Poetry Is For

Robinson has been a consistently serious poet. His experience, his temperament, and his theory of poetic inspiration all contribute to the elevation of the poet's calling. It would, therefore, be unusual if this attitude did not carry over into his conception of the function of poetry.

From scattered remarks and a few of his poems, it is possible to suggest some of his ideas as to the results to be expected from poetry. First of all, poetry expresses truth, but not the truth of the philosopher or the scientist. Robinson says, "It annoys me to hear people talk about my philosophy of life. I am not a philosopher. I don't intend to be one."[72] The implication of course is that he is a poet and that poetry and philosophy are two different things. However, Robinson would be the last to say that he was without a philosophy of life or that it was not a part of his poetry.

In a letter to Josephine Peabody concerning her *Wolf of Gubbio,* he speaks of the ethical element in poetry and finds even his own poetry too full of preaching. He says:

> I liked the *Wolf* because I liked it, not because it gave me "bread." The world doesn't want bread from poets, unless it is so completely disguised that they mistake it for cake; and while great poetry has nearly always an ethical value, history would seem to indicate that Apollo doesn't care a d-damn for the Uplift. You have done your best work when you have forgotten what a rotten place this world is. You needn't ever worry about the ethical presence in your own stuff, for there will always be rather too much than too little of it. And if this has a queer sound, coming as it does from such an incurable preacher as I am—why then, be sorry for me, and don't write any more *Singing Men.*[73]

In collecting her poetry and in writing in the future, Robinson suggests that she avoid "all hifalutin diction, and more or less nebulous generalizing about an entirely hypothetical human that has never existed and probably never will exist, and you will be a happy woman again. . . don't consume yourself in trying to reform the world. I don't mean to be discouraging but you can't do it."[74]

Although he appears to minimize the message element in this letter and suggests that the aesthetic experience is the chief aim, in the light of other comments, as in this case, he would seem to be attacking primarily the overtly didactic and the failure to objectify, embody in metaphor, abstract generalizations. Repeatedly throughout his career, he refers to poetry as a kind of knowledge, a kind of teacher, a seeker and purveyor of the truth in its own special way. Neff points out, "Miss Edith Brower . . . wrote to thank him for what the idealism of *The Torrent,* especially 'Two Sonnets,' had done to clarify her view of life. As he had hoped, his hard won insights could help others."[75] And

Robinson, referring to the same occasion, says, "My female correspondent has done wonders for me, and has proved to me that I possess the power of helping others, which after all, is about the greatest thing a man, or a book can do."[76] Several months later this idea is discussed at greater length in another letter in which Robinson allies himself with the great teachers and poets of all times: "If anything is worthy of a man's best and hardest effort that thing is the utterance of what he believes to be the truth. Of course I like a joke, and I like art for its own sake; but these things in themselves are not enough. Just as deliberate pathos. . . . for 'effect' alone—is almost always a mistake, so, I think, is mere objectivity. . . . at the best unsatisfactory."[77]

Robinson was too wise to think that anyone could know *the* truth; hence his qualifying "what he believes to be the truth." Robinson's truth can be reduced to philosophical abstractions from a study of his poetry; and when that is done one can be sure that he has not really discovered all the truth that the poet is concerned with. When thus reduced, these truths consist for the most part in a restatement of the old, old unanswerable questions that have teased mankind time out of mind.

Neff quotes Robinson to show his primary concern with human relationships and the existence of "A faint hope to make a few of us understand our fellow creatures a little better, and realize what a small difference there is after all between ourselves as we are and ourselves not only as we might have been but as we would have been if our temperamental make-up and environment had been a little different."[78] As late as 1920, the same principle is expressed in a letter to a friend, concerning the poetic function. "Meanwhile I shall have brightened the way for a few groping wanderers without lanterns, and shall have comforted them with the assurance, that, generally speaking, they haven't a damned thing to say about it."[79]

Time and again, in his references to other authors, Robinson emphasizes the influence and the power a work of art has for good or evil and for the understanding and reconciliation of life's conflicting elements.[80]

In this connection I cannot forbear quoting at some length Robinson's commentary upon John Donne, the enshrined idol and marking gauge of the New Critics. It is from a letter to John Hays Gardiner, long time friend and admirer of Robinson and professor of English at Harvard University.

> I find I have acquired a kind of artificial taste for your friend Donne but I shall never be able to share your enthusiasm. He is both dogmatic and ancient, like my stationery, and hardly to be considered as apart from his period—which is, to my mind, sufficient damnation for any writer—particularly a poet, who must be if he is to be anything, an interpreter of life. Donne, looking at him from the larger point of view, doesn't seem to interpret much more than a sort of half mystical

sexual uneasiness and a rather uninteresting religious enthusiasm which seems to have been quite the thing in those days for a fellow who had raised the devil for thirty-five or forty years and so worked up an appetite for symbols. Very likely I am wrong, as usual, but I can only tell you what I think.[81]

I do not know how well or how extensively Robinson read Donne, and it is obvious that his own extremely high moral standards were somewhat affronted. Whether his criticism tells us very much about Donne will depend somewhat on our own critical stand; however, it does tell us several things about Robinson. First a poet must be an interpreter of life; his vision must penetrate; and he must objectify what he sees. Secondly he must deal with fundamental human problems that will be valid for all times. Finally Robinson is quite willing, as usual, to admit that he may be wrong in his judgment.

That he is not a critic who damns merely on the grounds of the morality of poetry and poet, however, is witnessed by his sonnet "Verlaine." He does feel strongly that the touch of Apollo's wand confers a high degree and great responsibility, which must not be violated. He tells of

> A taste that would have tainted everything,
> . . . .
> The taste of death in life—which is the food
> Of art that has betrayed itself alive
> And is a food of hell. . . . [82]

Thomas Hood, in Robinson's sonnet to his fame, accepted the responsibility of his high calling as did George Crabbe in eminent degree, to whom Robinson pays tribute thus:

> Whether or not we read him, we can feel
> From time to time the vigor of his name
> Against us like a finger for the shame
> And emptiness of what our souls reveal
> In books that are as altars where we kneel
> To consecrate the flicker, not the flame.[83]

To summarize Robinson's somewhat ambiguous position as to the function of poetry, one would have to say that, although he recognizes the aesthetic aim as of great importance, his exalted opinion of the poetic art ultimately leads him to consider the expression of truth through the blinding flashes of poetic insight to be the supreme function of poetry.

---

1 E. A. Robinson, *Untriangulated Stars*, (Cambridge, Mass., 1947), 265.
2 E. A. Robinson, *Selected Letters* (New York, 1940), 9.
3 *Untriangulated Stars*, 120.
4 Hermann Hagedorn, *Edwin Arlington Robinson* (New York, 1938), 89.
5 E. A. Robinson, *Collected Poems* (New York, 1961), 77-8.
6 *Selected Letters*, 18-19.
7 *Ibid.*, 18-19.
8 Daniel G. Mason, "Early Letters of Edwin Arlington Robinson," *Virginia Quarterly Review*, XIII (1937), 233.

9 W. Burns, "Edwin Arlington Robinson in the Hands of the Reviewers," *Poet Lore*, II (1942), 164.
10 Hagedorn, 49.
11 Mason, 236.
12 *Untriangulated Stars*, 297-8.
13 E. A. Robinson, "The First Seven Years," *The Colophon*, Part IV, December, 1930, [p. 3 of article].
14 *Untriangulated Stars*, 187.
15 Burns, 171.
16 *Collected Poems*, 83.
17 *Ibid.*, 589-90.
18 W. T. Walsh, "Some Recollections of E. A. Robinson," *Catholic World*, CLV (1942), 531.
19 *Selected Letters*, 103.
20 Karl Schriftgiesser, "An American Poet Speaks His Mind," *Boston Evening Transcript Book Review Section* (Nov. 4, 1933), 1.
21 *Collected Poems*, 589.
22 Ellsworth Barnard, *Edwin Arlington Robinson*, (New York, 1952), 12.
23 Schriftgiesser, 1.
24 Emery E. Neff, *Edwin Arlington Robinson* (New York, 1948), 7.
25 Winfield T. Scott, "Robinson in Focus," *Poetry*, L (1945), 214.
26 Robinson, "The First Seven Years," [p. 1 of article].
27 The fascinating story of this translation, its problems, its joys, and the high hopes of using it to introduce himself as a poet that Robinson had unfolds in a series of early letters in *Untriangulated Stars*.
28 *Untriangulated Stars*, 255.
29 *Ibid.*, 127.
30 Robinson, "The First Seven Years," [p. 6 of article].
31 *Untriangulated Stars*, p. 297-8.
32 Daniel G. Mason, "Letters," *Yale Review*, XXV (1936), 863-4.
33 *Untriangulated Stars*, 227.
34 *Ibid.*, 20.
35 Mason, "Early Letters," 68.
36 Scott, 213.
37 Neff, 238.
38 Scott, 213.
39 Joyce Kilmer, "Edwin Arlington Robinson Defines Poetry," *New York Times Magazine Section* (April 9, 1916), 12.
40 Hagedorn, 23.
41 Robinson, "The First Seven Years," [pp. 6-7 of article].
42 *Untriangulated Stars*, 115-16.
43 *Selected Letters*, 96.
44 E. S. Fussell, "Robinson to Moody; Ten Unpublished Letters," *American Literature*, XXIII (1951), 180.
45 *Ibid.*, 183.
46 *Ibid.*, 178.
47 *Selected Letters*, 12-13.
48 *Untriangulated Stars*, 182.
49 Richards, 58.
50 Neff, 247.
51 Schriftgiesser, 1.
52 *Ibid.*
53 *Selected Letters*, 93.
54 *Untriangulated Stars*, 108-9.
55 *Ibid.*, 117.
56 *Ibid.*, 169.
57 *Selected Letters*, 32.
58 Hagedorn, 101.
59 Neff, 13.
60 *Selected Letters*, 93.
61 Henry S. Commager, "Traditionalism in American Literature," *Nineteenth Century*, CXLIV (1949), 324.
62 *Selected Letters*, 128.
63 *Collected Poems*, 31.
64 Schriftgiesser, 1.
65 Kilmer, 12.
66 Neff, 108-9.
67 *Selected Letters*, 111.
68 *Ibid.*, 67.
69 Kilmer, 12.
70 Schriftgiesser, 1.
71 *Collected Poems*, 29.
72 Schriftgiesser, p. 1.
73 *Selected Letters*, 82.
74 *Ibid.*
75 Neff, 79.
76 *Untriangulated Stars*, 281.
77 *Ibid.*, 289.
78 Neff, 167-8.
79 *Selected Letters*, p. 123.
80 Hardy—Mason, "Early Letters," 238; Moore — *Ibid.*; Bronte — Mason, "Letters," 862; Tolstoy—Robinson, *Untriangulated Stars*, 3; Albert Ross—*Ibid.*, 13; Wordsworth—*Ibid.*, 207.
81 *Selected Letters*, 15.
82 *Collected Poems*, 96.
83 *Ibid.*, 94.

ROBINSON'S "FOR A DEAD LADY": AN EXERCISE IN EVALUATION

CLYDE L. GRIMM

OVER A decade ago, Louis O. Coxe challenged admirers of E. A. Robinson's work to tell *why* they consider praiseworthy the poems they praise and to define "the kind of excellence readers who come to Robinson these days should expect."[1] Of course, the deficiency Coxe alleges is not peculiar to commentaries on Robinson's work alone: evaluation, as opposed to explication and other genres of criticism and scholarship, is the most troublesome and therefore least often attempted —and perhaps least often successful. But it seems to me that among "significant" poets Robinson has suffered more than most from this deficiency in criticism. Though he has certainly not suffered from want of praise, often of the highest order, his standing among American poets of the first rank remains tentative, due in large measure, I suspect, to a want of *substantial* praise, the kind supported by close analysis and specific demonstration of excellences.

"For a Dead Lady" is a case in point. Judging from the frequency with which it is anthologized and specially mentioned in studies of Robinson, it appears to be among his most highly regarded poems. Yet surprisingly little analysis has appeared in support of its alleged excellence. Reviews of *The Town Down the River* (1910), the first collection in which the poem appeared, established the prototype for most ensuing appraisals. Richard Le Gallienne called it "a beautiful dirge" and quoted the last four lines of the second stanza.[2] Another reviewer found many poems in the volume "worth quoting" but implicitly acknowledged the special worth of "For a Dead Lady" by quoting it alone and in its entirety.[3] Still a third reviewer, to illustrate Robinson's "verses of the rarest imaginable beauty," reprinted "For a Dead Lady" together with "Clavering" and "Uncle Ananias."[4] In the half-century

Reprinted by permission, *Colby Library Quarterly*, VII (December 1967), 535-547.

since these earliest notices, the same "let-the-magnificent-poem-speak-for-itself" type of criticism has prevailed. Ellsworth Barnard, for example, in the fullest systematic analysis of Robinson's work yet to appear, surpasses earlier critics only in the extravagance of his praise, calling the poem "indisputably one of the supreme lyrics of the language" but offering in support of this claim no evidence either of extraordinary originality or complexity in the thought and feeling it evokes or of unusual subtlety or intricacy in its technique or form.[5]

Before going on, let us examine the poem:

No more with overflowing light
Shall fill the eyes that now are faded,
Nor shall another's fringe with night
Their woman-hidden world as they did.
No more shall quiver down the days
The flowing wonder of her ways,
Whereof no language may requite
The shifting and the many-shaded.

The grace, divine, definitive,
Clings only as a faint forestalling;
The laugh that love could not forgive
Is hushed, and answers to no calling;
The forehead and the little ears
Have gone where Saturn keeps the years;
The breast where roses could not live
Has done with rising and with falling.

The beauty, shattered by the laws
That have creation in their keeping,
No longer trembles at applause,
Or over children that are sleeping;
And we who delve in beauty's lore
Know all that we have known before
Of what inexorable cause
Makes Time so vicious in his reaping.

Now, I gather that what this poem is generally regarded as doing is paying reverent tribute to a lady whose beauty, graciousness, and virtue were unsurpassed and, with some bitterness, asserting the injustice and mystery of death. (There has been some haggling over the lady's identity, with a number of people believing her to have been the poet's mother, and some over whether or not she was a flirt, but these disturbing notions have, I believe, been effectively discredited.[6]) I gather, too, that what is generally regarded as most original in Robinson's treatment of this traditional theme is the striking imagery evoking the beauties of the lady's person, manner, and character. Yet this is scarcely enough to establish the poem as a modern classic.

A considerable advance toward the kind of criticism needed has recently been made by Richard P. Adams, who is not content with merely asserting the fineness of the poem (i.e., " 'For a Dead Lady' is Robinson at his best, and his best is about the best there is") but seeks to define its excellence in specific terms and by detailed analysis.[7] Adams values Robinson's control of tone (i.e., "it never loses its tone"); the "vivid, concrete images"; and the "development, or increment, in the series of statements" about the lady's charms (i.e., her eyes, her movements, her emotions, the shape of her features, the color of life on her bosom) culminating in the summary word *beauty* at the beginning of the last stanza. He appears to value also the abrupt and shocking opposition of *shattered* which leads into the concluding statement of the mystery of Time's destruction of beauty. After what I find an unfruitful discussion of form, Adams concludes that the excellence of the poem derives primarily from "the superlative management of thematic imagery," by which Robinson achieves "a delicate but tense balance between the beauty of life and the pain of death." Whereas most readers have not found in the poem the compensation for the thought of death which is expected of an elegy, Adams thinks that this delicate balance permits us to regard the beauty of life itself as that compensation.

Though I disagree with very little of what Adams says, I think that a more thorough analysis is possible and even necessary in order to refine still further our understanding of Robinson's artistry. Once again, I take my cue from Coxe: "Robinson organizes his poems to a disarming extent, often building a structure that is so symmetrically proportioned that only the closest reading discovers the articulation" (p. 252). With this in mind, I have undertaken to read "For a Dead Lady" as closely as possible and to attach as much significance as possible to the various elements of structure. I may as well confess that I myself am not entirely persuaded by some of the "possibilities" I shall suggest, but I am convinced that if Robinson's best work really deserves and is to continue to receive the highest acclaim, critical analysis must drive it harder and farther toward the limits of its "articulation."

First of all, then, I think that the poem has a three-part rather than only a two-part "argument." Each stanza evokes an image or concept of ultimacy, an absolute that might be or has been worshipped by mankind or to which man otherwise might accommodate himself religiously or philosophically. The imagery of the first stanza clearly presents the lady as a goddess-like being, who presides over her own heterocosm ("woman-hidden world") and confronts her devotee the poet with just such sublime and incomprehensible wonders as are usually attributed to deity. The term *light* in the first line is, of course, Robinson's favorite metaphor for ultimate truth, wisdom, and grandeur, and the imagery of light dominates this stanza.

The second stanza, however, provides the real key to my interpretation, and its first two lines are crucial. The term *grace* is richly ambiguous. Most obviously, it denotes the graciousness of the lady and, with the modifiers *divine* and *definitive,* suggests her perfection in this regard and reinforces the deity-image of the first stanza. It may also suggest the meaning found in the phrase *grace period:* some temporary postponement of a deadline or temporary exemption from a debt or obligation. This meaning, it goes without saying, is clearly revelant to the transience-of-beauty theme in the poem. Most significant, however, is the common theological meaning of *grace:* that freely given and unmerited spiritual gift of the Christian God by which fallen man is enabled to purify his life and achieve salvation in eternity. Among the basic tenets of New England Puritanism, with which Robinson was surely acquainted, was "The Perseverance of the Saints," that is, a belief in the irresistibility and permanency of the special grace extended to the elect. Thus "The grace, divine, definitive" clearly invites us to recall a conventional Christian belief that extraordinary virtue (beauty of character) in mankind is attributable to the love and mercy of God and is a sign of his justness and power.

But sharply undercutting and reversing this implication is the following line with its image of deterioration, of pitifully futile adherence, of irresistible or inevitable withdrawal. Significantly, the only revision which Robinson made in the poem, after its first appearance in *Scribner's Magazine* in September 1909, was the substitution of *Clings* for *Comes.* The change was not only apt but necessary. It was more than a matter of replacing a "neutral" verb with a "charged" one. By reversing the direction of movement suggested by the image—from inward to outward, from entering to leaving, *Clings* is more consistent with the predominant focus on loss or termination and clarifies both the image itself and the attitude or tone of the poet. On the most literal level, the lines mean that only a slight and rapidly fading trace of the lady's former beauty (e.g., the rosy hue of her breast) remains and that the total transformation of her appearance into that of a cold and pale corpse is imminent. Equally fitting is the reading that the memory or vivid consciousness of her beauty is fading from the poet's mind, as the full realization of her death overcomes him. Most significant, however, is the implication that a belief in God's grace is rapidly fading from the poet's mind or indeed that the disparity between conventional reassurances of divine love, justice, and power and the destruction of this perfect human being has already led him to repudiate them. The sharp contrast between the alleged permanence of God's grace and the obvious impermanence of its manifestation in the dead lady's appearance indicates an ironic intent to challenge conventional platitudes by representing the orthodox Christian God as ineffectual or delusory.

The language of orthodoxy is, in fact, played upon ironically throughout the second stanza. This strategy is foreshadowed in the first stanza by repetition of the imperative third-person *shall,* which echoes the Decalogue's imperative "Thou shalt not . . . ." However, it is anticipated most clearly, almost explicitly, in the line "Whereof no language may requite." *Requite* itself carries theological connotations of sin, atonement, and reward. But the poet will not permit ("may") mere words—the empty, ineffectual platitudes of Christian doctrine—to obscure or compensate for the wanton destruction of the lady's flowing, shifting, many-shaded perfection. The ironic employment of this discredited language of accommodation begins in earnest with the image of fading "grace" in the opening lines of the second stanza. The third line (mistaken by some as evidence of a defect in the lady's character), if read as a continuation of this verbal irony, levels the bitter charge that the Christian God of infinite love and mercy could not or would not extend either to one whose bright laughter suggests the childlike innocence and purity most deserving of both (*hushed* connotes parental suppression of a child's carefree and spontaneous outbursts of delight). *Calling* in the next line carries the connotation of divinely ordained mission or duty, which the lady is prevented by death from answering or fulfilling. The line therefore suggests a contradiction between the notion of God's demands upon man and His failure or inability to provide man with the means or opportunity to meet them.

The ironic treatment of Christian orthodoxy continues in the couplet of this stanza, where to the suggestion of God's impotence Robinson adds the suggestion of His fictiveness or nonbeing. Conspicuously ignoring the Christian belief that a Father or Guardian oversees His human "children," the poet rather consigns the childlike lady (*little* reinforces the child-image) to the Roman god Saturn, who not only betrayed and deposed his father, Heaven, but also devoured his own children to prevent being superseded by them. Thus Robinson suggests that ultimacy is more accurately represented by the image of a jealous and unfeeling infanticide than by the image of a solicitous parent. Further evidence of Robinson's intent to repudiate the historic Christian revision or displacement of pagan myth may be inferred from his decision to allude to Saturn rather than his Greek counterpart, Kronos (*Kronos* or *Cronus* would conform as well to the iambic meter and would also provide functional alliteration, the doubled *k*-sound reinforcing the image of harsh destruction which emerges in the third stanza). As Greece gave way to Rome in Western history, worship of Kronos may be said to have given way to worship of Saturn, and as pagan Rome gave way to Christian Rome, worship of Saturn (though he shared the Pantheon with others) may be said likewise to have given way to worship of Christ. In fact, celebration of the Christian savior's nativity displaced celebration of the Saturnalia near the winter solstice in December. Thus Saturn may have been preferable because he was the immediate pagan predecessor of Christ and because allusion to him would therefore be more likely to recall this historic transition and to sharpen the irony of the poet's apparent indifference to it or tacit rejection of it. Finally, however, neither Kronos nor Saturn can be regarded as anything more than a mythic figure, a primitive personification of Time, which, to quote Bulfinch, "as it brings an end to all things which have had a beginning, may be said to devour its own offspring."[8] Thus neither is more reassuring—or less mythic—than the Christian personification of ultimacy. Indeed, as the last stanza will suggest, Time itself serves some abstract ultimate "cause," which in the poet's view prevails over all personal images of ultimacy.

The concluding lines of the second stanza develop the theme of repudiation still further by implying the inadequacy of the Christian view of man himself. The line "The breast where roses could not live" does indeed suggest more than a Renaissance conceit, as R. H. Super has urged, but certainly does not indicate, as he goes on to speculate, that the lady was a flirt.[9] The rose is not uncommonly employed as a symbol of the Christian view of the human heart, in which the shame, sorrow, and regret aroused by a sense of sin and the fallen condition of man are mingled with the ecstasy of love, joy, and gratitude inspired by God's mercy and Christ's loving self-sacrifice in raising man from spiritual degradation. If *roses* here carries this symbolic value, then we may say that the lady's heart ("breast") was entirely free of, indeed immune to, any sense of sin or evil, untouched by sorrow or regret, and overflowing instead with unmixed delight. One so perfectly innocent and pure could have no concern with salvation ("rising") because she would be unaware of the need for salvation ("falling"), nor would she comprehend the preoccupation of others with such matters or be entirely at home among them. Needless to say, they in turn might neither comprehend nor full appreciate her ("The laugh that love could not forgive" may suggest such a defect among her close associates, in addition to the meaning noted above). The tone of the idiom "to have done with" is often one of impatient annoyance, as with some troublesome or frustrating task or circumstance. *Has done with* may therefore reflect the poet's annoyance with conventional insistence upon sin and salvation coupled with blindness to or disregard of human perfection such as the lady's; it may also suggest his feeling that she is, in a way, better off for having escaped this inhospitable, stultifying milieu.

This scornful attitude toward shame and regret, in or out of a Christian context, appears again and again in Robinson's work and resembles closely the attitude of Emerson, whose influence on Robinson is widely acknowledged.

The second stanza, then, may be summarized as an ironic repudiation of Christian theology for its failure to acknowledge human perfection and to resolve convincingly the question of what ultimate purpose or concept of justice is served by its destruction. Indeed the ironic image of the Christian deity which emerges from this stanza appears inferior to the lady herself as an embodiment of perfection.

Appropriately, therefore, the opening of the third stanza substitutes *beauty* for *grace* as the proper term for the lady's perfection, which is thereby stripped of conventional theological connotations and presented as a purely humanistic-aesthetic conception. The beauty of the lady's defenseless, childlike innocence is once again evoked by the line "No longer trembles at applause" and then is complemented by the image of her beauty as loving and tender mother-protector, which contrasts sharply and ironically with both the earlier image of the defunct Christian "Father" and the following image of an impersonal "cause." Disentangled from the ineffectual platitudes and misleading contradictions by which Christians attempt to account for it, the destruction of such beauty is restated as an elemental mystery. The poet cannot affirm that the creation is in the keeping either of the Christian father-savior or of any other personal ultimate; his skepticism permits him to deduce and inclines him to affirm only some indifferent, amoral, indeterminate force. It can be "known" not as either the pagan or the Christian anthropomorphists have presumed but only as an abstraction, which causes the thought of death to be *felt* all the more agonizingly.

Thus neither conventional theology nor the skepticism born of modern science assuages the pain of the poet's loss. Yet, though the abstract "cause" born of skepticism proves the most powerful of the three ultimates by destroying both the lady and the poet's belief in her traditional protector, the lady herself or the "divine" beauty which she embodied remains the most compelling absolute and, for the poet, the most fitting object of worship.

If this seems a great deal to make the poem mean, I can again invoke the assistance of Coxe: "Robinson is a poet with a prose in view. Read 'Eros Turannos' or 'For a Dead Lady' or 'The Gift of God' and you will feel that the scope of a long naturalistic novel has emerged from a few stanzas" (p. 248). What I have suggested is no more than Coxe has invited one and all to find. The ideas are consistent with Robinson's "philosophy," as it is generally understood, and the compression of a prose argument of such scope into so few lines is just such as has always been recognized as a major characteristic and also a prime value of Robinson's art. But if a great poem should mean more than it "says," it should also, according to MacLeish's famous dictum, "be" more than it means. By now it is a commonplace to say that genuine poetry evokes a nonrational response—emotional and/or aesthetic—in addition to or instead of a merely intellectual one. "For a Dead Lady" certainly does so; in fact, since its ideas display no particular originality, the dramatic interplay of the poet's emotions becomes its primary interest. I do not pretend that the emotional structure of this or any other poem can be adequately accounted for by prose statement, but criticism is obliged at least to direct attention to this most basic aspect of lyric poetry.

As noted before, Adams has treated as a value the "delicate balance" Robinson achieves between the pleasurable emotion inspired by beauty and the painful one aroused by the thought of death. Again, however, I find somewhat greater complexity than this. The emotional structure of the poem, as might be expected, parallel the three-part argument, as the poet reacts emotionally to its ideas. His adoration of the lady, suggested by the deity-image of the first stanza, is clear enough, as is the mournful coloring provided by *No more* (echoing, as Adams says, Poe's "The Raven"). A dramatic development occurs, however, when the poet introduces the idea of non-requital. Though I frankly doubt that the ironic allusion to Christian platitudes, which I have suggested above, is likely to strike most readers immediately, nevertheless the connotations of *requite* are such as to create some suspense or dramatic anticipation. The gradual unfolding or revelation of its thematic appropriateness, as one becomes aware of the significant accumulation of terms having theological connotations, is likewise dramatic. The poet's tone reveals still more subtle shading, however, as we sense a dramatic tension between his bitter disillusionment with Christian reassurances and his peculiar reluctance to convey that disillusionment more overtly or to permit his bitterness unrestrained expression. It is as if some inhibition, perhaps some lingering uncertainty, prevents his making a firm and altogether unequivocal disavowal. The underlying bitterness does emerge more forcefully in the last stanza, especially in *shattered* and *vicious.* The sharp contrast between the violent destructiveness of the impersonal laws and the innocent tenderness of the lady suggests a deeply moving climax to the emotional experience the poet is undergoing. The poem closes abruptly with the understated expression of loss and helplessness, as if the poet could scarcely bear to contemplate any longer either the void left by the lady's passing or the void of the impersonal universe which he is inclined to affirm. Strangely, however, the personification of Time, indicated by *his* and by the conventional image of the reaper, suggests an irrepressible instinct to believe in, if only to blame, some personal ultimate. This, together with the understatement, indicates again a reluctance to make an unequivocal disavowal and implies perhaps a saving instinct to resist utter despair. Thus the tension in this subtle and complex dramatic structure is even more delicately balanced, its tone more astutely controlled, and its artistic value greater than Adams has hinted.

I shall conclude with a brief comment on the function of formal elements. The first stanza establishes a perfectly regular pattern of eight iambic tetrameter lines, interconnected by the rhyme scheme *ababccab*, with the *b*-lines having feminine rhymes requiring a ninth syllable. Odd-numbered lines have enjambement; even-numbered lines are end-stopped; there are no caesuras. Therefore, although short tetrameter lines tend to jingle, each successive pair of Robinson's lines moves unimpeded at a smooth and flowing pace. The feminine rhymes add to the end-stops extra "weight," which together with the regular and dignified pace contributes to the solemn effect of a dirge or hymn. The fifth and sixth lines draw together closely, because of the couplet-rhyme, as if, like the penultimate bars of a musical composition, preparing us for the conclusion, and thereby help to convey a more emphatic sense of closure and self-containment. The perfect regularity of this first stanza, including the perfectly fluid movement of the lines, enhances the visual image of the lady's perfection. Also contributing to the total impression of the lady's beauty is the preponderance of euphonious sound effects: the repeated assonances (chiefly long *o*'s and *e*'s and both long and short *i*'s) and the intricately woven patterns of alliteration (chiefly of *f*, *w*, and *sh*).

It is a further indication of Robinson's effort to adapt form to thought and feeling that neither of the other two stanzas displays such regularity (or such a pervasive use of sound effects). This is consistent with the reading that neither theism nor science provides an image of ultimacy so perfectly harmonious as the lady herself. Thus the opening line of the second stanza breaks sharply from the pattern of the first with two caesuras and an end-stop. The halting pace makes us read each of the modifiers of *grace* emphatically, so that the ironic reversal of the second line becomes all the more striking. The broken rhythm may also be said to enhance the sense of Christianity's broken promise and of the disharmony, both psychological and emotional, experienced by the poet. Another irregularity is the caesura of the fourth line, which is not, it should be noted, grammatically necessary. The forced pause creates an effect of ironic suspension, in this case signalling the poet's bitter view of the Christian belief in God's "calling." The third stanza, like the second, opens with a broken line, the caesura setting off *The beauty* exactly as *The grace* is set off above and perhaps calling attention to the meaningful difference I have suggested; the break also emphasizes the opposition between *beauty* and *shattered* which Adams has noted. Another forced pause breaks the pattern of enjambement in the third line, again suggesting ironic suspension; indeed this and the following line may be taken as an example of the rhetorical figure zeugma. *Trembles* with its first modifier suggests the emotion of the lady as child-recipient of affectionate approval but with its second modifier suggests the emotion of the parent-giver. The pause calls attention not only to this two-fold beauty of the lady as loved one and love-giver but also to the ironic contrast between her and both the unlovable, unloving laws of creation and the Christian Father, unloved by the poet because of His failure to demonstrate His love for the lady. A final departure from the pattern of the first stanza is the omission of the end-stop in the sixth line, permitting the unimpeded rush of the emotion-charged and barely restrained final statement.

To conclude this analysis of "For a Dead Lady," I am obliged to make explicit what I consider its values. In general, I value the poem's demand for a close reading—but only upon finding in it commensurate aesthetic rewards for such an effort: a subtle but coherent structure, all the more valuable because dramatically complex and moving; a sensitive and purposive selection of language to the end that meaningful and consistent patterns of connotation and imagery enrich the "argument"; and a more than mechanical or arbitrary employment of form. More subjectively, I value Robinson's poised treatment of matters which have tempted more than a few poets into expressions of rash thoughts and overwrought emotions; the Robinson who emerges from "For a Dead Lady" is a man sensitized but not disabled by the experience he records and the truth he perceives in it.

For these things I value "For a Dead Lady" very highly, and though it would not be entirely sound to infer from this one poem the general excellence of Robinson's work, one might with this poem in view seek such excellence elsewhere in his work with some confidence.

---

1 "E. A. Robinson: The Lost Tradition," *Sewanee Review*, LXII (Spring 1954), 247. Further citations are treated parenthetically in the text.
2 "Three American Poets," *Forum*, XLV (January 1911), 90.
3 Anon., "Three Poets of the Present," New York *Times* (February 12, 1911), Sec. 6, p. 79.
4 Anon., "Current Poetry," *Literary Digest*, XLII (March 4, 1911), 424-425.
5 *Edwin Arlington Robinson* (New York, 1952), 294, n. 17.
6 R. H. Super initiated the dispute in *Explicator*, III (June 1945), Item 60; Richard Crowder answered in *Explicator*, V (December 1946), Item 19; Super rebutted in *Explicator*, V (June 1947), Item 60; Edwin Fussell, *Explicator*, IX (March 1951), Item 33, and Barnard, 294, convincingly settled the matter, though a last word was had by Sylvia Hart and Estelle Paige, *Explicator*, X (May 1952), Item 51.
7 "The Failure of Edwin Arlington Robinson," *Tulane Studies in English*, X (1961), 141-144.
8 Thomas Bulfinch, *Bulfinch's Mythology*, Modern Library ed. (New York, n.d.), 10.
9 See note 6.

ROBINSON'S IMPULSE FOR NARRATIVE

J. VAIL FOY

ROBINSON'S single-minded devotion to a career as poet is so obvious a circumstance of his biography that one may overlook in the poet's apprenticeship two major experiments—the prose short story, or sketch as Robinson preferred to call it, and the play—that suggest why his major mature efforts in poetry, particularly after 1916, were in the form of extended blank-verse narratives: his chief concern in the later, long poems, as it had been in the earlier experiments, was with the dramatic as opposed to lyric presentation of the complexities he marveled at in the enigma of human character. Indeed, as one reads Robinson's early letters, one wonders what might have happened to the poet had his sketches and plays been commercially successful or had he received even significant critical praise for them. His lament to Harry DeForest Smith in 1895 is revealing:

> I have so much material in my head, and good material too, that the weight of it makes me dizzy at times; and then there is that fear that I may not do anything after all. My worst and most persistent enemy, though, is a constant inclination to write poetry. Sometimes I am half afraid the damned stuff will kill what little ability I have.[1]

His failures in prose fiction and drama, however, are significant only as they indicate the problems that Robinson had to overcome as he developed a narrative structure and technique of characterization to complement his indirect and allusive style of poetic expression.

As one considers the time and effort that Robinson spent for twenty years in writing sketches, plays, and even a novel (he tried to turn one of the plays into a novel but that effort has not survived), it seems inevitable that his poetry thereafter should reflect more than a little of his strong attraction toward dramatic presentation of his ideas as well as his attitude that character and its related problems were properly the center of the artist's deepest and most considered thought. Simi-

Reprinted by permission, *Colby Library Quarterly*, VIII (March 1969), 238-249.

larly, one might expect to find the blank verse of the later narratives the medium for an artist whose first extended poetic effort had been a blank-verse adaptation of *Antigone* (pp. 125, 172). And even a cursory listing of titles of the early poems shows characterizations predominant among them ("Richard Cory," "Aaron Stark," "Cliff Klingenhagen," "Reuben Bright," "Isaac and Archibald," "Aunt Imogen"), whether in sonnet form, in blank verse, or in the rhymed tetrameter of which Robinson was always fond. His later, major narratives, exclusively in blank verse after 1920, were merely end points of his natural lines of drift.

In the beginning, however, poetry had not seemed to Robinson the medium in which he could best cast his developing and expanding ideas. In his letters to Smith during the four years (1893-1897) of his prose experiments in Gardiner, one finds in the young artist a curious pride in his facility with the kind of poetry he was then writing; yet one also feels in that pride a kind of scorn for such productions, particularly because they were so fascinating and easy to do. Most of all, however, one notes the complaint that they were time-consuming and were interfering with his prose sketches. In fact, except for the adaptation of *Antigone,* which seemed to him significant, Robinson displays almost a resentment toward the sonnets and ballades, rondeaus, and villanelles, because they required—indeed, demanded—so much time. Yet, and significantly, he represented to Smith the urge to write verse as persistent and continuously compelling. As early as 1893 he was saying:

> I suppose I shall have to write a "Ballade of Dead Mariners." The idea, with three or four others, has been chasing me for some time, and I know of but one way to get rid of them—write them out. . . . The things may not be worth the trouble of the making, but there is a fascination about them that I cannot get over (pp. 111-112).

A few months later he was again "complaining" of this fascination, enclosing for Smith's opinion a copy of what was to become, after revisions, the most famous of his villanelles, "The House on the Hill":

> These old French forms always had a fascination for me which I never expect to outgrow. I don't know that I care to outgrow it, but still it interferes with my more serious work [prose sketches then in progress] to an unpleasant extent. When one of these things begin [*sic*] to run in my mind there is little rest for me until it is out. Fortunately, this one was made very rapidly (in about twenty minutes) so did not steal much of my time (p. 133).

But of the poems in his first published volume, *The Torrent and the Night Before* (1896), which was composed chiefly of such short rhymed pieces that together with his sonnets formed the bulk of his poetic output to that time, he was more enthusiastic about one of the three unrhymed efforts in the volume than about its companion pieces. His enthusiasm for "The Night Before" was probably heightened by the fact that the poem was his first extended narrative, originally "a tragic monologue written in unrhymed tetrameters." He had described it to Smith as "like *Evangeline,* with two feet left out" (p. 238), that is, dactyllic tetrameter. One is puzzled to know whether Robinson considered the published version as that meter, however, for he wrote to Smith a year after his initial description that he "had been rewriting that story of mine . . . in blank verse." Because the published version has the same opening line that he had quoted in each of the letters and because the rhythm of the lines in the poem is so obviously in the triple meters, it is difficult to believe that he considered the poem to be blank verse, despite the number of ten- and eleven-syllable lines it contains. Like his ten-syllable opening line, which is dactyllic tetrameter with opening and closing trochaic substitute feet (/u|/uu|/uu|/u), the other imperfect dactyllic lines do not conform to the basic iambic rhythm of blank verse.

Despite the pressures of his prose sketches, he had felt that this long monologue, like his other poems, had to be done:

> I have been too much occupied of late to do any writing except two sonnets and some ninety lines of a queer poem called "The Night Before." . . . the thing demands work—wasted work, most likely, but still work that I cannot seem to help doing. You will be glad, or sorry, to know that I have three prose tales well in my head and shall have them out as soon as I can settle myself down to such labor once more (pp. 158-159).

Then when reviews of the volume began to come in, he seemed concerned that reviewers had either ignored or were generally unimpressed with "The Night Before." Quoting to Smith excerpts from an otherwise gratifying review in the Denver *Times* (one of the best notices his first volume received), Robinson remarked on his disappointment with the general reception of his longest poem in the volume. The reviewer had written:

> "There are a few commonplace verses in the volume, such as 'Max Nordau,' 'The Night Before' (ach!) and 'For Calderon,' but it is unjust to judge a man by his worst traits or a writer by his poorest work" (p. 276).

Robinson observed wistfully to Smith:

> Of course "The Night Before" is purely objective, and may be called anything from pessimism to rot. I must confess that I haven't the slightest idea whether it is good for anything or not. I printed it to find out; but the opinions I have received are so conflicting that I am not much better off than I was before. The fact that you and Hubbell speak so well of it convinces me that it is nothing to be sorry for, but I am afraid it is one of those unfortunate narrative pieces which requires a second reading before it amounts to anything at all (pp. 273-274).

This effort, his last major dramatic monologue for nearly twenty years, was also the end of long unrhymed narratives for six years, and nearly the end of unrhymed verses for as long. Except for twenty-five octaves in blank verse and the reprinted "Walt Whitman," "The Wilderness," and "The Night Before" in his second volume, *The Children of the Night* in 1897 (thereafter, "The Night Before" was never again collected), Robinson published only rhymed verse until 1902; and not until 1915 did he publish another long dramatic monologue in blank verse, the justifiably famous "Ben Jonson Entertains a Man from Stratford," which, after some revisions, was reprinted in his best single volume, *The Man Against the Sky* (1916).

But as his first major effort, "The Night Before" illustrates Robinson's inability to devise an effective structure to express his conception of the character he was contriving. Writing to Smith during the construction of the poem, he seemed aware of the problems his inexperience in characterization was posing for him: "I don't know what it all amounts to, but there are some pretty good passages in it and they may lug it through" (p. 238). In the same letter he cited, but did not elaborate upon—unfortunately—a system of "opposites" on which he based the poem: "that is, creating a fictitious life in direct opposition to a real life [in general, presumably] which I know." Later, in one sentence, he related the stimulus for the poem, revealing, perhaps unconsciously, the major fault of the completed poem, a fault attributable not to his system, whatever it was, but to his inability at that time to handle effectively situations with which he had had no direct experience: "[The poem] reflects, in a measure, my present mood in the narration of things of which I know nothing except by instinctive fancy" (p. 161).

Unfortunately, the combined operations of his mood (which during that summer was a disturbed one) and his instinctive fancy on the dramatic situation in the poem produced mostly melodrama. Even if one grants the influence of the brandy that the good Dominie had brought to cheer the last hours of the murderer whose confession he was hearing, the erratic reactions of the condemned man appear not only extreme but so curiously compromised by certain of his statements that even an admiring reader might pause to wonder what the poet was up to. Though a careful examination of these reactions will demonstrate how wide of the mark Robinson went, his statements to Smith show clearly what effect he had intended:

> I think you may enjoy [the poem], but I must ask you not to expect too much and to make a strong effort not to laugh at the attempted intensity of the murderer's confession. The success of the poem will depend wholly upon the success of this intensity, which ought to increase from the start and end with a great smash (pp. 161-162).

Here Robinson singled out his problem but failed to see that the erratic nature of the murderer's intensity is what makes it appear ridiculous, not the intensity or "attempted intensity" itself. Although the poet tried to vary the emotional level of the murderer's statement so that he might build to his "grand smash," he made the elementary dramatic mistake of opening his scene at too high a pitch, which he then dropped slightly and in a very curious fashion, finally raising it again to a point where the murderer undergoes a brief but almost complete collapse at the thought of his impending execution. While the rapidity and abruptness of these changes make the action dramatically ineffective, the climax of emotional intensity in the first strophe is nowhere duplicated in the rest of the poem. The grand smash that Robinson envisioned as the climax of the action is not the climax of the condemned man's emotional intensity but rather a subdued return to the kind of terrified and questioning despair under which he had collapsed so ineffectively in the opening strophe.

As the poem begins, the condemned man has talked long enough with the priest and has drunk enough brandy to have worked himself into a mood of intense and rhetorical self-searching:

> Look you, Dominie, look you, and listen!
> Look in my face, first; search every line there!
> Mark every feature,—chin, lip, and forehead!
> Look in my eyes, and tell me the lesson
> You read there; measure my nose, and tell me
> Where I am wanting! A man's nose, Dominie
> Is often the cast of his inward spirit;
> So mark mine well. But why do you smile so?
> Pity or what? Is it written all over
> This face of mine, with a brute's confession?
> Nothing but sin there? nothing but hell-scars?
> Or is it because there is something better—
> A glimmer of good, maybe—or a shadow
> Of something that's followed me down from childhood—
> Followed me all these years and kept me,
> Spite of my slips and sins and follies,
> Just out of hell? Yes? something of that kind?
> And you smile for that? You're a good man, Dominie,
> The one good man in the world who knows me,—
> My one good friend in a world that mocks me,
> Here in this hard stone cage. But I leave it
> To-morrow. To-morrow! My God! Am I crying?
> Are these things tears? Tears! What! Am I frightened?
> I who swore I should go to the scaffold
> With big strong steps and—No more. I thank you,
> But no—I am all right now! No!—listen![2]

Two interpretations of this character immediately suggest themselves, even before the strophe continues: either he is a somewhat self-assured, slightly drunken, slightly cynical man, resigned to his own death, wishing merely to explain, perhaps even to justify, his sin, with the priest as a receptive but essentially passive audience; or he is a man in the middle stages of despair, frightened, not quite capable of accepting emotionally what is to happen to him and how he has come to be in this predicament, seeking the solace of talking to one who will listen sympathetically. In the first instance, his rather sudden collapse into tears is so unexpected, his appreciation of the priest's belief that some good remains of him is so pathetic, that the interpretation seems untenable; in the alternative interpretation, the intensity of his opening despair becomes ridiculous when he inserts the inconsistently whimsical remark about noses, with its pontifical conclusion, "So mark mine well."

Nor do the concluding lines of the strophe, with the strange, unmotivated shifts in person and mode, and a consequent shift in tone, serve to resolve this confusion:

> I am here to be hanged; to be hanged to-morrow
> At six o'clock, when the sun is rising.
> And why am I here? Not a soul can tell you
> But this poor shivering thing before you,
> This fluttering wreck of the man God made him,
> For God knows what wild reason. Hear me,
> And learn from my lips the truth of my story.
> There's nothing strange in what I shall tell you,
> Nothing mysterious, nothing unearthly,—
> But damnably human,—and you shall hear it.
> Not one of those little black lawyers guessed it;
> The judge, with his big bald head, never knew it;
> And the jury (God rest their poor souls!) never dreamed it.
> Once there were three in the world who could tell it;
> Now there are two. There'll be two tomorrow,—
> You, my friend, and—But there's the story:—(p. 72)

Quite aside from the speaker's self-commiseration in referring to himself as "this poor shivering thing, this fluttering wreck," here is a man, six lines from hysteria, referring to himself in the third person as coherently and forcefully as if he were completely recovered; yet the image he presents of himself is one of near collapse. Even taken figuratively, the description would be overstated, particularly since the shift to declamatory tone in the next two lines only serves to emphasize the incongruity of the characterization. Even if Robinson intended this shift from the first person to indicate the prisoner's objectification of his condition, it is improbable that a man in that state of mind could or would make such a shift; again, even if the murderer had regained complete control of his faculties, as he apparently had, the contrast between the strength and control with which he describes himself and the image which his description creates is too broad for effective characterization.

A third interpretation, suggested by Robinson's phrase "apparent intensity" in the letter to Smith, goes far to reconcile these contradictions, though it requires the closest reading of the text and an act of faith in the dramatic potential of the poem. Even then, the resulting characterization is not effective, but it does demonstrate at least certain of the complexities that a maturer Robinson was to exploit in the development of his later, great characters. The murderer is a man who, facing death which he fears desperately, has nevertheless decided to feign courage as he tells the priest the reasons for his actions. He sees shortly, however, from the man's smile that the priest understands enough about the nature of man to have penetrated his meaningless remark about noses for the bravado that it is (perhaps a pun on the notorious effect of liquor on the nose—he's been drinking brandy—or a reference to his actions—the murder of his wife's lover—as having cut off his nose to spite his face, though neither interpretation explains his following question to the priest as to why he smiles, a question inconsistent with a conscious pun or allusion) or to believe that even a murderer is not beyond salvation. In the face of this sympathy, the poseur breaks down and the essentially child-like nature of his feigned courage becomes apparent. His description of himself as having sworn to "go to the scaffold with big strong steps" is much like an adult's adjuration to a child to pluck up his courage and enter a darkened room "like a little man." The murderer's recovery after his breakdown differs from a child's in that the murderer can objectify himself as the weak, pathetic figure he is, although, again like a child, he is not in his fear ashamed of the figure he presents—he is just frightened and confused. Having decided to put aside the futile guise of courage, he determines to tell "the truth of my story." But whatever courage and relief he is able to muster by the accounting waver again and again during the recital.

The events of his life, presented in the extremes of illusion and disillusion, are expressed in diction and figures equally extreme and usually reflecting the romantic enthusiasm or despair normally ascribed to a sensitive and sheltered adolescent personality: acute instinctive perception without much emotional stability or intellectual understanding, yet with curious flashes of insight to show that he is learning, however slowly and painfully. Used to drop the pitch of intensity so that it may build again, these intervals of insight do much to temper the overintensity of the whole poem, though not enough to temper the extremes. Still, Robinson's treatment of this type of character differs here from the conventional treatment of individuals suffering from romantic despair—Housman's are prototypal, for example—in that Robinson does not endow his murderer with romantic fatalism. Recognizing his guilt, Robinson's murderer does not curse God and die, but remains naturally fearful and somewhat cowardly, very desperate, and manifests a questioning uncertainty that he is entirely to blame for the events leading to his plight. At the same time, he realizes the implications of his feeling that he is "the man God made him":

> You think me,
> I know, in this maundering way designing
> To lighten the load of my guilt and cast it
> Half on the shoulders of God. But hear me!
> I'm partly a man,—for all my weakness,—
> If weakness it were to stand and murder
> Before men's eyes the man who had murdered
> Me, and driven my burning forehead
> With horns for the world to laugh at. Trust me!
> And try to believe my words but a portion
> Of what God's purpose made me! The coward
> Within me cries for this; and I beg you
> Now, as I come to the end, to remember
> That women and men are on earth to travel
> All on a different road. Hereafter
> The roads may meet. . . . I trust in something—
> I know not what. . . . (p. 81)

The confusion that is the core of this character, as in many of Robinson's characters, lies deeper than the murderer's fears and doubts, even those about the nature and intention of a God that made him what he is, although it is derived essentially from his doubts. Terrified at the physical consequences of his deed ("Christ! did I say to-morrow? Is your brandy good for death?"), he is not particularly concerned about its moral consequences, primarily because he cannot reconcile his indifference to the fate of his victim and his understanding of the passions that drove him to kill. The conflict between passion and conscience is so unequal that he doubts the effectiveness of conscience—a "whisper" amid the shouts of passion—as a moral agent for most men. Although he talks about "the triumph of hate" as hell-inspired, he believes that those who hate live in an earthly hell and thereby "merit all grace that God can give." His sense of guilt, in consequence, is intellectual and does not arise from the emotional depths of conscience. What he has found mostly in those depths is a motivated passion to kill, and after the deed, a relative indifference toward his victim, indeed almost an indifference toward himself and his fate, for he has never told anyone but the priest *why* he killed the man (as interesting an attitude on his part as any in the poem, for his crime would probably have been judged differently had his motive been known: presumably he wished to protect his wife's name, though one must wonder whether it is not worse to be married to a murderer than to have cuckolded him). The condemned man's confession, then, for which he is never absolved, is a plea not for forgiveness or mercy, but for understanding and enlightenment in his confusion:

> But tell me,
> What does the whole thing mean? What are we,—
> Slaves of an awful ignorance? puppets
> Pulled by a fiend? or god, without knowing it?
> Do we shut ourselves from our own salvation,
> Or what do we do! I tell you, Dominie,
> There are times in the lives of us poor devils
> When heaven and hell get mixed. Though conscience
> May come like a whisper of Christ to warn us
> Away from our sins, it is lost or laughed at,—
> And then we fall. And for all who have fallen—
> Even for him—I hold no malice.
> Nor much compassion; a mightier mercy
> Than mine must shrive him. —And I—am going
> Into the light? —or into the darkness? (p. 84)

Here, as in many of Robinson's later characterizations, understanding of self, which is the same as wisdom, comes too late, if indeed it comes at all. But in "The Night Before," self-understanding is only half achieved—the murderer's despair does not result from his failure to accept what he knows about himself but, rather, from his inability to understand whether or not he is fully responsible. Though Robinson referred to the poem as a "tragic monologue," the murderer, without such understanding, can be only a pathetic figure, for tragedy implies both the power and exercise of a will not confused about the moral implications of its actions.

Whatever its merit as a poem, however, "The Night Before" stands as Robinson's earliest extended effort to achieve an effective dramatic presentation of the enigma of human character that was to him the artist's first concern. While his understanding of what was "dramatic" must have been influenced by Greek tragedy with its broad and sharply defined effects, and perhaps by the melodramatic effects of Wagnerian opera of which he was always fond, his tendency to invent plots and characters of considerable color had already been exhibited in some of his early prose sketches. How bizarre some of his situations were and how conscious he was of the artistic problems such invention posed, may be illustrated by his remarks to Smith about "Levy Condillac," one of his sketches in the mid-90s:

> It is not an easy task to kill a woman in childbirth with nervous prostration brought on by excessive clarinet playing on the part of an over-enthusiastic young husband, without bordering on the ridiculous. This is what I have been trying to do, and I have had the satisfaction of proving to myself that the thing can be done provided sufficient skill is exerted. Whether I can do it or not remains to be seen. Sometimes I fear that I am trying to straddle to the stars in this scheme of mine and may be obliged to come down a little before I realize anything. This will be hard, but not impossible when I set my reason to work (p. 130).

Robinson's problem from the beginning, then, had been to express his narrative impulse through an effective structure and thus allow his invention the range and depth that his increasingly complex conception of human character demanded. He had been aware in "The Night Before" of the limitations his inexperience posed for him in moving an original character through a purely imaginary situation. And although he did not receive the constructive criticism he had hoped for in publishing the poem, and accepted it as a failure, it was the beginning of the extended character studies that were to culminate in the book-length narratives that occupied him almost exclusively for the last twenty years of his life. Unfortunately, those longer works are all but unknown to the general reader who comes to Robinson through the anthologized shorter narratives, among which "Ben Jonson Entertains a Man from Stratford" is apt to be the longest representative.

How much Robinson had learned from the failure of "The Night Before" and how assiduously he had applied his talent to the extended characterization may be inferred from *Captain Craig,* published six years later (1902). While the volume's shorter blank-verse narratives —"Aunt Imogen" and "Isaac and Archibald"— exhibit the sure touch that the poet had exhibited in his more restricted portraits, many of them only sonnets, the longer narratives of the volume —"The Book of Annandale" and, particularly, the striking if uneven title poem, "Captain Craig"— clearly exemplify the directions in which Robinson's impulse for narrative was moving: the increased depth and complexity of the characterization and its supporting structure in "Captain Craig" is a clear forecast of the great characters Robinson was to move through the book-length blank-verse narratives that Ellsworth Barnard has aptly called "verse novels."

Robinson's experiments with the play would delay his beginning those productions for more than a decade, but after "Captain Craig" there could be no doubt that his impulse for narrative had found the right genre in which to express itself. The gallery of great characters that people the major narratives from *Merlin* (1917) to *King Jasper* (1935) is the measure of his success.

---

1 *Untriangulated Stars, Letters of Edwin Arlington Robinson to Harry De Forest Smith, 1890-1905*, editor, Denham Sutcliffe (Cambridge, 1947), 202. All subsequent page references are to this edition.

2 Edwin Arlington Robinson, *The Children of the Night* (New York, 1905), 71-72. All subsequent page references are to this edition, in which "The Night Before" is reprinted.

ROBINSON'S USE OF THE BIBLE

Nicholas Ayo

I

WHATEVER else the Bible might be, Robinson through the years appreciated it as great literature. Each of his Biblical poems ("The Three Taverns," "Lazarus," "Nicodemus," "The Prodigal Son," "Sisera," and "Young Gideon") capitalizes on dramatic elements in its source story. With a keen eye for a situation amenable to successful poetic treatment, he picked out of the Bible stories the crucial moment, the turning point—such as Paul's initial entry into Rome, or Lazarus' first words after his resurrection from the dead, or Nicodemus' painful moment of truth when he must choose whether or not to profess Jesus openly and break with the institutional religion and politics he was committed to. The dramatic effectiveness of the Biblical poems is naturally heightened by the reader's awareness, more or less conscious, of the jeopardy of the protagonist and the critical decisions that hang in the balance. Part of this emotional tension stems from the serious nature of the Biblical narratives, which Robinson, like any sensitive artist, tended to exploit. As one student of the Bible in literature reminds us, most Biblical stories "involve us as readers at a moral or moral-existentialist level which is quite different from the way in which, say, the farewell of Hector involves our common human nature."[1]

The predicaments of the protagonists in "Lazarus," "Nicodemus," and "Sisera" can hardly be overlooked; the dramatic situation of Paul in the more didactic "The Three Taverns," however, can easily be lost sight of. More than any other one person it is Paul who prepared the ground for the shifting of the center of Christianity from Jerusalem to Rome. As the Apostle of the Gentiles, he is the indefatigable champion of the universalism of Christianity already foreshadowed in the all-embracing colonization by the Roman Empire. On the vigil of his planned trail-blazing journey to Rome, he is arrested in Jerusalem. Many weeks later he comes as a prisoner into Rome, not as its prophet.

Reprinted by permission, *Colby Library Quarterly*, VIII (March 1969), 250-265.

Paul's reception there assumes a crucial importance for his career. Approaching the center of a civilization, he carries a message to initiate a world revolution in the spiritual order. Upon the outcome of the events in the capital city depends the entire future of that mission which is the electrifying purpose of his whole life. A moment of vital importance for mankind approaches. All is to be lost, or the world won, on the turn of the morrow's fate. For the habitual reader of the Bible, Robinson captures something of this momentous drama, and many of the lines of "The Three Taverns" take on added dimension in the light of Paul's predicament.

In his non-Biblical poems Robinson borrows widely from the Bible various quotations, paraphrases, and allusions that he thought would support or illustrate his meaning. Few of these borrowings, however, which can be found in the earliest poems as well as the latest, play a structural part. Most of the references to the context of the Scriptures function as decorative embellishment.

Among the books of the Old Testament employed, the largest number of references is to Genesis (about thirty), and there can be no doubt that the Garden of Eden was particularly meaningful for Robinson. Considering its short length, however, the book most alluded to is Daniel, where Robinson found a number of his favorite interests combined, viz., a mystery, a prophet, and a kingdom.

In the New Testament, on the other hand, the passages most frequently referred to concern various ethical dicta of the Gospels. By actual count, it is the exemplum in St. Matthew concerning houses built on sand compared to those on rock, and their respective fate when the rains come, that Robinson refers to more than to any other single passage. The poet made more extensive use of the third chapter of St. John, however, than any other single episode. Besides being the basis for "Nicodemus," it appears in several other poems. The Prologue to St. John is also cited frequently, and the parable of the sower is another favorite account. Many allusions to being a child again in order to find the Kingdom of God also stand out. As one would expect, both the Nativity story and the Passion story appear repeatedly.

Robinson's Biblical characters include more men than women. All of them would be considered reputable persons. There ars no villains. Even Sisera, as the underdog, elicits the sympathy of the reader. Among the major Biblical characters, however, the figure of the "prophet," taken in its most general meaning, stands out. All of the protagonists in the Biblical poems are isolated figures, whose vision of the truth must necessarily remain only partially understood by those to whom they must reveal it. The prophetic figure in Robinson moves alone, just as in "The Man Against the Sky," trusting in his *light* to discriminate between the true and the false—and that in spite of misleading clues. Paul is the prototype of the "prophet" in the Biblical poems; Lazarus, Nicodemus, Jael, and Gideon resemble him in various aspects. Lazarus, for example, receives a prophet's initiation in the experience of the miracle of resurrection, but because he cannot articulate his experience, he remains a dumb prophet. Nicodemus, knowing the truth but like Jonah fearing its consequences, represents the hesitant prophetic character. Although Jael receives Robinson's disapproval, at least implicitly, she is nonetheless the most enthusiastic "prophet" in the Biblical poems. The elder son in "The Prodigal Son" appeals to the future for the meaning of present events as a prophet would. Finally, Gideon may be considered the Old Testament equivalent of Nicodemus; both "prophets" seek to guarantee the presence of God and fail to find in themselves the resourcefulness to believe unflinchingly, even when given the help of external signs.

Part of the dramatic interest in Robinson's prophetic characters arises from the question uppermost in the reader's mind—how does a "prophet" know he is right? How can such a man assume, as he almost always must, that everyone else is wrong but himself? How the searching mind evaluates the sufficiency of the evidence to claim that *this* and not *that* is the truth, and how it resolves the hazardous ambiguities of taking one's conscience as the ultimate criterion of the validity of religious experience, must be considered a lifelong preoccupation with Robinson. It pervades not only the Biblical poems, but others as well, in which figures such as John Brown, Rembrandt, and Toussaint L'Ouverture endure similar difficulties and enjoy the same success in their roles as "prophets," whether political, social, or artistic. Moreover, with the secular "prophets," as with the religious, truth emerges only from the individual's faith in his own ability to see clearly.

In the character of the "prophet" Robinson enjoyed a privileged vantage point for contemplating some of the paradoxes that constitute much of the mystery of life. The prophet can explore the border between what is subjective and objective, between the rights of the individual and obligations to society, and between conscience and law. His struggle to preserve spiritual integrity through suffering and doubt readily leads to character revelation.

Robinson not only borrowed stories from the Bible, but he also capitalized on myths which the authors of the Bible had adapted to their purposes. Most of the discussion in the Biblical poems focuses around one major theme—the myth or "mystery of rebirth." Although the setting and the characters change, the dominant emphasis remains with the metamorphosis of soul, with the passage through some form of death to a higher form of life. Because such a passage can only be vaguely described, Robinson could harmonize it, not only with Biblical doctrine such as the fall and the grace-giving redemption, but also with broader accounts concerning a search for new life, such as the Grail legends and various myths of Eastern religions. Ramifications of the rebirth theme, therefore, readily extend outside the Biblical poems. For example, the Arthurian trilogy narrates in great detail the search for a passage from darkness to light, and from death to life of a higher spiritual order. Though the Grail legend serves Robinson well, the most profound rebirth stories—not necessarily the most poetic—come from the Bible, where the Grail legend itself had roots.

The "mystery of rebirth" that so appealed to Robinson receives its most forceful Biblical expression in the interview between Jesus and Nicodemus. "Except a man be born again, he cannot see the kingdom of God" (John 3:3). The poem devoted to Nicodemus, however, is not the only manifestation of the rebirth theme. In "The Three Taverns" Paul testifies to the passage from death to life in his conversion to the Gospel. Similarly, Lazarus descends into the tomb, which is transformed into a womb of birth issuing in a renewed life that holds at least some glimmer of meaning for human existence. Only by dying, therefore, by going through the doors of death as the several characters in *Matthias* approach the dark cave with the Egyptian door, can a man be reborn as Lazarus is, as Jesus is from the dead, or as Nicodemus is told he must be reborn. Each man must find the passage through death—whether physical, psychological, or spiritual—to a new life, and thus be reborn.

Quite logically Robinson links up the idea of rebirth with several Gospel passages that emphasize the need to become a child again in order to enter the kingdom of God. To become a child again is, of course, to be born again. The quest for spiritual childhood appears frequently, especially in the long poems. Its most characteristic expression, however, is found in the Biblical poems. Accordingly, Lazarus searches for the assurance that finding a "father" would give. The only outcome of his search—the only outcome Robinson admits—is the knowledge that he must be content to have faith in a "father" who transcends the apparent absurdity of this life. One cannot expect a miracle to give any guarantee.

Robinson does not speak explicitly of a "father" in his poems, but prefers to talk of becoming a child again. It is clear, however, that what characterizes childhood is dependence on an all-knowing, all-powerful, all loving parent who provides life and protects his child from death. "The Prodigal Son" portrays, of course, the classic account of a son's truly finding his father whose everlasting compassion could never be exhausted: "For this my son was dead, and is alive again;

he was lost, and is found. And they began to be merry" (Luke 15:24). Nicodemus, on the other hand, represents the theologian, the rational mind invited to go beyond reason. He speaks for the adult world—as does Caiaphas—the world with knowledge but no belief in a "father." If he is to be saved, Nicodemus must recognize the incomplete nature of his adult knowledge and return to the child's belief in an ultimate wisdom. His spiritual convictions must now spring from within himself, and not from the tradition and learning he acquired through his education and position. So a child grows from within. That it takes courage to be a child again, to believe that life has meaning in spite of faith-shattering experiences, is an important contention of the Biblical poems. Perhaps "Nicodemus," the last of Robinson's searching Biblical poems, best reflects his own conviction that one cannot expect all men to have the courage to believe—even in themselves.

The search for a "father" extends beyond the Biblical poems. In *Roman Bartholow,* for example, the protagonist seeks a psychological "father." The search is for a quasi-religious "father" in *Matthias at the Door.* Even if religious faith were proved an illusion, these poems argue, faith in some form is indispensable. As Pascal expressed man's recurrent need for a "father," if there were no God, man would have to invent one.

In the non-Biblical poems that show the impact of the Bible the "mystery of rebirth" also appears, although its expression is naturally not so completely developed. Robinson's interest in the Garden of Eden centers upon the fall from the innocence of "childhood" to the condition of the adult. Whether or not the fall of the soul as presented in his poems is the result of conscious sin, or the simple outcome of the experience of maturity, cannot be discussed here. However that may be, Robinson's preoccupation with innocence and the fall merges with one of the main streams of American literary thought running through Hawthorne, Melville, Henry James, and Faulkner among its noteworthy exponents.

The imagery of Eden gives way to other garden images. "Unless the grain of wheat die," for example, together with the parable of the sower with its implications of a final harvest, underline the theme of rebirth and offer shadowy prefigurations of the Lazarus and Nicodemus stories. Perhaps Robinson's most poetic analysis of a casualty in encountering the "mystery of rebirth" is Fernando Nash in the Bible-orientated *The Man Who Died Twice.* In an attempt to avoid relinquishing his habit of self-indulgence, he loses the inspiration to write a great symphony. In repentance, however, Nash achieves a spiritual triumph after all. "Unless a man lose his life he shall not find it" represents a distillation of the "mystery of rebirth" that Robinson never tired of borrowing from the Bible. No other myth—and its significance to the poet may extend beyond myth—in the Scriptures played such an important part in his poems.

The truths in Scripture held a wisdom that Robinson recognized as something special, if not unique. He would not have argued whether or not the Bible was essentially different from any other religious literature of permanent value—such a question was far too theological. He contented himself to say that he read the Bible for a number of reasons. And although Robinson was not a learned student of the Bible, he made efforts to use it accurately. Similar care was not always shown with some of the other literary sources he employed. In the Arthurian legends, for example, he assumed more liberty with the story of Camelot than he did with the accounts in the Bible, although it should be noted that the Arthurian legends were handed down in variant versions that doubtless invited eclectic borrowing. Nor can evidence of a detailed knowledge of appropriate written sources be found in poems such as "John Brown," "Rembrandt to Rembrandt," or "Ponce de Leon," that would compare with the Biblical poems.

"The Three Taverns" is the best example in Robinson of an elaborate Biblical mosaic. In the judicious combination of various elements of Pauline doctrine, Robinson highlights the substance of Paul's Epistles and puts it in a form readily understandable for a modern reader with some familiarity with the Bible. "The Three Taverns" is a remarkable tribute to the Bible in the accuracy which Robinson took pains to preserve in creating a poem that reflects the extraordinary literary merits of the Epistles themselves. Although such fidelity to Biblical texts and such sensitivity to Biblical doctrine do not prove religious belief, they argue that the author treated the Bible with a care that he lavished on no other literary source.

Robinson's niece Ruth recalled in an interview that the poet wanted to be remembered for two qualities he cherished in his life and work, namely reverence for other persons, and a continual search for the truth. To what extent the truth in the Bible was made more attractive by the needs of his personal life remains a question open to debate. For what it may be worth, however, the periods of significant Biblical efforts—the late 1890s, 1918-1920, and 1928-1929—correspond to periods of painful circumstances in his life.

Without doubt there were far better stories as stories in the Bible that Robinson overlooked. Moreover, we know that he composed "Nicodemus" because he felt that he had not done enough in his lifetime to explore the religious dimensions of human existence. The autobiographical concern of this poem has been generally recognized by commentators, and it is noteworthy that the poet "liked his 'Nicodemus' and was greatly pleased to have it praised by certain friends whose judgment he trusted."[2] On the other hand there is little doubt that Robinson's accurate use of the Bible was partly motivated by the desire to take refuge in the safety of impersonal historical statement. The open-endedness of "Nicodemus," consequently, which does not unequivocally take a stand, may fairly be judged a partial evasion of responsibility—although it must be remembered that it is a poem after all, and not a creed.

Since Robinson early rejected verbal formulation of religious beliefs, I think it is futile to attempt satisfactorily to assemble his religious tenets, either from his life and letters, or especially from his poems. Without doubt the Bible held an important, though probably not a decisive, place in his total religious view. It certain held a pervasive place in his poems. As Edwin Fussell wisely concluded, the Bible certainly played a part in the formulation of the poet's unique vision, "But the most important results of Robinson's familiarity with the Bible were finally poetic."[3] On the other hand, the open-ended quality of the Biblical poems reflected Robinson's personal search for genuine faith. Characteristically, his interest in these poems centered on the crisis of decision, rather than on a triumphant discovery or affirmation of belief that he never experienced himself. Since authentic religious faith, nevertheless, is known to have its own inexpressible dark nights, one ought to be careful not to pass over lightly Robinson's religious commitment. And since the individual of today often repeats in capsule form the religious experience of the group of yesterday, it may not be out of place to suggest that Robinson, as a spokesman for the contemporary soul in the process of searching the Christian tradition, represents a world that serious men must encounter at some time in their life.

Roy Harvey Pearce conveniently divides American poets into two groups, those for whom the "Adamic" point of view dominates, or the "mythic."[4] In the Biblical poems, Robinson's prophet-protagonists represent "Adamic" figures, but the poet's attempt to place them in a Biblical frame of reference reaches out for the stability of the "mythic" community and religious tradition. Although Robinson fails in his affirmation, and he certainly does and though his work shows consequent poetic shortcomings, he nevertheless attempts a crucial synthesis. Furthermore, an author and his attitudes are revealed by the kind of subject he writes about, whether or not he succeeds with it, or is compelled to profess his subject as meaningful outside the references of the poem itself.

II

Robinson's thorough development of the Scriptural stories in the Biblical poems and the fidelity he shows to the story outline in combining Scriptural texts, sometimes from different parts of the Bible, create the impression that these poems share in the "authoritative reality" of Biblical quotation itself. As a result, the historical milieu of the Bible functions as a constant background. Because Robinson's Biblical allusions are so reminiscent to a reader familiar with the Bible, the echo of parallel texts reverberates in the poems. Consequently, many lines of "The Three Taverns," to cite the best example, which is a carefully composed mosaic of over two hundred Biblical allusions, could substitute for an apocryphal Pauline Epistle, although the poem taken as a whole reveals its twentieth-century origin. According to James Sims, to whom I am indebted for the concept "authoritative reality," Milton's accurate and pervasive use of "Biblical echo, paraphrase, allusion, idiomatic structure, and tone" similarly creates a dense atmosphere of Biblical reality that makes the invented parts of his epic poems seem authentic and probable. Robinson creates such a credibility for "The Three Taverns," and for the remaining Biblical poems to a lesser degree, by so immersing them in the events, attitudes, and even language of the Bible.

Since the New Testament accounts of Lazarus and Nicodemus are less complete than its account of Paul, it is not surprising that the corresponding Biblical poems show more expansion of details than "The Thee Taverns." Robinson, however, does not alter the Scriptures until his last two Biblical poems, "Sisera" and "Young Gideon." And even in "Sisera," where the poet invents a number of episodes to fill in the gaps, he does not distort the story outline. Robinson actually alters details of the Biblical story only in "Young Gideon," and in some respects he rewrites the Gideon story. Fussell maintains that "Young Gideon" and "Lazarus," which are based on meager Biblical details, illustrate Robinson's characteristic treatment of the Bible. Although it is true that Robinson alters the Gideon story, he does not, strictly speaking, alter the Lazarus story. Because the Gospel details are sketchy, he necessarily expands the Lazarus account, and in places uses it as a point of departure. Robinson includes, however, virtually every Gospel reference to Lazarus, Martha, and Mary, and his own invention in no way changed the general outline of the Biblical story. Expansion, and not alteration, is Robinson's characteristic way of handling a Biblical story.

Besides the six Biblical poems (seven poems if one includes "Calvary") the influence of the Bible can be found in varying degrees in approximately one hundred of Robinson's poems, or almost half of his total composition. Throughout the *Collected Poems* I have been able to discover about 250 references to the Bible, not counting the same number in the Biblical poems themselves. The bulk of these references are allusions to particular passages in the Bible; quotations and close paraphrases of the Scripture number only about thirty. The largest concentration of Biblical references is found in the volumes published during the years 1916-1924, a period which represents the middle years of his writing career.

In the non-Biblical poems Robinson did not contribute a great deal to his borrowings from the Bible. Among the earlier poems, such as "Captain Craig" and "The Revealer," he began to employ what I call a "complex simile," which made the Biblical allusion a structural part of the poem instead of merely an embellishment. Furthermore, some of the complex similes were used as foils; Robinson on occasion used the context of the Bible for an ironic contrast. "The Gift of God" is a good example, and "Cassandra," "Llewellyn and the Tree," and "An Island" would serve as well. Because many of the short poems in Robinson adumbrate the longer poems of his later period—"Credo" prefigures "The Man Against the Sky," for instance—there is reason to think that the complex similes foreshadow the Biblical poems themselves, which assume their function.

All of the Biblical poems show that the appropriate source stories were adapted to expand the psychological dimensions that are almost entirely lacking in the more objective narratives of the Bible. This psychological expansion is achieved through the focus of a limited point of view and through the development of the inner consciousness of the characters.

Turning now to the limited point of view, Robinson imposed a number of restrictions upon the information which the characters within the poem possess. What they know of the course of events is limited to what the historical characters could have known at the time of the action in the poem. Edwin Fussell noted the advantages of what he calls the "agnostic point of view" especially in "Lazarus" and "Nicodemus." A particularly modern adaptation, this "limited point of view" enhances the dramatic qualities of the narrative by creating suspense, and often a certain amount of irony, since the reader enjoys more knowledge than the characters within the poem. In addition, Robinson is able to present an impersonal and objective interpretation of the Bible. Without committing himself, he can offer the reader an imaginative grasp of the central religious elements of the Bible story.

Because of the development of the inner consciousness of the characters, Robinson's Biblical poems represent for the most part spiritual biographies. Since the Scriptures could provide him with only an historical framework, he invented most of the inner life of his characters. Robinson, like hosts of other writers, tended to intellectualize his own experiences, and it is not surprising that he does the same for his poetic characters. Rollo Brown reports telling Robinson he "believed there was something in Miguel de Unamuno's theory that all fictional characters are somewhat autobiographical, since they are only the projection of cardinal qualities in the author magnified to the required proportions." The poet apparently was disturbed "as if [Brown] had suggested that every tragic character in his poetry was only some representation of the tragic in his own life."[5] Although Robinson is by no means always and everywhere autobiographical, Hagedorn's observation that he was "inclined to universalize emotions peculiar to his own hypersensitive nature" is worthy of attention.[6]

III

In his longer poems Robinson needed the support of a story structure. The Arthurian poems enjoy their success largely because the "mythic" elements supported the psychological. Most of the poet's later verse novels, such as *Cavender's House* and *The Glory of the Nightingales,* lacked this support. They were too amorphous, too cerebral, and they created an overly private world of psychological drama reminiscent of Henry James's similar impasse. Robinson's Biblical poems, however, enjoyed ample support from Christian "myth," regardless of the incorporation of any doctrinal values. As it happened, the peak of Robinson's successful blend of the "mythic" and the psychological occurred about 1920 with the publication of two of his most esteemed volumes, *Lancelot* and *The Three Taverns.*

Though Robinson needed the support of the Bible, he circumscribed his borrowings from it. He preferred a narrow range of characters and emotions which he could treat exhaustively. Most of the Bible stories he chose were ideally suited. Episodic as they were, they limited the subject from necessity, and the poet made a virtue of remaining within those bounds. The objective atmosphere, moreover, created by the "authoritative reality" and the "limited point of view" of the poems tended to emphasize the overall meaning of the Biblical episode.

"The Three Taverns" best illustrates Robinson's detailed familiarity with the Bible, the functional accuracy of his borrowings, and his sensitive elaboration of only pivotal—and paradoxical—points in St. Paul's character and teaching, such as the law and freedom, faith and charity, the word and the Word. It is a superb religious poem from the point of view of its spiritual sensitivity. The blank verse style is austere and masterfully controlled as befits religious feeling at once ardent and thoughtful. The poem has much of the virtue of Gregorian chant; the music is completely subordinated to the meaning of the words, and the total effect is one of simple unity rich in wisdom.

Yvor Winters, perhaps the most perceptive critic of the Biblical poems, maintained that the style and subject were perfectly matched in

"The Three Taverns" to create "one of the greatest poems of its kind and length in English."[7] Ellsworth Barnard considered the poem to be "a recreation of the Apostle Paul that perhaps comes as near to transplanting the essence of the Epistles into modern idiom as will ever be possible."[8] And the consensus among Robinson's chief critics was unanimous when Edwin Fussell concluded that "The Three Taverns" was "probably the best as poem" among the Biblical poems (p. 162).

At the same time as Robinson was attracted by St. Paul, he was intrigued also with Lazarus, and wrote a poem that began where the Gospel account ended. In "Lazarus" the limits of word expression are approached, for neither the poet nor Lazarus, who is his creature, can describe the experience of death. No man has returned from beyond the grave except Lazarus in the Gospel, whose silent voice frequently tempts artists to put words in his mouth. As a poem of deep religious feeling and psychological truth, with profound touches of inter-personal sensitivity among the characters, "Lazarus" is an impressive achievement. Its method is to isolate the mystery of death by a series of negatives, often only implied, which, while never revealing the unknown, encircle it with conclusions about what death must not be. As a result the reader is left to contemplate what remains unknown, yet confined in the center of the poem's roundabout progression. Because Robinson pressed against the frontiers of the verbal world, his poem strains. Perhaps the Lazarus story cannot be told. However that may be, Robinson's effort remains a powerful religious poem, calculated to engender surprise and serious reflection in a sympathetic reader. Even with the inherent weakness of the subject, Winters thought the poem deserved the rank of "great," for it has "great power and the style is controlled in every line" (p. 138).

In my judgment, none of the Biblical poems except "The Three Taverns," can compare with "Nicodemus" for depth of religious understanding. As a didactic poem which presents a poignant understanding of the perennial struggle between reason and faith, it has no equal in Robinson. Yvor Winters thought that "Nicodemus" was a partial failure. Although "excellent in its plan" and "for the most part respectable in style, though a brief emotional outburst from Nicodemus near the end is very weak" the style was too "relaxed and a trifle flat as compared to the style of the greater poems" to place it among Robinson's "important works" (p. 140). While it may be argued whether "Nicodemus" is inferior to "The Three Taverns" or to "Lazarus," there is no doubt that it is quite different. Its sense of urgency, for example, is in contrast to the cerebral tone of its sister poem "Lazarus." Moreover, "Nicodemus" does not have the sparse economy and the muscle of the earlier Biblical poems, and if these characteristic traits of Robinson's best poetry are valued as indispensable, it suffers in the comparison. But depth of mind and feeling it has in abundance.

Only Edwin Fussell wrote at some length about "The Prodigal Son," and he concluded that it was a failure: "Some of the lines are both trite and trivial. Robinson was rarely so empty, except in such a situation, when his skeptical restriction of materials left him too little with which to work" (p. 166). I find no reason to qualify these remarks. The poem is decidedly inferior in imagination, although it does not seem to be carelessly written.

The Old Testament poems lack the power and seriousness of the earlier New Testament ones. They are largely neglected by the critics and generally assumed to be inferior. "Sisera" can be read as serious religious poetry, although it is open to the criticism of having a vague resolution. As sophisticated comedy, however, an approach which Robinson hinted but the critics have not pursued, it has many merits. Robinson's later verse novels, *Talifer, Amaranth,* and *King Jasper,* are definitely comic-serious works and must be read with their ambivalent nature in mind.

Robinson's use of the Bible in the non-Biblical poems shows a lack of flexibility and daring in the imaginative manipulation of the Bible's almost inexhaustible material. Most of the borrowings—often rare or bizarre references—are simply decorative embellishment. Because the "complex simile" he used at one time introduces a more symbolic usage, it is unfortunate that Robinson did not further exploit it.

Finally, as must be apparent to the reader, even the major Biblical poems were by no means an unqualified success. Even though the Biblical story outline gave Robinson's psychological imagination a necessary support, it also confined the area open to exploration. Consequently, the Biblical poems easily became too analytical, and there was little attempt at a bold synthesis of ideas or images as, for example in William Vaughn Moody's *The Death of Eve* or Robinson Jeffers' *Dear Judas.* Furthermore, Robinson's minimal affirmation missed completely the spirit of the "good news" that pervades the Gospel. The Biblical poems lacked color and vitality, and even their didactic success was often achieved at the cost of being overly abstract. Despite their shortcomings, as religious poems of a didactic nature, they deserve more acclaim than they have yet received.

More significantly, perhaps, Robinson's Biblical poems represent an interest in religion not thought so characteristic of the poet or of the 1920s when he composed them. Robinson wrote about 1500 lines of poetry concerning explicitly Biblical situations and personages after 1920. Of his approximately 450 pages of short and medium-length poetry, the Biblical poems total one-tenth. Under the impact of scientific and other upheavals, religion did not disappear from the American literary scene, although it underwent important modifications, which have become more evident as our perspective improves with the passage of time. Religious concerns and spiritual values endure under many guises in the works of major writers, such as Dreiser, O'Neill and Robinson, despite first impressions often to the contrary. Generally overlooked in Robinson's total poetical production, the Biblical poems hold a noteworthy place in the literary history of the period, and they may acquire a higher aesthetic reputation as qualified critics give them more attention. The course of American poetry and the role of religion in it during the first half of the twentieth century have not yet been adequately studied. Robinson, of course, must be considered one of the most important poets in such an account; in my judgment, no thoughtful and carefully executed religious poetry of didactic nature comparable to "The Three Taverns," "Lazarus," and "Nicodemus" may be found in all of American literature.

---

1 Amos Wilder, *Theology and Modern Literature* (Cambridge, Mass., 1958), 68.
2 Esther W. Bates, *Edwin Arlington Robinson and His Manuscripts* (Waterville, Me., 1944), 23.
3 *Edwin Arlington Robinson: The Literary Background of a Traditional Poet* (Berkeley, 1954), 170.
4 *The Continuity of American Poetry* (Princeton, 1961).
5 *Next Door to a Poet* (New York, 1937), 60.
6 Hermann Hagedorn, *Edwin Arlington Robinson: A Biography* (New York, 1938), 287.
7 *Edwin Arlington Robinson* (Norfolk, Conn., 1946), 136.
8 *Edwin Arlington Robinson: A Critical Study* (New York, 1952), 91.

E. A. ROBINSON'S IDEA OF GOD

DAVID H. BURTON

THE PROBLEM of God in the poetry of Edwin Arlington Robinson is to a large extent the problem of God in a modern scientific society where traditionalism remains vital to the way of life of countless of its members. Focusing on the idea of God, or Divine Force, in the work of a poet-intellectual like Robinson therefore not only provides a better awareness of the total worth of his verse; it helps to locate him explicitly in the growth of American thought. By the time of Robinson's death in 1935 American thought had been greatly influenced by an interaction of philosophical and scientific teachings and traditional ways of approaching the major human issues that had not achieved a stable synthesis. This interaction was a momentous one, and while Robinson's verse composed but a small segment of the total experience his art revealed something of the subtle uncertainty that featured it. Being wholly artist the poet was unaffectedly intellectual. He mirrored aspects of the contemporary American mind with an innocence, a directness, and an honesty that render his commitments and his doubts symptomatic of the American of his time, the years that witnessed the modern transformation of American thought.

In this regard Robinson's approach to God in his poetry was, perhaps, as illuminating as any aspect of his total poetic expression. His attraction to the God of his fathers and the ethical values that inhered in the ancient religion was inimical to his philosophical awareness and the instruction of science. This contention remained a feature of his poetry, unresolved quite as much as it continued unresolved in the larger context of the American mind. The endurance of a traditional religious concept of God and the appeals of philosophical and scientific assertions about the probability and the probable nature of some Divine Force created a tension in both the poet and his poetry. Without this

Reprinted by permission, *Colby Library Quarterly*, VIII (June 1969), 280-294.

conflict Robinson would be considerably less interesting as a poet, and also less important as an intellectual whose keenness to enjoy both the assurances of a scientific world and the reassurances of the old faith was an instructive detail in the larger canvas of American thought.

Three major influences were at work on Robinson, affecting his vision of the Divine, all of them intrinsic to the development of American thought in his lifetime. The Self of Idealism, the "no-God" of science, and the Father of traditional Christianity were all discernible in various passages of his poetry, explaining Robinson's reluctance, to his very last days, to be very specific about the nature of his deity. His penchant for philosophical Idealism is well known. Two of his best poems, "The Children of the Night" and "The Man Against the Sky" contain noteworthy evidences of his fondness for an Idealistic interpretation of life and of God. A letter to his friend, Harry DeForest Smith, in 1896, leaves no doubt of his Idealistic sympathies. In it he wrote:

> . . . my ideas are getting to be so thoroughly ideal, that the collecting of anything but wisdom often seems like going back into ignorance and barbarism. Carlyle has given me a brush lately, and I am just beginning to see what he was driving at in his *Sartor Resartus.* If the book is anything it is a denial of the existence of matter as anything but a manifestation of thought. Christianity is the same thing, and so is illuminated common sense.[1]

The consequences of his contact with Idealism were persuasively present in Robinson's general reluctance to be definite about the nature and quality of God, while insisting on the actuality of the divine in various ways. He remained unwilling to submit finally to a pantheistic absolute, however. Knowing well the argument that the taproot of the subconscious went down to God, the one Self called God or the Absolute, he was not entirely convinced. He followed the line of argument without adopting its conclusions, reserving the right to interpret the existence and the function of God as accumulating thought and experience might suggest.

His enthusiasm for Idealism was stubbornly subdued by science, much as Robinson himself was subdued by life. His cosmic pessimism, his fatalism, his verging agnosticism—and his work shows signs of all these traits—perhaps were born as much of personal defeat as they were the products of a world scientifically measured. Yet the infiltration of scientific ideas had important effects after all. The tenets of science struck hard at both an Idealistic and a religious conception of God. They also encouraged in Robinson's poetry a recourse to scientific methodology that scorned first principles in favor of what the specific and individual facts might yield by way of wisdom in showing man why he must accept his lot. The realism of his verse he owed to the scientific temper, and in such poems as "How Annandale Went Out" and "Lost Anchors" life viewed as a quaint adventure of the protoplasm was an overriding feature. Turning again to his letters there is a passage written to Harry Smith in 1893 that conveyed his feelings.

> This life is a curious mess, after all. Sometimes I sit here by my fire and wonder how it is all coming out. I look upon the millions who lived and died a thousand years ago and wonder if it makes much difference how it comes out, after all. I do not look pessimistically upon the matter. I am inclined to regard it more in the light of a big joke—whose joke it is, or whether it is a good one, I cannot tell (*US*, 80).

As late as 1934 Robinson found himself with much the same thought. To Laura Richards he observed:

> I'm afraid, on the whole, that there isn't much comfort in nature as a visible evidence of God's infinite love. It [the world] appears to me to be a shambles and a torture-chamber from the insects up — or should we say down? The insects will have the world some day, and maybe they will eat everything that's on it, and then eat each other. For some reason or other this makes me think of an epitaph by Thomas Hardy. You may know it?
>
> "I'm Smith of Stoke. Aged sixty-odd,
> I lived without a dame
> From youth-time on; and would to God
> My dad had done the same."[2]

In such moods even the stern God of his Puritan forebears enjoyed small place because the poet could find little meaning to life itself.

In many ways Robinson was a Puritan and therefore a Christian, and though he formally rejected the orthodoxy of early New England, strong evidences of its mark on him are everywhere in his poetry. The problem of sin, the weight of conscience, the ultimacy of self-knowledge were all part of Robinson's thought. Preoccupation with such themes often led him to some of his best verse. In "Siege Perilous" the poet-moralist warned that men must not be seduced by the easy way of materialism, even though the world was replete with good men confronted by misfortune and men of indifferent virtue enjoying the world's prosperity. Instead, man must trust his conscience and his God. If he does this, he can ignore the rest of men:

> There fell one day upon his eyes a light
> Ethereal, and he heard no more men speaking.[3]

The power of conscience was the very marrow of the old New England theology and Robinson sang such songs of an inner necessity. His Christianity did not include a willingness or a need to define God metaphysically, or to discuss the nature of the Heavenly City. Rather it addressed itself to man in his moral relationship: to God and to his fellowmen. At times Robinson displayed an essentially religious conviction of man, and by inference, of God, espousing a kind of tendential Christian theology.

A degree of caution is in order in characterizing Robinson's adherence to a traditional view of God, for the very reason that he declined to be specific very often about the subject. In his poetry God is not so much a person as a force, a Divine Force for Good, which motivates men and turns them in the direction of God. But for Robinson, man's vision is not an awareness of the majesty of the Almighty but the need of man to know himself, and thereby to attain a meaning beyond himself. This is the Divine Force for Good that Robinson discovered and so often revealed in the tangled lives of men. His reluctance to personalize God is attributable both to philosophical Idealism, which tended to simplify the Divine Force for Good to the point where a single word, such as Self or Absolute, sufficed to identify the deity, and to the sway of scientific agnosticism in which God was unknown and perhaps did not exist at all. Occasionally Robinson's verse personalized God, but more typically his deity remained "the great Whatever-it-is" (*SL*, 142).

The interplay between the Self of Idealism and the God of traditionalism, with lingering evidence of the doubts about the existence of a deity at all, when examined in some detail spells out Robinson's appreciation of the Divine Force for Good in the world of men. His shorter verse — his "songs with souls"— present an initial way of understanding this. Robinson retained an affinity for short verse throughout his career so that this particular poetic form encompasses the full range of his thought. So far it would seem clear that uncertainty about the "eternal verities" was a typical starting point for him:

> We know not, dying, what we may be, dead;
> We know not, living, what we are, alive.[4]

These lines, written in 1890, aptly pronounce this intellectual indecision. But it was the confusion that drove Robinson to sing of the need of belief and in his verse to delineate men who were seeking fulfillment. "The Children of the Night" is an example. The poem is a simple confession of faith in God undertaken by Robinson as an individual who is sure of man's essential dignity and his eternal destiny. It is a destiny culminating in God, the Light, spoken of in the poem. To Robinson the Light and the Divine are synonymous. The initial use of the figure of Light is instructive in that it suggests the presence of both Idealistic and Christian versions of the divine. In one place the Light is identified with Self.

> So let us in ourselves revere
> The Self that is the Universe!

Yet the poet does not remain satisfied with the extent of this assertion. He seems drawn irresistibly to the God of his fathers. In sensing the futility of life he allows for the traditional God, from his own lonely station as a man and on the premises that men use with respect to God:

> If there be nothing, good or bad,
> But chaos for a soul to trust, —
> God counts it for a soul gone mad,
> And if God be God, He is just.
> And if God be God, He is Love.

Yet the apparent traditionalism of this profession should not obscure the fact that the poem proposes to endorse no finalized way of judging God, relying instead on the "common creed of common sense." In "The Children of the Night" Robinson took occasion to flay formal religious confessions of God:

> we have played enough
> With creeds that make a fiend of Him.[5]

This passage suggests not alone the influence of Idealism but the antagonisms bred by the failures of formalized religion and the pretensions of the Higher Criticism as well. In summary, "The Children of the Night" may well be called "the breakdown of the old belief and the endeavor to find life without it,"[6] but enough of the traditional concept of God remains to render the poem a fine example of the interplay of the conflicting ideas that dominated Robinson's version of God.

The tension arising from the interplay of conflicting principles served, at times, to bring Robinson closer to an agnostic position, as, for example, in "The Man Against the Sky." In this poem was represented the whole human race in one man, a modern Everyman, in whom were cast up the doubts, the fears, and the aspirations of twentieth-century scientific man. The hero of the poem was real in that these feelings and convictions had been part of his earthly labor. In one man he is all men,

> As if he were the last god going home
> Unto his last desire (*CP*, 60).

An indisputably religious piece, "The Man Against the Sky" nonetheless represented a diluted version (and vision) of God. God became only the Word, a final destination of humankind dimly realized. The deity of the poem is not so much ill-defined as undefined. It was not the Self of Idealism nor was it after the fashion of the Biblical God. At most Robinson chose to profess the divine in a negative manner, an Infinity defying human comprehension:

> The Word itself, the living word
> That none alive has ever heard
> Or ever spelt (*CP*, 68).

For "the man against the sky" the Word was sufficient. The foundation of the belief explored here was akin to intuition, its most tangible expression was the mainspring of an ethical code, that is, a Divine Force for Good in the lives of men.

The poem, "Captain Craig," stands out as an affecting delineation of this concept of a Divine Force for Good. Doubtful that he could know very much about God, Robinson was equally sure that he could recognize the divine elements in men. In "Captain Craig" he set forth his idealized view of a man, revealing how this Divine Force ought to play itself out in human affairs. The character of Craig becomes an epitome of man's dignity:

> 'Nothing is there more marvelous than man',
> Said Sophocles; and he lived long ago (*CP*, 117).

And "What power a man has in him to put forth," marvels Craig (*CP*, 117). The poet has Craig relate how a soldier by his kindness saved a young man from suicide. Pondering the incident Craig speaks of the power for good that is in men that is not the result of wealth or worldly well-being. Does man's purpose terminate with advancing the brotherhood of man? The evidence in "Captain Craig" implies that above this brotherhood Robinson recognized a form of a divine Fatherhood. Craig is made to avow the existence of God and he tells something of His nature. The deity is termed God, or Truth. God is inscrutable and He is all-just and all-loving.

> "There is no luck,
> No fate, no fortune for us, but the old
> Unanswering and inviolable price
> Gets paid: God sells himself eternally,
> But never gives a crust" (*CP*, 121-122).

This appears to be the same God as found in "The Children of the Night," whose make-up Robinson there chose to define as justice and love. God "sells" himself in his love for mankind, but men must be disposed to love God in return. This is presented as part of God's justice, He never gives even a crust unless men are willing to receive Him.

"Captain Craig" also contains a statement concerning the passage of man to God. The more obvious means was love for fellow human beings, yet in the poem Robinson asserted that charity is best based on faith, a mystic supra-rational belief. This faith should not be conceived in fear, furthermore, but in a complete and utter trust in God, a

> "wiser kind of joy that you shall have
> Never, until you learn to laugh with God" (*CP*, 119)

Robinson probes the phenomenon of faith. He shows it to be a simple trust in God and a desire to carry out His will. Such a faith is not always a gratuitous gift.

> "It is the flesh
> That ails us, for the spirit knows no qualm,
> No failure, no down-falling: so climb high" (*CP*, 151).

God is reached not " 'alone through flesh contempt / Or through flesh reverence' " (*CP*, 153). This ascent to God is made easier by a firmness of faith. The stronger the faith, the more certain the salvation, a conviction movingly analogized in Craig's dream of his encounter with the Carpenter from Nazareth (*CP*, 141-142). "Captain Craig" demands action emanating from faith so that all men may be led to the Light (*CP*, 158). Clearly Robinson appears at home with the God of tradition in these passages. Yet it is well to remember that what he has to say about God is inspired not by the deity of Idealism or the God of the Testaments, but by his realization of the Divine Force for Good in men's lives. It is from the human situation that the poet implies a personal God that seems quite traditional at times; it is not from some *a priori* notion of the divine that Robinson deduces his judgment of man. This may be the same as saying that he admired the Christian ethic while resisting the accompanying concept of God. But it is the old God that we discover him in the process of resisting, and in some ways none too successfully. In any case, the Divine Force for Good was the everyday experience of God for E. A. Robinson.

Other of the poet's "songs with souls" tell of the conflicting elements in his approach to the divine. In "Credo" he wrote:

> For through it all—above, beyond it all—
> I know the far-sent message of the years,
> I feel the coming glory of the Light (*CP*, 94).

In such a passage the inscription of Idealism is convincing. Yet consider, in contrast, the fervent message, the agonized faith of "Calvary," with its final question:

> Tell me, O Lord—tell me, O Lord, how long
> Are we to keep Christ writhing on the cross! (*CP*, 83).

If read out of the context of his total poetry "Calvary" appeals to us as a poem worthy of one who confessed the Father in the Son. Is it fair to suggest with respect to the kind of God Robinson believed in sufficiently to include in his verse that there were times when he could only accept "the Self that was the universe," and that at other times nothing else would satisfy him than a belief in "The Master who toiled along to Calvary?" Neither the Idealistic vein nor the Christian mood dominated, however; neither was as consistent as Robinson's acknowledgement of the deity as a Divine Force for Good.

Two of Robinson's Arthurian pieces, *Merlin* and *Lancelot,* afford some further exemplification of his idea of God. Though they are set in abstracted medieval surroundings, the poet does not portray in these poems anything resembling the medieval Christian view of God. Much of medieval religious sense is present but with an ethical and not a theological accent. The characters whom Robinson develops in the poems are not the stereotypes of chivalry but men and women highly individualized yet with a universal projection. They are at home in the moral quandaries in which Robinson places them while at the same time they manage to suggest in their moral dilemmas a dimension larger than life itself.

Merlin tells the story of the doom of Camelot. Robinson used this well-known theme to examine the consequences of sin, the sins of Arthur the King. His intention is not to condemn the sinner; the consequences of the sin as these are observable in life seem sufficient for him. In *Merlin* the effects of Arthur's sins are the ruin of Camelot. The quality that pervades the story is Fate. As Merlin himself says: "On Fate there is no vengeance / Even for God." But Fate in the poem is based on an abstracted concept of fate as the wages of sin which are inescapable, saving Robinson from the necessary imputation of fatalism and making it consistent with his implied traditionalism in the poem with respect to God. Robinson commented once that in *Merlin* he was not simply an evangel of ruin as he proclaimed an end to Camelot. "When you have read it," he told Mrs. Louis Ledoux, " . . . you mustn't forget the redemption—even if you don't see it" (*SL*, 97). Something of the same thing can be observed of *Merlin* with respect to Robinson's idea of God. By utilizing a medieval setting he could draw upon the Christian estimate of God with no need on his part to be very precise about it. But the traditional God is there, even if it is not readily visible.

Lancelot emphasized the Light as *Merlin* did Fate. Once again the figures in the work are not wooden characters whose attraction to the Light is a studied conclusion merely to be chronicled. Robinson left his subjects free to reject the Light, if they so desired, in a very human way. Lancelot was allowed to elect either the Light or his love for Guinevere, and the knight faced his choice like any ordinary mortal,

> A moth between a window and a star
> Not wholly lured by one or led by the other (*CP*, 415).

And in an all too human fashion he laments that he can not have both the Light and his love for Guinevere. What was the Light that led Lancelot away from the world to personal sacrifice in order to achieve it? Guinevere says, and Lancelot agrees, that it was not a Light of any worldly kind, nor was it the Light of Rome. It appeared, rather, as a unique and ethereal Gleam from "another state," "nor one that we may name." The Light is the Grail of the *Morte d'Arthur* given a psychological figure. But it is still mystic and still miracle-working. Robinson wrote to Hermann Hagedorn that the Light of Lancelot was "simply the Light of the Grail, interpreted universally as a spiritual realization of Things and their significance" (*SL*, 113). His distaste for metaphysics permitted him no more concrete statement of it than "one we may not name." To understand Robinson's traditional God in *Lancelot* requires an emphasis on values. The thrust of the poem is not so much the nature of the Light, though it was clearly a spiritual Something, as it is the absolute merit of faith as the practical means of achieving a higher spiritual condition. As in *Merlin* the explicit medieval setting enables Robinson to execute a combination of varying views of God. Where else but in the medieval world could the nature of the traditional notion of the divine be more naturally assumed, yet allow the poet to be true to his own personal uncertainty about God? He is content to term God the Light. Nevertheless, the final determination by Lancelot to follow the Light strikes us as very similar to medieval man's passage to God and so reinforces the image of the Christian deity in this example of Robinson's poetic thought.

A major portion of Robinson's later work, poetry completed after *Merlin* and *Lancelot,* took the form of dramatic narratives. These poems reaffirmed a moral foundation to life, but they were notable as well for a hesitancy to avow an absolute God, or immortality. The spiritual message of the dramatic narratives was oftentimes obscure. Of the significance of human values these poems spoke with an immediate and experiential certainty; of the nature of God or of the existence of God at all, doubts were simultaneously raised. What emerged most consistently in these poems was a sense of the weight and power of conscience, the tool of self-knowledge. The age-old faults of man—pride, hatred, lust, spiritual complacency—were all incisively portrayed along with the varying efforts to achieve salvation on the part of the characters involved. In this collection of poems there were some amazing variations with respect to Robinson's estimate of the nature of God. For example, the deity of Fernando Nash in *The Man Who Died Twice,* as often as he was described, was verily the God of Revelation. At the other extreme, *The Glory of the Nightingales* lacked altogether any affirmation of God.

Roman Bartholow was one of the first of these studies exploring the spiritual state of the times and reiterating the lesson of *Lancelot* that man of his nature seeks a spiritual goal. The sense of sin symbolized in *Merlin* also figured prominently, bringing the total human dilemma into focus. Simply told, *Roman Bartholow* was the story of modern man's saturation with materialism and his attempts to overcome this condition. The poem revealed in an important way Robinson's grasp of values in that it narrated the personal triumph of a morally sick man. Bartholow faced a spiritual impasse:

> Like one above a dungeon where for years
> Body and soul had fought futility
> In vain for their deliverance (*CP*, 733).

He was able to find himself and rise above his weaknesses because he came to a belief in God. The figuration assigned to the deity,

> Power
> That filled him as a light fills a buried room
> When earth is lifted and the sun comes in (*CP*, 733).

delimited knowledge of the divine nature. Yet in thanksgiving for his deliverance through faith Bartholow invoked God, hinting at some form of a personal deity. *Roman Bartholow* had three important ingredients that were consistent in Robinson's religious verse: a sense of sin or failure, a need to believe in Something, outside of man, and a passage to God on the strength of faith. But the poet hesitated to personalize the deity, save by faint implication, preserving his preferences for a Divine Force for Good as the essence of his awareness of the goal of man's spiritual desire.

"Avon's Harvest" was another poem in which Robinson's moral intention was not projected in a highly symbolic form but told as a simple tale of the reality of sin in an average life. The sin of Avon was one of hatred. In the end the remorse of conscience he felt for his misdeeds killed him. He was unable to find any healing medicine.

> "I'm witness to the poison, but the cure
> Of my complaint is not, for me, in Time.
> There may be doctors in eternity
> To deal with it, but they are not here now" (*CP*, 559).

Much of Avon's doubt about God was traceable to the influence of science. In pondering the possibility of an afterlife he alternated between the unknowable God and the "no-God." Referring to divine knowledge of those aspects of life inexplicable to men, Avon remarked:

> "If such an one there be. If there be none,
> All's well—and over. Rather vain expense,
> One might affirm—yet there is nothing lost.
> Science be praised that there is nothing lost (*CP*, 567).

Such was the tone of Robinson's statement of the nature of God in "Avon's Harvest."

In *The Man Who Died Twice* the notion of God was more clearly expressed, better defined in fact than in most of Robinson's poetry. His definition was indirect for he was concerned primarily with the sins of his protagonist, Fernando Nash; but the drama of redemption recounted was very close to the traditional experience of man's salvation by God and because of man's free belief in Him. For Fernando Nash God was a personal being, offended by sin; divine justice required a complete dedication of the sinner if he were to overcome his faults and come to God. This passage to God is what gave meaning to life for the repentant. In Robinson's poetic phrase man became "God's too fallible image." Man was crushed by remorse because he was given to see his actions as an offense to the all-high Person; God was a being to whom Nash prayed for help, for he came to understand that he was of God, "a half-hatched bird of paradise." After a long inner struggle Nash at last found God and saw the wisdom of forsaking the world. While not defining God as such, Robinson has left an indelible impression of God, as Western men have often viewed Him, in *The Man Who Died Twice.*

It has been argued that in *Cavender's House* Robinson emancipated himself from the Christian theme of salvation, forgiveness and redemption, by resorting to "natural justice," "the inevitable consequences of sin."[7] Certainly the conception of God was far less developed and meaningful than it was in *The Man Who Died Twice.* The existence of God, or Purpose or Law, the poet was ready enough to affirm, but it is equally plain that the nature of the deity was not considered very important or very relevant. The traditional and the agnostic elements both received enunciation so that no firm insistence on the nature of God, even by indirection, is likely. Yet the God, or Purpose or Law, which binds men was real enough in *Cavender's House.* The sin of Cavender was traditionally conceived, his "tower of self," an unexceptional form of pride. Furthermore, he was willing to accept the moral sanctions that men are wont to attach to sin. There was simply no redeeming God at work.

The absence of a Divine Force for Good in the lives of the people in *The Glory of the Nightingales* enables us to appreciate the humanistic morality Robinson at times so much favored. In all his dramatic narratives the problems were entirely human ones. The resolution of such a problem in *The Glory of the Nightingales* was in these same human terms. The greed of the wealthy Nightingale, which encompassed the ruin of his physician-friend, Malory, was the human fault around which the poem was structured. Nightingale atoned for his misdeeds through his confession to Malory that he had failed to act with appropriate human dignity. In order to recover his true stature as a man he told Malory of his willingness to endow a hospital, affording himself human expiation for his life, wrongly spent. His salvation was discovered in an exclusively human way. The absence of God in the poem does not suggest at all that the human resolution utilized by Robinson to demonstrate salvation or healing has any less meaning for the people involved because there is no God directly or indirectly part of the drama. To Robinson human redemption could be fully satisfying. The purpose of God is further denied in that part of the power of the poem came from Nightingale's inability to understand or to accept the conventional ideas of sin and divine redemption.

What conclusions may be drawn about Robinson's idea of God? A consistent awareness of man's frailty and his struggle against that condition in order to achieve some kind of self-mastery and self-fulfillment are the starting points for recognizing Robinson's acceptance of a divinity. Usually for him human fulfillment is explained by reference to the Divine Force for Good in the lives of men. There is some power and purpose that form part of the universe, accounting both for man's desire for self-satisfaction of a high moral order and imparting to him the stamina to achieve his special dignity. At this level of definition Robinson's belief in a deity is not open to question. Beyond this definition, however, conflicts must arise about how far he went to the direction of defining God. Perhaps some useful distinction can be made between Robinson's traditional, well-limned God and his ill-defined deity of Idealism and the scientific temper by distinguishing between what Robinson wanted in God and what he was able to accept intellectually. That he wanted (and in ways, needed) the God of Revelation seems practically certain. That is why he wrote, subconsciously perhaps, as though there was such a deity and his belief in him was quite real. But the positive thrust of philosophical Idealism and the negative effects of scientific thought prevented him from enjoying the anthropomorphic consolations for humanity that belief in a personal God held out. His heart and his mind were at war. Nor did the fully mature artist move finally in one direction or another. All three major sources of his idea of God he continued to draw on throughout his total verse; the passing years witnessed a retention of an indefinite idea of God. Like his own generation of Americans, Robinson in his poetry revealed a need for God, whether out of historic habit or something deeper that had given rise to that habit. Yet he remained puzzled as to God's existence and knowability according to any worldly form. He struggled with this difficulty to the end of his life, not unlike the man in one of his poems, walking up "Wood Street from Cheapside" in search of an answer.

---

1 E. A. Robinson, *Untriangulated Stars, Letters of Edwin Arlington Robinson to Harry DeForest Smith, 1890-1905*, Denham Sutcliffe, editor (Cambridge, Mass., 1947), 263. All subsequent page references (*US*) are to this edition.

2 E. A. Robinson, *Selected Letters of Edwin Arlington Robinson*, Ridgely Torrence, editor (New York, 1940), 177. All subsequent page references (*SL*) are to this edition.
3 E. A. Robinson, *Collected Poems of Edwin Arlington Robinson* (New York, 1948), 41. All subsequent page references (*CP*) are to this edition.
4 E. A. Robinson, "Thalia," first published in the *Reporter Monthly*, Gardiner, Maine, March 29, 1890. Cited in Charles Beecher Hogan, *A Bibliography of Edwin Arlington Robinson* (New Haven, Conn., 1936), 167.
5 E. A. Robinson, *The Children of the Night* (Boston, 1897), 12.
6 Amy Lowell, *Poetry and Poets* (Boston, 1930), 26.
7 Estelle Kaplan, *Philosophy in the Poetry of Edwin Arlington Robinson* (New York, 1940), 102.

FORMULATION OF E. A. ROBINSON'S PRINCIPLES OF POETRY

ROBERT D. STEVICK

THE CRITICAL task of formulating the principles of poetry with which E. A. Robinson worked was not performed by the poet himself. He can hardly even be said to have assisted in that task. Robinson did not, so far as is recorded, write a formal essay setting forth, as a systemic set of statements, a theory of poetry, nor did he explain his own poetry.[1] He could not be induced to deliver a lecture of any sort, on any subject. He did not associate himself with any poetic movement or any group of poets whose tenets may be imputed to him. Unlike such of his predecessors as Bryant or James Russell Lowell, or such contemporaries and successors as Amy Lowell, T. S. Eliot, or Ezra Pound, he did not write literary crticism. He refused a request to write something in connection with the posthumous publication of some works by his admired friend William Vaughn Moody: "It seems to me that we poor devils who are condemned to write poetry should write it, and not talk about it."[2] On another occasion he said: "I believe so firmly that poetry that is good for anything speaks for itself that I feel foolish when I try to talk about it."[3] In retrospect he told Carl Van Doren much the same thing: "I am inclined to believe that poetry-makers should stick to their trade and leave criticism to others . . . . [T]hat has been my attitude, in spite of a few lapses, for the past thirty years."[4] After he became well known (after his first *Collected Poems* in 1922 and especially after the publication of *Tristram* in 1927), Robinson received apparently quite a number of inquiries from literary scholars regarding his poetic theory. His usual response seems to be typified by his reply to such an inquiry by Harry Hayden Clark: "So far as I can make out, I haven't any literary theory or aim in literature except to do as well as I can what insists on being done. I have had to make this unsatisfactory sort of reply to many similar requests."[5]

Reprinted by permission, *Colby Library Quarterly*, VIII (June 1969), 295-308.

Informal statements provide a few guidelines for formulating Robinson's poetic principles, but they are far less helpful than we might wish. He apparently did not keep notebooks, journals, or other personal records in which his ideas about poetry might have been set down. The "few lapses" he confessed to Carl Van Doren in criticizing others' poems appear venial indeed. None seems to have taken the form of a systematic pronouncement; unless his criticism was conveyed in a letter, there hardly is any record from which to draw any principles. Even so Boswellian a reporter as Chard Powers Smith admits to being tells us only the following. Robinson undertook to criticize the typescript of Smith's proposed first book of poems.

> I stood by his chair, and we went through it. Besides the two he didn't like, he had indicated bad spots in half a dozen others, and he explained them. If he hadn't pointed out the flaws I should not have noticed them, for his marks were pencil dots in the margins, hardly visible . . . . It would be hard for me to persuade a bibliographer that these were the corrections of Edwin Arlington Robinson![6]

Memoirs, biographies, recollections of conversations, and other types of reportorial evidence also fail in recording statements of the principles operative in Robinson's composition of poetry. Typically: "He hates to walk. He wears a soft hat. He never talks about his own poetry. He never criticizes other people's poetry."[7] They do contain, however, a number of cryptic hints and, together with Robinson's letters, provide important evidence. "He never ceased to marvel at Professor Charles Cestre," particularly for *An Introduction to Edwin Arlington Robinson* (1930); "That Frenchman knows what I am up to. And somehow he always has."[8] "[H]e says a great deal that I have been waiting for someone to say—not only the praise, which in itself doesn't always amount to much, but simple statements of what I have been trying to do."[9] The few poems Robinson wrote on the subject of poetry also provide some oblique evidence about his poetic principles.

To recall Robinson's historical context, theorizing about poetry was not the fashion among poets when Robinson began to write verse. The "renaissance" of American poetry, with its abundance of theories of one aspect or another of poetry, began when Robinson was about forty years old, when he had been writing for twenty years or longer. When we make due allowance for Robinson's reticence and still find that even when confronted by poetic theories developed by his younger contemporaries he had little to say on the nature of poetry, we must infer one thing: despite his complete commitment of effort and interest to the writing of poetry, Robinson never formulated, never articulated poetic theory. The following assertion seems to be nothing if not candid: "I have absolutely no theories."[10]

That Robinson's principles were intuitively held and intuitively formulated is established by his remarks on poetry and poems as well as his remarks on poetic theory. His statements regarding diction in poetry serve suitably as a paradigm; diction is the most prominent topic of his remarks—in writing and in reporting conversation—about poetry. "I demand *a certain something* in the arrangement of words, and more in their selection"[11] is one way he put it; or, his persistent concern was for "the *right* selection and arrangement of words" (my italics). Nothing, perhaps, is more characteristic of Robinson's statements, both within his poetry and without, than the "definite indefiniteness" of a phrase such a *a certain something;* the definition of that something is never brought beyond the felt into the said: it remains nonverbalized. In the same way, the rightness of selection and arrangement of words never has definition either by rules and all too seldom has definition by example. The sense without the prescription for the "right word" underlies countless other of Robinson's remarks, of which the following are but two. In 1930 Robinson recalled that around 1896

> time had no special significance for me, . . . a fisher of words who thought nothing of fishing for two weeks to catch a stanza, or even a line,[12] that I might throw back into the squirming sea of language . . . . I wanted fish that were smooth and shining and subtle, and very much alive, and not too strange; and presently, after long patience and many rejections, they began to bite.[13]

The other remark is an early one, in which Robinson complained that "those verses which ought to go like bees and things . . . want to go like camels. It is hunting for hours after one word and then not getting it that plays the devil with a man's gray matter and makes him half ready to doubt the kindness of the Scheme."[14] On the face of it, Robinson's numerous remarks about archaism in diction would seem to be a marked exception to the intuitive nature of his poetic principles. In letters, conversations, and even in revisions of his own early poems (notably "Horace to Leuconoë," an early version printed in *Untriangulated Stars,* 19-20), rejection of archaic words and constructions is a recurrent note: but the grounds for rejection of them remain as unspecific as they are unshifting.

As with diction, so with the nature and purpose of poetry. All Robinson's statements are plainly personal, and do not form parts of a poetic theory linked to such disciplines as aesthetics, anthropology, linguistics, or psychology. When writing of poetic inspiration he used again the indefinitely designative words such as *something*: "I discovered long ago that an artist is just a sort of living whistle through which Something blows."[15] Or, he used expressions that are not allowed merely to pass as metaphors but, by their being persistently capitalized, are transformed into place-markers in the geography of intuition:

In the great shuffle of transmitted characteristics, traits, aptitudes, the man who fixes on something definite in life that he must do, at the expense of everything else, if necessary, has presumably got something that, for him, should be recognized as the Inner Fire. For him, that is the Gleam, the Vision, and the Word. He'd better follow it.[16]

For its purpose, poetry should have "ethical value"—though it should not be propaganda or crusading for social change. "Message" is a term Robinson himself used repeatedly, and in a sense indicated by such remarks as these:

If printed lines are good for anything, they are bound to be picked up some time; and then, if some poor devil of a man or woman feels any better or any stronger for anything I have said, I shall find no fault with the scheme or anything in it.[17]

Or,

I suppose that a part of it might be described as a faint hope of making a few of us understand our fellow creatures a little better, and to realize what a small difference there is after all between ourselves as we are and ourselves not only as we might have been but would have been if our physical and temperamental make-up had been a little different.[18]

It must be added, however, that the "message" or purposive element is attenuated in some of his poems that Robinson regarded most highly. Miss Bates tells us that, talking of his sonnets, he explained that some of them "were written for their idea, or because they held up some fragment of humanity for a moment's contemplation, or because they turned a light on some aspect of life"; but he added that these "did not have so much in the way of beauty" as the opening lines of "Many Are Called."[19]

In sum, Robinson's poems do not seem to be what they are because of a specific theory that controlled the writing of them, especially a theory of the nature of poetry, or of meter, or of any other of the technical aspects of verse. He seems not to have held to any metaphysic of art that either constrained or guided the construction of poems. Robert Frost recalls that he and Robinson, talking together about poetry during their early acquaintance, "didn't care how arrant a reformer or experimentalist a man was if he gave us real poems. For ourselves, we should hate to be read for any theory upon which we might be supposed to write. We doubted any poem could persist for any theory upon which it might have been written."[20]

Formulation of Robinson's poetic principles thus falls by default to scholars and critics who, it may be observed, have for the most part presented their findings in format more appropriate to the lecture hall or classroom than to the study or workshop. That so much of the study of Robinson's poems has been based on published texts—particularly those of the final *Collected Poems*—without attention to the extant manuscripts is a symptom of the limitations within which students of Robinson's poetry have tended to work.

Within those limitations much good work has of course been done. In so far as the poet's subjects may be construed to reveal by implication a set of principles, those principles have been well canvassed in the catalogues of Robinson's subject types; Barnard has provided the fullest inventory of the much-noted "failure" types, for example. As important a point as any is that Robinson avoided using himself as subject for poems, as a matter of principle, it seems; but that principle may or may not belong to his poetics. The poet's characteristic attitude toward his subjects has also been well formulated, though again there is some question of how far the consistency with which the stance of the poet in his poems is maintained throughout the large corpus of verse should properly be construed as constituting one of his principles of poetry: that the mode of expression can be termed "austere," "tragic," having "high seriousness," or being pervaded by "New England chill" may indeed be more informative about Robinson in his role as poet than about the principles with which he operated in writing his poetry.

Surely the best—the most informative—statements thus far offered concerning the poetic principles Robinson held, however restricted to intuitive existence, have to do with style. On the one hand, the poet's characteristic indirection of expression has been discussed extensively. By many, especially since Cestre's *An Introduction to Edwin Arlington Robinson* (1930), it has been admired as the source of Robinson's finest poetic effects. Redman termed the oblique approach as almost Robinson's signature.[21] Aiken regarded *The Man Against the Sky* as Robinson's first volume to show mature development of the technique of the "vague phrase."[22] Many, though, have regarded the indirectness of expression, as well as of representation and exposition, as the poet's besetting sin: to it Winters attributed Robinson's obscurity and Fussell attributed Robinson's ambiguity and obliquity.[23] Whatever they attribute to it in respect to poetic value, all who have written about Robinson's style nevertheless agree that it is indirect and that it forms part of the essence of his poetry. On the other hand, the term "plain" is most often use to describe another aspect of Robinson's style. Repeatedly it has been remarked that the diction is unornamented, that a paraphrasable element is always present, that (as Mark Van Doren put it) the style of expression is difficult but is never obscure.[24]

When all this has been said, however, formulation of Robinson's principles of poetry seems somehow far from exhaustive; and, I think, most of the formulations, sound as they are and important as they must be, do not converge toward the central principles which in Robinson's case we must regard as a set of dispositions with respect to the writing of verse. The principal signposts pointing to the central principles are to be recognized, it seems, precisely in the poet's persistent refusal—probably his inability, finally—to formulate a theory of poetry. *In his historical context* he seems to have begun and to have persisted in writing within the great tradition of English verse that had its rise in the Renaissance; his writings, whether in their metrical forms, the presence of paraphrasable elements, or other matters, continue in that main tradition, and show distinctive features arising only from his attempts to revitalize that tradition—in rejecting archaism and other types of poetic diction, in turning to subjects whose poetic credentials were good if not yet widely recognized, and so on. There is no need to formulate a theory when one works within a well established tradition: one learns his trade as a craftsman, not as a philosopher.

So it is not enough, for example, to say that Robinson employed traditional verse forms, if it is his principles of poetry that one is seeking to formulate. That he did master the technicalities of the major traditional verse forms—and some of the intricate French forms as well—and that he used them with meticulous care throughout his writing career, imply one of his crucial principles of poetry: that meter is not merely decorative, that it does not have an independent communicative ability, or whatever, but that fixed (traditional) metrical form is an essential element from which genuine poetry is synthesized. From a matrix of defined verse form and an initial "something to say," he seems to have created his poetry from "an almost endless succession of periphrases that [came] nearer and nearer to metered language until he achieve[d] what he want[ed]."[25] His typical remarks such as the one about being a "fisher of words" can have, in fact, little meaning as we regard Robinson fishing for words not in isolation, but for a context precisely defined by conditions of meter in addition to syntax and semantics; otherwise we should have to regard his lifetime of spending hours hunting for words as the result of deficiency of verbal facility.

That this "traditional" principle regarding meter was operative, and crucially so, may be inferred not only from the ubiquitous precision of Robinson's syllable-count and rhyme, but from manuscript evidence as well. "Many Are Called" offers an excellent and compact example. An early version (first written version?) shows the first four lines and the sixth of the octet, the first line of the sestet and the final phrases set down as, with minor exceptions, they remained in the published version, according to Léonie Adams' analysis. "Two lines in the octet are given in a variant and the rest was to be filled in."[26] At one stage part of the octet read thus:

> And though fame-hungry multitudes have tried
> In ecstasy, in anguish and in vain,
> To summon him, their bones remain outside.

This was rewritten then as follows:

> And though melodious multitudes have tried
> In ecstasy, in anguish, and in vain,
> With invocation sacred and profane
> To lure him, even the loudest are outside.

Miss Adams' comment on this (which necessarily implicates the rest of the sonnet as well) deserves to be quoted in full:

> in suppressing "fame-hungry"—an unfortunate word in this position, redundant to and slightly distorting his meaning—Robinson somewhat obscured this meaning. For his Apollo is conceived not directly as inspiring but as rewarding accomplishment. By his use of light in place of "definitive laurel," the other aspect is of course suggested, and both meanings—that of fame and that of achievement—are included. Yet by shifting, as some interpreters do, the surface emphasis to the incidence of genius (inspiration), the last line becomes absurd. Inspiration, unlike fame, is not a property of the dead. Such hovering yet concentration of meaning, without disturbance of logic, is characteristic; and read so that the final irony is the postponement from the "called" of all certitude, not only is the poem more climactic and cohesive, but some dignity from the "patient dead" balances the mockery of the octet's close.[27]

Some further analysis of revisions will reveal even more about the principle by which meter operated, together with other factors, to produce this outstanding sonnet.

The changes were made within one unit of the sonnet: neither the conceptual framework nor the syntactic structure is altered. This unit, in turn, is a unit in the rhyme-pattern, the second quatrain repeating the *a b b a* pattern of the first four lines; and the quatrain is a single, complete syntactic unit. The changes are *inside* the frame. "Fame-hungry" was certainly the more accurate, concrete term, but it gave way to the vague, allusive term "melodious." There were apparently at least three reasons for this. First, the new term brings into the line an alliteration, a device Robinson habitually used; not only here is this the result of revision, but in the last line of the quatrain two terms were changed with a consequent introduction of a second alliteration. Second, "melodious" makes more regular the accent-pattern; Robinson always exercised considerable freedom in position of accent in a metrical line, but this sonnet is otherwise regular in accent-pattern except for an inversion beginning the sestet. Third, Robinson had no objection, as his poems generally show, to using a term we may describe as "denoting by indirection," provided he felt the denotation was accessible and the implications of the indirections could be controlled. This is what Miss Adams' comment (above) points out. "Melodious," as Robinson probably thought of it here, leads by a series of associations to "poets," "singers," then to a characteristic of poets; the particular characteristic "fame-hungry" is isolated by the rest of the poem which describes Apollo's reign and habits. This is certainly indirection and does invite the misinterpretations Miss Adams notes.

Further, in comparing the two versions, we find the addition of the third line of this quatrain, "With invocation sacred and profane." The limited number of rhyme-words in this kind of octet may have determined the choice of these words; once introduced, however, they had an effect on the concluding line of this unit. For one thing, "invocation," fitting as the mode of communication of the "multitude" with "The Lord Apollo," renders the original verbal element "to summon" entirely inappropriate. Once the term "invocation" was established (as opposed, say, to "supplication") and the notion of "fame-hungry" was still implied, a term such as "lure" had the only appropriate connotations. Then, once "lure" was settled on, the tone of "bones remained outside"—fitting perhaps with the tone of "summon"—required change. The idea of "loudest" now became consonant with "invocation" and the choice of this particular word was probably influenced once again by its creation of alliteration within the line.

The principle of utilizing a fixed (and traditional) metrical form as a synthesizing element in creating verse inevitably leads, as in the notes above, to consideration of other factors such as diction and allusion. And on these matters Robinson's principles of poetry are the same as those of any excellent poet or writer, that perfect adjustment of referential elements, both denotative and suggestive, must be attained. On these principles, therefore, little more need be said here.

But let us return to the matters of style. In light of Robinson's principles of meter we have inferred, can his style be formulated more precisely and completely than it has been heretofore? I think it can be, with the help of analytic tools developed especially in the past two decades. At this stage only a sketch of procedure will have to serve.

A first point is that Robinson's principle of using the rhythms of prose (as it has often been designated) can be restated more accurately in terms of syntax, for it is not rhythms, after all, of prose but those of verse that controlled his composition: characteristically he signaled overtly and completely the relations obtaining among the forms (the "words") of his poetic utterances. It is not merely the word order of expository prose that he regularly employs, but the form-words (prepositions, conjunctions, relative forms) signaling relations between sentence constituents as well that he employs as fully as one reasonably may. Complete explicitness of sentence structure, then (as opposed to "prose rhythm"), is one of his stylistic principles. A prime illustration is a one-sentence poem, "Octave XII":

With conscious eyes not yet sincere enough
To pierce the glimmering cloud that fluctuates
Between me and the glorifying light
That screens itself with knowledge, I discern
The searching rays of wisdom that reach through
The mist of shame's infirm credulity,
And infinitely wonder if hard words
Like mine have any message for the dead.

One may parse this poem by any technique he wishes, and find the syntactic relations always fully specified—as with the three *that*'s, for instance, introducing clauses. There is nothing inferential or ambiguous in the task of construing the syntactic structure. (Robinson's prose, we may notice as well, is exactly the same in this respect as his verse.) Thus, both meter and syntax are fully fixed and specified. Both tend to affect a reader in much the same way. Since both are clear, complete, and essential to comprehending verse utterance, a reader gets from them a sense of linguistic and metric security in respect to comprehension.

A second point is that within the secure meter and syntax of all his poetic constructions there is a play of semantics for major classes of words (nouns, adjectives, verbs, essentially), and a play of reference for other classes, particularly pronominal forms. "Luke Havergal" is notorious for the variety of interpretations it has engendered; one may suspect that the strategically placed *wh-* forms ("wait for *what* will come," "to *where* she is") and the quasi-specification of "western gate" by an extended "there where" statement is the main source of both the fascination the poem holds and the diversity of its interpretations. For a single, compact illustration of the referential waywardness of words within a firm structural frame, however, "Octave XI" is perhaps the most useful.

Still through the dusk of dead, blank-legended,
And unremunerative years we search
To get where life begins, and still we groan
Because we do not find the living spark
Where no spark ever was; and thus we die,
Still searching, like poor old astronomers
Who totter off to bed and go to sleep,
To dream of untriangulated stars.

Reducing this poem to its simplest and apparent paraphrase still leaves several possible meanings: Our search for where life begins does not succeed; and, like astronomers who are unable to triangulate certain stars, we are haunted by our failure. The meaning pattern and the syntactic structure are clear in outline. The multiple meanings arise from semantic and referential play.

What is the object of the search? "Where life begins" may mean the origin of life in terms of biological evolution: Darwin's hypothesis was still an issue when Robinson wrote the poem. It may mean the origin of an individual's life in terms of his soul: from what state and under what conditions does one's soul enter into (and create) his life? It may mean the defining limits which determine the real nature of (human) life. Again, "we do not find the living spark." "Living spark" may have meanings to match those of "where life begins"; it may be some sort of initial vital impulse, the soul's uniting with body, or that which constitutes the essence of (human) life.

Why does our search fail? Because we search in darkness ("dusk")? Because the years have no inscriptions that could supply the answer (they are "blank-legended")? Because years simply will not repay our efforts by rewarding the search? Does our search fail because the "living spark" never existed, or existed but was not where we looked for it, or because we are looking for the wrong thing? For that matter, what are "dead" years: those which are past, those which—because they are dead—can tell us nothing, those which no longer contain the "*living* spark" for which we search? Are the years "blank-legended" because they are dead, because years cannot really be inscribed, or because our vision cannot see the legend written on them? Are they "unremunerative" because "dead" or because "blank-legended" or because all past years are unremunerative? Or perhaps they are our own years which are "dead, blank-legended, and unremunerative" because we have misused them (willfully or not).

Must this search forever fail? "Still" occurs twice in the first four lines, and can take either of its basic meanings: we search (and groan) forever, always; we are searching up to the present and will continue to do so in the future. The verb forms may indicate a limited present time (at least a span of time not indefinitely extended into the future) or they may indicate a "universal" truth, hence imply that the searching will continue forever. The verb forms and the adverbs suggest parallel possibilities of meaning. "And thus we die" at first appears to dispel the ambiguity of this answer; but "we" again may be not only the poet and his readers, but all mankind who will die without succeeding in the search. There is yet one more possibility: when we die still searching, does our search then cease, or may it be satisfied only after death?

This last conjecture of meaning perhaps leads us too far: the last three and a half lines suggest that we end our search without success only to be haunted by our failure. Yet the failure does not cancel all possibility of success. The failure, after all, is one of providing rational or logical structure for that which is not yet included within our general rational accounting of the universe, whether in completing the process of mapping the stars, or in discovering "where life begins." If the analogy between "we" and "astronomers" is a true one, the latter part suggests, beneath the surface meaning and tone, that stars nevertheless can be triangulated, therefore a generic "we" can find ultimately "where life begins." Once more, there are submeanings that keep open the hope of success: "dusk" may be not only the dimness that precedes night, but the period just before dawn; the latter is also suggested by the time at which astronomers go to bed.

The two central principles of Robinson's intuitively held poetics, I believe, are that meter and syntax should be as completely defined as possible with traditional verse form for the first and with the devices of ordinary (literate and cultivated) language for the second; and that full, thoroughly exploited semantic and referential play should operate within the rigorous metric-syntactic framework. From these most of the other principles Robinson did not articulate can be derived or inferred: the indefiniteness of key words, the negative definitions, the rendering of psychological effect with its cause left implicit, and so on. In all, Robinson's principles of poetry did not produce brilliant lyric effects, they did not weave elaborate (or exotic) tissues of allusions, echoes, and suggestions, they never conveyed the immediacy of dramatic voice. They generated, rather, a characteristically ruminative poetry, modest, intellectual, "public," and at its best, that "conjunction of a few inevitable words"[28] which we, with Robinson, may count as genuine poetry.

---

1 Besides absence of any formal statements in surviving papers and the absence of reference to Robinson's having set down a formulation of his poetic principles, the impressions of those who knew Robinson corroborate the negative assertion—which must always stand as tentative. (I regret not having had the opportunity to examine *Edwin Arlington Robinson's Letters to Edith Brower*, ed. Richard Cary, which has not reached me at time of final revision of this paper.) A main point made by Chard Powers Smith in his recent biography is that, whether in philosophy or in poetics, the logic or system that inheres in theory was not characteristic of Robinson (*Where the Light Falls. A Portrait of Edwin Arlington Robinson*, New York, 1965).

2 *Selected Letters of Edwin Arlington Robinson*, ed. Ridgely Torrence (New York, 1940), 90.

3 Ellsworth Barnard, *Edwin Arlington Robinson: A Critical Study* (New York, 1952), 1.

4 *Three Worlds* (New York, 1936), 161.

5 Clark, ed., *Major American Poets* (New York, 1936), 946.

6 Smith, 20-21.

7 John Farrar, ed., *The Literary Spotlight* (New York, 1924), 119.

8 Rollo Walter Brown, *Next Door to a Poet* (New York, 1937), 7.

9 *Selected Letters*, 161-162.

10 *Ibid.*, 93.

11 *Untriangulated Stars: Letters of Edwin Arlington Robinson to Harry De Forest Smith, 1890-1905*, ed. Denham Sutcliffe (Cambridge, Massachusetts, 1947), 115.

12 Robinson says much the same thing in *Selected Letters*, 103.

13 "The First Seven Years," *The Colophons*, IV (1930), n.p.

14 *Untriangulated Stars*, 236.

15 Barnard, 12.

16 Hermann Hagedorn, *Edwin Arlington Robinson: A Biography* (New York, 1938), [vii].

17 *Untriangulated Stars*, 247.

18 Barnard, 20.

19 Esther Willard Bates, *Edwin Arlington Robinson and His Manuscripts*, (Waterville, Maine, 1944), 22.

20 Introduction to Robinson's *King Jasper* (New York, 1935), ix-x.
21 Ben Ray Redman, *Edwin Arlington Robinson* (New York, 1926), 40.
22 Conrad Aiken, "The Poetry of Mr. E. A. Robinson," *Freeman*, IV (September 21, 1921), 43-46.
23 Yvor Winters, *Edwin Arlington Robinson* (Norfolk, Connecticut, 1946), and Edwin S. Fussell, *Edwin Arlington Robinson: The Literary Background of a Traditional Poet* (Berkeley, 1954).
24 *Edwin Arlington Robinson* (New York, 1927), 54-55.
25 John Crowe Ransom, *The New Criticism* (Norfolk, Connecticut, 1941), 303-304.
26 "The Ledoux Collection of Edwin Arlington Robinson Manuscripts," *Library of Congress Quarterly Journal of Current Acquisitions*, VII (November, 1949), 11.
27 *Ibid.*, 13.
28 *Selected Letters*, 103.

THE PLAYS OF EDWIN ARLINGTON ROBINSON

IRVING D. SUSS

THE UNFORTUNATE fact is that Edwin Arlington Robinson was driven to the writing of plays more by his need for money and hope for a quick Broadway success than by any deep urgency to find dramatic expression for his view of life. Years without a poem sold and publication underwritten by friends when his poems did appear in print convinced Robinson that poetry would pay not even for the sauce, let alone the dinner. His sister-in-law and his three young nieces needed his assistance, and the income from his sinecure at the Custom House in New York evidently could not cover his own expenses during the first decade of the century. He saw potentially high profits from the stage as a solution to his financial problems, and he turned as intensely as he could to playwriting.

His two published plays, *Van Zorn* (1914) and *The Porcupine* (1915), were aimed at the commercial theatre, though Robinson rationalized their theatrical and, indeed, their dramatic inadequacies by suggesting that their target was rather the reform of the crass inanities of the contemporary theatre. To be sure, there is some reason for seeing Robinson along with his friends William Vaughn Moody, Percy MacKaye, and Ridgely Torrence as liberators of the stage, but Robinson's theatrical taste would put into question his competence for helping to accomplish that. His earlier interest in the stage was conventional. His friend and biographer, Hermann Hagedorn, says Robinson enjoyed even dull plays and saw in the theatre an escape from life like alcohol.[1] This comment would seem to be justified on the basis of the poet's announced approval of the artificial problem plays of the currently popular James A. Herne and Henry Arthur Jones. A more startling disclosure of his taste in drama appeared in a comparison he drew for

Reprinted by permission, *Colby Library Quarterly*, VIII (September 1969), 347-363.

Mrs. Louis V. Ledoux, who had written admiringly about a production of Gilbert and Sullivan's *The Pirates of Penzance.* Although he had forgotten most of the operetta except the policeman's chorus, he liked the musical "better in some ways than the last act of *Prometheus Unbound,* which somehow," he wrote, "doesn't quite come off."[2] What might imply a wider and deeper approach to drama on his part was an early attempt to write an English version of *Antigone* based on a literal translation, but his interest in that play flagged.[3]

Despite his apparently conventional theatrical views, his clearly desperate need for money and a public for his writings during the early 1900s might have inspired him to compose a masterpiece for the stage; what stood massively in the way of that possibility was his feeling that every line of prose he wrote obstructed his yearning to write poetry. If art does grow out of frustration, it would have needed frustration in another mode to fertilize his dramatic imagination.

His own view of why he turned to playwriting obscured what seems to be the reality and emphasized a different motive. In 1913, shortly after he had completed yet another draft of *Van Zorn* and just after receiving an unencouraging letter about *The Porcupine* from Winthrop Ames, the director-producer, Robinson wrote: "I see now that my past three years of floundering in prose have been due to nothing more serious than the fact that I had temporarily written myself out."[4] The fact that six years elapsed between the publication of *The Town Down the River* in 1910 and *The Man Against the Sky* in 1916 might bear out this conclusion. Later, when once again the current was running full and swift, he would be publishing a volume every two years at most.

From 1905 until a production of one of his two published plays in 1917 Robinson was intermittently involved in playwriting, but his dramatic effort was concentrated in the years between 1906 and 1913. He had "high hopes" of a comedy he was planning in 1905,[5] but unless Robinson was referring to one of the plays later published, that particular comedy did not go beyond the planning. Nor have manuscripts turned up for the "play after play" that, according to his biographer, failed "to find . . . a production."[6] Whether he actually did finish more than two plays is open to question. He may possibly have written a one-act drama entitled *Terra Firma* for Henry Miller, the actor-producer, in 1906 or 1907,[7] but others were no more real than flickers of intention, as he admitted: "I thought some time ago that I had other plays in sight, but I can see now that they are not only far off, but gradually dissolve into nothing."[8]

What may have prompted him to devote so much of his time to drama was the brilliant theatrical success of Moody's *The Great Divide* in 1906[9] and the accomplishment of MacKaye, whose *Jeanne d'Arc* that same year is said to have saved the season for Sothern and Marlowe.[10] These two, with Torrence and Robinson, used to talk among themselves about regenerating the hackneyed commercial theatre. Together they would demolish the Broadway Philistines. Hopeful and elated by this public response—to Moody's play especially—Robinson in early 1907 started serious work on *Van Zorn,* originally titled *Ferguson's Ivory Tower.* While one draft of *Van Zorn* was making the rounds of producers' offices, he began *The Porcupine.*[11]

Robinson persisted with rueful obstinacy for the next several years in wrestling with the uncongenial dramatic mode. In December of 1911 he wrote to MacKaye's daughter: "Tell your father that E.A. has gone crazy again and is writing another bad play."[12] And the following summer from the MacDowell Colony at Peterborough, New Hampshire, he wrote Hagedorn that he was ready to work on a new comedy and hoped to have "the scaffolding all up" before returning to New York.[13] This was his year of resolution and ambition. As time went on he came to see his playwriting merely as a way of filling the void of exhausted poetic inspiration, but in 1912 and into the spring of 1913, deeply discouraged about his prospects for making money in the theatre,[14] he could yet not bring himself to refuse the hurdle of the theatrical challenge. He would have to leap that hurdle, he felt, before he could reach again the free field of poetry.[15]

He pressed and badgered friends, producers, and publishers to win a public for the tentatively completed plays. For years he nagged at the plays themselves, once even called *Van Zorn* an "impossible play,"[16] and eventually made both plays into novels that could not find publishers. He left Scribner's for Macmillan, with the publication of his plays as the price for the rights to his poems. After all the struggle, the years of revision, the pathetic search for approbation as he circulated the manuscripts, one of the plays, *Van Zorn,* was at last produced—by a stock company at the Y.M.C.A. in Brooklyn.

Five years after he had begun *Van Zorn* he was still revising it, and in letters to friends he had constantly to reassure himself that he could write a play. He was reducing the first act to "less formidable proportions"[17] and depending on his friend John Blair to circulate the play among the theatrical managers.[18] His reaction to the criticism of his friends shifted as his own uncertainty about the plays developed over the years into sad awareness of the truth. In one letter he talks about John Blair's "enthusiasm" for *Van Zorn;*[19] less than a month later he is complaining that "Blair tells me that my play will act, but he doesn't like the people in it very much. I don't think he is more than half-right in his interpretation of them, but I am hardly in a position to say much."[20] He continued to tinker with *Van Zorn,* and six months later he had still not had a final copy typed.[21] As the certainty of failure grew, Robinson became more and more defensive.

The Porcupine was no more successful than *Van Zorn* in finding production or publication quickly. When it was first written in 1907, Robinson read it to Moody, who found it a "stunning play." Moody went on in a letter to his wife to say, "It is really a very strong play, and handles with a wonderful deftness and lightness of touch. I am going tomorrow to beard Charles Frohman in his den, with it in my hand and try and hypnotize him into taking it."[22] Moody kept his promise and in Frohman's office "swore the daylight black and blue cracking up *The Porcupine*."[23] Two days later Frohman had returned the play with the notation oddly worded but unmistakable in meaning: "not available for stage."[24] Winthrop Ames, too, had a look at *The Porcupine*, and Robinson reported his reaction this way: "He professes to like [*The Porcupine*] immensely himself but thinks it would pass over the heads of an audience and leave them wondering what it was all about. He may be right; I don't pretend to know."[25] But he did know. When he sent Ames's letter to another friend two days later his comment became: "I think he is right."[26] His conclusions accorded with what he had written a few weeks before to Kermit Roosevelt: "When I have satisfied myself and all my friends that I cannot write a play, I shall probably have the good sense to go back to poetry."[27]

But the ego was bruised, and defenses were raised: "It isn't that I can't write a play, so far as the technique goes—in fact, I believe it is admitted that I can—but I cannot hit the popular chord, and for the simple reason that there is no popular impulse in *me*."[28] It is likely that the parenthetical clause here cherished the memory of a comment of Moody's five years earlier after both Moody and MacKaye had followed their original theatrical successes with failures. "You have got the technique better than any of us," Moody wrote then, "and it is only a question of time when you will strike it and strike it hard."[29] For Robinson *Van Zorn* was still a "writhing demon," and *The Porcupine* had "a real odor of the stage." But he said, "I may be wrong—probably I am."[30] He would not chance further failure by trying to write more plays, but he would not admit equivocally the end of his hope by filing *Van Zorn* and *The Porcupine* away. He continued to dream of a production even after both plays had been published.

The publication of *Van Zorn* in September 1914 and *The Porcupine* just a year later liberated him for the poetry he always felt was at the center of his life. The years he had spent on the plays and on the novels he tried to derive from them he saw as "literary gallivanting."[31] What he could bring himself to say when he considered the two plays finished was that the years spent on them were years of waste: "I feel that I have given the thing a fair trial and that it would be unfair to . . . waste any more of my life doing something for which I have come to see that I am not fitted."[32]

He admired the cover of the advance copy of *Van Zorn* in early August 1914, but he was concentrating on his new book of poems. And in answer to an admiring letter from Kermit Roosevelt about the play, he could not refrain from referring with some of his earlier touchiness to the less than wholehearted approval that had greeted the book elsewhere. The play, he told Roosevelt, "seems to be giving trouble to several otherwise worthy people. It remains to be seen whether it is simply a failure, or whether it is so different from most plays in subject matter and construction that some time will be required for its assimilation."[33] But the heat of his defense had diminished.

Not all of Robinson's correspondents felt so kindly toward *Van Zorn* as did Roosevelt. His long-time typist, Esther Willard Bates, thought that in an ideal production it might be "possible that certain qualities might come to life and light that would explain the author's dogged faith in his own playwriting."[34] After publication of the play she wrote Robinson that she had "failed to understand *Van Zorn*," and her confession brought this swift reply:

> I'm sorry, too, that you, like so many others, have missed what I was driving at in the play. It was written for the stage—too much so, in fact—and I fear the stage will (or would) be absolutely necessary to make the thing intelligible. Van Zorn is supposed to believe that he has 'found his destiny' in Villa Vannevar, but finds in Act II that he has been working unconsciously for Lucas, who is equally ignorant of what is going on. Villa knows by this time that Van Z. is in love with her, and this fact, together with the realization that she is going to get Lucas after all, and through the unconscious sacrifice of a man who would probably have got her himself, if Lucas hadn't been in the way, shakes her up considerably. I suppose the trouble is that I tried to do too much. The play is for the most part the working of character upon character, the plot being left, more or less, to reveal itself by inference. If the thing has vitality enough to be 'cussed and discussed' sufficiently, people will come eventually to understand and accept it. Otherwise it will probably die an easy death, if not a sudden one. I made a misleading mistake, too, in calling it a comedy. So far as Van Z is concerned, it is a tragedy; and it is supposed to open or partly open all sorts of trap doors and windows that will give people glimpses into their own cellars and dooryards, and incidentally a fairly good view of the sun, moon and stars.
>
> In one sense it is more a poem than a play. In another sense, the good Lord only knows what it is, or what it is worth. In the light of my experience with other things of mine, I can only say that I don't believe that I could feel quite as I do about it, if there wasn't something in it. But the only sensible thing for me to do now is to forget it and work at other things—which will, in all probability, be about as intelligible as Van Z.[35]

The play is neither so complex as Robinson suggests nor so opaque as Mrs. Bates leads one to believe. The four leading figures are Weldon Farnham, a fashionably successful portrait painter; his fiancée, Villa

Vannevar, a brittle sophisticate with depths of feeling and perception beneath the shining surface; Villa's former fiancé, the unstable genius, George Lucas; and Van Zorn, a mysterious millionaire and catalyst in the crucible of "Destiny." The central symbol of the play is a portrait of Villa just completed by Farnham which rests on its easel facing away from the audience during the first and third acts in Farnham's studio. In the second act—in Villa's sitting room—another portrait, a picture of her alcoholic uncle, is the dialogue spring that prompts exploration of the past relationship between Villa and Lucas. The repetition of the device does not function to accentuate a dramatic rhythm; nor are the two portraits conjoined on the symbolic level. They are there baldly for the convenience of the playwright, who, as poet, responds to the purely visual and not to the tensions within the visual out of which drama might be created. The point becomes clear if we stand the portraits in *Van Zorn* alongside those in, say, Pirandello's *Henry IV*. In the Italian play the portraits are at the heart of the metaphysical problem of real and unreal time, which is one of the central concerns of the drama. Not the portraits but the tensions in the situation indicated by the portraits is the focus, and if we did not hear a word spoken, we should have been aware of a dramatic action.

It might be argued that the invisible portrait of Villa sets up suspense simply because we wonder what is on the face of the canvas turned away from us. But drama does not occur out of suspense alone. A central theme of *Van Zorn* is the horror of the meretricious, and verbally the painting is a central instance of that theme. But obviously, since we never see it, the painting cannot dramatize the theme. The practical problem that faced Robinson here is the virtual impossibility of conveying to an audience largely unattuned to the often subtle differences between good and bad painting the idea that Farnham was an artist of genius who was wasting himself in creating works aimed merely at satisfying the popular taste. The audience, seeing the painting, would of course have responded in the way of popular taste, and would have found appealing in it what Van Zorn found bad.

In Farnham's Greenwich Village studio at the opening of the play the artist and his friend Otto Mink, a novelist and man-about-town, talk of the painting, of destiny, and of the other characters in the play who are expected. Lucas, a weary and cadaverous alcoholic (a self portrait?) arrives, is astonished but controlled at hearing the news that Farnham and Villa are engaged, joins the other two in a drink, and then listens to Otto's mild reproof: "Why don't you try to find out where you are, and stop pickling your brains with rum?"[36] The others arrive—Villa, her aunt Mrs. Lovett, and then Van Zorn. Van Zorn's silent reaction to Villa, their teasing banter, and his declaration to

Farnham that his destiny has brought him to Villa at that moment establish one of the currents in the plot that centers on the lady. Farnham's half-hearted love for his fiancée flows into that stream too, and so, at last, does the old love between Villa and Lucas. The second focus is upon Van Zorn, who perceives the potential in the wasted genius of Lucas, the wasted integrity in the success of Farnham, and the wasted love in Villa's engagement to the artist.

Lucas comes to call on Villa later that day, sends up a blank calling card, talks evasively about going on a journey—"going west," as he puts it—and is just about to leave when Van Zorn appears and insists on talking privately with him. In this conversation Van Zorn makes it clear that he understands the direction of Lucas' journey. Lucas, feeling in Van Zorn's interest a compelling reason to reconsider his suicidal intention, accepts a check from the millionaire to help his rehabilitation and hands over to Van Zorn the vial of poison he had carried with him. The second major dialogue in the act is between Villa and Van Zorn, who extracts from her the admission that her relationship with Farnham can lead only to the dark and that she is still in love with Lucas. What becomes apparent is Van Zorn's love for Villa and the strength in his denial of his own desire as he smooths the way for a reconciliation between Villa and Lucas.

During the dialogue between Van Zorn and Villa, Otto enters to reveal that Lucas has just refused a drink! The reformation is established! This incident sums up the failure of the play. None of the incidents in the play is so strong as Robinson imagined it was. Just as the refusal of one drink is hardly credible or large enough dramatically to signal the reformation of an alcoholic, so also is the action in the final moments of the third act weak and unconvincing.

The first action in Act III comes only after eight pages of static dialogue between Farnham and Van Zorn, dialogue on Van Zorn's part full of innuendo about Lucas' reformation and Farnham's destiny. Then, just prior to the entrance of Villa and Lucas, Van Zorn returns to Farnham the engagement ring the artist had given to Villa. Eventually Lucas accepts Villa and Farnham accepts Villa's rejection—rather more quietly than one would expect. Otto, who arrives on the scene to hear the news, approves of the rearrangement, and the stage is cleared for the final confrontation between Van Zorn and Farnham.

In the final moments of the play Robinson achieves a truly dramatic instance—an accomplishment that had eluded him before. Supporting the conclusion of the play is the revelation from Van Zorn that with Villa's decision to marry Lucas he has lost any reason for living—that without talent and without motive now he must face himself. Farnham, at Van Zorn's request, gives his friend the painting of Villa. Deliberately Van Zorn cuts the head and shoulders from the canvas, cuts the image of Villa from the painting that now is his, and then shreds and burns it all. The episode is dramatic not because it is melodramatic (it is that, too), but because in the first place it suggests the emptiness Van Zorn feels and his personal strength in tearing from himself what might make him weak, and in the second place the action proves to Farnham the possibility of deep sacrifice, the potentiality of human strength and, with the destruction of the painting, the transience and emptiness of the meretricious, whether in art or love. In thus bringing Farnham to a crisis of awareness the play does what drama ought to do. But, if what has just been described is to occur meaningfully, it must occur within a context dramatically whole and wholly moving. Obviously, there may be drama within a single incident, but a single incident does not create a drama.

The leading motif of the play is what Robinson calls "destiny," and probably the poet's intention was to weave a rich and suggestive tapestry around that theme. The theme is personified in Van Zorn himself, but only partially, for Van Zorn is conceived as subject to "destiny" as well as "destiny" itself. In the play we hear the word for the first time from Otto, the author of elegant books, who is the friend and confidant of all the principals. He has just been criticizing Farnham's easy accession to popularity. "What have I done?" Farnham asks.

"You? You haven't done anything," Otto answers. "Destiny, or something or other has done it for you." To which Farnham replies: "But I don't believe much in destiny. I believe in work."[37] A few lines later, however, Farnham says: "I'll take back a part of what I said, Otto. There may be a large element of destiny in my—we'll say my very great good fortune."[38] The word appears with little excuse in other parts of the play. In the first act, for instance, Farnham, indicating some photographs of a bust of Poe, announces to the company at large, ironically, "*He* could tell you something about Destiny, if he were alive."[39] And again, later in the act in a reference to Lucas' alcoholism, Farnham, looking at Van Zorn, comments: "As for poor Mr. Lucas, this man . . . will tell you that he is in the hands of Destiny—gin-rickeys and all."[40]

Farnham's typically jocular attitude toward "destiny"— his view of "destiny" as chance or luck, and his implicit faith in man's capacity to create his own situation—is the first term in the dramatic equation that is fully stated at the conclusion of the play when Farnham, having lost Villa to Lucas, comes to the opposite awareness. The reiteration of the word in the play does not achieve the aura of mystery and the depth of intensity that Robinson must have wanted to surround the idea. Well toward the end of the last act, after the crisis of rearranged lives has occurred, Farnham and Otto and Van Zorn all use the word "destiny" as though it meant nothing more than a future event.

The implications beyond this are found in the characterization of Van Zorn. The elements in the play that present Van Zorn as the figure of fate, vague and deliberately mysterious though they are, yet compel the attention. For example, the others in the play talk of Van Zorn's immense wealth and the tantalizing source of it; they talk of his unexpected appearances and unannounced departures; they talk of the strong and strange impression he makes. In his presence and at the prompting of little more than a conventional question (Van Zorn [*Indulgently*]: "I will ask if you care enough to begin the game all over again, and let the past sink.").[41] Lucas hands over the poison that was intended for his suicide. What undercuts the dramatic aim here is Van Zorn's presenting Lucas with money in exchange for the poison. The large effect of presence and force dwindles to a Lord Bountiful gesture.

Van Zorn begs comparison with Gorki's *The Lower Depths* and sentimentalized plays on the same theme of the mysterious stranger who changes lives such as *The Passing of the Third Floor Back* and *The Servant in the House.* Its allegiance is to the last two as they celebrated the softer verities—truth and true love, honesty and honest self-appraisal. A better comparison would be with Robinson's poem "Flammonde." In its narrative detail the poem about a man of mystery who comes to Tilbury Town and moves the people there to new kindness and new understanding is not more convincing to the contemporary sensibility than *Van Zorn.* But the imagery imbedded in a series of rhetorical questions in the penultimate section of the poem succeeds in creating the sense of strange power that burgeons when human beings touch the deepest currents within each other. *Van Zorn* aims at this effect but does not achieve it.

Robinson's second play, *The Porcupine,* is most clearly seen perhaps as three geometrical configurations with the characters at the angles. Viewed in this way, the play reveals its fundamental flaw: the configurations are tangential merely, and despite the fact that certain of the characters appear in more than one of the configurations, the groupings are not interlocked. The four-angled figure farthest from the center of focus is composed of the family doctor, Ben; the woman he wants to marry, Alma, who has chosen to remain a spinster because the man she is in love with married another; Stuart, the man Alma loves, who has wasted ten years of his life in marriage to a brazen and possibly unfaithful coquette; and Stuart's wife Louise. The complication among these four is easily unraveled by Alma's brother Larry whose insight and wealth permit him to provide Stuart's wife with what she wants most: money and the exciting life of a metropolis. Dr. Ben remains peripheral, never in dramatic confrontation with the others. Louise yields without demur to Larry's proposition that she disappear into the city with his financial support. Stuart is glad his wife has chosen to leave, and the true love between him and Alma promises to flourish as the play ends.

Closer to the center of the play is a triangle involving Louise, Larry's half-brother Rollo who is infatuated with her, and Rollo's wife Rachel, the porcupine of the play. Larry's arrangement to get Louise off the scene concludes the incipient scandal between her and Rollo. Within this configuration there is a minor conflict between Rollo and Louise as he pursues his infatuation and she turns away any serious advances, though she continues to toy with him.

The important drama in *The Porcupine* lies in the figure involving Rollo, Rachel and Larry. Rachel was and is in love with Larry. Years before, pregnant with his child when he disappeared, she married in desperation his half-brother Rollo, who was deeply in love with her. Robinson creates in the relationship between Rollo and Rachel the sense of sexual and emotional frustration that governs Rollo's life; what Rachel has refused him over the years he yearns to find elsewhere. Rachel's cold and prickly rejection of her husband accounts for the title of the play. The portrayal of Rachel's sense of guilt is one of Robinson's successful efforts in playwriting. He is less successful in motivating Rachel's revelation to Larry that the child who lies ill in an adjoining room is his; and he is less successful still in making believable Rachel's suicide by poison—the concluding action of the play. More than *Van Zorn* the later play suffers from melodramatic effects: Rachel steals the poison from the doctor's medicine bag and hides the vial in a bookcase. After she swallows the poison, she stands, arms outstretched, whispering her lover's name before the door of the sickroom where Larry is entertaining the sick child with joyous violin music.

The Porcupine is essentially *Van Zorn* retold. If any additional proof were needed for the theory that every dramatist or would-be dramatist has but a single play to write, this play of Robinson's would furnish it. Like Van Zorn, Larry is a manipulator of the other characters. He comes with a portentous slogan from *Ecclesiastes* ("Or ever the silver cord be loosed or the golden bowl be broken"— the Preacher's foretelling of doomsday), and envisions himself as the providential one, the "weaver of a silver cord, whereby the golden bowl may not suffer destruction."[42] He talks of "the Powers" as Van Zorn spoke of "destiny," though for Larry "the Powers" are forces that exact payment for human actions.[43] What Larry has become during his ten years' absence is disguised under the whimsical costume he affects during the first part of the play: a pea jacket, a pair of dingy rubber boots, and a pair of old trousers. To his sister Alma and his half-brother Rollo he appears to be a profligate come home to sponge on the family, and consequently his attempts to guide lives, his insouciance, his cryptic references to himself as a force in the universe do not go down easily with the others. At midpoint of the play, he reveals himself as a wealthy builder. But neither the disguise nor the revelation are motivated. There is a saving irony in the fact that as an arranger of the lives of others with special insight, as he thinks, into the realities and necessities of life, he is surprised when he learns from Rachel of her continuing love and hears that the sick child is his own. His decision to take Rachel and the child away with him is more revealing of his obtuseness than of his good heart.

If *Van Zorn* is closely akin to the sentimental mystery of *The Passing of the Third Floor, The Porcupine* has some interesting plot resemblances to Ibsen's *The Wild Duck.* In the Scandinavian play a character with a Christ complex is responsible for the death of a child and the shattering of a marriage of convenience as he insists on stripping away the illusions that had made life acceptable for the family he destroys. Like Rachel's child, the daughter in Ibsen's play was not fathered by the husband, and similarly the marriages in the two plays were arranged to cover the pregnancies. The death of the child in *The Wild Duck* and Rachel's impending death are both suicides. Furthermore, the manipulators in both plays—and this is the strongest resemblance between the two works—are treated ironically by the authors as they make the point that human agents who tamper with the lives of others are blind to their own conditions and the effects of their actions. In the final analysis, despite these surface similarities, the plays are fundamentally different: Ibsen's chief concern is man's need for illusion; Robinson's play scratches about the pathos of love denied.

When Robinson thought of a play, he thought of a plot, not only at first in accordance with Aristotle's injunction, but last, too. His test for judging whether his friends understood the plays was to ask them for a resume. "I am beginning to realize, considerably to my chagrin," he wrote Edith Brower, "that the very people who read [*Van Zorn*] . . . in MS. praised it, and seemed to understand it, could not have known what it was really about. I am going to be mean enough to ask you to give me the briefest possible sketch of the plot, or rather the situation, as you understand it. If you 'fall down' you needn't be at all worried, for you will be one of a rather large company." He thought he could have cleared up the confusion in "fewer than a dozen short speeches."[44] During the next month several other letters to Miss Brower reiterate the point. Once he gave a woman precisely one minute to summarize the plot of *Van Zorn*; she failed. With some exasperation he then told Miss Brower to put the play away and forget it.[45]

The sad and angry acceptance of the failure of *Van Zorn* came in a letter at the end of the year to Miss Brower. Robinson drew a gravestone with a skull and crossbones over the parody of his hero's name: X. Melchizedek Van Zorn. And then, below the dates 1906-1914, the years he had worked on the play, the epitaph: "And only five people knew what AILED HIM."[46] The letter below the drawing tells that even his resourceful friend herself had flunked the test.

> It's all over as I thought. What you say is well enough so far as it goes, but like most readers, say eight out of ten, you seem to have missed the plot itself, . . . Apparently you have been so much interested in Lucas's drinking that you have not stopped to consider why VZ should take up so much room or so much time . . . . I'm . . . a little mad at myself for working eight years over a thing and only to find it a puzzle for the public. I can only suppose that the plot is so simple and so obvious that you didn't notice it, and yet a sufficient number do get it to convince me that I'm not altogether an idiot.[47]

A little more than a year later, in January 1916, he acknowledged the failure of *The Porcupine,* too, and at the same time sustained his faith in both. Perhaps it would be more correct to say he was confirmed in his estimate of the low state of perception among his readers. "Both plays have fallen utterly flat," he told Miss Brower, "and the few people who have read them—with one or two exceptions—don't even know what they are about. I may as well confess that all this leaves me a bit bewildered, for they seem to me at least to be interesting. I still nourish a more or less idiotic faith in their coming to life some day."[48]

One of the exceptions was Robert Frost whose comments on *Van Zorn* must certainly have heartened Robinson. Frost read the play twice over and did not find it at all perplexing. He spoke glowingly of the dialogue: "It is good writing, or better than that, good speaking caught alive—every sentence of it. The speaking tones are all there on the printed page, nothing is left for the actor but to recognize and give them. And the action is in the speech where it should be, and not along beside it in antics for the body to perform." Having said that, Frost went on to wonder whether the best sentences were not those that conveyed their own tone without the aid of italicized interpretive directions from the author. Would Robinson, flushed with the pleasure of such praise, have noticed then that practically every speech in the play did have such directions?[49]

Some reviewers found elements to commend in the plays when they were published, but the comments were generally restrained. None of them were so fulsome as William Lyon Phelps's remarks memorializing Robinson at the annual meeting of the American Academy of Arts and

Letters in 1936. *Van Zorn,* Phelps said, "is not only very fine as drama and as literature, but it exhibits a side of his talents usually unknown; it had the bad luck to appear in 1914."[50] If the war in Europe smothered the publication of the play, what can be said about the performances which came at the end of February in 1917, just prior to America's actual involvement?

Van Zorn was the first production of the newly organized Brooklyn Community Theatre Company. Without a permanent theatre of its own, the group rented the auditorium of the Brooklyn Y.M.C.A., which had previously been used only for amateur theatricals. There was some question as to whether or not the fire department would permit its use by a professional troupe, but the license was finally forthcoming. Advertisements for the play ran in the Brooklyn *Eagle* during the week before the performances, *without* the author's name. Nothing is said about Robinson attending rehearsals, but he did appear at the opening. How much of his impression answered to his pride it is impossible to tell, of course, but the negative tone of a letter to Josephine Preston Peabody is revealing:

> The thing is given under the worst imaginable conditions, but those who see it sit through it and appear to be interested, and possibly a little bewildered. At any rate I have the satisfaction of knowing that I wasn't an ass in believing it would act. It comes out just as I saw it in my mind's eye—only a little more so. It isn't a bad show, but I doubt if there will ever be much of a public for it.[51]

The public was much more interested in the competing theatrical fare: Eva Tanguay was playing that week, and so was a popular comedy, *So Long, Letty,* in addition to a spate of burlesque shows, including *Puss, Puss* at the Casino Theatre. Yet in the Brooklyn *Eagle* Tuesday, February 27, the day after the opening, Robinson's play won the headline over all other reviews, including one on a revival of *Henry VIII,* starring Sir Herbert Beerbohm Tree. But that was playing in Manhattan. The reviewer noted that a small audience called the actors forward five times at the end, and he agreed that they deserved the kudos. The extremely brief comments on the play in this long review were perfunctory for the most part. The critic thought Van Zorn, the fatalist, "something of an ass," as Robinson had drawn him, but he found "genuine drama in the second act when Lucas hands over the vial of poison . . . . This scene was well written and splendidly acted."[52] The short shrift given the play by this reviewer was echoed more politely by Hermann Hagedorn twenty-two years later: "At no point did the story come to life. The characters were like exquisite engravings talking."[53]

The Porcupine has never been produced.

---

1 Hermann Hagedorn, *Edwin Arlington Robinson, A Biography* (New York, 1939), 239.
2 [Ridgely Torrence, editor]. *Selected Letters of Edwin Arlington Robinson* (New York, 1940), [to Mrs. Louis V. Ledoux, 26 June 1913], 86.
3 Lucy Dickinson Fryxell, *Edwin Arlington Robinson as Dramatist and Dramatic Poet* (University of Kentucky doctoral dissertation, 1955), 10.
4 *Letters* [to John Hays Gardiner, 9 March 1913], 79.
5 Hagedorn, 209.
6 *Ibid.*, 273.
7 Fryxell, 10-11.
8 *Letters* [to Gardiner, 9 March 1913], 79.
9 Charles T. Davis, *The Poetic Drama of Moody, Robinson, Torrence and MacKaye 1894-1909* (New York University doctoral dissertation, 1950), 15-16.
10 Fryxell, 10.
11 Hagedorn, 240-243.
12 William Vaughn Moody, *Letters to Harriet* (Boston, 1935), 418n.
13 *Letters* [to Hagedorn, 18 September 1912], 74.
14 Letters [to Gardiner, 9 March 1913], 79.
15 Hagedorn, 277.
16 *Ibid.*, 256.
17 *Letters* [to Louis V. Ledoux, 1 October 1912], 76.
18 *Ibid.* [to Hagedorn, 18 September 1912], 74.
19 *Ibid.*
20 *Ibid.* [to Ledoux, 1 October 1912], 76.
21 *Ibid.* [to Lewis M. Isaacs, 7 March 1913], 78.
22 Moody, [13 October 1907], 342-343.
23 *Ibid.* [16 October 1907], 344.
24 *Ibid.* [excerpt from letter to Percy MacKaye], 423n.
25 *Letters* [to Isaacs, 7 March 1913], 78.
26 *Ibid.* [to Gardiner, 9 March 1913], 79.
27 *Ibid.* [to Kermit Roosevelt, 23 February 1913], 77.
28 *Ibid.* [to Gardiner, 9 March 1913], 79.
29 Hagedorn, 246.
30 *Ibid.*, 277.
31 *Letters* [to Isaacs, 7 March 1913], 78.
32 *Ibid.* [to Gardiner, 9 March 1913], 79-80.
33 *Ibid.* [to Roosevelt, 28 June 1915], 87.
34 Esther Willard Bates, *Edwin Arlington Robinson and His Manuscripts* (Waterville, Maine 1944), 8.
35 *Ibid.*, 8-9. (I have silently followed certain inconsequential corrections from the annotated copy of Howard G. Schmitt, owner of the manuscript.)
36 Edwin Arlington Robinson, *Van Zorn* (New York, 1914) 19-20.
37 *Ibid.*, 5.
38 *Ibid.*, 6.
39 *Ibid.*, 35.
40 *Ibid.*, 41.
41 *Ibid.*, 91-92.
42 Edwin Arlington Robinson, *The Porcupine* (New York, 1915), 14-15.
43 *Ibid.*, 20-21.
44 Richard Cary, editor, *Edwin Arlington Robinson's Letters to Edith Brower* (Cambridge, 1968), [30 November 1914], 157-158.
45 *Ibid.* [7 December 1914], 158.
46 *Ibid.* [1914], 159.
47 *Ibid.*, 160.
48 *Ibid.* [17 January 1916], 166.
49 Lawrance Thompson, editor, *Selected Letters of Robert Frost* (New York, 1964) [to Robinson, 13 June 1915], 180.
50 "Memorial Remarks on Edwin Arlington Robinson by Professor William Lyon Phelps," New York *Herald Tribune* (13 November 1936), 25.
51 *Letters* [to Josephine Peabody, 31 March 1917], 100.
52 Brooklyn *Daily Eagle* (27 February 1917), 10.
53 Hagedorn, 321.

THE OCTAVES OF E. A. ROBINSON

RONALD MORAN

IN APRIL 1897 Edwin Arlington Robinson told Edith Brower that he had written forty Octaves, adding, "but I do not think they will be very well received." And, as Richard Cary says, "He was right."[1] In light of Robinson's splendid achievements in the short lyric and narrative forms, it is not surprising that his Octaves, neither lyrical nor narrative in manner, have been generally excluded from discussions of his poetry. Yet in one area of inquiry, the Octaves are indispensable: written when he was twenty-six and twenty-seven, they provide us with, as no other single body of his work does, statements in poetry that disclose his beliefs on the function of poetry, the presence of God, the state of the age, the condition of man, and most importantly, the Octaves introduce us in his poetry to idealism as the basis for a life-style. We can say with authority that the speaker of the Octaves is Robinson, not a persona. For these reasons, the Octaves demand the attention of the serious student of Robinson. As collateral benefits there are some instances of remarkable writing (e.g., "like poor old astronomers / Who totter off to bed and go to sleep / To dream of untriangulated stars" (XI); "Like scattered lamps in unfrequented streets" (VIII). But it would be misleading, perhaps even dishonest, to argue that the Octaves contain many instances of Robinson's best work.

There are twenty-eight Octaves extant: a series of twenty-three in *Collected Poems*; two originally included in the series first published in *The Children of the Night,* but later deleted for *Collected Poems*; two printed together under the title "Two Octaves" in *The Children of the Night*; and one printed in the February 26, 1897 issue of the Boston *Evening Transcript* and later reprinted in Charles Beecher Hogan's *A Bibliography of Edwin Arlington Robinson.* The term *octave,* as Robinson uses it, means a poem consisting of eight lines of blank verse; there are no other special properties. Neither does there seem to

Reprinted by permission, *Colby Library Quarterly,* VIII (September 1969), 363-370.

be any literary precedent to the form. Robinson, of course, had been writing sonnets before the Octaves, which could account for his choice of title, as could his fondness for music.

Since the Octaves are intense, personal statements, it would seem important to cite some of the circumstances in Robinson's life during 1896-1897 that may indeed have influenced him to write this curious body of poetry, curious especially when we consider that his shorter poems are frequently ordered by suggestion rather than by the kind of statement characteristic of the Octaves. By 1896 his brother Dean was already addicted to drugs; Herman, his other brother, was taking alcohol in order to escape financial failures; the marital life of Emma Shepherd and Herman was becoming increasingly strained. In *Where the Light Falls,* Chard Powers Smith discusses, in as thorough a fashion as possible, the triangle relationship involving Emma, Herman, and the poet, a triangle whose lines never actually intersected, though Robinson apparently was in love with Emma. Smith tells of asking Ridgely Torrence shortly after Robinson's death: "Was E. A. celibate all his life?" "Hell, no," said Ridgely. "Was there one great love?" "Yes," he said. "It started back in Gardiner, and he fought it out in the *Octaves*."[2] Smith concludes that only two or three of the Octaves "can be directly associated with Emma, though she probably knew that the personal aspect of the passion behind them was for her" (p. 170). Certainly the death of Robinson's mother on November 22, 1896 is responsible as well for some of the intensity and for some of the attitudes set forth in the Octaves. In the March 15, 1897 letter to Harry de Forest Smith, Robinson mentioned the strains under which he was living and, presumably, writing: "The past three months of my life, however, are quite another thing. If they had come two years ago, or even one, I think they would have finished me."[3] Why they did not finish him is revealed in those Octaves given over to idealism.

The Octaves can be grouped sensibly into categories according to primary subject matter: (1) poetry; (2) God; (3) condition of the times and state of man; (4) idealism. These categories are by no means mutually exclusive, for an Octave may involve more than one of the above subjects, but the categories do provide an external ordering device in the absence of an internal one. A few of the Octaves seem to follow others, but there does not appear to be in the sequence of twenty-three in the *Collected Poems* an overall design waiting to be discovered. The five Octaves independent of the sequence fit into the same categories.

Robinson did not write essays concerning the nature and purpose of poetry; neither did he lecture publicly on the subject of poetry or, for that matter on anything. It is therefore interesting for us to read his comments on poetry in his letters and particularly interesting to examine the several Octaves on the subject of poetry. We know from his letters that Robinson hoped his poems would be of practical value to readers, that his poems would make the lives of his readers more fruitful. Two excerpts from letters to Harry de Forest Smith, dated respectively May 13, 1896 and February 3, 1897, bear on this discussion:

> If printed lines are good for anything, they are bound to be picked up some time; and then, if some poor devil of a man or woman feels any better or any stronger for anything that I have said, I shall have no fault to find with the scheme or anything in it. I am inclined to be a trifle solemn in my verses, but I intend that there shall always be at least a suggestion of something wiser than hatred and something better than despair (p. 247).
>
> * * *
>
> I also make free to say that many of my verses [were] written with a conscious hope that they might make some despairing devil a little stronger and a little better satisfied with things—not as they are, but as they are to be (p. 273).

The Octave originally numbered I in the initial series in *The Children of the Night* reiterates in its closing lines the poet's concern for his audience:

> To get at the eternal strength of things,
> And fearlessly to make strong songs of it,
> Is, to my mind, the mission of that man
> The world would call a poet. He may sing
> But roughly, and withal ungraciously;
> But if he touch to life the one right chord
> Wherein God's music slumbers, and awake
> To truth one drowsed ambition, he sings well.

The analogy of poetry to music and the allusion to God are found as well in Octave XIX, which begins with this indictment of poetry then currently in vogue:

> Nor jewelled phrase nor mere mellifluous rhyme
> Reverberates aright, or ever shall,
> One cadence of that infinite plain-song
> Which is itself all music.

Robinson continues in XIX that "Stronger notes / Than any that have ever touched the world" are needed; they must "ring like hammer-blows, / Right-echoed of a chime primordial, / On anvils, in the gleaming of God's forge." In Octave XX Robinson says that the poet must "work with something else than pen and ink" in order to "acknowledge and include / The foregleam and the glory of the real." These tools, he tells us, are "unseen implements that have no names."

One of the clear impressions we receive from the Octaves is Robinson's deep and sincere belief in God. Whether God is pantheistic, Christian, or what-have-you is never apparent. God in the Octaves is frequently introduced by light imagery, the same as, or at least closely related to, the light imagery Robinson uses in those Octaves setting forth his idealism. In some of the Octaves, such as XIX and XXII, God figures only in an image capacity; in others, notably I, VI, and VII, God's greatness is the subject. Octave I is exemplary of this latter grouping:

> We thrill too strangely at the master's touch;
> We shrink too sadly from the larger self
> Which for its own completeness agitates
> And undermines us; we do not feel—
> We dare not feel it yet—the splendid shame
> Of uncreated failure; we forget,
> The while we groan, that God's accomplishment
> Is always and unfailingly at hand.

The incompleteness of man described in Octave I and the sad condition of the age provide subject matter for a number of the Octaves. Here are several passages that illustrate the scope and tone of Robinson's indictments: "the days / Of most of us [are] affrighted and diseased . . . In this the prentice-age of discontent, / Rebelliousness, faint-heartedness, and shame" ("Two Octaves, I"); "the fulgid sun looks down / Upon a stagnant earth where listless men / Laboriously dawdle, curse and sweat, / Disqualified, unsatisfied, inert" ("Two Octaves, II); "The legion life that riots in mankind / Goes ever plunging upward, up and down . . . And ever led resourcelessly along / To brainless carnage by drunk trumpeters" (II); "To me the groaning of world-worshippers / Rings like a lonely music played in hell" (III). Octave XVI is extreme and inclusive enough to deserve reproduction:

> Something as one with eyes that look below
> The battle-smoke to glimpse the foeman's charge.
> We through the dusk of downward years may scan
> The onslaught that awaits this idiot world
> Where blood pays blood for nothing, and where life
> Pays life to madness, till at last the ports
> Of gilded helplessness be battered through
> By the still crash of salvatory steel.

Robinson employs military imagery in three additional Octaves (II, IV, V) in which man and the times are objects of his invective. The image "downward years" to indicate old age is to reappear later in the brilliant lyric "Eros Turannos."

In the March 15 letter Robinson wrote, "a glimpse of the real light through the clouds of time . . . makes me wish to live and see it out" (pp. 278-279). In a world where people and conditions seemed to demand only negative response, Robinson found the positive, and it is in the Octaves that the positive is first voiced with consistency in his poetry. The affirmation of idealism in the Octaves as an "unsystematized" philosophy to which he could hold firm is paralleled by passages in his letters to Smith during the time he was working on the Octaves. On November 6, 1896 he wrote: "They [postage stamps] are so obviously material and my ideas are getting to be so thoroughly ideal, that the collecting of anything but wisdom seems like going back into ignorance and barbarism" (p. 263). On December 7, 1896 he wrote: "She [his mother] has gone ahead and I am glad for her. You see I have come to look on death as a deliverance and an advancement . . . and I am very glad to be able to stand up and say that I am an idealist. Perhaps idealism is the philosophy of desperation, but I do not think so. To me it is the only logical and satisfactory theory of life" (p. 264). Octave X is a poetic version of the above attitude toward death, though in the poem Robinson substitutes a "dead man" in the place of his mother:

> Where does a dead man go?—The dead man dies;
> But the free life that would no longer feed
> On fagots of outburned and shattered flesh
> Wakes to a thrilled invisible advance,
> Unchained (or fettered else) of memory;
> And when the dead man goes it seems to me
> 'T were better for us all to do away
> With weeping, and be glad that he is gone.

The March 15 letter, which Chard Powers Smith calls the "prose equivalent" (p. 161) of the Octaves, contains a passage which suggests that by then Robinson had begun to live according to idealism:

> I am not going crazy, for I see some things she [his mother] did not see—some things she could not see; but I am going to lose all those pleasures which are said to make up the happiness of this life and I'm glad of it. I'm glad to say that I am strong enough to do without them. There is a pleasure—a joy—that is greater than all these little selfish notions and I have found the way to it through idealism (pp. 279-280).

This idealism—the life within rather than the life without—is the subject of Octave V:

> There is one battle-field whereon we fall
> Triumphant and unconquered; but, alas!
> We are too fleshly fearful of ourselves
> To fight there till our days are whirled and blurred
> By sorrow, and the ministering wheels
> Of anguish take us eastward, where the clouds
> Of human gloom are lost against the gleam
> That shines on Thought's impenetrable mail.

We are unwilling to wage war against those materialistic forces that must be overcome before we can know the light of idealism, the "gleam / That shines." Paradoxically the defeat we suffer is prerequisite to our inward triumph. The "gleam / That shines" is synonymous with the "compensate spirit-gleams" in Octave VIII, the "glorifying light" in XII, the "foregleam" in XX, "God's highways gleaming" in XXII, and it is perhaps synonymous with the "gleaming of God's forge" in Octave XIX. The idealism of the Octaves seems to be based, at least in part, on the conception Robinson has of the glory of God, for the similarities in light imagery to describe both idealism and the attributes of God are more than coincidental. There is also in the Octaves an inner peace commensurate with the knowledge, wisdom, truth, and love that idealism radiates to man. This inner peace is perhaps best exemplified in the closing lines of Octave XVII: "The soul itself must insulate the Real, / Or ever you do cherish in this life— / In this life or in any life—repose."

Chard Powers Smith recognizes and charts to an extent the significant role idealism plays in the Octaves. Smith is convinced that Robinson's commitment to idealism must not be considered his final philosophical position. And, Smith cautions, Robinson never negated the "*reality* of Matter" (p. 289). In fact, Robinson acknowledged in the March 15 letter the "temporal necessities" of life, though he did so ironically: "The age is all right, material progress is all right, Herbert Spencer is all right, hell is all right" (p. 278). Smith concludes that Robinson's idealism "was no more than an assertion of his preference for the life of the mind within 'thought's impenetrable mail,' the contemplation by his outer conscious self of his inner unconscious self whose subsensuous activity was a mood, a mood of universal clairvoyance composite of being, perceiving, and loving" (p. 290).

The Octaves should be read as somewhat random entries in a journal chronicling the attitudes a sensitive, intelligent young man held during a time in which his family seemed to be disintegrating. The Octaves tell us something about Robinson's feelings on the subject of poetry; they affirm his belief in "God's accomplishment [that] is always and unfailingly at hand"; they register his disgust with the age and with man's inability to make something of it and himself; and they contain the genesis of his idealism. Although there is no consistent design to the Octaves, the last, XXIII in the *Collected Poems* series, serves as a conclusion in that the poet has come to meaningful terms with himself:

> Here by the windy docks I stand alone,
> But yet companioned. There the vessel goes,
> And there my friend goes with it; but the wake
> That melts and ebbs between that friend and me
> Love's earnest is of Life's all-purposeful
> And all-triumphant sailing, when the ships
> Of Wisdom loose their fretful chains and swing
> Forever from the crumpled wharves of Time.

This serenity and confidence, quite far-removed tonally from the near frenetic quality of a number of these pieces, appropriately conclude the Octaves.

---

1 Richard Cary, "E. A. Robinson as Soothsayer," *Colby Library Quarterly,* VI (June 1963), 237.

2 Chard Powers Smith, *Where the Light Falls* (New York, 1965), 57. All subsequent page references are to this edition.

3 *Untriangulated Stars,* editor, Denham Sutcliffe (Cambridge, Mass., 1947), 279. All subsequent page references are to this edition.

E. A. ROBINSON'S YANKEE CONSCIENCE

W. R. Robinson

The best works of art are the expression of man's struggle to free himself from this condition, but the effect of our art is merely to make this low state comfortable and that higher state to be forgotten.
Henry David Thoreau

Obvious as it may be, the fact that Edwin Arlington Robinson, born and reared in Maine, was a New Englander must be heavily underscored. For not only did New England constitute the primordial physical environment for his human life and poetic career, but it also impressed itself upon his being, as in the normal course of events it naturally would, as an ineluctable spiritual presence and moral force. He acknowledged the degree to which his native region occupied his imagination in "New England," a sonnet, first published in *The Outlook* in 1923 and collected in *Dionysus in Doubt* (1925), explicitly devoted to appraising it:

Here where the wind is always north-north-east
And children learn to walk on frozen toes,
Wonder begets an envy of all those
Who boil elsewhere with such a lyric yeast
Of love that you will hear them at a feast
Where demons would appeal for some repose,
Still clamoring where the chalice overflows
And crying wildest who have drunk the least.

Passion is here a soilure of the wits,
We're told, and Love a cross for them to bear;
Joy shivers in the corner where she knits
And Conscience always has the rocking-chair,
Cheerful as when she tortured into fits
The first cat that was ever killed by Care.

The poem opens by noting that the region, continuously swept by frigid winds, inhospitably endures man, and he survives against its mer-

Reprinted by permission, *Colby Library Quarterly*, VIII (September 1969), 371-385.

ciless change only because, accommodating himself to its hostile reality, he learns "to walk on frozen toes." The warmth available to him in this alien habitat, the poem further implies, originates from a man-made fire in a man-made edifice. Yet the social order erected by intelligence upon the freezing land, rivaling it in coldness, treats him as an unwelcome intruder, too. New England's Conscience interjects itself between the inspiring heat source and the humane powers, and from there zealously protects Yankee wits from soilure by Passion, banishes Love as a cross of compassion it refuses to bear, and kills Joy with Care. Contrary to its nature and name (which etymologically means "knowledge in association with"), it is obsessed with dividing and dominating, and takes its "cheer" accordingly from the sadism, suppression, and negation with which it forces the impulses toward freedom and unity "to shiver in the corner." It so thoroughly dominates the speaker of the poem, in fact, that the utterance he manages to make amounts to little more, at least on the surface, than a defensive reaction to its aggressiveness. Exerting enough pressure upon him to threaten his survival, it harasses him, as the frigid land does the people, into resorting to his intelligence to ward off New England's annihilating cold. But while it prods him into intellectual awakening, it also keeps his attention absorbed in it, so that not only does it compel him to write but also to write about the region. His life, quite evidently, arises from and is brought to an existential crisis in the confrontation.

New England decidedly figures as more than an accidental subject in this sonnet. Here—and in general for Robinson's imagination, it is safe to say—the very life of his art depends upon the kind of relationship his imagination establishes with its environment, that is, New England's spiritual presence and moral force. And, indeed, "New England" seems to have disposed of that matter rather nicely: it gives all the appearances of flatly repudiating the region for its moral callousness while itself issuing from a liberated spirit dissociated totally from it. Certainly Conscience, despite its authoritative zeal and its considerable success in intimidating the warm feelings, fails to squelch completely the vital urges: the poem, written in protest of its inhumanity, does defy its moral tyranny in castigating New England as a place and a community.

The gestures it makes of a free spirit declaring its untrammelled independence and about to strike out on its own belies, however, the profounder moral forces at work in the poem. For despite the one-sidedness of the assertion its speaker makes, the poem renders the continuation of a moral quarrel in which New England functions as the speaker's antagonist. Having "told," New England is being told back. This quarrel definitely takes precedence over the sensory and sensual, even though the poem's bias thematically favors the hedonistic pleasures of the unspoiled, uninhibited creature. Armoring itself in New England qualities, the poem, in effect, walks on frozen toes—its form, the highly stylized sonnet, is rational and conventional; its argument, witty, or intellectually assertive; its diction, abstract, as is its major figure of speech, personification; and its manner, laconic. Its poetic "cheer," not unlike Conscience's cheer, comes from coldly torturing words with indirectness, compression and irony. And this pleasure has crowded out those of the passion, love, and joy it thematically affirms. Judging by appearances, by the poem's explicit features, it would be more accurate to say that instead of repudiating New England the poem is New England, for it so adopts external circumstances that in outer characteristics the poem and region are indistinguishable.

But "New England" is anything but chauvinistic. In it a stubborn New Englander perversely turns upon his native ground the very qualities it prides itself upon, and it is this friction between the two that readily stands out as the salient fact in the imagination's relationship to its environment. Their superficial similarity does not cancel out that friction but rather, through the contradiction it introduces, hints of complex ironies. Apparently forced into adopting its characteristics in self-defense, the imagination has been trapped by the environment into internalizing its discriminations. The speaker keeps a tight intellectual lid upon the child's open innocence and eager spontaneity; the cat's undomesticable and solitary way; the sun, heat, feast, and drink of the pagan vision; as well as passion, love, and joy—all essential virtues of the imagination. No "lyric yeast of love" or anything else leavens the poem. Rather, an intransigent moral order superimposes itself upon the interior life of the imagination as well as the person, producing a consciousness intellectually and morally self-repressive. The frigid wind blowing down across New England and New England's divisive Conscience have opened a deep schism within the human being as well as between the individual and society.

As a result wit wars with wonder, conscience and intellect with the imagination—or, more accurately, the wits and the conscience are in the turmoil of a civil insurrection, one side within each exploiting its resources to defend propriety, the other enjoyment. They contend for possession of wonder, which one would force to "knit" dutifully and provide a practical garment for protection against the cold and the other would free in order that the spirit might rejoice in its natural warmth. But the immediate effect of this war within consciousness is that the one extreme of coldness badgers wonder into dreaming up its antithesis, an irrelevant, impotent fantasy of hot pagan indulgence. In this way New England has profoundly and complexly ingrained itself in the speaker's being and the poem. Instilled with its excesses and deficiencies, both are as cold as New England's Conscience, and both thereby extend its moral dualism, no matter how grudgingly. As a consequence, his argument, ultimately, is as much with himself as with New England, and, as culpable as it is, he stands, ironically, as condemned as the environment by his own conscience.

The poem's external features are considerably more than a skin-deep disguise to keep out of harm's way. In fact, its intellectualism so pervades it that "New England" cannot elude classification as a poem of the intellect. An even more obvious sign that its external qualities and implied quarrel that this is the case is the simple fact that the speaker makes assertions: his main act, what mainly happens in the poem, is that he uses language to describe a state of affairs. And in doing that he is engaged in baring the truth, the intellect's preeminent value. Since his crucial subject is Conscience, all his assertions and implied judgments "tell it like it morally is"; the poem, in other words, renders the imagination's moral predicament. As is inevitable from the point of view of the dichotomizing intellect, the moral phenomenon, exemplified in the poem by the incompatibility of wit and wonder, appears to consist of two incompatible worlds. The depth to which Robinson plumbed the moral truth in this direction is perhaps best attested to by Henri Bergson in *The Two Sources of Morality and Religion,* published in 1936, one year after Robinson's death, so if anything a conceptual extension of rather than an influence upon his poetry. (John Dewey's *Human Nature and Conduct,* 1922, also could serve in this respect.) In Bergson's theoretical formulations, the two incompatible moral worlds are designated "pressure" and "aspiration." Eternally irreconcilable, the first exerts itself multifariously, as Bergson defines it, in support of impersonal obligation, duty, habit, intellect, the abstract, law, order, restraint, repose, and a closed system; the second radiantly moves through vision, emotion, attraction, will, the concrete, creativity, action, joy, liberation, and possibility of an open universe.

But the complexity of the antagonists introduces a minimally novel moral truth compared to the insight recorded in "New England," and confirmed by Bergson, that both alternatives are groundless or rationally indefensible. Neither has a determinable priority or is backed up by infallible authority—in part because, as the philosophers were pointing out with their notion of the naturalistic fallacy, what is cannot provide a reason for what ought to be, and in part, and more devastatingly, because it is evident that there is not any such thing as "reality," a rock bottom to the world that could be used to measure the good even if the preceding were not true. Moral phenomena are unsponsored; their careers are a play of powers, precepts and principles being instruments within the struggle for supremacy. Values exist autonomously in a world generated by their own energy. Accordingly, in "New England" wit and wonder both derive their energy from the man-made fire, and the fire favors neither. When it breaks and divides, it sets in motion a moral drama in which the imagination and the intellect or society are on their own. And this absence of justification for its self-assertion largely explains the imagination's diffidence in the poem.

Yet the imagination does assert itself. Whereas Conscience with its selfish exclusiveness does its best to obstruct innovative moral action, still the imagination, intuiting its good, acts upon an instinct for self-preservation, so that although Janus-like the speaker faces in two moral directions simultaneously, he is not impaled in immobility upon the proverbial horns of his dilemma. The ironic and unsponsored condition, deep as it cuts, does not constitute the complete moral truth in the imagination's existential morality. There remains to be taken into account the fact that the imagination speaks out in this poem of the intellect.

Beneath the overt dualism of "New England" lies perforce, as a precondition of the poem's existence, a still more complex bond between the imagination and its environment than occurs on the intellectual plane. The coldness of the locale infused itself into the community erected upon it and the community in turn instilled that coldness, in the form of intellectual and moral aloofness, in the speaker, who begot a cold poem. In effect, a generative act, or a series of generative acts, has transpired during which, overall, the land has been transmuted into a poem, with the essential qualities of the former being handed down generation by generation to the latter. The land, New England, the speaker, and the poem are all blood kin, organically linked in a descending chain of increasing concreteness. Thus their primordial family trait, even beyond their coldness, resides in their creativeness, most notably present in the poem, since the relation between New England and the speaker occupies its foreground, in what transpires between the environment and the imagination. There Conscience reproduced itself in a conscience. In spite of itself, its aspiration prevailed over its pressure. The speaker and the poem are replicas of New England, therefore; begotten by and of it, they inherit and bear its Conscience and so perpetuate its character and urges.

Working beneath and around the surface friction, the imagination discovered and established a living bond with the world from which it emerged. It lives, as do the poem and Robinson's art, only if this vital connection prevails over the disjunctive force because, without a heaven or hereafter, decidedly absent from the poem, as a source or alternative, everything it has, including its creative power, comes from the "local" environment. It lives in so far as the world lives within it and it assumes a living responsibility to the world. The imagination and the environment survive as mutually interdependent functions of one another as long as their life line is intact. Of necessity, the speaker is involved in New England's destiny and it moves toward fuller realization through him; it inhabits him as he inhabits it, or his intellect participates in the life of his imagination as his imagination functions by means of it. The poem and its environment, as a consequence, are not only outwardly indistinguishable but inwardly, too: it is an incarnation of New England's spirit.

The most immediate concrete result of the generative event, then, is that an intently moral environment propagated itself in an imagination that sensed, as Thoreau did, that "Our whole life is startlingly moral." That is what it basically meant for Robinson to be a New Englander. But at the same time that also entailed his sensing that what New England said contradicted what it did. In its pronouncements it insisted upon austerity, repression, and conformity, and exerted its pressure to confine aspiration in set molds, yet in performing the creative act itself it set the example of innovation. Thus while Robinson's imagination abstractly understood itself to be duty bound, a strong upsurge of aspiration stirred within it.

Now the consequence of this contradiction, this tug of values, was not debilitation but liberation, not despair but possibility. It made the imagination a free moral agent, doomed to be moral but not predestined to make any given moral choice. The condition of its freedom is acknowledged in "New England" by the absence of time, history, or the past. The poem exists in the eternal present tense, the Now. The environment's authority depends solely upon its power to enforce its will, not upon any ancestral gods or traditional taboos. Nor is the imagination self-righteous. For both, historical guilt has been replaced by existential guilt, and both the environment and the imagination suffer from a deficiency of being. But the imagination suffers less an existential deficiency than the environment, since it, or the speaker, is a particularized creative agent. A mirror image of the environment, nevertheless he is different from it. The generative chain progressed from the unconscious land through the abstractly conscious society to the creatively conscious specific human being and finally to the poem. Endowed with the most highly individuated consciousness, the speaker stands apart as a distillation and enhancement of the environment. His special kind of consciousness allows him transcendent awareness of his environment and himself, and his free will and imagination make it possible for him to do something about the deficiencies he perceives in both. Once he becomes autonomous, the umbilical cord cut, he assumes the burden of employing his freedom to go forward, after the example of the environment in generating him, into greater life.

It follows as a correlative from the demise of historical guilt that only the future matters, but not in the sense of a terminal state to be reached eventually. The imagination is not going anywhere in time; it aims at refinement, not historical progress. Its good, it instinctively knows, lies in the intensification of life, so it works to manifest the spirit of life through further distillation and enhancement of it by means of aesthetic form, the most vividly individuated mode of existence. For this purpose its self-assertion constitutes an "inside narrative" focused appropriately upon its living truth and the intellect functions in an ancillary role to bring the creative chain to a culmination in consciousness objectified. (This accent in "New England" on knowing itself, or self-consciousness, gives way in different kinds of poems, it has to be kept in mind, to accent upon the creative freedom for which it is a preparation.)

Freedom for the imagination means having to choose. That is its inescapable existential moral burden. But coupled with the fact that neither the imagination nor the environment were sponsored by an authority on high and that the two dynamically contend for dominance, it meant also that on any given occasion Robinson had to choose one over the other. (And the wavering of his imagination in moral point of view and emphasis from poem to poem throughout his career reflects this plight.) Aware that such was his moral predicament, Henri Bergson, again conceptually articulating Robinson's poetic insights, made this choice:

> we must search below the social accretions, get down to Life, of which human societies, as indeed the human species altogether, are but manifestations. But this is not going far enough; we must delve deeper still if we want to understand, not only how society "constrains" individuals, but again how the individual can set up as a judge and wrest from it a moral transformation.

Although aspiration shivers in the corner in "New England" rather than being openly acted upon, nevertheless the speaker makes Bergson's choice. Wit clearly holds dominion over wonder and casts the poem in the reflective mode, yet the poem's heart belongs to passion, love, and joy, even if the imagination can manage no more overtly than to state their plight and must affirm its loyalty ironically.

A poet committed to the values of the imagination, Robinson heeded what New England did above what it said. His art is a choice as well as a record of his choosing and choices, and to have chosen poetry was to prefer the active and constructive, the assertive and affirmative moral alternative. In "New England," by virtue of its being a poem, the liberating and unitive powers, despite appearances to the contrary, ultimately prevail over the divisive and diminishing ones. The poem, like the land, New England, and the speaker, in line with their generative acts, which opt for the concrete and individual, freedom and life within the world, values the created and creative. Contingency is acknowledged tacitly as a condition of these values, and in that way in addition to tracing its emergence from its ground, its evolution from the abstract into its particularized form, it acclaims a finite art and finite man in a creative universe over two decades before Jean-Paul Sartre announced a program dedicated to that in 1947.

Life's most startling moment for his imagination occurred, as a consequence, when wonder, no matter how unobtrusively, assumed dominance over wit. This is the moment George Bernard Shaw singles out as "turning a child into a man" when he has Tanner, in *Man and Superman,* reject the first experience of erotic love, the Romantic's wellspring, as the origin of the imagination's life with the argument:

> No: the change that came to me was the birth in me of moral passion; and I declare that according to my experience moral passion is the only real passion . . . . [This] mightiest of the passions dignified all the other passions, gave them conscience and meaning, found them a mob of appetites and organized them into an army of purposes and principles. My soul was born of that passion . . . . You have no imagination, Ann . . . . The moral passion has taken my destructiveness in hand and directed it to moral ends. I have become a reformer, and, like all reformers, an iconoclast.

Like Tanner, Robinson assumed his New England birthright, his imagination came of age as a self-reliant agent, when it knew itself charged to be moral in this way. When morality became a passion for him in Shaw's sense, not righteousness or condemnation, not even the knowledge and dissemination of moral principles, but being and above all doing good were his paramount concern.

Henry David Thoreau, the archetypal New England, bore this moral passion, of course, long before Robinson did, and in *Walden* he carried out and defined in doing so the task the New England tradition prescribed for both himself and Robinson. The morally impassioned man, he saw, is a Columbus of "continents and seas in the moral world." Calling him to adventure, the moral life commands exploration into moral possibility, not obedience to already entrenched codes. The truly moral conscience, correspondingly, values above all else novelty, variously imaged by Thoreau as the new day dawning, spring, life resurrected, and the elated spirit. Such a conscience, "in an effort to throw off sleep," like Tanner, thrusts its reforming and iconoclastic fervor vigorously forward to uproot moral lethargy wherever it may be found. It knows that "while wholly involved in nature," for instance, that nature "must be overcome"; and that the soul must "transcend and redeem" itself, climbing constantly up what Emerson called the spiral of forms. This aspiration arises, inexplicably, when emerging from its source, consciousness perceives the "higher laws," and then alienated from its previous sufficiency, it simultaneously beholds in disgust man's and the world's imperfections. At that moment of moral awakening, conscience urgently enlists in a moral revolution dedicated to making man and the world over for the better. New England primed Robinson's imagination to discover that neither of them were good enough as they are, and thereby bound it, as it did Thoreau's, to quarrel with the region and itself in a relentless, continuous moral crusade. It demanded that his imagination by means of radical, uncompromising moral questioning come alive and stay alive. Which is precisely what New England's Conscience cannot do: rocking, moving without advancing, it administers a moribund or dead morality with the intent of obstructing the living conscience's passion for moral exploration.

Contrary to its conscious intentions, New England, acting compulsively to save itself from the self-inflicted death toward which Conscience inherently tends, blindly but wisely elected an individuated consciousness to insure the success of its aspiration in overcoming its wit's fearful resistance to regeneration. And to act successfully upon its choice of life, to rejuvenate while keeping intact the region's moral life, Robinson's imagination, in turn, was confronted with the problem of tapping the vital matrix and imitating while enhancing life's miraculous feat of continuously regenerating itself. His work is hypocrisy and a sham if, say, Thoreau had exhausted the possibilities of moral exploration within New England's moral world or Robinson was simply incapable of extending its moral frontier.

Neither Thoreau nor any other New England literary ancestor had fulfilled the region's moral aspiration, however, and Robinson was aware that they had not, as numerous comments in his letters, and those on Thoreau especially, reveal. Both he and Thoreau shared a common foe in the "Puritan Ethic," which enthroned money, respectability, worldly success in general—the outer signs of virtue—as man's chief good, and they were both devoted to demolishing that illusion and supplanting it with realistic living values. But otherwise their moral assignments differed rather markedly, so that though a powerful energy source to draw upon, Thoreau's achievement no longer sufficed. His escape from civilization, Robinson noticed quickly, aggravated the tendency of the Puritan Ethic to drive people apart and divorce them from their own humanity. That was the inescapable consequence of his sacrificing human relations to the transcendental consummation he ardently sought. Thoreau was committed, like Robinson, to bringing the mind into a creative conjunction with the vital, and he managed to do that to a degree by assigning the imagination hegemony over the intellect ("the imagination, give it the least license," he wrote, "dives deeper and soars higher than Nature goes"), reverencing the wild as well as the spiritual in himself, preferring words with dirt clinging to their roots, and scrutinizing the concrete, be it Walden Pond, a thawing railroad embankment, or a decomposing carcass of a horse, with scientific diligence. The commitment is there, to be sure, but the aspiration for rarefied intellectual values has priority over it. His strongest urge compels him to polarize moral alternatives into extremes, blatantly evident in his isolating himself in a natural setting to carry out his moral adventuring.

Moreover, his moral truth, as qualified by his style, is characterized by an uncompromising fervor, and he leaps over links in the generative chain—man's social and sexual being—to attain the saintly lucidity and purity his spirit desired. Even though he knew that relations were the heart of the matter ("Children," he said, "who play life, discern its true laws and relations," and "not till we have lost the world, do we begin to find ourselves, and realize where we are and the infinite extent of our relations"), he so simplified moral relations that the categorical dominance he assigns to cosmic enlightenment limits him to illuminating the precondition of the mind necessary for facing directly and embracing fully the complex moral fact, which encompasses all man's relations and especially those of man with man and to himself.

For Robinson the cosmic alternative, at least after his early poems, had lost its allure. Human existence was more complicated than such a clear-cut choice allowed for, he sensed, probably because Realism and science had installed objectivity as the arbiter of all knowledge, including the moral, and thereby made all intellectual and moral certitude obsolete. His moral adventuring had to proceed, his imagination acknowledges in "New England," without recourse to moral absolutes; it is trapped in society and beyond that in relativity—that is, in relationships. Relations are its "reality" and it must make do with them.

This predicament is conveniently described by Irving Babbitt, the academic defender of rational values for Robinson's generation, in his essay "Genius and Taste." He blames the decline in reason's prerogatives as a moral authority, and therefore of moral absolutes, upon Romanticism's permissiveness, which, he argues, had unleashed a gathering moral disintegration that could be checked only with a renewed dedication to "restraint" or "a proportioned and disciplined view of life" attainable through a return to "standards" or a "supersensuous truth" recognized as having "an outer authority" with "veto power" for imposing "control upon impulse," "order upon energy." Reason loses its credentials as a moral authority because "the illusions of a higher reality" are "not given to man to seize directly"; actually a composite of "reality" and "illusion," the supersensuous truth of standards is the province of the imagination, which "governs the world." Thus the man of reason admits frankly that responsibility for determining the good falls not upon reason but "the ethical and generalizing imagination." He admits that in his moral quandary he depends upon the artist to keep him spiritually afloat and so unashamedly reiterates Emerson's call for the poet, the man of imagination, to illuminate man's way in the new world.

Objectivity and its concomitant relativity, the ontological conditions of "New England," freed Robinson's imagination from the categorical dominance of reason but in doing that set it loose on an uncharted moral frontier. And without what Babbitt called "traditional moorings," the classical confidence of intellect, his imagination had to trust itself. Nothing was predetermined for it except that it be moral or relate; otherwise its life was in its own hands, its relations were its own doings. And since relating—synthesizing it has been more commonly called—is what the imagination by nature does, its solo explorations in the moral world perforce articulate the morality of the imagination.

Which "New England" does, for, however covertly, its subject is itself and it is a self-definition for both the poem and the imagination that begot it. Through articulating itself, Robinson's imagination posits the laws of the imagination as the laws of the universe, a generalization that W. B. Yeats insisted upon also in "The Symbolism of Poetry." In that way it supplies the "standards" Babbitt anxiously appealed for to head off what Robinson himself once referred to as "the dark and awful chaos of the night," but those new standards are the "absolutes" of relations, of life, not of reason. All his imagination could take for granted in its crusade, as imaged in "New England," is the fire that burns within it, and in the end all that it could know was that it was involved inextricably in the living process. To be a New Englander was to be scarred by its moral fire, and once burned by it, he was Fate's lieutenant, paradoxically doomed to be free and in his freedom to bear the potency and purposes of his region onward. Since poetry was his calling, his moral adventuring, his getting down to life and wresting from society a moral transformation, his contributing to the greater freedom of the individual in the world, his more fully extending living relationships and bringing to further realization the morality of life, had to be done in poems. His burden was to be a good poet and write a good poetry.

Robinson's life and letters, suffused with moral if not moralistic concern, leave no doubt of the depth and intensity of his moral passion.

That passion equally pervades his poetry, where it erupts in manifold ways—for example, didactically in poems such as "Zola," "Cassandra," and "Dionysus in Doubt," which rail at the world's evils; ironically in poems such as "John Evereldown" and "Miniver Cheevy," in which upstart passions are derided, the imagination, in effect, chastizing its own boisterousness; and implicitly in such poems as "The Night Before," "Isaac and Archibald," "The Book of Annandale," and "Nicodemus," to mention only the shorter poems. This diversity, resulting from an initial ambivalence toward the relative superiority of the values of Thought—a frequent word, capitalized, in his early poetry—over those of Life, reflects the tortuous path he negotiated in getting down to life. Though he began in moral uncertainty about what was involved in a commitment to life, that commitment is unquestionable, since abundant evidence of it is to be found in the arrangement of the poems in his first two volumes of poetry in a progression from poems of Thought to poems of Life or poems thematically assertive of life in such phrases as "touch to life," "to know enough to be alive," "life is a game that must be played," and "to get to where life begins"; and in his evolution from poems about solitary figures or of solitary statements in the first two volumes to "marriage" poems, poems treating complex interpersonal relations, in *Captain Craig*.

Robinson's commitment to life provides the prevailing drive or aspiration of his imagination from the beginning of his career but traditional attitudes he inherited initially blocked his acting upon it to create poems of life. To clarify and realize its commitment, his imagination had to move beyond "poems of the mind"— didactic poems, vehicles by which a knowledgeable consciousness self-righteously lectures wrongdoers and aggravates the divorce of thought from life, and also the ironic character study, where the discordance between thought and life is even more pronounced than in the didactic poems. No creative transaction occurs explicitly within either of them or even underlines the ironic type, the most fully and exclusively intellectual, and so sterile from the vitalistic point of view, in Robinson's poetry. Clarity comes to it, and a resolution to the animosity between thought and life, not in poems like "New England," which are limited to telling the moral truth and implying the unitive and creative desideratum, but in the poems of life—of being or structure if a metaphysical or aesthetic identification should be preferred—that increase in number as Robinson's career progresses until decisively dominant and that are his most distinctive and significant poetic achievement. In them, his imagination, eluding Conscience and Care and positioning itself next to the fire, its inspiriting source, does its most daring moral adventuring. In them the "downward flash of something new and fierce, / That ever strives to clear, but never clears / The dimness of a charmed antiquity" in "Boston," as in "New England," wins its way into the open and his imagination succeeds in rejuvenating while keeping intact New England's moral life, indeed, in pushing its moral frontier beyond where any of his ancestors or contemporaries had gotten to and to a point as yet unsurpassed.

HE SHOUTS TO SEE THEM SCAMPER SO: E. A. ROBINSON AND THE FRENCH FORMS

PETER DECHERT

THE OUTLINES of young Win Robinson's poetic involvement with Alanson Tucker Schumann, the homeopathic physician who lived next door to the Robinson family and wrote reams of verse, have been suggested in Hagedorn's biography and elsewhere.[1]

In later years Robinson wrote warmly of "my old friend Dr. A. T. Schumann, who was himself a prolific writer of sonnets, ballades and rondeaus, and a master of poetic technique. As I shall never know the extent of my indebtedness to his interest and belief in my work, or to my unconscious absorption of his technical enthusiasm, I am glad . . . to acknowledge a debt that I cannot even estimate. . . . I am sure that he was one of the most remarkable metrical technicians that ever lived, and an invaluable friend to me in those years of apprenticeship."[2]

Hagedorn tells of an incident during an informal evening at which Robinson and Schumann were present. When, "in the course of conversation, the doctor or one of his companions casually remarked that 'the perfect boozers live in Maine,' the rhythmic line was snatched up as the theme and refrain of a rondeau."[3] Emery Neff carried this tale farther, drawing the conclusion that Robinson's "humor was a bond with his fellow townsmen. When he began to experiment with the French forms, he caught up a phrase from conversation, 'the perfect boozers live in Maine,' for the refrain of a rondeau."[4]

The rondeau, as a verse form, of course requires a two- or three-stress catch-line; the four-stress line cited by both biographers actually became the refrain line of a "Ballade of the Maine Law":

> We have an elephantine law
> In our remote and frigid state,

Reprinted by permission, *Colby Library Quarterly*, VIII (September 1969), 386-398.

Framed, we are told, without a flaw,
  Rum's ravage to annihilate.
  We recognize its worthy weight
(Haply they do in France and Spain),
  Yet—why should we prevaricate?—
The perfect boozers are in Maine.

The judge protrudes his ample maw—
  He seems, though little, to be great—
And with a voice harsh like a saw,
  Decides vague issues to create.
  With unctuous phiz and hairless pate,
The lawyer vilifies in vain:
  The parsons from the pulpit prate;—
The perfect boozers are in Maine.

The seller sneers with coarse guffaw
  And swaggers with defiant gait;
The officer, with brutal paw,
  Drags the limp victim to his fate;
  The justice rules with look sedate,—
How ponderous the mental strain!—
  Pay, peach, or lounge incarcerate! . . .
The perfect boozers are in Maine.

ENVOY

How not the nuisance to abate
  Each drunken year we find again:—
Hence we aver that, up to date,
  The perfect boozers are in Maine.

Both biographers also erred in attributing this poem to Robinson: it was written by Schumann, and published under his name in the Gardiner *Reporter-Journal*.[5]

On October 5, 1893, Robinson wrote Harry Smith that "Schumann has written a 'Ballade of the Law,' with the refrain, 'He sells his soul for a paltry fee.' It is a very good thing, though perhaps a little strong in places. . . . He has another on doctors, 'This marvellous medical man.' "[6] This is the "Ballade of the Law," which Robinson admired:

A shameful farce is your splendid law,
  The world will know if it stop to think;
Yet it holds the timid in servile awe,
  And causes the valiant to quake and shrink.
  As vague and keen is a lawyer's wink
As a flash of foam on a fickle sea;
  And while the jurymen stare and blink,
He sells his soul for a paltry fee.

Mayhap he's a man with a massive jaw,
  And the head of an ape and the teeth of a mink;
With a hoarse voice harsh as a raven's caw,
  And the hairy phiz of the missing link;
  With a bullet eye as black as ink,
And a poll as bare as a polished pea;
  Perchance of the church he's the pride and pink:—
He sells his soul for a paltry fee.

Or his speech is as sharp as the hiss of a saw,
  Or as thin as the pelf that he loves to chink;
Or he talks with his hand with a clutch and a claw
  And his lies are as foul as a filthy sink;
  Tho' he lean, tho' he leer, tho' he pose, tho' he prink,
Tho' he fret, tho' he fume, tho' he fawn, may be,—
  Tho' squelched by the Court, and forced to slink,
He sells his soul for a paltry fee.

Envoy

His home is a hut near hell's red brink;
  And when he succumbs to death's decree,
To his ear as he drops comes the chill gold's clink;
  He sells his soul for a paltry fee!

The "Ballade of Gardiner," whose title Schumann wisely changed to "A Ballade of Physic" when he published it in the Springfield *Republican,* is of the same style, as its envoy can indicate:

His cordials come from Tokay,
  His drugs are from Biblical Dan:
Potatoes are often his pay—
  This marvellous medical man.

Still another ballade, "Shooting Stars," is a member of this genre:

When ardent summer skies are bright
  With myriad friendly lamps that glow
Down from their dark, mysterious height
  To charm the shrouded earth below—
  Lost in a faith we do not know,
Nor human discord ever jars
  With eyes that wide and wider grow,
He sits and waits for shooting stars.

And when they slide across the night
  Like arrows from a Titan's bow,
He shudders for supreme delight
  And shouts to see them scamper so,
  No sneering science comes to show
The poor brain crossed with silly scars;
  But flushed with joys that overflow,
He sits and waits for shooting stars.

We call him an unlovely wight;
  But if his wit be something slow,
Nor ever weary of the sight
  That Adam saw so long ago—
  Released from knowledge and its woe,
No gloom his constant rapture mars:—
  Oblivious from head to toe,
He sits and waits for shooting stars.

Envoy

Nor is it yet for us, I trow,
  To mock him, or to shut the bars
Of scorn against him—even though
  He sits and waits for shooting stars.

This poem is not Schumann's, however, but Robinson's. Published first in the *Globe* for December 1896, it has been reprinted in Hogan's *Bibliography* (173-174).

"Shooting Stars," although its opening and closing lines point toward Robinson's almost unique diction in his more mature poetry, does not represent the sort of verse that he later cared to perpetuate. He never reprinted it. In fact, he almost surely wrote it some considerable time before it was published; the *Globe* had a habit of holding poems for years before printing them. But he had been working an apprenticeship with the ballade form. His "Ballade of the White Ship" was printed in the Harvard *Advocate* for October 1891; reworked, it appeared as "Ballade of a Ship" in *The Children of the Night* before, like the "Ballade of Dead Friends," being excluded from the later collections.

Only two ballades were allowed to remain in the *Collected Poems,* both of which had appeared earlier in *The Torrent and the Night Before.* One, "Ballade by the Fire," is an exercise in irrevocable fate tempered by nostalgia, sentiments which too often occurred in his mentor Schumann's verse; with its envoy

> Life is the game that must be played:
> This truth at least, good friends, we know;
> So live and laugh, nor be dismayed
> As one by one the phantoms go[7]

it hardly seems worth taking very seriously.

The second, "Ballade of Broken Flutes,"[8] was in fact dedicated to Schumann. This poem has been seen as a statement of Robinson's rejection of poetry in favor of prose as a medium for self-expression (it must be remembered that he spent some time in the 1890s trying to master the short story); it might just as easily be seen as rejecting the sterility of the French forms because they seemed incapable of handling complex contemporary thought, the "broken flutes of Arcady" representing the uselessly formal pastoral quality of the archaic forms. Robinson's thinking was growing more complex than Schumann's ever became. In this view, this ballade probably anticipates a point that will be discussed in a moment.

Robinson seems never to have taken the triolet at all seriously, his only remaining one being the offhand

> Silent they stand against the wall,
> The mouldering boots of other days.[9]

This *jeu d'esprit* was written early in 1891, and if one may be allowed to make a serious deduction from a single piece of frivolity it seems to me to indicate a lack of understanding about the essential nature of the triolet, where the particular joy of the game is to shift the context about so that the refrain lines accrete new meaning at each reappearance. This observation is entirely applicable to Schumann's triolets (of which far too many remain) as well. At one point, indeed, Schumann retold the story of Christ in a triolet sequence, with awesomely disastrous results. One of his lighter efforts may better serve to give the flavor of the triolet style to which he exposed Robinson; it also serves to show that even minor poets are not immune to editorial annoyance:

Who told you, my friend,
To tinker my verses?
To trim and to mend,
Who told you, my friend?
I pray you to end
Your mischievous mercies!
Who told you, my friend,
To tinker my verses?

With its "sassy" rhyme of "mercies" and "verses," this triolet has a certain felicitous appeal, but like Robinson's boot epic it fails to make really effective use of the refrain.

Schumann was particularly addicted to writing in the rondeau form, which he equated with the sonnet:

Two formal stars begem the sky of song,
The lofty sonnet and the high rondeau;
Both in their course imperially go. . .

From Robinson's practice, we must assume that he did not agree with the Schumann equation, although his only surviving rondeau shows reasonable facility:

In Harvard 5 the deathless lore
That haunts old Avon's classic shore
Wakens the long triumphant strain
Of Pride and Passion, Mirth and Pain,
That fed the Poet's mind of yore.
Time's magic glass is turned once more
And back the sands of ages pour,
While shades of mouldered monarchs reign
In Harvard 5.

Thin spirits flutter through the door,
Quaint phantoms flit across the floor;
Now Fancy marks the crimson stain
Of Murder. . . and there falls again
The fateful gloom of Elsinore
In Harvard 5.[10]

But this is no more than an exercise: it shows only that Robinson had studied the technique of the rondeau well enough to apply it in an offhand manner when the spirit moved him to a piece of occasional verse. He seems never to have fallen into Schumann's attitude of ascribing moment to the form.

He did, however, write one serious poem which seems unquestionably to owe its structural basis to the rondeau. Much of the aural effect of "Luke Havergal" derives from the fact that its long stanzas end in truncated echo lines. Unlike the short refrain lines of the rondeau, which echo the beginning phrase of the first line of the poem, those in "Luke Havergal" repeat the closing syllables of the first line of each stanza. Structurally, nevertheless, this device is quite close to that of the rondeau. And each of the four seven and one-half line stanzas is almost the structural equivalent of the opening long stanza of a formal rondeau, even to the rhyme scheme that Robinson employed, the only differences being that the entire seventh line echoes the entire first with the eighth line (the half-line) serving as re-echo, and that there is one less line than in the eight and one-half line opening section of a rondeau. A comparison of the opening stanza of "Luke Havergal" with the beginning of "In Harvard 5" quoted above will show the similarities, as well as the differences:

Go to the western gate, Luke Havergal,
There where the vines cling crimson on the wall,
And in the twilight wait for what will come.
The leaves will whisper there of her, and some,
Like flying words, will strike you as they fall;
But go, and if you listen she will call.
Go to the western gate, Luke Havergal—
Luke Havergal.[11]

This poem has provided commentators with all sorts of leads to chew on. Fussell has found its roots in Poe and Longfellow,[12] for example. While the tone of the poem may be similar to the examples he cites, the tone in fact derives largely from the technique Robinson used (the thought, the "situation," is relatively banal, as it often is even in great poems, which depend on the method of expression to carry them over the hump of pathos), and this technique in turn has much more obvious roots in the rondeau than it has in the work of other poets. That Robinson was successful in so modifying the structure as to adapt it to the mood which he wanted to express is a measure of the technical resources that he had acquired during his apprenticeship. By the time that he wrote "Luke Havergal," he had advanced beyond Schumann's capabilities.

If Robinson did not himself take the formal rondeau structure very seriously, he actually suppressed one of his poems because it had mistakenly been taken seriously by several reviewers. He never reprinted the rondel, "Poem for Max Nordau," after *The Torrent,* although we can easily enough see it as another example, like "In Harvard 5," of his adapting a French form for satirical ends:

Dun shades quiver down the lone long fallow,
And the scared night shudders at the brown owl's cry;
The bleak reeds rattle as the winds whirl by,
And frayed leaves flutter through the clumped shrubs callow.

Chill dews clinging on the low cold mallow
Make a steel-keen shimmer where the spent stems lie;
Dun shades quiver down the lone long fallow,
And the scared night shudders at the brown owl's cry.

Pale stars peering through the clouds curled shallow
Make a thin still flicker in a foul round sky;
Black damp shadows through the hushed air fly;
The lewd gloom wakens to a moon-sad sallow,
Dun shades quiver down the lone long fallow.[13]

Considering the repetitive demands of the rondel form, "Poem for Max Nordau" is not an unsuccessful effort. But these formal demands, like those of the triolet, are hardly suited to the expression of the sort of things that Robinson increasingly felt that he had to say during the 1890s. Certainly, from the evidence that remains, and particularly from its facility, there seems to be no doubt that in his formative years Robinson did work diligently in the strict forms, under Schumann's aegis. He wrote to Smith of fiddling "too much over sonnets and ballades,"[14] although he soon enough rejected the latter in favor of the former. And in 1894, sending Smith an early draft of his villanelle "The House on the Hill," he added that "These old French forms always had a fascination for me which I never expect to outgrow. . . . When one of the things begin [*sic*] to run in my mind there is little rest for me until it is out."[15]

Fortunately, he did outgrow the fascination. In fact, his "Villanelle of Change,"[16] one of the two villanelles in the *Collected Poems,* seems (as do most of Schumann's villanelles) to be little more than a five-finger exercise, as, on the evidence of what he had written Smith, he may very well have regarded it himself. "The House on the Hill,"[17] however, went through at least one major reworking and several minor revisions during its almost three years of growth. Apparently Robinson took it more seriously than he did most of his French form efforts, and it demonstrates not only the possibilities of this metier, but also the weaknesses that probably led him to abandon these forms.

In the earliest version of "The House on the Hill," found in a letter to Smith dated February 25, 1894, it is subtitled "(Villanelle of Departure)." Robinson noted that it was "made [yesterday] very quickly (in about twenty minutes)" and "is a little mystical perhaps . . . an attempt to show the poetry of the commonplace." Its second and third stanzas combine two of his early, relatively simple, attitudes toward death, with the quasi-religious echoing the fatalistic:

Malign them as we may,
  We cannot do them ill:
They are all gone away.

Are we more fit than they
  To meet the Master's will?—
There is nothing more to say.

Implicit in this version is the idea that Robinson was writing about a strongly specific "departure," a single set of deaths, and the "they" comes through as a specific family group; this implication is reinforced in the next stanza as well, particularly by the "the" in the second line:

What matters it who stray
  Around the sunken sill?—
They are all gone away.

The version sent to Smith was printed in the *Globe* with slight alterations in punctuation, but Robinson's one verbal change—"the sunken sill" became "that sunken sill"—made the particularization of the poem's theme even more apparent.

It is also interesting to see that at least two aspects of this early version indicate the continuing influence of Schumann on Robinson. The first, the "Master" theme, closely echoes Schumann's probably spurious religiosity; while "What matters it who stray" is pure Schumannesque diction, an example of the sort of rhetorical absurdities found in almost all of his poems. It seems obvious that Robinson, soon after writing this first version, realized the vapidity of such expressions and made a conscious effort to suit his diction more realistically to his subject matter, whether or not in the direction of a "poetry of the commonplace."

The other striking attribute of this early version of "The House on the Hill" is that, for all its "mystical" quality, it is still an occasional poem. That is, it is—as I have said—motivated by a specific subject. Schumann's attitude, the conventional one, toward the French forms was that they were primarily suited to the celebration of the specific; and Robinson in this instance seems to agree.

One of the things that makes a major poet, however—or a novelist, for that matter—is the urge, and the ability, to universalize. On the evidence at hand, Robinson, either instinctively or otherwise, began to realize this transformation from the particular to the universal in the period between early 1894, when he wrote "The House on the Hill," and 1896, when he sent *The Torrent and the Night Before* to the printer with a much reworked version which is practically identical to the one finally included in the *Collected Poems*.

Indeed, the most striking aspect of this revision is the way in which

Robinson worked to substitute universality for particularization. The three stanzas quoted above, which are the most changed, now read:

Through broken walls and gray
  The winds blow bleak and shrill:
They are all gone away.

Nor is there one today
  To speak them good or ill:
There is nothing more to say.

Why is it then we stray
  Around the sunken sill?
They are all gone away.

The "one," the "we," the "they" here are much more ephemeral individuals than the corresponding figures in the early draft. "That sunken sill" has reverted to "the," and its placement in the stream of developing thought does not seem to insist nearly so strongly on its being unique. "The winds," by being plural, are also a strong universal symbol.

But a shift toward the generality of experience is not the only new note here. The two early attitudes toward death have both been erased; in their place, Robinson arrived at the idea of death as simple finality, not only of actual existence, but even of remembered existence: no one recalls the "they" who went away, for "good or ill." They have not gone, but vanished. This, of course, reflects his final mature attitude, one which continues relatively unchanged down through all the long blank verse narratives to *King Jasper.* The accretion of maturity over a two and one-half year period demonstrated by the development of "The House on the Hill" almost surely echoes a biographical maturing whose discussion is beyond our present scope. One clue, however: remembering that the implied formula "death equals forgetting" is equally validly stated "forgetting equals death," we can also remember the combination of factors which seemed to Robinson during these years to be isolating him as an individual.

In the process of revision, the nature of "The House on the Hill" changed from an occasional piece with an overtone of mysticism, if we accept Robinson's jocular evaluation, to a personal philosophical statement. Poetically it progressed along the line between jingle and tone poem as a result of Robinson's increased perception of his actual subject matter, and also because its verbal structure shifted from rhetoric toward the communication of specific images and felt ideas rather than conventional ones. Like Poe's "Raven," however, it in many ways succeeds despite itself: it is a tour de force still, as indeed must be the case with poems cast into one or another of the French forms, and perfecting it seems to have been among Robinson's final struggles with these restrictive forms. There is no evidence that he attempted anything serious in any of them after about 1895.

Very little in the ultimate *Collected Poems* indicates Robinson's involvement with the stubborn formalities to which Schumann had introduced him. Only the technical facility of the two ballades and the two villanelles can lead us to infer hundreds of earlier attempts, almost all aborted, abandoned, or destroyed. Fortunately a few poems like "In Harvard 5," "Shooting Stars," the Boots triolet and "Poem for Max Nordau" remain to demonstrate that these conjectured hundreds did exist.

For the expert who wants to analyze the developing facility of a fine poet, it is frustrating to think of so much evidence, all gone. For the person who is interested in poetry as an end result, however, there probably is no need to mourn the juvenilia that we lack. The little that remains is poor enough to cause us to doubt the quality of the rest.

Poor, that is, as poetic expression. Robinson's handling of the forms was competent enough. Probably the missing rondeaus, rondels, ballades and villanelles were not, at their happiest, unlike the hundreds of Schumann's that we still do have. At their best, which is fairly represented by the two ballades which were quoted earlier in this essay, Schumann's poems were technically effortless, and their content could be both amusing and trenchantly caustic. Many of Schumann's neighbors also lived in Tilbury Town. But in the end, Robinson settled on the sonnet as the form best suited for the observations that he wanted to make.

It seems likely to me that the maturing Robinson found the jingle-effects of French form structure to be at cross-purposes with the increasing seriousness of what he had to say in the later 1890s. Life was beginning to close in on him. For the first time, he had been—or had imagined himself to be—in love: not once, but allegedly at least three times, with Mabel Moore, with Rosalind Richards, and with his brother's fiancée.

His mother died only days before he received the printed copies of his first book. Herman had lost the family fortune, such as it was. Harry Smith had married "on the night of a friend's wedding," and Robinson felt that he had finally become estranged from all of the few close friends that he had chosen over the years. Jobless in a job-oriented society, he was approaching thirty with a goal, but with no assurance of achievement.

From his experience with the French forms and from his other early practice, Robinson by this time had developed and honed the ability to express himself easily and to the point in structured verse. Far harder to construct as vehicles for meaning than the sonnet, the several French forms demand much of any poet if he is to use them to communicate anything but the barrenest of conventional sentiments, and "The House on the Hill" shows how far Robinson had come from being satisfied with entirely ephemeral purposes. The shape of his early verse no longer was congruent with the shape of his thoughts. But time spent in mastering strict formality is not time wasted, no matter if the forms themselves are ultimately abandoned for less meticulous structures.

Under the circumstances, then, and especially considering Schumann's often over-facile handling of them, it is not hard to believe that the French forms finally seemed too frivolous to Robinson, too lightweight to bear the reflective burden that he was now ready to impose on his verse. They had served their purposes by developing his facility at stanzafied self-expression and by allowing him an outlet for jejeune thoughts and humor; ultimately, however, they were playthings to be outgrown. He had had done with shouting at their scampering.

Shortly after *The Torrent and the Night Before* was printed, Robinson wrote his friend Art Gledhill that he had discovered that he must "write whatever I think is appropriate to the subject and let tradition go to the deuce,"[18] and to Smith he added "Of course I like a joke, and I like art for its own sake; but these things in themselves are not enough."[19]

He was writing his epitaph for the French forms.

---

1 Hermann Hagedorn, *Edwin Arlington Robinson* (New York, 1938).
2 "The First Seven Years," *Colophon*, I (Part Four, 1930), n.p.
3 Hagedorn, 47.
4 *Edwin Arlington Robinson* (New York, 1948), 89-90.
5 Quoted from an undated clipping found in the Schumann collection in the Gardiner, Maine, Public Library in 1953. All other quotations from Schumann in this essay are from manuscript or newspaper versions of his poems in the Gardiner material.
6 Denham Sutcliffe, editor, *Untriangulated Stars: Letters of Edwin Arlington Robinson to Harry De Forest Smith, 1890-1905* (Cambridge, Mass., 1947), 110.
7 *Collected Poems* (New York, 1937), 76-77.
8 *Ibid.*, 77-78.
9 Estelle Kaplan, *Philosophy in the Poetry of Edwin Arlington Robinson* (New York, 1940), 6.
10 Donald Hall, editor, *The Harvard Advocate Anthology* (New York, 1950), 55-56.
11 *CP* (1937), 74.
12 Edwin S. Fussell, *Edwin Arlington Robinson* (Berkeley, 1954), 16-17, 20-21.
13 *The Torrent and the Night Before* (Gardiner, Maine, 1896), 33.
14 *Untriangulated Stars*, 115.
15 *Ibid.*, 133.
16 *CP* (1937), 80-81.
17 *Ibid.*, 81-82. Earlier versions appear in the letter to Smith cited in note 15, in the *Globe*, and in *The Torrent*.
18 Ridgely Torrence, editor, *Selected Letters of Edwin Arlington Robinson* (New York, 1940), 13.
19 *Untriangulated Stars*, 289.

"THE WORLD IS . . . A KIND OF SPIRITUAL KINDERGARTEN"

PAUL H. MORRILL

NO READER of Edwin Arlington Robinson's poems can escape the realization that people were his most important interest. All kinds of people attracted him. He "tried them on," so to speak, in several tempers, sizes and shapes, from lonely old women and crass butchers to artists and industrial magnates. His poems, from his first publication in 1896, are about human beings, not landscapes or colors, or subjective speculation. Robinson wrote of his first book:

> You won't find much in the way of natural description. There is very little tinkling water, and there is not a red-bellied robin in the whole collection. When it comes to "nightingales and roses" I am not "in it" nor have I the smallest desire to be. I sing in my own particular manner of Heaven and Hell, and now and then of natural things (supposing they exist) of a more prosy connotation than those generally admitted to the domain of meter.[1]

His commentators agree unanimously, if not with equanimity as to his aims and results, that his "subject" was first and foremost people.

This interest has resulted in Robinson being labeled a psychological poet, meaning primarily for his readers that Robinson stood or fell generally on his particular analytical style. Some critics rely for this statement upon the method the poet used in presenting his individuals. Others believe that it was his content, his studies of failures, mistaken idealists, and unsure lovers (to cite a few examples), which earned him the title "psychological poet."

This paper will review Robinson's content and methods of characterization, his varied people and their problems—in the total context of his work. The selections made are arbitrary and narrowed down to individuals who best exemplify the psychological categories or illustrate

Reprinted by permission, *Colby Library Quarterly*, VIII (December 1969).

most clearly this aspect of the poet. We hope to show possible categories of people, although no warrant exists to confine them to particular niches. The emphasis is upon the "psychological" in Robinson, not upon categories or philosophy. There is nothing here of the biography of the poet, though his life offers more than enough for speculation.[2] Nor are Robinson's debts, mental or material, or the results of his study, especially treated. The rationale has been that a reading of Robinson's poetry, looking particularly at the characters, their concerns and ideas, their hopes and fears, their interpersonal relationships might result in new and fuller reactions for the reader.

The title quotation indicates the genesis of this review. Early in his career, soon after his first poems appeared, Robinson made this statement in answer to a critical article:

> I am sorry to learn that I have painted myself in such lugubrious colors. The world is not a prison house but a kind of spiritual kindergarten where millions of bewildered infants are trying to spell God with the wrong blocks.[3]

One can see at once the chain of speculation that this vivid figure sets in motion. The idea that a poet considered the world a kindergarten, and people in it children, made putting "tags" upon his cast of portraits almost a game. And the additional words of his metaphor, "blocks" and "spell God," gave rise to a set of categories to explain or contain his people. Finally, and most important, the words "bewildered infants" seemed to epitomize nearly every person that the poet brought to life in his writing. A pattern seemed to be apparent; at least the suggestion of children and infantile behavior, in a world of misplaced motives and ideas, made the title, the "psychological poet," pertinent.

The problem became one of explanation. How did the poet show the "children"; of what stuff were their problems constructed; by what means did they achieve or fail to achieve their goals; and what were their aims?

If, then, Robinson has infantile characters in *content,* and uses a psychological *method* of presentation, what part of or how does this affect his readers? Or to rephrase the query: how successful is Robinson in stating in literary form conceptions of psychic character? Is he dealing with "neurotic personality" *patterns* current in his time? Using these interpretations, can the Robinson characters be cited which appear to exemplify psychological views of individuality?

It is not the intention of this essay to minimize other approaches to Robinson; nor is it suggested that Robinson consciously or unconsciously measured his subjects by psychological theories. It is doubtful, also, that specific theories of psychology can be demonstrated in the case of the poet. On the other hand, since the term "psychological" is applied to him, there is relevance in noting whether such insight into his people enhances the value and illuminates the coherence of his work.

The poet is convincing in his exposition of infantilism in reactions against others and against creeds and standards of their culture. He appears to be posing this question: what are the conditions which make for infantile personalities? The answer given to that query, in part, is the reason why criticism of his work has taken both negative and affirmative stands. At one reading Robinson appears only to be viewing infantilism sympathetically but objectively without comment. At another reading, he seems to be exhibiting the conditions which give rise to anxiety and fears and presenting attitudes and means of overcoming these frustrations.

By treating of people's mental states to a high degree, using a style in which he can be observer and analyst (even to the extent that several observers are "physicians"— with their own problems; see "How Annandale Went Out"), Robinson offers a cast of persons who hear voices, talk to the unseen, dream a variety of fantasies and nightmares. As his kindergarten figure suggests, his people are either trying to reach the wrong goals or are using the wrong methods to achieve their goals. Some, by not observing the norms of society, may actually be behaving maturely. Others are possessed with uncertainties because they know that their way is not satisfactory to their inner selves. They have problems of love and affection and understanding, in and out of marriage, with relatives and friends. Others strive for power and its symbol, possessions: want it when unobtainable, are hated or hate themselves in the power role, or find that it is not truly what they are seeking. Man, as a creator, feels the distrust and antagonism of society, questions the area or degree of fame, lives with or rejects the personal expression which satisfies society and not himself. Others react violently in their relations with their fellows, kill or are killed, commit suicide, become completely unrational, respond abnormally to life's problems, have dreams, nightmares, tantrums, are consumed by jealousy and hatred. And many of his *dramatis personae* appear to be types, either historical or symbolical, who illustrate psychological concepts.[4]

There seems to be agreement among readers in discussing Robinson's approach to his poetic world that most of the characters have some bewildering flaw in their make-up.[5] Herein, also, lies the elements of the pessimism with which he has been charged.[6] As a rule, sociologists and students of human difficulties agree that all of us are subject to peculiar attitudes, prejudices, blindspots, and degrees of infantilism— essentially human attitudes.[7] Robinson's people, despite their flaws and their difficulties, real and imaginary, attempt to overcome or sublimate their faults, to accommodate, to achieve a measure of balanced successful living. In this they reflect Robinson's "incurable optimism."[8]

The scope of Robinson's psychological landscape may be obtained from his own comments on his work; a survey of representative characters in the poems; classification of problems his people faced; and some illustrations which make the kindergarten statement most applicable as a reference in Robinson's study.

For discussion of the characters in this orientation, the following categories seem most pertinent: *characters involved in problems of giving and receiving affection:* demanding and jealous love, compulsive love, competitive love, mother love; *characters evidencing problems of self-evaluation or assertion* (success-failure themes): power, possession, and prestige problems, unwillingness to face difficulties; *characters concerned with their creative place in society:* the artist in material world, the creative self at odds with social order; *aberrations; pathological characters:* victims of delusions, neurotic anxieties, etc.; and, throughout, characters who are *archetypal* in nature or effect.

Fifty-three short and medium length poems, and eleven longer narrative poems are especially illustrative of characters in difficult situations, struggling to adjust themselves to life. In an earlier effort, I summarized the method, content, and effect of these poems. It is included at the end of this paper to suggest further exploration.

Robinson never explained his kindergarten statement in any formal way. Nor can it be proven that the poet consciously held to a consistent application of this idea, although he reiterated his interest in infantilism and mental insight in letters and other statements. He did feel strongly that he should not be expected to interpret himself in analytical or discursive terms. He always wished, when accused of "obscurity," that people would simply read his poems "one word after another."

To his friend, Harry Smith, Robinson wrote:

> Your good letter came Thursday and I was somewhat amused at your remarks on my perceptive powers. I do not think I get a very clear view of the wrinkles on the cerebrum of the men and women I meet, though I generally form some idea of their characters before a very long acquaintance. There is more in every person's soul than we think. Even happy mortals we term ordinary or commonplace act their own mental tragedies and live a far deeper and wider life than we are inclined to believe possible in the light of our prejudices. I might name one or two examples, but it is not always best to be too specific on paper . . . . I do not always mean all that I say, but I must acknowledge the dismal truth that the majority of mankind interests me only as studies.[9]

When we consider the word "studies" there can be little doubt that Robinson worked in this fashion. For example, his Reuben Bright, a butcher, obviously illustrates the point: a man normally considered unfeeling is profoundly grieved by the death of his wife and reacts violently. Robinson's poem "Neighbors" admirably presents his version of gossip. Later he wrote:

I hate self-praise, or much of it, but it really seems to me that I have brought out the idea of the occasional realization of the questionable supremacy of ourselves over those we most despise in a moderately new way. If there is a little poetry in it, then all the better. There is poetry in all types of humanity — even in lawyers and horse jockeys — if we are willing to search it out; and I have tried to find a little for the poor fellows in my hell, which is an exceedingly worldly transitory one.[10]

There is no corroboration in Robinson's statements to set up divisions or classifications of his poetic persons; yet the classifications do seem to exist, and the people, in his earliest writings of Tilbury Town, continued with him in various forms through all his work.

From the first book, published at the age of twenty-seven to the last after his death at sixty-five, arranged roughly in chronological order, the poems show a steady preoccupation with bewildered people in a world of difficulties. At the same time there is an artistic progression in method from shorter views to longer, more complex structures. The effect is movement from maturity to greater maturity, from constrained shorter accounts of personal cataclysms to narrations of people with more intricate if not deeper problems.

Running through all the poems, no matter how they are classified, are psychological themes which we may regard as intrinsic to Robinson. Most readers recognize this as did Theis who wrote early in the *Forum*:

He is not unfamiliar with the windings and complexities of the human soul. On the contrary, he is often even rather fond of what are called psychological states, as in the long narrative poem called "The Book of Annandale" . . . complete portrait of types that on the surface seem utterly unadapted to poetic treatment.[11]

Thirty years later, Samuel Beers wrote:

No one can read Robinson's poetry with psychiatric insight and not come away without a sharpening of his own sense. Robinson knew the . . . labyrinthian problems of married folk . . . tortured neurosis of unfulfilled love . . . hidden worth of ostracized hermits . . . acquaintance with the peculiar persons who walk city streets.[12]

Finally these psychological "studies" should be considered as contributing to the richness of Robinson's ethical and aesthetic purposes. In all the relationships of man in the world, with himself and others, and with the ultimate, the psychological import augments the moral value and buttresses the philosophic. The artist who sets out to create a work of permanence is akin to Captain Craig, the mendicant philosopher, or the Everyman in *The Man Against the Sky*, in the search for surety of mind.

Seldom can characters be filed under a single heading, and the theme and substance of many poems are interwoven. There are points of comparison between the shorter earlier poem, "The Clinging Vine" and the later more involved work, *Cavender's House.* What these characters share is the search for understanding and love, often without a true conception of the meaning of giving and receiving affection. The precise little drama of the husband and wife in "The Clinging Vine" depicts the flickering and dying of a love as seen through the eyes of an external observer. *Cavender's House* brings to a climax the pathological compulsions of a jealous murdering husband—a fuller narrative rich in detail with excellent (stream of consciousness) self-examination.

Similar threads link the vivid "Richard Cory" of Tilbury Town and the more involved *Matthias at the Door.* Both of these poems, regardless of length and method, are concerned with the evaluation of the self. Both may be considered in the kindergarten structure of Robinson as material successes but spiritual failures. Robinson said of Matthias that it "is about a man who assumed that he was perfect until he discovered that he wasn't." Similarly, *King Jasper,* the allegorical study of commercial power which destroys love and friends, parallels the earlier work, "Bokardo."

Studies of aberrants vary as do the archetypal and historical figures, but relationships in the Tilbury Town groups, such as "John Evereldown" and "Flammonde" are included in broader and larger works of later years.

The central question for Robinson's creative people was how each reconciled his artistic drives—whatever "light" or "demon" demanded he do—with the mores of society. Like Henry James, Robinson was aware of his profession. Its mark was on him all his life; as a consequence he wrote considerably of creative men in relation to society. *The Man Who Died Twice* and *Amaranth* are classic accounts of the content of the artistic mind. Llewellyn Jones said of the first of these that

> it is another story of Mr. Robinson's often treated human types, the man of high spiritual impulse who is nevertheless either spiritually or materially a failure . . . if it is a beautiful example of his insight into the creative mind.[13]

Ulrich wrote that it is the psychological revelation of the hero, Fernando Nash: "The ruin of a potential world shaker."[14]

However, in noting the similarities and parallels in the content of the (psychological) characterizations of Robinson, the reader must not lose sight of differences: differences of time which alter their effect; differences which affect the style, length, and approach. In method Robinson at first chose to make short records as an observer of externals, allowing his characters to develop their "childishness" before the eyes of the reader, principally by what *they did.* Later Robinson—although no less concerned with the theory of self-revelation of his characters—augments the scope of observation. He illuminates the thoughts and actions that govern people by amplified analysis, a broader frame of reference, and by varied use of monologue and dialogue. "Richard Cory" is a mannered portrait of sixteen lines. The observers ("We") are the people of the community (with the implication that only a few of the "We" in the community really care or seek to understand the case). In a later work with similarities of content, a painful feeling of inadequacies hangs over *Matthias at the Door*—a man set "apart / Because, being who he was, and as he was / His natural station would inevitably / Be somewhat on an eminence, like his house." Here Robinson's method is a broad and deep probe into Matthias' anxieties and fears through his own words, those of his wife, and several others in his social ken. The element of surprised disbelief in "Richard Cory" which is the hallmark of the "observer" is replaced in *Matthias at the Door* by an entirely different set of concerns governed principally by the method of disclosure.

Some readers hold that Robinson's work is best summed up in the body of his earlier and/or shorter poems. The "padded verbosity" they read into the later and longer narrative poems only makes the study of his work more difficult, less rewarding. But, because of the links mentioned, readers should examine more or all of Robinson for psychological characteristics before a final accounting can be rendered. It is possible to read "Richard Cory" only, but it would ignore much that is rewarding and psychologically apt.

Robinson maintained his psychological method and content in all his poetry; his "studies" are as much a touchstone of his work as is James's "point of view." He sustained control, so to speak, by supplying the objective observer, by combinations of observer-commentator, and by letting the reader participate in the internal thoughts of the "children." In "Flammonde," for example, Robinson conceives his archetypal "hero" through the puzzled eyes of an observer in the community. In "Gift of God," a mother, ambitious and selfish, is visualized in comments about her son by an omniscient person. A dramatic monologue of deep intensity in "The Clinging Vine" conveys the rebuff and humiliation of a woman trapped by crippling jealousy. A compulsive voice, about which there has been much question, calls "Luke Havergal" to his destiny. The confessional on spiritual and artistic values in "Tasker Norcross" comes to us by the method of a dialogue between the principal subject and an analytic companion. By a process of abreaction the characters of *Roman Bartholow* conduct self-analysis in dialogue and dream sequences. In "Avon's Harvest" a man's hatred and fear are plumbed in the presence of a physician-analyst.

In these poems, poems sustained in mood and revelatory of psychological state and tensions, Robinson meshes content and method, uses and foreshadows the "internal monologue," infuses poetry into the atmosphere of the mind. Truly, as a critic says, writing in the *Bookman*: "He ferrets out the soul of humanity and turns it over and over with analytical interest, making his acute deductions and stabbing truths come home to his reader with a phrase . . . He is an alchemist refining gold out of the chaos of modern life.[15] In the analysis of this chaos and the evocation of the spirit of contemporary life, Robinson presents a huge cast: the infantile; the neurotic; those without respect for other individuals; those blind to love; devoid of tenderness; those selfish in motive and action; those self-seeking for power and for possessions; those who use or are used by others; those who choose wrongly or are lacking in positive effort; persons who teeter in a world of fear, in an agony of anxiety or wasted passions; those consumed by nightmares residing in their own selves; people who wander in and out of reality in search of answers; those fearful that they may encounter the truth about themselves. In all of this, though armed with high ethical and moral values, Robinson seldom sits in judgment; nor does he hold up to the reader one course of conduct as the only "truth." He seeks to set forth his observation and testimony with fundamental insight into all lives, not to be a moralist or a pessimist, or ironic, etc., as certain critics insist. All are present, as appropriate to the content and the method: to come through any experience to a knowledge of oneself. We are always aware of a fine intelligence at work, an intelligence that insists realistically upon our understanding of the maximum that can be known. At the same time, as Boynton saw the themes,[16] his poems often refuted popular codes: charity is often only self-egoism, marriage may be slavery of the worst sort, emotional love is full of pitfalls, life is often tortured and nightmarish, the bad can and does triumph over good.

Not only has Robinson paralleled or augmented the form and content of contemporary "interior monologue," he anticipated in a number of instances the idea that the subconscious is an essence of life. Study of his poetry suggests that what Robinson meant by "light" was not only rational understanding, or emotional power of the self—an aid for one to go beyond the possible.

In addition, Robinson presents with vision and clarity the concept of personality as an organization of biosocial processes, relations, and experiences. As readers we are in "a kind of spiritual kindergarten where millions of bewildered infants are trying to spell God with the wrong blocks." The "orientation" offers a highly charged principle upon which Robinson's work may be projected. According to this idea, experiences are derived from and essentially consist of interpersonal relations, both real or fantastic (imaginary), or a blend of both. Such experience may be public and overt, or more or less private; but it always occurs in a social context, apparently having a discoverable reference to others. Robinson is prophetic of these beliefs and goes further to suggest that the choice of the "wrong block" and the effort made to "spell God" may lead to bewilderment, even neurosis, that wrong efforts or wrong goals will alienate one from his "real self." This self, for the poet, both in the average person and in the creative soul, is the active unique center of personality. In "Rembrandt to Rembrandt," for example, Robinson calls this "his daemon," the only part of man that can grow and wants to grow. Furthermore, Robinson makes clear what one modern philosopher has stated:

> in life, there is misery as well as happiness, failure no less than success; and . . . tragedy underlies the truth that human hopes must measure themselves against unfeeling necessity . . . tragic wisdom is the knowledge of evil . . . by purging man of the original sin of self-sufficiency, tragedy makes him sociable and compassionate . . . so that he can love without craving, strive without fretfulness, rise to success without falling into pride, fail without losing heart.[17]

This, then, is the basic question Robinson asks: what are the factors that make for disturbances in these persons? His world contains conditions which give rise to anxiety: either external fears of enemies or competitors; social fears or hostilities arising from injustice; dependence or internal suppressions of desires because of class or tradition leading to repressions and neurotic attitudes in life. That is why discussion of Robinson's "children," as they exemplify distinctive attitudes toward love and self, competition, anxiety, and fear, will bring into focus the ultimate truth that in this world love belongs only to those who can give it, and that those who cannot give it out of their own egoism are incapable of recognizing it when they receive it. The opposite side of the Robinson kindergarten shows an order of reality in human life: that the success standards of the majority lead to far greater demolition of personality than are normally imagined.

An Approach to Robinson's Psychological Methods and Content.

The date given for each poem is that indicated in the *Collected Poems* (1948).

For brevity in this listing, the method is indicated in the following code: WE-I indicates an external, community observation; there are several kinds of observers; A stands for the doctor-analyst type. N for the straightforward narrator; OC indicates an observer who is also a commentator; MON will stand for external monologue (often with implied dialogue); ExD indicates straight narrative dialogue; DN equals a dream told on the surface by a narrator. For internal accounts the following code will show the method: IM indicates internal monologue, including a stream-of-consciousness effect; ID stands for a variation in narration, the beneath-the-surface dialogue; FN stands for dreams or fantasies told, as if internal, by a narrator. Combinations of these codes may be used for several poems, as the approach of the poet varies.

	Aspect	*Poem*	*Date*	*Method*
I.	THE SEARCH FOR AFFECTION AND UNDERSTANDING			
	a. demanding love	The Clinging Vine	1916	MON
		The Unforgiven	1916	MON
		Eros Turannos	1916	WE-I
		Llewellyn and the Tree	1916	WE-I/OC/ExD
		The Woman and the Wife	1902	ExD
	b. compulsive love	John Evereldown	1897	ID
		Luke Havergal	1897	IM
		Reuben Bright	1897	WE-I
		The Mill	1920	WE-I
	c. love blocked by love of another	The Book of Annandale	1902	IM
		Mortmain	1925	ExD
		Annandale Again	1932	OC
	d. lover's jealousy	The Whip	1910	WE-I/OC
		Cavender's House	1929	ED/FM
	e. old vs. young	Rahel to Varnhagen	1920	ExD
	f. competitive love	Guinevere and Alexandra	1925	ExD
		Lisette and Eileen	1916	MON
	g. age	Veteran Sirens	1916	OC
		The Poor Relation	1916	OC/N
	h. love of children	The Gift of God	1916	WE-I/OC
		Aunt Imogen	1902	OC/N
		Partnership	1902	IM
	i. gradations of love	*Merlin*	1917	N/ExD
		Launcelot	1920	N/ExD
		Tristram	1927	N/ExD
II.	THE QUEST FOR POWER			
	a. distinctive power motives	*King Jasper*	1935	N/ExD/FN
		The Glory of the Nightingales	1930	N/ExD/IM/FN
	b. destruction of friends	Bokardo	1916	MON
		An Old Story	1897	MON
III.	MAN, AS THE CREATOR, IN HIS SOCIETY			
	a. material success, spiritual failure	Richard Cory	1897	WE-I
		Ben Jonson Entertains a Man from Stratford	1916	MON
		Tasker Norcross	1920	MON/OC
		Saint-Nitouche	1902	WE-I
	b. combines power with spiritual and love problems	*Roman Bartholow*	1923	ExD/N
		Cavender's House	1929	ED/FN
		Matthias at the Door	1931	ExD/N
	c. misers of material things	Aaron Stark	1890	WE-I
		Vickery's Mountain	1910	WE-I/OC
	d. material failures, spiritual success	Flammonde	1916	WE-I
		Captain Craig	1902	ExD/N
	e. artist in society	Rembrandt	1921	IM
		Amaranth	1934	N/IM/FN/ID
		The Man Who Died Twice	1924	N/OC/FN

	Aspect	*Poem*	*Date*	*Method*
IV.	ABERRANTS			
	a. pathological	John Evereldown	1897	ID
		Luke Havergal	1897	IM
		Reuben Bright	1897	WE-I
		The Growth of Lorraine	1902	OC
		The Whip	1910	WE-I/OC
		Miniver Cheevy	1910	WE-I
		The Mill	1920	WE-I
		Roman Bartholow	1923	ExD/N
		Avon's Harvest	1921	ExD/OC/FN
		Cavender's House	1929	ED/FN
		The Man Who Died Twice	1924	N/OC/FN
		Amaranth	1934	N/IM/FN/ID
		Mr. Flood's Party	1921	ExD/FN
		Matthias at the Door	1931	ExD/N
		Cliff Klingenhagen	1890	ExD
	b. archetypal figures	Flammonde	1916	WE-I
		The Man Against the Sky	1916	N
		The Wandering Jew	1920	WE-I/OC
		The Valley of the Shadow	1920	N
		Amaranth	1934	N/IM/FN/ID
		King Jasper	1935	N/ExD/FN
		Captain Craig	1902	ExD/N
		The Three Taverns	1920	MON
		John Brown	1920	MON
		The Revealer	1910	WE-I
		The Gift of God	1916	WE-I/OC
		Cassandra	1916	N

---

1 Ridgely Torrence, editor, *Selected Letters of Edwin Arlington Robinson* (New York, 1940), 12-13.
2 Chard Powers Smith, *Where the Light Falls: A Portrait of Edwin Arlington Robinson* (New York, 1965).
3 Ben Ray Redman, *Edwin Arlington Robinson* (New York, 1926), 20.
4 Through all of this, it is understood, of course, that Robinson was not a psychologist in a scientific sense: the term is not meant to suggest that he made literal scientific studies of the processes of the human mind or the phenomena of consciousness and behavior.
5 Lloyd Morris, *The Poetry of Edwin Arlington Robinson* (New York 1923), 112.
6 Herbert Gorman, *The Procession of Masks* (Boston, 1923), 39.
7 Kurt Lewin, "Frontiers in Group Dynamics," *Human Relations*, I (June 1947), 9; Robin Williams, Jr., *The Reduction of Integrated Tensions* (New York, 1947), 83-84.
8 Robinson's own expression for himself. See *Selected Letters*, 111.
9 Denham Sutcliffe, editor, *Untriangulated Stars: Letters of Edwin Arlington Robinson to Harry De Forest Smith, 1890-1905* (Cambridge, Mass., 1947), 134.
10 *Untriangulated Stars*, 108.
11 O. F. Theis, "Edwin Arlington Robinson," *Forum*, LI (February 1914), 306, 309.
12 Samuel G. Beers, "A Poet for Pastors," *Religion in Life*, XII (Summer 1943), 424-425.
13 "Edwin Arlington Robinson," *Macmillan pamphlet* (New York, 1926), 11.
14 Dorothy Ulrich, "Edwin Arlington Robinson," *Avocations*, II (June 1938), 252.
15 *Macmillan pamphlet*, 16.
16 Percy H. Boynton, *Some Contemporary Americans* (Chicago, 1924), 16-32.
17 Raphael Demos, *Time* LII (October 18, 1948), 64.

Cary, Richard, 1909- *comp.*
Appreciation of Edwin Arlington Robinson; 28 interpretive essays. Waterville, Me., Colby College Press [1969]

xiii, 356 p. port. 24 cm.

Includes bibliographies.

1. Robinson, Edwin Arlington, 1869-1935. I. Title.

PS3535.O25Z617 811'.5'2 74-15276
MARC

Library of Congress 70 [4]